MARXIST IDEOLOGY AND SOVIET CRIMINAL LAW

MARXIST IDEOLOGY
AND
SOVIET CRIMINAL LAW

R. W. MAKEPEACE LL.B, LL.M, PhD
Lecturer in Law at the Hatfield Polytechnic

CROOM HELM   LONDON

BARNES & NOBLE BOOKS
TOTOWA, NEW JERSEY

© 1980 R.W. Makepeace
Croom Helm Ltd, 2-10 St John's Road, London SW11

British Library Cataloguing in Publication Data

Makepeace, R W
    Marxist ideology and Soviet criminal law.
    1. Criminal law — Russia
    2. Law and socialism
    I. Title
    345'.47   [Law]
    ISBN 0-7099-0183-6

First published in the USA 1980 by
Barnes & Noble Books
81 Adams Drive
Totowa, New Jersey, 07512

ISBN: 0-389-20099-9

343.094
M 235 m

Printed and bound in Great Britain by
REDWOOD BURN LIMITED   81- 7553
Trowbridge & Esher

CONTENTS

TO S.

PREFACE

As its title suggests, this book is about the relationship between certain areas of philosophy and law. To enable comparison, there is in effect a historical survey of the criminal law of the Soviet Union which has had to be highly selective considering the breadth of the field. The reader may notice some greater detail in aspects of chapters dealing with the early period. This is caused by three factors: first, the connection or supposed connection between theory and practice is easier to trace in those years; secondly, there are other sources of information on more recent developments easily available, and I view this book as a guide to further study; and finally, I found my interest in the early period developed as my researches progressed. However, I feel that an overall balance has been achieved, especially as pertinent areas such as criminology and sentencing policy are more fully considered in later chapters. The work is a product of research undertaken at The London School of Economics and Political Science, and I would like to thank Professor Ivo Lapenna for the great help he gave to me as my supervisor, and Mrs E. Gottlieb and Dr B.S. Johnson for their great efforts to teach me Russian.

To my colleagues at The Hatfield Polytechnic, particularly Rosalind Brooke, for the many helpful suggestions they made, to the Polytechnic for financial assistance, and especially to my wife, I am greatly indebted.

R.W.M.
The Hatfield Polytechnic
Hertford

GLOSSARY

Besprizornye — homeless youths and children (caused by collectivisation
and the war)

CEC — Central Executive Committee (see VTsIK)

Cheka — abbreviation for Extraordinary Commission for the Struggle with
Counterrevolution, Sabotage and Speculation

Equivalence — the linking of particular penalties to particular crimes or
types of crime

GPU — State Political Administration (secret police)

Gubernia — province

Kolkhoz — collective farm

Kolkhozniki — collective farm workers

Kolkhozsentr — central co-ordinating agency for the collective farms

Krai — territory

NEP — New Economic Policy

NKVD — People's Commissariat for Internal Affairs

Oblas† — region

OGPU — Unified State Political Administration (secret police)

PCJ — People's Commissariat of Justice

Procuracy — prosecutor's office

Raions — district

RCP (B) — Russian Communist Party (Bolsheviks) (earlier name for CPSU)

RSDLP — Russian Social Democratic Labour Party (earlier name for
CPSU)

RSFSR — Russian Socialist Federated Soviet Republic

Sostav — the 'composition' or 'make-up' of a crime. It includes the value
or interest injured, elements characterising the criminal and the social
danger of the act, and guilt.

Sovarkom — Council of People's Commissars

Sovkhoz — state farm

Vecheka — 'All-Russian' variant of the Cheka (see above)

VTsIK — All-Russian Central Executive Committee (one of the main
organs of government).

INTRODUCTION

This book is about differences between theory and practice in the
Soviet Union — a statement which in itself implies the existence of
such differences. This should come as no surprise to those who have
studied the country, its political and social systems, but may perhaps
have a different effect on those uninitiated into the relevant intricacies.
'Intricacies' is for once not too strong a term to use, as the special
arguments and terminology involved create a complex situation where
truth inhabits a labyrinth. To guide oneself, an analytical approach is
necessary, and the first thing one has to decide upon is what exactly is
meant by 'theory'?

The most obvious answer is 'Marxist theory', but on this, especially
considering its attached political importance, there is something far
from unanimity. It would, therefore, seem both reasonable and
necessary to consider what was said by Marx and Engels before one can
decide what is in accord with the originators and what is not. This task,
made difficult enough by the quantity and quality of the subsequent
variations, is not facilitated by the existence of possible differences in
the approaches of Marx and Engels, and the very relevant point that
Marx looked upon his work as an 'approach to further understanding'
rather than a 'theory'. Although in assessing the developments that
followed, one does tend to label Marx's pronouncements a 'theory',
both these totally fundamental factors have not been overlooked.

Of all the revisionists, the list of which may well include Engels —
if the theory is not seen as a joint work — Lenin is of special
importance to this study. Soviet and Lenin's own practice has always
been to thoroughly condemn 'revisionism', but the concept can be very
difficult to define, and as already hinted, Engels may be among the
accused.

In the Soviet Union, the work of Marx and Engels is seen as a joint
opus, and any changes made by Lenin (although they are not bluntly
admitted to be this) are treated as a legitimate part of the traditional
theory. Further alterations made by the leader of the time, the prime
example being Stalin, are also considered in the same manner, until
later criticisms led to the rejection of inconvenient sections. A more
balanced view would be to recognise the changes wrought by successive
leaders. For example, Lenin tended to be highly selective in the writings

of Marx he used, and often Engels is the more quoted of the two.

Part of the problem that Lenin, and to a lesser extent Stalin, had to meet was the difference between the actual situation of Russia, particularly in economic development, and the type of country that had been envisaged by Marx as ripe for the socialist revolution. The disparity between the two – and to the present writer *the* fundamental problem – has been the main cause of theoretical distortions, and has given a reason, or excuse, for many horrendous events and illegalities in Soviet history. The attempt to make the theory fit a situation to which it did not apply is a central part of this study and has been given periodic reconsideration throughout. As already mentioned, the economic development of the country is a useful and important pointer in assessing the practicalities of the situation in Marxist terms, and has therefore been regularly appraised, albeit somewhat superficially.

The pre-eminence of the Communist Party of the Soviet Union in the affairs of the country is such that the history of the Party cannot be overlooked, but for the sake of brevity, its changing (or unchanging) role in society and its social composition have been the main areas of interest. The regime governing the Soviet Union was meant to be the dictatorship of the proletariat, but this soon became one of the Party, so the practical effect of its basic role as the guiding force of society should therefore be analysed, and as the Party is meant to represent the people, its social composition and development must be considered.

The area of substantive law chosen for this study is Soviet criminal law. Why should one choose criminal law? One answer would be to say that it is easier in many respects to look at criminal law, as it is a more self-contained subject than many, which facilitates both breadth and depth of approach. Apart from this important but negative reason, there is one overwhelmingly positive argument for so doing. Marx's 'theory' covers all aspects of society, so when what purports to be a legitimate development of this is to be evaluated, the political and social controls exercised by or in the name of the state are of prime significance. Criminal law is a major, if not the major, way in which these control mechanisms are implemented, and is therefore an above average guide to subsequent practice. Also, although Marx and Engels did not say a great deal about law, and many aspects have to be deduced from state theory, what was said usually referred to criminal law, due to its central importance in society, and so makes assessment easier. Within the subject of criminal law, certain areas have been chosen as being of particular interest. Counter-revolutionary crime is one of these, as it relates to the protection of the regime, and as this is really to do with control over, rather than by, society, it is highly pertinent. Similarly, crimes indicating society's reaction, for example hooliganism, have been extensively considered. It will become increasingly clear that at different times in its history, the regime has emphasised particular crimes as being more unacceptable, but there are also reasonably clear continuous trends throughout the entire period, and efforts have been made to trace these, and deduce why they have been of special concern.

Most of the material for the study of substantive law consists of decrees, but other wider pronouncements such as constitutions, Party rules etc. have been incorporated where it was thought necessary or helpful. Criminology, and sentencing policy, can both offer insight into the theory and reality of Soviet practice, and have been studied in some depth. Certain changes of an administrative, institutional nature, for example courts, procuracy and other agencies are included as being of some consequence, while in the early period, some – the Cheka and revolutionary tribunals – have to be studied in more detail.

Due to the very great number of decrees involved, All-Union laws and Russian Republican legislation have been the prime areas of study, but these are of special importance in this controlled society, and other Republican legislation has been mentioned where it was felt to be of help or interest.

Consideration of the theory begins with Marx and traces subsequent changes. It is hoped that, taken together, the above-mentioned institutional and substantive aspects of law will offer a representative picture of Soviet criminal legal development with which to compare the original theory, and the corresponding contemporary theory.

The purposes of the book are partly descriptive: one aims to see how the theory has altered, how the practice has unfolded, and what is the connection, if any, between the 'theory' of Marx and that which has evolved, and the way in which a theory of a particular period affects the law and its implementation. It is also hoped to draw more general deductions on the possibilities of prescribing action from theory. This is especially pertinent to the Soviet situation as (i) one particular theory, whatever its origins, has an unusual pre-eminence; (ii) the theory is said to affect all areas of life; and (iii) at least in its original version, one could not artificially impose the 'theory' on a situation, as it was really an 'approach', a description of how society developed.

MARXIST THEORY ON LAW AND CRIME

The Relationship between Infrastructure and Superstructure

This relationship can too easily be seen as a one-sided determinism with the infrastructure as the source of all development, but as is often the case with simplifications of complex theories, this is only a partial truth. A comparatively clear and concise account of historical materialism was set out by Marx in his Preface to *A Contribution to the Critique of Political Economy*:

> In the social production of their life men enter into definite relations that are indispensable and independent of their will, relations of production which correspond to a definite stage of development of their material productive forces. The sum total of these relations of production constitutes the economic structure of society, the real foundation, on which rises a legal and political superstructure and to which correspond definite forms of social consciousness. The mode of production of material life conditions the social, political and intellectual life process in general. It is not the consciousness of men that determines their being, but, on the contrary, their social being that determines their consciousness. At a certain stage of their development, the material forces of production in society come into conflict with the existing relations of production or — what is but a legal expression of the same thing — with the property relations within which they have been at work before. From forms of development of the productive forces these relations turn into their fetters. Then begins an epoch of social revolution. With the change of the economic foundation the entire immense superstructure is more or less rapidly transformed.[1]

The inclusion of this admittedly long quotation can be excused on the grounds that the sometimes subtle relationships between the constituent elements can be more easily seen if it is read as a whole.

As the 'relations of production' correspond to the stage of development of the 'material productive forces', the latter must be the more basic concept. Acton,[2] who says he takes a technological approach to the problem, describes the productive forces as the skills, tools and experience handed on by one generation to the next. Is one to conclude that the productive forces, whatever they precisely may be, are the ultimate determining factor? In the Preface reference is made to the 'economic structure of society' which is made up of the 'totality of relations of production', and that this economic structure is the 'real foundation on which legal and political superstructures arise'. This may mean that the determining factor is a wider concept than the productive forces, i.e. the 'economic structure'.

Hook[3] takes this approach, but Acton[4] and Bober[5] say that the economic structure is not the determining factor; it is the productive forces which fulfil this role. Plamenatz[6] concludes that the Acton-Bober approach is more in keeping with what Marx and Engels have to say when describing their theory, but that Hook's view is very plausible and often seems to agree with their explanations of actual social change and transformation. If one takes the narrower approach, and considers that the productive forces are the ultimate determining factor, questions on the importance of superstructural concepts still arise — 'still' because they would almost certainly be implicit in the 'economic structure of society' — as the determining sequence partly consists of the relations of production.

Different stages in the development of the productive forces give rise to corresponding productive relationships and these then determine the superstructure. Questions can arise here over (i) whether the relations of production are actually determined and actually do determine the superstructure — Plamenatz[7] gives examples of land cultivation in different societies that would seem to indicate the determination has not taken place; and (ii) whether there are elements of the superstructure in the relations of production which are, of course, part of the base.

The influence of the superstructure is discussed by Wetter,[8] who gives detailed consideration to the dialectical interplay between the various concepts and elements of the theory. He characterises the productive forces as the relationship between man and nature, and the relations of production as that between man and man. The mode of production, made up of the forces and relations, determines the superstructure, changes in the latter resulting from changes in the former. The dialectical tension between the components of the mode can explain changes in the mode, but how do changes in the productive forces, being the most basic element, occur? Are elements imported into this concept to enable change, for if so they will most probably originate in the superstructure. Wetter also discusses the theoretical developments made by Lenin and Stalin, an important outcome of which is a strengthening belief in the role of the superstructure.

The purpose of the above discussion was to show that the infrastructure and superstructure cannot be entirely separated, and that there is some inter-reaction. The whole question really revolves around any influence the superstructure has on the base as the latter's influence is fundamental to the theory.

Engels' Four Letters

These are of particular interest to the problem at hand. Chronologically, the first of these letters was that to Bloch[9] in which, after saying that the *'ultimately* determining factor in history is the production and reproduction of real life', Engels continues, 'More than this neither Marx nor I have ever asserted. Hence if somebody twists this into saying that the economic factor is the *only* determining one, he transforms that proposition into a meaningless, abstract, senseless phrase.' The superstructure is said to interact with the base, and exercises influence upon the 'course of the historical struggles and in many cases preponderate in determining their *form*'.[10] Later in the same letter he wrote, 'Marx and I are ourselves partly to blame for the fact that the younger people lay more stress on the economic side than is due to it,' because of lack of time to discuss and investigate all the factors.[11]

On 27 October 1890, Engels wrote to Conrad Schmidt, 'On the whole, the economic movement prevails, but it has also to endure reactions from the political movement which it itself set up and endowed with relative independence.'[12] He referred to an 'interaction of two unequal forces', and outlined three ways in which the state power (a superstructural concept) could react upon economic development –

> in the same direction, and then things move more rapidly; it can move in the opposite direction, in which case nowadays it will go to pieces in the long run in every great people; or it can prevent the economic development from proceeding along certain lines, and prescribe other lines.[13]

In the letter to Mehring, written on 14 July 1893, he wrote, 'once a historic element has been brought into the world by other, ultimately economic causes, it reacts, can react on its environment and even on the causes that have given rise to it.'[14] Finally, the letter to Borgius,[15] written on 25 January 1894, contains the lines:

Political, juridical, philosophical, religious, literary, artistic, etc. development is based on economic development. But all these react upon one another and also upon the economic basis. It is not that the economic condition is the *cause, solely active*, while everything else is only passive effect. There is, rather, interaction on the basis of economic necessity, which *ultimately* always asserts itself.[16]

Bober's treatment of the letters is somewhat negative. He says that 'Those who contend that the two philosophers give a prominent place to noneconomic factors invariably cite these letters as conclusive proof,'[17] but after giving the letters detailed consideration he concludes:

> The general impression which these letters make. . .comes to the familiar formula that while institutions and ideas have a part in history, their influence is of such a subordinate character that social events and changes are explicable mainly in terms of economics.[18]

Bober's reasons for coming to this conclusion seem to revolve around the fact that the economic forces were thought to be the ultimate determinant, and as any other conclusion would have been totally irregular in the terms of the theory, this in itself is to be expected. The degree of influence had by the superstructure is impossible to quantify precisely, and it may be impossible to agree as to whether they have been given a 'prominent place'. Bober would seem to imply that if changes are caused 'mainly' by economic factors, then other factors cannot have an important role to play.

There may be a semantic problem here, but taken at its face value, the statement is unacceptable because a belief in the ultimate determining quality of the economic forces does not preclude the possibility that other factors can be important. Engels states this clearly in the letters.

It could be suggested that Engels is introducing a new element into the theory by placing so much emphasis on superstructural influences, but his explanations are convincing, and the flexibility inherent in this view is in accord with Marx's principle that the 'theory' was not a theory, but an 'approach'.

Law as Part of the Superstructure

Marx disclosed such a belief as early as 1849, saying in his speech at the trial of the Rhenish democrats, that it was a legal fiction to base law on society and to believe that it reflected the needs and conditions of society.

> As soon as it ceases to fit the social conditions, it becomes simply a bundle of paper. You cannot make the old laws the foundation of the new social development any more than these old laws created the old social conditions.[19]

In 'The Poverty of Philosophy' he wrote, 'Legislation, political as well as civil, could do no more than give expression to the will of the economic conditions';[20] and in the introduction to his *Contribution to the Critique of Political Economy* reference is made to the view that 'each mode of production produces its specific legal relations, political forms, etc.'[21] Engels clearly endorsed this principle – 'If the state and public law are determined by economic relations, so, too, of course is private law, which indeed in essence only sanctions the existing economic relations between individuals which are normal in the circumstances.'[22] Law, as part of the superstructure, will basically be determined by the mode of production, but does the system of law have any independence and can it affect other parts of the superstructure or the infrastructure itself? As law was not given a great deal of consideration by Marx or Engels, the extent of the dependence or independence of law has to be deduced to some extent from comments made about the superstructure as a whole. However, Engels did follow his above-mentioned statement in 'Ludwig Feuerbach' on the law, sanctioning the existing economic relations with the information that the forms in which this can happen 'vary considerably', giving the examples of England, where feudal laws have been given a bourgeois content, and the modification of Roman law by Western European jurists; and concludes, 'If, therefore, bourgeois legal rules merely express the economic life conditions of society in legal form, then they can do so well or ill according to the circumstances.'[23] There would seem to be, therefore, some degree of flexibility open to the legal system. Exactly from where this has come is debatable, but not its existence. It may be as well, at this point, to remind oneself that law is also the 'will of the ruling class', which may suggest a contradiction. This suggestion evaporates when one considers that the will of the ruling class is itself part of the superstructure and is itself determined by the mode of production.

Wetter[24] divides the superstructure into two main parts, one political and legal, the other ideological, partly basing his approach on comments such as: 'The sum total of these relations of production constitutes the economic structure of society, the real foundation, on which rises a legal and political superstructure and to which correspond definite forms of social consciousness.'[25] These latterly mentioned 'forms' constitute the ideological part. It is sometimes thought that the political-legal part of the superstructure has a certain pre-eminence, being more directly influenced by the base and exerting the same over other parts of the superstructure. This view no more detracts from the belief that the economic base is the ultimate determining factor than the premiss that the superstructure acts upon itself, as it is merely a more sophisticated variation of this latter, widely accepted proposition. It would appear to be a reasonable deduction to make from Marx's writings, and could be of use in understanding the relationship between the infrastructure and superstructure.

Conclusions

It should now be clear that in explaining the relationship between superstructure and base, Marxist theory does not postulate a one-sided determinism. Various pertinent factors have been considered:

(i) If the economic structure as a whole, rather than the productive forces, is the ultimate determining factor, superstructural concepts and influences would become part of the determining factor. On the evidence of what Marx and Engels wrote, it is more probable that the productive forces alone are the ultimate determining factor.
(ii) Wetter mentioned a philosophical problem with the dialectic, that is, how does change occur in the productive forces without the introduction of outside influences? Later Soviet theory would indicate superstructural elements have some part in this.
(iii) The relations of production, for example, as analysed by Acton and Plamenatz, seem to contain concepts belonging to the superstructure, and although the productive forces are the ultimate determining factor, the relations of production are, of course, part of the base.
(iv) It would seem to be universally accepted that the superstructure can influence itself, and it is possible that the political-legal part may have a greater role in this.

Engels' four letters deal with the problem and state unequivocally that the superstructure does have an active part to play. One agrees with

Engels' own statement that this was not always clearly stated in the writings, and his explanations are believable. The theory did not preclude any such superstructural independence, but the letters do give the concept greater emphasis. The suggestion that Engels was a revisionist — if indeed he, the co-author of the theory could in any case be described as such — is not supported. Any differences between Marx and Engels, notably the more philosophical approach of the former and his view that the theory was an 'approach' tends, in this particular instance, to uphold a belief in flexibility. Economic determinism does not exclude the possibility of the superstructure having a considerable effect; all it stipulates is that the economic base is the ultimate determining factor.

This introductory discussion has left out many important economic and philosophical criticisms of the theory, but it is only necessary to consider those aspects of the theory pertinent to law and crime, and not to criticise the theory *per se.* One concludes that law is part of the superstructure, and is determined by the base, but like all parts of the superstructure, has some influence on itself, other parts of the superstructure, and the base itself. The view that law (and politics) is an especially important part of the superstructure only emphasises this influence. While investigating Soviet practice on law one will have to allow for variations, as the theory permits them within limits. The degree of the variations will be seen and considered later, in the main part of the book.

The Theory of State and Law

Marx and Engels did not develop comprehensive theories about either of these two concepts, and, moreover, the state was given greater consideration, so in some degree the approach to law has to be deduced from that to the state. Such action is instructive and can be defended on the grounds that the two concepts have much in common.

Relevant Aspects of State Theory

The birth of the state was given close analysis by Engels in his 'Origin of the Family, Private Property and the State', the basic premiss being that state and class come into existence at the same time — 'The old society, built on groups based on ties of sex, bursts asunder in the collision of the newly developed social classes; in its place a new society appears, constituted in a state.'[26] The purpose of the state was to 'sanctify private property' and to 'perpetuate, not only the newly-arising class division of society, but also the right of the possessing class to exploit the non-possessing classes and the rule of the former over the latter'.[27] The root cause of the birth of the state was the division of labour, as that had resulted in the appearance of classes. However, Plamenatz[28] believes that the division of labour does not necessarily lead to the formation of classes in the Marxist sense as division does not in itself produce exploitation, an element indispensable to a Marxist class system.

Although, from the above, one would assume that the existence of classes is a prerequisite to the existence of the state, some writings would seem to indicate otherwise. Engels, in his introduction to 'The Civil War in France' says:

> Society had created its own organs to look after its common interests, originally through simple divisions of labour. But these organs, at whose head was the state power, had in the course of time, in pursuance of their own special interests, transformed themselves from the servants of society into the masters of society.[29]

Earlier, in *Anti-Duhring*, he says the state was first used 'to safeguard their common interests (e.g. irrigation in the East) and for protection against external enemies' and only acquires 'the function of maintaining by force the conditions of existence and domination of the ruling class against the subject class'.[30] These statements would seem to indicate the possibility of a state not controlled by a class, but working for the whole society. One cannot clearly deduce that the society is classless as division of labour had occurred in the first example, and this may mean classes had appeared; and in the *Anti-Duhring* example, Engels said that the state acquired the functions it did acquire because of the advent of classes.

Bloom[31] mentions the possibility of the birth of the state being due to conquest, relying on the statement by Engels concerning the German conquest of Roman provinces — 'the organs of the gentile constitution had to be transferred into organs of state.' A substitute state for the deceased Roman one had to be found. The immediate cause was conquest, but classes were in existence, and as the state was to be used by the Germans to facilitate their rule, it was to be the 'weapon of the ruling class'.

The main theory on the birth of the state says that it arrives with the birth of classes. The proposition that the state may originally be supra-class and later becomes subverted to the needs of one class is not orthodox by Soviet standards and could be related to Pashukanis' theory of the state coming into being because of a compromise between the classes. However, in the writings of Marx and Engels there is some evidence in favour of the possibility of non-class states. A very important concept to mention at this point is that of 'depoliticisation', which can explain, or begin to explain, apparent anomalies in the theory, and will be considered in detail with the 'withering away' of state and law. Does the possibility of supra-class states mean that law could be supra-class, for both are supposedly class entities and it is of great importance to decide whether their existence is to depend on that of classes?

The role of the state in society has two main explanations, the orthodox of which says that the state is an implement of the ruling class, which uses it to enforce its will, to maintain its rule. Many statements of Marx and Engels uphold this approach; for example, *The German Ideology* says, 'it is nothing more than the form of organisation which the bourgeois necessarily adopt both for internal and external purposes, for the mutual guarantee of their property and interests,' and later, 'the State is the form in which the individuals of a ruling class assert their common interests, and in which the whole of civil society of an epoch is epitomised.'[32] Perhaps the most famous reference is from the Manifesto, 'The executive of the modern state is but a committee for managing the common affairs of the whole bourgeoisie.'[33]

The second of the two main explanations of the role of the state is not so widely accepted by any means, and is centered on the concept of the 'state above society', and could be considered in terms of exceptions to the principle that the state is a weapon of the ruling class. The main or e is that of autocratic personal rule exemplified by the pre-1789 French monarchy and most of all by Bonapartism. Marx, when speaking of Louis Napoleon's rise to power, wrote in the 'Eighteenth Brumaire', 'France, therefore, seems to have escaped the despotism of a class only to fall back beneath the despotism of an individual,' and 'The struggle seems to be settled in such a way that all classes, equally impotent and equally mute, fall on their knees before the rifle butt,'[34] adding that 'only under the second Bonaparte does the state seem to have made itself completely independent.'[35] Marx does link Bonaparte with a class — the smallholding peasants — so is this a class state or not? Miliband[36] says it has an unusual degree of independence, but still has a definite class aspect. The actual degree of this independence is of course difficult to define, but he feels that

Engels went 'much farther than anything Marx had in mind' when he (Engels) spoke of playing off 'the proletariat against the bourgeoisie' and vice versa, so that the state power, in acting as mediator to these nearly balanced classes, appears to be independent.[37] The major class theory of the state has other exceptions, more partial than the above: for example, in 'The Class Struggles in France' Marx refers to control by a section of a class — 'It was not the French bourgeoisie that ruled under Louis Philippe, but *one* faction of it' (the 'finance aristocracy').[38]

Sanderson[39] refers to examples of competition within the ruling class, for example when Marx, in a lecture 'On the question of free trade' explained that the repeal of the Corn Laws was due to the desire of the industrial capitalists to undermine the position of the landowners, and in retaliation, they joined with the proletariat in passing the Ten Hours Bill, designed to reduce profits in manufacturing industry.

A final exception is where the economically dominant class does not produce the actual rulers of the state — 'The Whigs are the *aristocratic representatives* of the bourgeoisie,' and in exchange for power, these representatives make concessions to the middle class, enabling it to further its aims.[40] In this situation, Marx said that only those concessions that had become 'unavoidable and undelayable' are given, which means that there will be a considerable brake upon development. Also, one should note that the economically dominant class maintains its dominance, as it can oust its representatives if it so wishes.

Sanderson[41] discusses the fall of the Party of Order and its split into bourgeois factions, explaining that its fall occurred when, as representatives, they ceased to reflect the wishes of the represented. This is not parallel to the example of the Whigs, mentioned above, as two classes were involved there, whereas here only one is involved, and it really amounts to another type of non-uniformity within the ruling class.

The role of law, at least in so far as the statements made by Marx and Engels refer to it, does not give rise to those problems advanced by the role of the state, as the references always affirm that law is the will of the ruling class and that its role is to facilitate that rule.

The Manifesto contains the celebrated lines:

> Your very ideas are but the outgrowth of the conditions of your bourgeois production and bourgeois property, just as your jurisprudence is but the will of your class made into law for all, a will whose essential character and direction are determined by the economic conditions of existence of your class.[42]

This links the concept of law as part of the superstructure, and therefore determined by the base, with that of law as the will of the ruling class, this latter concept containing elements of the former as the will is itself determined, ultimately, by the base.

The German Ideology contains the assertion that as the basis of state power is really economically determined,

> The individuals who rule in these conditions, besides having to constitute their power in the form of the *State*, have to give their will, which is determined by these definite conditions, a universal expression as the will of the State, as law — an expression whose content is always determined by the relations of this class, as the civil and criminal law demonstrates in the clearest possible way.[43]

There are other similar passages, concerned with the bourgeoisie using the law to their own advantage, many of which are contained in *The Condition of the Working Class in England* and *Capital*.

It has been stated that some points concerning the theory of law have to be deduced from state theory. The exceptions to the class controlled state, such as Bonapartism, have no parallels with regard to law in the writings of Marx and Engels, and therefore one can only speculate over the possibilities of law above class, law reflecting the requirements of a faction of the ruling class, etc. If these could in any way exist, it would mean that the law in a given situation would not necessarily relate to the needs of the ruling class, or at least to all of it. Perhaps the state and law need not always be *simply* the devices of the ruling class.

The transition period, dictatorship of the proletariat, and 'withering away' of state and law are closely interrelated and are conveniently considered together. Marx, in his 'Critique of the Gotha Programme' wrote that:

> Between capitalist and communist society lies the period of the revolutionary transmutation of the one into the other.
> Corresponding to this is also a political transition period, in which the state can be nothing but the *revolutionary dictatorship of the proletariat.*[44]

In the Paris Manuscripts, and elsewhere, Marx writes of the existence of an intermediate stage of development called 'vulgar communism' or 'socialism', which will have some characteristics of the bourgeois era, society not having developed into full communism. These 'characteristics' may well include state and law in the usual class sense. The relationship between the transition period and vulgar communism is that the latter comes in the later stages of the former.

Supported by common sense, as one could not expect society to change instantaneously, the existence of the transition period is not a source of great controversy, but what actually happens in this period is such a source. A crucial concept is that of 'withering away', the most famous exposition of which occurs in *Anti-Duhring*, where Engels says that as soon as the state becomes truly representative of society, when there is no longer a subject class and the 'struggle for individual existence based on the former anarchy of production' has ceased, the state becomes ' superfluous' – 'the government of persons is replaced by the administration of things and the conduct of the processes of production. The state is not "abolished". *It withers away*.'[45] This 'withering away' is supposedly to take place during the transition period, at the end of which the state, and the law for that matter, no longer exist. It is impossible to closely relate the stage of withering away to the time scale of the transition period; all one can say is that the state and law should be less in evidence in the later stages of the transition period, and these include 'socialism', than in the earlier ones. There should be neither state nor law under communism.

The transition period is also characterised by the dictatorship of the proletariat. Draper[46] writes that Marx, who used the term sporadically and did not fully develop the concept, had introduced the idea of the proletarian class as dictator in contradistinction to Louis Blanc, Blanqui, *et al.* who favoured a temporary dictatorship by a group over the proletariat. Draper thinks that the dictatorship of the proletariat is a 'social description'[47] and is not about the form of government, relying for this view on such statements as that in the 'Critique of the Gotha Programme' where Marx criticises the Programme for remaining within the present state system, making changes to the government machine, not to society itself. This is the context in which Marx says that when he writes 'state' he does not mean 'government machinery', and therefore Miliband's view that 'the dictatorship of the proletariat is *both* a statement of the class character of the proletarian power *and* a description of the political power itself'[48] is preferred.

Although Engels[49] (and Lenin for that matter) referred to the Paris Commune as an example of the dictatorship, Marx did not think of it as such, mainly because it was a localised event and not a national phase. In a letter of 22 February 1881 to Domela Nieuwenhuis, Marx referred to the 'difficulties of a government that has just come into being', and said that a socialist government must take immediate action against the bourgeoisie to gain sufficient time for permanent action, but as far as the Paris Commune was concerned, 'this was merely the rising of a city under exceptional conditions.'[50]

However, actions taken by the Paris Commune to de-institutionalise political power are almost certainly part of the programme of the dictatorship, and constitute part of the programme of the dictatorship, and constitute an important part of the measures necessary in the dictatorship, and constitute an important part of the measures necessary in the transition period. Obviously some sort of organisation would be necessary to introduce these measures, and the need for such an entity − a state, perhaps − can cause problems with regard to the withering away of the state and law, that is to take place in the transition period. This is centred on the meaning of 'withering away'. Avineri[51] finds a 'marked difference' between Marx's and Engels' terminology in this area, Engels using a biological simile, 'der Staat wird nicht "abgeschaft", er stirbt ab,' in *Anti-Duhring*, while Marx always refers to the 'abolition and transcendence' − 'Aufhebung' − of the state, a philosophical term with dialectical overtones. Adamiak,[52] following Bloom,[53] considered the relative positions of Marx and Engels on this matter and concluded that they were similar. However, he adds that they were not anarchistic, and that the state was to play a very important part in the future society. Adamiak's premiss is that Marx believes in the abolition of 'political power' rather than the 'state' *per se*, and supports this view with references such as Marx saying the working class will establish 'an association which will exclude classes and their antagonism, and there will be no more political power properly so-called, since political power is precisely the official expression of antagonism in civil society';[54] and 'political power, properly so called, is merely the organised power of one class for oppressing the other.'[55] The terms 'political power' and 'state' are sometimes treated as synonymous when they are actually not the same. So in the Manifesto when mention is made of the 'public power' losing its 'political character', no more is meant than that, and one will be left with a public power without a political character. As political power is the suppression of one class by another, once classes have disappeared, so will political power. The ownership of the means of production is a major aspect of the class system, and one of the factors constituting the dying out of the classes is the extension of state ownership. The gradual development that is foreseen in this area − witness the Manifesto's ten measures, especially 'Extension of factories and instruments of production owned by the state' — would seem to comply with the measured disappearance of class and political power in the transition period. Adamiak[56] explains the 'anarchistic' statements made by Marx in terms of the rivalry between Marxism and anarchism, at times acute, and Bloom[57] pointed out that Marx's most anarchistic statements were made when attacking anarchists. Popper[58] suggests that Marx competed with the anarchists partially by using special terminology, for example calling a particular concept of a class-political state 'the state'.

In Marx's review of Emile de Girardin's 'Le socialisme et l'impôt' (in which the practical abolition of the state by simplification of functions and coercion by means of a self-regulatory tax system was postulated), he said:

> The abolition of the state has meaning only for communists, as the necessary result of the abolition of classes, with which the necessity of the organised force of one class for the suppression of other classes falls away of itself.[59]

Also note the reference to 'the abolition of classes, and thus to eliminate the power of the state. . .and to transform the governmental functions into simple administrative functions' in Marx's reply to Bakunin's Sonvillier Circular.[60]

However, in private pronouncements Marx was more revealing. In the 'Critique of the Gotha Programme', which was never intended for publication, he says, 'freedom consists in transforming the state from an organ standing above society into one completely subordinated to society'; 'what transformation will the state organisation undergo in a communist society? In other words what social functions will remain in existence there that are analogous to present state functions'; and he refers to 'the future state of communist society'.[61]

Engels, in a letter to Bebel written between 18 and 28 March 1875, wrote:

> so long as the proletariat still *uses* the state, it does not use it in the interests of freedom but in order to hold down its adversaries, and as soon as it becomes possible to speak of freedom, the state as such ceases to exist.[62]

Even the famous line, 'The state is not abolished. *It withers away*,' was not in the first edition of *Anti-Duhring*, but was added later by Engels to further refute anarchism. This could explain any doubts that arise over why it does not exactly fit the context at that point.

One is drawn to conclude on the subject of 'withering away' that it is a centrally important, yet complex, concept. The basic position seems relatively simple – between capitalist and communist society there is a transition period, the latter part of which can be termed 'socialism'; during this period, state and law were thought to 'wither', beginning this process with the commencement of the transition period and completing it by the end of the period. The existence of state and law during the period followed on from the premiss that classes still subsisted, a difference being that the ruling class was now the proletariat in its dictatorship phase – the dictatorship of the proletariat was held by Marx to be the equivalent of the dictatorship of the bourgeoisie which was professed to exist under the 'democracy' of bourgeois, capitalist states – and was not to be considered as the antithesis to 'true' democracy. As the proletariat would overcome the opposing classes and society would be reorganised, it would no longer exercise its dictatorship. The dictatorship would wither with the state and law.

Some type of entity for the purpose of carrying out the necessary controls of the future society, however minimal they may be, would seem to be required. Marx and Engels not only suggest this, but in some of their statements go much further than this. The concept of political power, and the use of special vocabulary by Marx and Engels, would seem to be highly relevant to this discussion. Political power is linked to the subordination of one class by another. Therefore, if there are no classes, there can be no political power, and a gradual dying out of classes would be paralleled by a gradual reduction of political power. If one approaches the theories on the birth and role of the state in this way, exceptions and anomalies can be explained by distinguishing between (i) a *state*, which exists where there is a ruling class (and, of course, this implies the existence of class(es) to be ruled); and (ii) an *organisation*, which is the structure or entity that carries out the necessary co-ordination in a non-class society. Hence, in pre-class primitive societies, there is an organisation, but not a state. Once classes form, political power and suppression emerge, and the organisation is used by the ruling class, it becomes a state. In the situation where Bonapartism or factionalism has taken place, the degree of political power has lessened as the position of the ruling class *vis-à-vis* the ruled has, for whatever reason, weakened, and the state tends towards the organisation.

Under communism, there will be no political power as there will be no classes, and therefore there can be no state; but there is to be an 'organisation'. This explains the references to 'future state' and the like, and allows for the existence of a future regulatory, but non-political, entity. The 'withering away' is the withering away of political power, and will transform the state into an 'organisation'.

In considering law in this context, one has to allow for the possibility of non-political law — 'rules', to exist in the future society. *Law* is the will of the ruling class as determined by the mode of production, *rules* are purely regulatory and have no class content. What has been said about the birth, role and withering away of the state can be applied by analogy to law — as law loses its political character, its class content, it becomes rules, the process being an aspect of the withering away.

Present society has examples of these classless regulations, the obvious example being traffic rules. The existence of 'rules' under communism will enable the necessary organising of society to take place. They will be able to include a much wider range of regulations than may be immediately thought from the examples in present society, because the class base of society will have gone, so, for example, anything relating to 'criminal' matters will not be founded on class. Exactly how much regulation and how many rules will be needed is impossible to predict, but at the very least, an explanation for the existence of such classless but vital rules as on which side of the road one has to drive, is now possible.

Marx and Engels on Crime

Concentrating as they did on questions of political economy and capital-labour relations, Marx and Engels did not produce a comprehensive theory on the subject of crime, but several interesting and informative concepts can be detected in their writings. Not surprisingly, one fundamental point that soon emerges from any investigation is the rejection of any formal approach to crime. In an article — 'Capital Punishment' — appearing in the *New York Daily Tribune* on 18 February 1853, Marx discussed Kant and Hegel with regard to punishment, and concluded that their theories, especially Hegel's, considered the criminal as 'a free and self determining being', which had the merit of recognising human dignity as an abstraction, but sanctioned the existing values in society. For Marx, the concept of free will obscures the true picture, that of the individual with 'multifarious social circumstances pressing upon him'.[63] *The German Ideology* warns against taking a narrow formal approach, saying that 'visionaries who see in right and law the domination of some independently existing, general will can see in crime the mere violation of right and law.'[64] In a passage in the *Theories in Surplus Value*, 'the apologist's conception of the productivity of all professions', Marx ironically discusses the many improvements brought about by crime, and finishes by quoting from Mandeville's 'Fable of the Bees', in which the author says that evil is the originator of art and science, and the moment evil ceases, society must be 'spoiled if not totally dissolved'. In this excerpt, which could mislead a casual reader, Marx is attacking the 'bourgeois' idea that society is divided into good and evil, by pointing out how many upright citizens are indirectly given employment by crime. It is also an attack on functionalist approaches to crime which can lead to the conclusion that crime is necessary. Marx directs this attack via the concept of 'productive labour', defining it in terms of surplus value rather than considering the contribution made to the production of wealth. (Note that Hirst[65] discusses theft, prostitution and illegal services, and criminal enterprises in terms of the role they play in production relations, following Marx's approach.)

After having noted what Marx and Engels were careful to warn against, one has to consider the various principles and comments made by them, that help in forming a representative picture of their 'theory', or whatever there is of one. A basic point to note is that the capitalist system is believed to be the fundamental cause of crime. This is stated many times by Engels in *The Condition of the Working Class in England*:

> The contempt for the existing social order is most conspicuous in its extreme form — that of offences against the law. If the influences demoralising to the working-man act more powerfully, more concentratedly than usual, he becomes an offender as certainly as water abandons the fluid for the vaprous state at 80 degrees, Reaumur. Under the brutal and brutalising treatment of the bourgeoisie, the working-man becomes precisely as much a thing without volition as water, and is subject to the laws of Nature with precisely the same necessity; at a certain point all freedom ceases.[66]

Directly after this passage, Engels says that as the proletariat has expanded, so has crime increased, for 'nearly all crime arises within the proletariat'.

The effects of unemployment:

> Every improvement in machinery throws workers out of employment, and the greater the advance, the more numerous the unemployed; each great improvement produces, therefore, upon a number of workers the effect of a commercial crisis, creates want, wretchedness and crime;[67]

and bad housing:

> What physical and moral atmosphere reigns in these holes I need not state. Each of these houses is a focus of crime, the scene of deeds against which human nature revolts, which would have perhaps never been executed but for this forced centralisation of vice;[68]

were emphasised. Both of these factors are caused by the system, and such general influences are accompanied by individual cases where need, with the same underlying cause, has given rise to crimes — for example two boys, 'in a starving condition', stealing a half-cooked calf's foot from a shop.[69]

The concept of law as the will of the ruling class as determined by the mode of production is pertinent here, for as Engels says, 'Let the ruling class see to it that these frightful conditions are ameliorated, or let it surrender the administration of the common interests to the labouring-class,'[70] which indicates that there is a certain latitude of action possible. The rather odd language used here is probably due to the early date at which this work was written (1844-5), for the idea that the ruling class could give up power in this way would seem strange in the light of the developed theory.

Up to now, we have seen a theory that explains the causes of crime in terms of the bad conditions produced by the capitalist system, and the individual seems to have little choice in his actions, to the extent of being likened to the boiling of water. This has led to the situation where Marx and Engels are considered to be one-sided economic determinists, but it should be carefully noted that further investigation leads one to consider modifications of varying importance.

One such qualification is the concept of individual or group rebellion against the system. There is some sort of link between these two forms of action, as, generally, the former develops into the latter when the accompanying class situation changes. In either case, the reason for the offences is said to be based on need, or 'defence'. For example, Engels says:

> The attempts of the Irish to save themselves from the present ruin, on the other hand, take the form of crimes. These are the order of the day in the agricultural districts, and are nearly always directed against the most immediate enemies, the landlords' agents, or their obedient servants, the Protestant intruders.[71]

Individual rebellion, incorporating the view of crime as the 'struggle of the isolated individual against the prevailing conditions',[72] generally leads on to group action, which can take the form of riots and machine smashing. As stated, class development seems to influence this:

> The manufacturing and mining proletariat emerged early from the first stage of resistance to our social order, the direct rebellion of the individual by the perpetration of crime; but the peasants are still in this stage at the present time.[73]

Once a class has emerged from this stage, a more organised and sophisticated approach is followed, which must involve a union approach and perhaps crime in a highly purposeful way. This can lead to a fall in the crime rate, but the examples of this given by Marx and Engels tend to be explained in terms of changing conditions, such as the decline in crime in Ireland in the 1850s which was 'simply the consequence of a famine, an exodus, and a general combination of circumstances favourable to the demand for Irish labour'.[74]

Another possible dimension to the basic economic determinism approach is that of 'social reaction', which is mentioned in this same article:

> Violations of law are generally the offspring of economical agencies beyond the control of the legislator, but, as the working of the Juvenile Offender's Act testifies. . .it depends to some degree on official society to stamp certain violations of its rules as crimes or as transgressions only. The difference of nomenclature, so far as from being indifferent, decides on the fate of thousands of men, and the moral tone of society. Law itself may not only punish crime, but improvise it, and the law of professional lawyers is very apt to work in this direction.[75]

This would seem to show an awareness of the possibility of 'labelling' producing deviance, and could be accompanied by Engels' earlier comment that 'society creates a *demand* for crime, which is met by a corresponding *supply*' and 'the gap created by the arrest, transportation, or execution of a certain number of criminals is promptly filled by other criminals — just as every gap in the population is at once filled by new arrivals.'[76]

Punishment is briefly mentioned by Marx and Engels, by the former as early as 1844 in 'Bruno Bauer, "Die Fähigkeit Frei zu Werden"', where he wrote:

> Here again the supreme condition of man is his legal status, his relationship to laws which are valid for him, not because they are laws of his own will and nature, but because they are dominant, and any infraction of them will be *avenged.*[77]

In *Anti-Duhring*, when attacking Duhring's alleged ignorance of the law, Engels says that Duhring's reference to the basis of criminal law as being revenge is not new, 'and that the "natural basis" of criminal law is *revenge* — an assertion of which in any case the only thing new is its mystical wrapping of "natural basis".'[78]

Marx's 'Capital Punishment' article contains a more detailed definition of punishment, 'punishment is nothing but a means of society to defend itself against the infraction of its vital conditions, whatever may be their character.'[79] This 'social defence' approach has to be considered in the light of state and law being class entities, for the defence of society is really the defence of the ruling class.

The final factor to consider is that of the 'lumpenproletariat':

> The 'dangerous class', the social scum, that passively rotting mass thrown off by the lowest layers of old society, may, here and there, be swept into the movement by a proletarian revolution, its conditions of life, however, prepare it far more for the bribed tool of reactionary intrigue.[80]

These harsh comments on the criminal classes, for they form part of the lumpenproletariat, contrast with statements on the 'isolated individual struggling against the prevailing conditions', but a clue to the different attitude may lie in the words 'bribed tool of reactionary intrigue'. Marx explained how the provisional government in France had formed 24 guards battalions made up of individuals who 'belonged for the most part to the *lumpenproletariat*, which in all big towns forms a mass sharply differentiated from the industrial proletariat, a recruiting ground for thieves and criminals of all kinds',[81] and he goes on to explain how they were used against the proletariat. In the 'Eighteenth Brumaire' there are numerous derogatory references to the lumpenproletariat being bought by Bonaparte. At one point Marx calls Bonaparte and his government lumpenproletarians![82] Engels, in his Preface to the 'Peasant War in Germany', says the lumpenproletariat is 'the worst of all the possible allies. This rabble is absolutely venal and absolutely brazen,'[83] adding that the French workers were correct in shooting a few of them!

It should be more than obvious that Marx and Engels hold distinctly adverse views on the lumpenproletariat. There is some obscurity about the composition of this group, as the Manifesto refers to the 'lowest layers of the old society', the 'Eighteenth Brumaire' contains a reference to the 'peasant lumpenproletariat',[84] and Engels speaks of the 'scum of depraved elements from all classes'.[85] There are many references to the view that thieves and criminals form part of this group.[86] Hirst[87] gives a reasonable explanation of this attitude to the lumpenproletariat when he says Marx and Engels tended to look at everything from a political viewpoint, and as this group could be a danger to the proletariat because of their possible use to reactionaries, they were to be totally condemned.

Summary

There is no comprehensive theory of crime, but it is possible to draw some pertinent conclusions. The role of the capitalist system is of primary importance, as features produced by this system, such as unemployment and poor housing conditions, are a direct cause of crime. As these influences act upon the individual, it sometimes seems that he has no choice but to be criminal, for the economic determinism that is certainly part of Marx and Engels' approach does receive a degree of emphasis. However, other factors are given consideration and the inclusion of social reaction, the effect of labelling and the concept of individual and group rebellion may add some credence to their beliefs, for economic determinism alone would be unsatisfactory.

Modern criminology believes that '*either* positive or negative relationships with economic conditions may be supported,'[88] and it is generally believed that complex factors are involved.

The role of the ruling class affects the concept of punishment. This basically consists of revenge on the part of the ruling class towards members of subjugated classes who have broken the rules. However, this is not to say that revenge is the sole purpose, for general and specific deterrence would be closely allied to this, and re-education may be admitted, although its aims would, of course, support the dominance of the ruling class. Note that it is that class as a whole that is supported, hence the law acting against individual members of the ruling class who commit crimes. In such cases, although the offenders will not normally be acting against the existence of the ruling class *per se*, their actions are not advantageous to the ruling class as a group, and so for the greater good they must be punished.

As stated, offences committed by members of the ruling class will not normally be political. Is this so in regard to offences committed by others? Hirst[89] says such actions are 'not *in effect* forms of political rebellion against the existing order but a more or less reactionary accommodation to them', but machine smashing has a political aspect, and Engels does say that one could be surprised that the bourgeoisie do not fear a 'universal outburst',[90] so politics may have to be considered. Politics would seem to be the only explanation of Marx and Engels' attitude to the lumpenproletariat. The criminal classes form part of this group, and without a political explanation it is difficult to rationalise the contradiction between the generally exonerative attitude to criminals and the attitude to the lumpenproletariat.

Under communism, classes will no longer exist, and one can deduce that many causes of crime will not exist — certainly, of course, those caused by the capitalist system itself. Plamenatz[91] says that crime will be 'virtually unknown', for the

> motives will be less urgent and frequent, and the offender will be more easily brought to his senses by the need to regain the good opinion of his neighbours. The assumption is that he lives in a society that is not divided, where men are not one another's victims, where no man is an outcast or an inferior merely because of his position in society. In a society of this kind, crime is much more clearly irrational, much more clearly against the interests of the criminal.

Plamenatz is concerned that this picture of no alienation and no need for organised force may not be the true one, for he feels that Marx may have been mistaken in thinking that alienation was so much a part of capitalist society, when it may be due to the 'scale and complexity of industrial society'.[92] It may not automatically disappear under communism. We are, therefore, led to ask what sort of crime will wither away in the development towards communism, and what will remain? Certainly 'political crimes' in the Marxist sense will go. These are crimes caused by the existence of classes, obvious examples being infringements of property rights, labour relations, and many types of contractual rights. Crimes caused by the pressures and disparities within society would supposedly not exist, as communist society has none of these problems. Equally, certain types of offence would exist under communism, such as traffic violations, those brought about by negligence, etc., and could be termed 'deviations' rather than 'crimes'.

What Plamenatz is asking is whether or not some crimes thought to be caused by the capitalist system will be caused by the communist system; for they may not be caused by the capitalist system in itself, but by collective living, an industrial society, or whatever. Perhaps one has to allow for the existence of some unacceptable behaviour under communism, but it is impossible to be very specific about quantity or quality.

Notes

1. K. Marx and F. Engels, *Selected Works*, in three volumes (henceforth referred to as *MESW*) (Moscow, 1973), vol. I, pp. 503-4.
2. H.B. Acton, *The Illusion of the Epoch* (London, 1973), p. 133.
3. S. Hook, *Towards the Understanding of Karl Marx* (London, 1936).
4. Ibid.
5. M.M. Bober, *Karl Marx's Interpretation of History* (Cambridge, Mass., 1948).
6. J. Plamenatz, *Man and Society*, 5th imp. (London, 1966), vol. II, p. 276.
7. Ibid., pp. 22-3.
8. G. Wetter, *Soviet Ideology Today* (London, 1966), pp. 168 *et seq.*
9. Written 21-22 September 1890.
10. *MESW*, III, p. 487.
11. Ibid., p. 488.
12. Ibid., p. 491.
13. Ibid., pp. 491-2.
14. Ibid., p. 497.
15. Previously this was thought to be to Starkenburg, and may be listed as such.
16. Ibid., p. 502.
17. Bober, *Karl Marx's Interpretation of History*, p. 306.
18. Ibid., p. 310.
19. *Articles from the Neue Rheinische Zeitung, 1848-49* (Moscow, 1972), p. 232.
20. K. Marx and F. Engels, *Collected Works* (henceforth referred to as *Coll. Works*) (London, 1975-in progress), vol. 6, p. 147.
21. *Contribution to Critique of Political Economy* (London, 1971), p. 193.
22. 'Ludwig Feuerbach and the End of Classical German Philosophy' in *MESW*, vol. III, p. 370.

23. Ibid., p. 371.

24. Ibid.

25. *MESW*, vol. I, p. 503 (from 'Preface', see above).

26. *MESW*, vol. III, p. 192.

27. Ibid., p. 275.

28. *Man and Society,* vol. II, p. 353.

29. *MESW*, vol. II, p. 187.

30. F. Engels, *Anti-Duhring* (Moscow, 1969), p. 179.

31. S.F. Bloom, 'The "Withering Away of the State"', *Jour. of Hist. of Ideas* (1946), p. 116.

32. *MESW*, vol. I, pp. 77-8.

33. Ibid., pp. 110-11.

34. Ibid., p. 476.

35. Ibid., p. 478.

36. R. Miliband, 'Marx and the State', *Socialist Register* (1965), p. 285.

37. *MESW*, vol. III, p. 328.

38. Ibid., vol. I, p. 206.

39. J. Sanderson, 'Marx and Engels on the State', *Western Political Quarterly* (1963), p. 950.

40. From Miliband, 'Marx and the State', p. 294, note 34.

41. Ibid., pp. 950-1.

42. *MESW*, vol. I, p. 123.

43. K. Marx and F. Engels, *The German Ideology* (London, 1965), p. 366.

44. *MESW*, vol. III, p. 26.

45. *Anti-Duhring*, p. 333.

46. H. Draper, 'Marx and the Dictatorship of the Proletariat', *New Politics*, vol. I, p. 95 *et seq.*

47. Ibid., p. 102.

48. Ibid., p. 289.

49. For example in his 1891 introduction to 'The Civil War in France'.

50. K. Marx and F. Engels, *Selected Correspondence* (Moscow, 1975), p. 318.

51. S. Avineri, *The Social and Political Thought of Karl Marx* (Cambridge, 1968), p. 202 *et seq.*

52. R. Adamiak, 'The "Withering Away" of the State: A Reconsideration', *The Journal of Politics*, vol. 32, p. 3.

53. Ibid.

54. 'Poverty of Philosophy', in *Coll. Works*, vol. 6, p. 212.

55. *MESW*, vol. I, p. 127.

56. Ibid., pp. 10 *et seq.*

57. Ibid., p. 114.

58. K.R. Popper, *The Open Society and Its Enemies* (London, 1966), vol. II, note 8 to Chapter 17.

59. See Bloom, 'The "Withering Away of the State", p. 114.

60. See Adamiak, 'The "Withering Away" of the State: A Reconsideration', p. 13.

61. *MESW*, vol. III, pp. 25-6.

62. Ibid., p. 35.

63. *Coll. Works*, vol. 1, pp. 387-8.

64. *German Ideology*, p. 367.

65. P.Q. Hirst, 'Marx and Engels on Law, Crime, and Morality', *Economy and Society*, vol. I.

66. F. Engels, *The Condition of the Working Class in England* (Moscow, 1973), p. 168.

67. Ibid., p. 173.

68. Ibid., p. 105.

69. Ibid., p. 70.

70. Ibid., p. 148.

71. *Condition of the Working Class in England*, p. 310.

72. *German Ideology* p. 367.

73. *Condition of the Working Class in England*, p. 302.

74. Article by Marx, 'Population, Crime and Pauperism', appearing in the *New York Daily Tribune* in September 1859, in K. Marx and F. Engels, *On Ireland* (Moscow, 1971), p. 93.

75. Ibid., pp. 92-3.

76. 'Outlines of a Critique of Political Economy', in W.O. Henderson (ed.), *Engels: Selected Writings* (London, 1967), p. 176.

77. T.B. Bottomore, *Karl Marx: Early Writings* (London, 1963), p. 38.

78. *Anti-Duhring*, p. 130.

79. T.B. Bottomore and M. Rubel (eds.), *Karl Marx: Selected Writings in Sociology and Social Philosophy* (London, 1963), p. 234.

80. *MESW*, vol. I, p. 118 (the Manifesto).

81. 'The Class Struggles in France', *MESW*, vol. I, p. 219.

82. Ibid., p. 485.

83. Ibid., vol. II, p. 163.

84. *MESW*, vol. I, p. 483.

85. Ibid., vol. II, p. 163.

86. E.g. ibid., vol. I, p. 219, and p. 442.

87. Hirst, 'Marx and Engels', pp. 41-2.

88. I. Taylor, P. Walton and J. Young, *The New Criminology* (London, 1973), p. 218.

89. Hirst, 'Marx and Engels', p. 43.

90. *Condition of the Working Class in England*, p. 171.

91. J. Plamenatz, *Man and Society*, vol. II, p. 374.

92. Ibid., pp. 376 *et seq.*

2 LENIN

The Russian Situation

Due to the great preponderance of peasants in the social composition
of the country, the greatest problem for believers in the occurrence of
a socialist revolution (in the Marxist sense) in the relatively foreseeable
future was this position and role of the peasantry. The Mensheviks and
Bolsheviks, being Marxist, were initially less interested in the peasantry
than the Socialist Revolutionaries — the revolutionary peasant party —
and took a more 'political' attitude. The former saw the coming
revolution to be one heralding capitalism, the bourgeois rather than
socialist revolution. They envisaged themselves as the opposition in a
bourgeois democratic republic. This 'conservatism' led to little support
in the country, where land distribution was understandably popular.
Their attitude was, however, certainly prima facie orthodox, as Marx's
main position seemed to indicate that capitalism had to fully develop
before the socialist revolution could take place. This was a depressing
outlook for Russian revolutionaries, at least those of a Marxist nature,
and various schools of thought in Russia adopted alternatives which
allowed for the socialist revolution to occur before the development of
full capitalism. It was in reply to Tkachov, one such believer, that
Engels wrote his 'Russia and the Social Revolution', containing the
distinctly unequivocal remark that 'A person who says that this
(socialist) revolution can be carried easier in a country which has no
proletariat or bourgeoisie, proves by this statement that he still has to
learn the ABC of socialism.'[1]

The 1859 Preface, by saying 'In broad outlines Asiatic, ancient,
feudal, and modern bourgeois modes of production can be designated
as progressive epochs in the economic formation of society'[2] had
helped, rightly or wrongly, towards the formation of the view that
history was a series of automatically successive epochs. Marx and
Engels had then made further difficulties by referring to Russia as
'semi-Asiatic', which tended to link it with the Asiatic mode of
production, which was supposedly characterised in its early stages by
a lack of private ownership in property, and later by the prevalence of
small, self-sustaining village communities. The existence in Russia of
village communities with a degree of communal ownership was a cause
for much speculation. Engels, in his reply to Tkachov noted above, said

39

that he thought them significant, but their predominance 'does not prove by any means that this drive [i.e. for association] makes possible a jump directly from the artel to the socialist society'.[3] He did think that some sort of revolution was at hand, but twenty years later, when reconsidering this article, still remained inconclusive – 'it will hasten the victory of the modern industrial proletariat, without which contemporary Russia cannot achieve a socialist Transformation arising either out of a village community or out of capitalism.'[4]

Marx himself had been consulted on this question by Vera Zasulich, and after drafting several replies, finally concluded that

> this community is the fulcrum of Russia's social revival, but in order that it might function in this way one would first have to eliminate the destructive influences which assail it from every quarter and then to ensure the conditions normal for spontaneous development.[5]

At the time, this reply, in seeming to support development from the village communities, was embarrassing to the Marxists in Russia who had contended that capitalism had begun to develop already, and this short cut, if it was one, could not apply.

This had followed his earlier comments in a letter to the editorial board of *Otechestvenniye Zapiski*, refuting Mikhailovsky, in which he had said that 'If Russia continues to pursue the path she has followed since 1861, she will lose the finest chance ever offered by history to a people and undergo all the fatal vicissitudes of the capitalist regime.'[6] The Preface to the Russian edition of the Communist Manifesto stated 'If the Russian Revolution becomes the signal for a proletarian revolution in the West, so that both complement each other, the present Russian common ownership of land may serve as a starting-point for a communist development.'[7] Although one gathers from these statements that the schema in the Preface and *Capital* were not to be universally applied, all the statements call for the cessation of change in the village communities. This did not happen. Changes were taking place at the time the statements were made, and even more so in the period up to the Revolution. Therefore, apart from the lack of any supporting revolutions, which seem to be another prerequisite, historical events would seem to preclude the possibility of development to communism directly from the village communities, even if it were possible in theory.

Lenin's view of the situation contained both Menshevik and Trotskyite concepts. In opposition to the former's belief that the proletariat would support the underdeveloped bourgeoisie, and undergo political, social and economic education to prepare it for the socialist revolution, Trotsky developed the celebrated theory of 'permanent revolution'. This says that the revolution is happening too late to be a purely bourgeois event, as that class will have to depend on the proletariat and the peasantry to carry through the revolution, and once this has happened, the course of events would lead the bourgeois revolution forward into a proletarian one. The two would be 'telescoped'. The theory is international in that European insurrections are expected. Indeed, Trotsky, in his 'Permanent Revolution' says, 'Socialist construction is conceivable only on the foundation of the class struggle, on a national and international scale,' and 'The completion of the socialist revolution within national limits is unthinkable.'[8]

Lenin, in 'Two Tactics', follows the Menshevik belief in that the coming revolution would be bourgeois, but says that the role of the proletariat need not be so secondary. However, unless the proletariat rouses the peasantry to revolutionary consciousness, the bourgeois element would prevail, and the proletariat would leave no 'imprint' on the revolution – 'Nothing but a revolutionary-democratic dictatorship of the proletariat and peasantry can prevent this.'[9] 'Instability' of both the bourgeoisie and peasantry is mentioned as a possibly dangerous factor, but an alliance with the latter was of great practical importance to the proletariat, as the peasantry was of far greater numerical significance. Lenin, and Trotsky, visualised this alliance as unequal, in that the proletariat was to lead; Lenin refers to the 'persuasion of the peasants by the workers'.[10] Critics said this would be an impossible alliance, but although he warned that 'the peasantry, as a landowning class, will play the same treacherous, unstable part as is now being played by the bourgeoisie,'[11] Lenin thought a bond with the workers would be possible as the peasantry is aware that 'only the proletariat is capable of supporting the peasantry to the end.'[12] This concept of a 'revolutionary-democratic dictatorship of the proletariat' is a variation from the original theory, but Marx may have hinted at something similar when, in the 'Eighteenth Brumaire', he says the French peasants 'find their natural ally and leader in the *urban proletariat*, whose task is the overthrow of the bourgeois order'.[13] M. Liebman refers to an article of September 1905, in which Lenin says:

From the democratic revolution we shall at once, and precisely in accordance with the measure of our strength, the strength of the class-conscious and organised proletariat, begin to pass to the socialist revolution. We stand for uninterrupted revolution. We shall not stop half-way.[14]

However, despite such Trotskyite leanings, the April Theses caused a great deal of surprise when Lenin indicated that the

specific feature of the present situation in Russia is that the country is *passing* from the first stage of the revolution — which, owing to the insufficient class-consciousness and organisation of the proletariat, placed power in the hands of the bourgeoisie — to its *second* stage, which must place power in the hands of the proletariat and the poorest sections of the peasants.[15]

The immediate reaction was unfavourable to Lenin as many, for example Kamenev writing in *Pravda*, thought that the bourgeois revolution could not be already completed, but Lenin's view eventually prevailed. One should note that Lenin, like Trotsky, saw the Russian Revolution as part of a world situation, the more developed Western European countries being ready for the socialist revolution. The relationship between Russia and Western countries was illustrated in an article of November 1917, in which Lenin says:

The proletariat will at once utilise this ridding of bourgeois Russia of tsarism and the rule of the landowners, not to aid the rich peasants in their struggle against the rural workers, but to bring about the socialist revolution in alliance with the proletarians of Europe.[16]

One can see that Lenin's attitude to the revolution moved from a basically Menshevik to a basically Trotskyite outlook, and many aspects of Trotsky's theory were incorporated into Lenin's. Marx's opinion as to whether Russia could accelerate the movement to socialism depended on supporting revolutions. Lenin agreed with this and yet the revolutions did not occur. Trotsky's theory of permanent revolution was not derived from Marx; Trotsky considered Marxism a 'method' rather than an outline for all future development, and using a 'Marxist' approach to the Russian problem, arrived at his theory. Lenin uses this ingenious theory to attach Marxist terms to the Russian situation. For example, he says the February Revolution was bourgeois, the October proletarian, and his modifications are too radical to remain 'Marxist':

they are 'Leninist'.

Some Important Aspects of Lenin's Theory

Starting with a concept of the 'dictatorship of the proletariat' similar
to that of Marx, Lenin increasingly emphasises its importance and that
of the transition period. Carew-Hunt[17] considers this to have happened
in three stages, the first of which centres about 'Two Tactics', where
Lenin says it will be 'a democratic, not a socialist dictatorship. It will
be unable (without a series of intermediate stages of revolutionary
development) to affect the foundations of capitalism.'[18] One should
remember that, at this stage, Lenin believes that the coming revolution
will be bourgeois. In the 'State and Revolution' imposed restrictions
are stressed:

> *Simultaneously* with an immense expansion of democracy, which
> *for the first time* becomes democracy for the people, and not
> democracy for the money-bags, the dictatorship of the proletariat
> imposes a series of restrictions on the freedom of the oppressors,
> the exploiters, the capitalists.[19]

The aim is to achieve true freedom by opposing the enemies of
freedom, but Lenin says that there will be no suppression and violence
when the free, democratic society has been achieved. On the nature of
the dictatorship, he wrote, 'We cannot imagine democracy, even
proletarian democracy, without representative institutions, but we can
and *must* imagine democracy without parliamentarism.'[20] Lenin looked
upon parliaments as 'talking-shops' and aimed at 'working bodies'
similar to the Paris Commune. This attitude brought Lenin into conflict
with Kautsky, who wrote 'The Dictatorship of the Proletariat' in reply,
which in turn elicited 'The Proletarian Revolution and the Renegade
Kautsky', in which the dictatorship is further emphasised, becoming,
the very *essence* of Marx's doctrine'.[21] Its purpose is left in no doubt —
'to break down the resistance of the bourgeoisie; — to inspire the
reactionaries with fear; — to maintain the authority of the armed
people against the bourgeoisie; that the proletariat may forcibly hold
down its adversaries.'[22]

This growing emphasis on the dictatorship may be due to practical
experience, as 'Kautsky' was written in November 1918, and perhaps
Lenin found force to be of great use when he had to run the country.

However, a more probable cause for its growing importance is the contemporary change in Lenin's view of the forthcoming revolution, for the dictatorship of the proletariat is to occur in the transition period, that is after a proletarian revolution, and would be, therefore, of little interest so long as the revolution was seen to be bourgeois. Even when this was thought to be the case, Lenin attached more importance to the part played by the proletariat than did Marx and Engels, so one may conclude that another relevant factor is the former's greater preoccupation with practical problems, whether immediate or in the future.

A final point to note here is that the dictatorship, whatever its importance, is considered by Lenin to be a 'rule unrestricted by any laws' based on force[23] – 'The revolutionary dictatorship of the proletariat is rule won and maintained by the use of violence by the proletariat against the bourgeoisie, rule that is unrestricted by any laws.'[24] The closely related concept of the 'withering away' of the state is considered in some detail when, in 'The State and Revolution', the famous passage in *Anti-Duhring* is analysed. There, he says the bourgeois state is abolished by the revolution, and it is the subsequent proletarian state that withers away. Later, he writes of two stages in development, socialism and communism, the latter, of course, being the more developed.

In deciding what Lenin means by the withering away of the state, a concept of central importance is that of class, which Lenin, in agreement with Marx, linked to the means of production – 'The abolition of classes means placing *all* citizens on an *equal* footing with regard to the *means of production*.'[25] This would involve the means of production being owned by the whole of society, as it is the ownership of the means of production that decides class membership. 'Only in communist society,. . .when there are no classes. . . *only* then "the state ceases to exist".'[26] This is closely following Marx's approach, and does not preclude the existence of a social organisation, not class based, in the future society, where public participation is to be important:

> We are not utopians, and do not in the least deny the possibility and inevitability of excesses on the part of *individual persons*, or the need to stop *such* excesses. In the first place, however, no special machine, no special apparatus of suppression is needed for this; this will be done by the armed people themselves.[27]

Just as public participation is important in communist society, it is instrumental in the withering away process that leads to that society. Lenin speaks of 'the gradual abolition of the state by systematically drawing on ever greater numbers of citizens, and subsequently *each and every* citizen, into the direct and *daily* performance of their share of the burdens of administering the state';[28] and 'enlisting the mass organisations of the working people in constant and unfailing participation in the administration of the state'.[29]

Summary

Lenin placed increasing emphasis on the dictatorship of the proletariat, an emphasis which affected the importance of the role of law in the transition period, as law is the will of the ruling class and during the period of the dictatorship, there is such a ruling class, the proletariat. Although considerable use is to be made of law in the transition period, the dictatorship is not bound by law and, considering that the use of suppression and violence is openly avowed, there is an obvious possibility that an authoritarian regime, unable to be criticised, could form.

The withering away can be seen in class terms, with public participation having an important role. During the transition period classes die out, and as law is seen by Lenin to be a class phenomenon,[30] it will die out. This does not exclude the possible existence of 'rules', i.e. 'non-class law', outlined above.[31] The law of the transition period should gradually acquire the character of 'rules' as it loses its class nature — this happening as the proletariat consolidates its position and society reforms.

There is a certain lack of clarity, or a complication, in the Russian situation due to the need for a worker-peasant alliance. The spirit of a dictatorship of the proletariat is perhaps kept alive by the leading role assigned to that class in the alliance, but one is left with some doubts over the exact nature of the class relationship, doubts due to a modification of Marx's theory made necessary by practical considerations.

Lenin and the Party

Lenin's attitude to the party is partially based on his concept of class consciousness. The more developed Western proletariat could have parties of the entire class, but in Russia, the newly emergent proletariat had not evolved a class consciousness, which had to be 'imported' into the class by *déclassé* intellectuals. Lenin relied on this course of action and rejected any emphasis on 'spontaneity' – important to Rosa Luxemburg and the Mensheviks. However, Lenin believed that the masses play a crucial role in that their full participation turns consciousness into power, and the mood of the masses, the social conditions and spontaneity are all relevant to the basic requirement of a 'revolutionary situation'.

The pamphlet 'What is to be done?', written in 1902, is of great importance with regard to the party, as in it Lenin attacks spontaneity and khvostism – the belief that the party should follow the masses – calling for an organisation with 'a stable organisation of leaders' and consisting 'chiefly of people professionally engaged in revolutionary activity',[32] partly, one may add, due to the need to prevent police infiltration. Moreover:

> As against the populists, he conceived of this party as proletarian; as against the 'legal Marxists', as a party of action as well as of theory; and as against the 'economists' as a party with a political as well as an economic programme.[33]

Lenin was not the originator of the well organised secret party, but he introduced it to Marxism, Marx having visualised the masses acting openly. Conquest says that Marx and Engels' famous dictum, 'The emancipation of the working class is the task of the working class itself,' received decisive amendment,[34] but one should note that Lenin considered the party to be part of the working class, i.e. its 'vanguard', and that the change is in line with Lenin's more 'voluntarist' approach.

This concept of the party is reflected in Lenin's definition of party member, discussed at the Second Congress in 1903. The differences between Lenin's definition and Martov's was one of the causes of the famous schism – the former utilised 'personal participation', the latter 'regular co-operation' in their respective formulae.

In 'One Step Forward, Two Steps Back', written in 1904 in reply to all the criticism he received after the Congress, he reiterated his views on the size and nature of the party, saying it must be conspiratorial, hierarchical and centralised, also agreeing with Plekhanov that the party would not be subservient to any transcendental democratic principles, but that such principles should be 'exclusively subordinated' to the party.[35]

Apart from certain, almost anarchistic, trends in 'The State and

Revolution', Lenin followed and developed these beliefs, until by 1920 ('Left-Wing Communism') he says that one of the conditions fundamental to Bolshevik success is 'the strictest, truly iron discipline' prevailing in the party, and that 'absolute centralisation and rigorous discipline in the proletariat are an essential condition of victory over the bourgeoisie'.[36] This spirit was incorporated into the 'Theses of the Communist International' approved by the Second Comintern Congress in July/August 1920; and the concept of 'democratic centralism' was embodied into Article 21 of the 1920 'Twenty-One Conditions of Admission to the Comintern', but of course with this principle, it is important as to whether it is democracy or centralism that is to be emphasised.

Hindsight has shown that Lenin's concept of the party laid the foundations for the dictatorship of one man. However, contemplation of an elite, hierarchical, centralised, professional and secretive organisation led Plekhanov, Rosa Luxemburg, Trotsky, Vera Zasulich *et al.* to foresee such a result and therefore attack Lenin's ideas. Plekhanov, in the 'Journal of a Social Democrat', made the perceptive comment that if the Bolshevik conception prevailed, 'everything will in the last resort revolve around one man who *ex providentia* will unite all the powers in himself.'[37] Lenin's view was formed by the theoretical questions that have been mentioned, and practical problems that had to be overcome if any headway was to be made. The Leninist party was well suited to the practical situation, not surprisingly if one remembers Lenin's usual preoccupations, preoccupations which were particularly decisive here.

The Dictatorship of the Party

On achieving power, the Bolsheviks were faced with a considerable problem. If they entered into a coalition government, they would be abdicating power, giving up something they had longed for, but if they did not, civil war and repression were a distinct possibility. Zinoviev and Kamenev supported the acquisition of a broader base by joining with the Mensheviks and Social Revolutionaries. However, the majority of the party, led by Lenin and Trotsky, thought the party should govern alone, allowing other parties a minor role. The supporters of the minority view left the Sovnarkom and the Central Committee, saying a non-coalition 'can maintain itself only by means of political terror' and that it would 'alienate the proletarian masses and cause their withdrawal from political leadership; it will lead to the establishment of an irresponsible regime and to the ruin of the revolution and the country.'[38]

The elimination of the other political parties was gradual, and did not involve a particular decree outlawing them. On 14 June 1918, the VTsIK expelled the Right SR and Menshevik members for supposed counter-revolutionary and anti-Soviet activity, leaving only the Left SRs in a coalition which lasted three months, brought to an end by disagreements over the Treaty of Brest-Litovsk and grain confiscations, which resulted in the July uprising and subsequent terror. Later in 1918, 'loyal' Mensheviks and SRs willing to repudiate 'internal and external revolution' were readmitted to the VTsIK (the latter three months after the Mensheviks). They were expected to follow the Bolshevik line, and were in a peculiar limbo until Kronstadt, when a great many were exiled. From 1921-2, the Bolsheviks had sole control.

With opposition inside and outside the Party, Lenin often took a conciliatory line, as one can see from Zinoviev and Kamenev, and the Left, Military and Workers' Oppositions, but he was ruthless in pressing his own views forward, and did not hesitate to denounce any criticism that was not felt to be 'constructive'. Precedents were set.

The process of taking power drew attention to certain problems. What was the basis of the Party's right to govern for the proletariat, and what was to be the relationship between the government and the Party? One has to start from the premiss that the Party is said to be the 'vanguard of the proletariat', the repository of its consciousness. The theory of consent required to change the dictatorship of the proletariat into one of the Party was constructed by Lenin, and more especially by Stalin.

The former had claimed that the Party was the authentic spokesman of the will of the masses, and had the task of upholding the interests of the workers and to represent those of the entire working-class movement. Stalin further developed this theory, saying:

The Party cannot be a real party if it limits itself to registering what the masses of the working class feel and think. . .if it is unable to raise the masses to the level of understanding the class interests of the proletariat. The Party must stand at the head of the working class: it must lead the proletariat, and not drag at the tail of the spontaneous movement.[39]

As all important political and organisational questions were coming to be decided via guiding directions from the Party, and there were to be no competing entities for power, the dictatorship of the proletariat would tend to become that of the Party. Shapiro says, 'The onset of totalitarianism was inherent in the determination which the bolsheviks showed from the first to tolerate no rivals for power, and no independent institutions.'[40]

Practical problems concerning the control of the government by the Party were to be considered after Sverdlov's death – with Lenin concluding that there was no problem. The emphasis up to then had been on the system of soviets, not the Party, and as Sverdlov, in his capacity as Secretary of the Central Committee and Chairman of the CEC of the Congress of Soviets, had been able to use the machinery of the latter, that of the former had atrophied.

Some, for example Preobrazhensky, had suggested the abolition of the Party, while others had thought it needed strengthening. At the Eighth Party Congress that followed soon after Sverdlov's death in March 1919, the 'Resolution on Organisational Matters' said that the Party and governmental bodies were no longer to be integrated. The Party was to give directions via its members within the soviets. This did not revolutionise the position, as the control was still there, and the problem of how a dictatorial party with a monopoly of political power was to control the soviets, and yet allow them autonomy, was not – and could not – be resolved.

Lenin and Legality

Lenin's post-revolutionary writings contain many calls to uphold legality. 'To The Population' (18 Nov. 1917)[41] says:

> Establish the strictest revolutionary law and order, mercilessly suppress any attempts to create anarchy by drunkards, hooligans, counter-revolutionary officer cadets, Kornilovites and their like. . . Arrest and hand over to the revolutionary courts all who dare to injure the people's cause irrespective of whether the injury is manifested in sabotaging production (damage, delay and subversion), or in hoarding grain and products or holding up shipments of grain, disorganising the railways, etc.[42]

Later that year, Lenin concerns himself with incidents involving looted landed estates, calling for prosecutions and to be kept informed of any sentences.[43] The Petrograd Committee of the Party is asked for '100 reliable party members' to help stop looting,[44] itself a great cause of concern, a committee having been recently set up to deal with it, and a counter-revolutionary group allocating large sums of money to further looting had been discovered.

'Red tape' and bureaucratic methods were often attacked, the 'Instructions of the Council of Labour and Defence' directed laws against red tape,[45] red tape was linked to bribery, Lenin saying that the Party needed purging of those who practised either;[46] and the Commissariat of Justice was periodically accused of not fighting this problem.[47]

More examples of individual cases include Lenin's call for a 'rigorous investigation' and a subsequent arrest of the murderers who had entered the Mariinskaia Hospital and killed Shingarov and Kokoshin;[48] and the instruction to Bonch-Brugevich about drunken sailors illegally arresting officers and carrying out searches, and asking for action and names.[49]

On 4 May 1918, Lenin wrote to Kursky saying a law against bribery was urgently needed, and mentioned the not inconsiderable sentence of ten years' imprisonment plus ten years' compulsory labour.[50] This was the result of the six-month sentences passed by the Moscow Revolutionary Tribunal on Moscow Committee of Investigation members who had accepted bribes, and led to the decree 'On Bribery'[51] which Feldbrugge[52] describes as one of those decrees of the early period that 'stand out by their technical merits and appear to bear the mark of the professional lawyer'.

Telegrams ask a local executive committee to check 'very strictly' the behaviour of anti-profiteer detachments and what they do with items requisitioned,[53] and a land department is informed that forcing peasants to do communal work is illegal, punishable with 'all the severity of revolutionary law'.[54] Dzerzhinsky is to institute a '*very strict* investigation' into a case where peasants had come to Lenin with complaints and were subsequently arrested,[55] and Lacis is told the Cheka in the Ukraine needs scrutinising as 'hangers on' etc. have gathered around it.[56]

Finally, one should note the 'Rough Thesis of a Decision on the Strict Observance of the Laws' drawn up by Lenin on 2 November 1918. The first part of this said that 'Legality must be raised and observed since the basis of the law in the R.S.F.S.R. has been established,' and laws against counter-revolutionaries can be passed but they must be 'specific'.[57] The use of this particular word is perhaps enigmatic, as the Resolution of the All-Russia CEC, dated 16 January 1918, says all power is to go to soviets and Soviet institutions:

Accordingly, any attempt by any person or institution whatsoever
to usurp any of the functions of state power will be regarded as a
counter-revolutionary act. All such attempts will be suppressed by
every means at the disposal of the Soviet power, including the use of
armed force.[58]

The definition here is very wide, perhaps unavoidably so, and we shall
see that whatever Lenin did mean by 'specific', it did not generally
result in closely defined acts.

All these numerous calls for the upholding of legality, the use made
of the law, are accompanied by various speeches, letters and
communications in which Lenin seems to condone the commission of
illegal acts, acts undermining legality. It is worth while considering what
is meant by 'legality' at this point. The term is discussed in 'Lenin, Law
and Legality'[59] by Lapenna, who outlines the basic requirements as
(i) the existence of a legal system which provides adequate solutions for
all possible legal relations; (ii) a system of guarantees for protection
against arbitrariness and abuses; and (iii) an adherence to minimum
legal standards recognised by all the civilised nations of a given epoch.
This is a useful framework with which to compare the real situation.

An early example of a call to arbitrary action is Lenin's urging of
soldiers to 'shoot the Traitors on the spot'[60] in event of betrayal or
attack during fraternisation, in his speech at the All-Russia CED on 23
November 1917. This is an almost military situation and could be
excused on these grounds, but giving authority to adopt 'the most
revolutionary measures' to ensure the movement of grain from Siberia
to Petrograd, accusing railwaymen of sabotage, and saying the 'most
ruthless revolutionary measures' should be taken[61] does not have any
such qualifying factors. The language used indicates that some form of
severe measures are to be used, but these are not in any real sense
defined — 'revolutionary' can mean many things. On 9 August 1918,
Lenin ordered 'ruthless mass terror' against 'kulaks, priests and
whiteguards',[62] and three days later he speaks of the 'ruthless'
suppression of kulaks.[63] Apart from ill-defined measures, these have a
further imprecise element, 'kulak'. Theoretically, these were of course
a particular type of peasant, at the top of the old peasant economic
hierarchy, and suffered considerable disapproval — 'The kulak steals
other people's money and other people's labour.'[64] However, in
practice anyone could be termed 'kulak' and dealt with accordingly,
so severe unlimited measures could be freely applied to all.

Many of the instructions involving severe actions are written in such imprecise terms, another good example being the telegram of 7 July 1918 charging Natsovenus to shoot any foreigner helping the enemy, and to shoot citizens of the RSFSR who are plundering 'directly or indirectly'.[65]

Summing up, one notices that in Lenin's post-revolutionary writings, extending as they do from October/November 1917 to his death, there is a lack of uniformity, where differing emphases occur, reflecting a wide variety of interests. One sees a person in a revolutionary situation, organising many governmental functions and trying to do everything himself. There are many calls to uphold legality, not surprisingly as 'the basis of the law in the R.S.F.S.R. has been established'.[66] The new legality is 'revolutionary legality', supposedly that of the proletariat — the law is 'their' will, and therefore must be upheld. However, there are also many utterances ordering actions that would undermine legality, in that they would not be free from arbitrariness or abuse, nor adhere to minimum recognised legal standards. These are directed against situations or people that Lenin would consider deleterious to the revolution.

The use of law against such cases is supported by theory — the degree of ruthlessness being due to the extremely serious nature of the situation. However, it is easy to excuse the means by reference to the end, and the injustice and danger of such arbitrary actions cannot be overlooked.

The examples of personal intercession by Lenin, especially perhaps those involving Gorky,[67] are, one believes, typical of many individuals who treat impersonal situations with whatever action they feel necessary, but react differently when they become privately involved. 'Justice' can appear in a different guise when one is personally concerned.

Conclusions

One may think that the most basic problem that Lenin had to face was the adoption of theory to the practicalities of the Russian situation. In deciding whether he really did have to do this, one has to consider carefully what Marx and Engels had to say on the matter.

Marx had concluded that Russia may be able to avoid certain phases of development undergone by the more advanced Western European countries, because of the existence of the peasant communities with their degree of communal ownership. However, specific mention was made of the need not to further undermine these communities, and of the necessity of supporting revolutions occurring abroad. In the years following this statement, both of these stipulations were not complied with, as changes that were taking place when Marx wrote continued to the point when before the Stolypin reforms half the communes investigated in European Russia had stopped the periodic land redistribution that had been one of their most promising features. As to the supporting revolutions: of course they did not occur.

Despite these fatal drawbacks, Lenin, moving from a Menshevik to a Trotskyite approach, incorporated parts of Trotsky's (and Parvus') theory into his own and eventually arrived at the view that the October Revolution was the socialist one for which all had been waiting. Again it was assumed that other revolutions would occur – in the Western democracies this was implicit in the theory of permanent revolution. But this was not to be the case.

Any Marxist alternative to Marx's opinion that the communes may be a starting point has to rely on the classical theory – i.e. the socialist revolution will take place when capitalism has reached the required stage of development. As the Western countries were considered to be nearer that stage than Russia, one has to assume that the economy of the latter had to become more like those of the former. Capitalism had to develop.

In the first half of the nineteenth century, Russia had fallen behind the countries of Western Europe. This had occurred for several reasons and once it had done so, the situation worsened: Russia became more backward because it was behind to begin with. Changes came about after the Crimean War, the most important being the emancipation of the peasants, a most necessary measure, but one which brought many problems. The labour pool formed from landless peasants would enable industry to expand if measures were taken in this direction, and from the late 1880s this took place, Witte playing a leading role. The more advanced countries were also instrumental, not by having supporting revolutions, but by supplying capital. This was carried to such an extent that it is doubtful whether the loans could ever be repaid. This question was never resolved, however, as the loans were repudiated by the Bolsheviks after they had taken power.

In the 1900s there were periods of stagnation, but generally the period was one of growth. However, by 1913, it is said that industry contributed only one-fifth of the national income and only employed 5 per cent of the total labour force – hardly a position of advanced capitalism. As to agriculture, although there had been reforms, these did not help all peasants, for a 'wager on the strong' could not be expected to advantage the poor, so the situation still had much room for improvement.

One can summarise by saying that although the country was undergoing capitalist development, it was far behind the Western countries, and could not be said to be 'capitalist' as such. As the socialist revolution was supposedly to happen in the most advanced countries first, Russia was not the most promising ground for this to occur. Keeping this in mind, Lenin's audacious premiss that the February Revolution was that introducing capitalism, and that of October, socialism, seems singularly unconvincing. Unless the basic approach is greatly modified, there would obviously be no time for the necessary economic development. If this can be explained away by 'modifications' to the theory, then these must be such to label it Leninist rather than Marxist.

Turning to aspects within Lenin's theory, his emphasis on the importance of the dictatorship of the proletariat in the transition period, and the corresponding de-emphasis on the 'withering away', indicate an increasingly important role for law, as the transition period is a law-containing period, with the proletariat as the ruling class. Usually this law is termed 'special' because it is not used for the suppression of a majority by a minority, but in many respects it is theoretically similar to law in bourgeois states. The 'withering away' is described in the special terminology used by Marx and Engels, and one should distinguish between 'law' and 'rules', as between 'state' and 'organisation', for the future society is to have the latter two respectively, being as they are apolitical, classless concepts. In effect, the position is as before: the final elimination of law and state depends on that of politics, which in turn depends on that of class. The event must be seen in these terms, and not in any simplistic manner which may leave the impression that there will be no regulatory influences at all. The Party is Lenin's great creation, and his view of it is linked to his belief that class consciousness has to be brought to the proletariat from outside. The centralised, hierarchical party is the 'vanguard of the proletariat', speaks for the proletariat, and is the repository of its will. To some extent under Lenin, and more so with Stalin, accommodations were made to make the party synonymous with the proletariat: the dictatorship of the proletariat becomes that of the party, then that of the party summit.

When Lenin came to power, many of his actions were totally in accord with his theory — for example, he made many calls to uphold legality, which complied with the replacement of the old ruling class by the new, and 'its' dictatorship becoming the basis of legality. However, many of his actions should be viewed in the light of the actual situation. Severe penalties, wide definitions, particular interests — 'red tape', bribery — illuminate the dictatorship in action, 'unfettered by any laws'.

In conclusion, four points can be made.

(i) There are strong doubts as to whether Marx's theory or approach can be applied in the first place, for although individual action can to some extent advance or retard the historical forces, certain stages of economic development are a prerequisite to the corresponding social reactions. Russia could not have a socialist revolution because Lenin wanted one, and in any case, there had been no supporting revolutions abroad.

(ii) There have been important changes of emphasis in the theory, and although the lack of guidance given by Marx and Engels can make assessment difficult, the changes are certainly significant.

(iii) It is very important to realise that the Party is not the proletariat, nor is it the summit of the party. Apart from the theoretical problems posed by this assertion, such as how the consciousness and will of a class can be assigned to a group, there is a paradox in the situation where the party represents the wishes and aspirations of the proletariat and yet does not allow any choice to indicate their actual nature. One may add that this concept of a party would be alien to Marx himself, as he showed total contempt to even sympathetic political parties, in line with his view that the proletariat would free itself. Marx is distinctly more deterministic than Lenin.

(iv) In so far as it has been considered, which is not to any great extent, Lenin has been comparatively orthodox in his treatment and use of law, but this will be examined in greater detail later.

Notes

1. P.W. Blackstock and B.F. Haselitz (eds.), *Karl Marx and Friedrich Engels: The Russian Menace to Europe* (Glencoe, Illinois, 1952), p. 205.

2. *MESW*, vol. I, p. 504.

3. Blackstock and Haselitz, *Russian Menace to Europe*, p. 210.

4. Ibid., p. 241.

5. *Selected Correspondence*, p. 320.

6. Ibid., p. 292.

7. *MESW*, vol. I, pp. 100-1. Written on 21 Jan. 1882.

8. In C. Wright Mills, *The Marxists* (London, 1963), p. 274.

9. V.I. Lenin, *Selected Works* (3 volumes) (henceforth *SW*) (Moscow, 1975), vol. I, p. 461.

10. *SW*, vol. III, p. 188.

11. Ibid., vol. I, p. 524.

12. Ibid., p. 523.

13. *MESW*, vol. I, p. 482.

14. M. Liebman, *Leninism under Lenin* (London, 1975), p. 83.

15. *SW*, vol. II, p. 30 (written in April 1917).

16. See Liebman, *Leninism*, p. 181.

17. R.N. Carew Hunt, *The Theory and Practice of Communism* (London, 1963), pp. 180 *et seq.*

18. *SW*, vol. I, pp. 457-8.

19. Ibid., vol. II, p. 302.

20. Ibid., p. 272.

21. Ibid., vol. III, p. 20.

22. Ibid., p. 36.

23. Ibid., p. 22.

24. Ibid., p. 23.

25. *Collected Works* (London 1960-70), vol. 20, p. 146.

26. *SW*, vol. II, p. 302.

27. Ibid., p. 304.

28. *Coll. W*, vol. 27, p. 156.

29. *SW*, vol. III, p. 106.

30. E.g. 'What is law? The expression of the will of the ruling classes' in *Coll. W*, vol. 15, p. 172.

31. See Chapter One.

32. *SW*, vol. I, pp. 187-8.

33. Carew Hunt, *Theory and Practice of Communism*, pp. 185-6.

34. R. Conquest, *Lenin* (London, 1972), p. 39.

35. *SW*, vol. I, pp. 260-1.

36. Ibid., vol. III, p. 293.

37. In E.H. Carr, *The Bolshevik Revolution* (London, 1966), vol. I, p. 45.

38. In M. Fainsod, *How Russia is Ruled* (Cambridge, Mass., 1963), p. 133.

39. 'The Foundations of Leninism' in B. Franklin (ed.), *The Essential Stalin* (London, 1973), p. 172.

40. L. Schapiro, *The Communist Party of the Soviet Union* (London, 1970), p. 325.

41. All dates are given in New Style versions unless otherwise stated.

42. *Coll. W*, vol. 26, p. 297.

43. Ibid., vol. 35, p. 327.

44. Ibid., vol. 44, entry no. 10.

45. Ibid., vol. 32, p. 390.

46. Ibid., vol. 33, p. 77.

47. E.g. letter to Kursky, in ibid., vol. 35, p. 521.

48. Ibid., vol. 44, entry no. 20.

49. Ibid., entry no. 22.

50. Ibid., vol. 35, p. 331.

51. 9 May 1918.

52. F.J. Feldbrugge, *Soviet Criminal Law: General Part* (Leyden, 1964), p. 28.

53. *Coll. W*, vol. 44, p. 187.

54. Ibid., p. 209.

55. Ibid., p. 213.

56. Ibid., p. 245.

57. Ibid., vol. 42, p. 110.
58. Ibid., vol. 26, p. 428.
59. In L. Schapiro and P. Reddaway (eds.), *Lenin: the Man, the Theorist, the Leader* (London, 1967).
60. *Coll. W*, vol. 26, p. 318.
61. Ibid., vol. 44, pp. 55 and 56.
62. Ibid., vol. 36, p. 489.
63. Ibid., vol. 44, p. 129.
64. Ibid., vol. 29, p. 31.
65. Ibid., vol. 44, pp. 114-15.
66. Ibid., vol. 42, p. 110 (noted above).
67. See ibid., vol. 44, p. 210, involving a friend of Gorky, one Ivan Volny.

3 CRIME AND PUNISHMENT IN THE FIRST PERIOD – 1917-1921

This is a very unsettled and disorganised period due to the historical circumstances. However, a surprising amount of organisational activity occurred, especially regarding the administration of justice. Substantive law did not receive such close attention, with decrees having an unassimilated, unplanned appearance, dealing on an individual basis with particular problems that had arisen; but the role of prerevolutionary law and legal consciousness received more systematic treatment. Similarly, attitudes to certain types of offence and offender are directly attributable to theory, which progressed during this era under Lenin's guidance.

Due no doubt to Lenin's presence, other theoreticians did not greatly deviate from the accepted path, and we find law seen as a temporary repressive force, and

> With the final suppression of the bourgeoisie the function of the proletarian 'law' will gradually diminish and be replaced by the organisational rules of economic life. . .The organs of law will be transformed into economic administrative organs. Judges will be replaced increasingly by workers, overseers, and bookkeepers.[1]

Mass participation, the involvement of members of the public in administration, played an important role immediately after the revolution, there being little else to run the necessary institutions and agencies, but became less significant with increased organisation and centralisation. The Basic Principles were to speak of destroying the state 'as an agency of persuasion, and the law as a function of the state', not of destroying the state and law *per se*, perhaps indicating a belief in their modified existence in the future. Crime, at least that which was class-based, was to disappear with inequality and the class system, but in this, as in the other aforementioned areas, one sees the beginning of the divergence between theory and practice.

Exercising Power

As would be expected, on taking power the Bolsheviks had to face
important practical problems as well as those of theory. The result of
the elections for the Constituent Assembly was one, for out of 707
deputies, 370 were SRs, 175 Bolsheviks, 40 Left SRs, 17 Kadets and
16 Mensheviks.[2] The Bolsheviks obtained under one-quarter of all the
votes cast, but conveniently dealt with the situation by the simple
expedient of withdrawing (together with the Left SRs) and then
refusing access to all others, so limiting the life of the Assembly to all
of one day. Lenin had obviously meant it when he wrote, 'Naturally,
the interests of this revolution stand higher than the formal rights of
the Constituent Assembly.'[3] It is important to note and perhaps of
special interest when one remembers that all the other parties, apart
from the Kadets, could be termed 'socialist', that Lenin, together with
a majority of the Party, thought the Bolsheviks should rule alone, and
not in coalition with other parties — the view of Kamenev and Zinoviev,
amongst others. The elimination of the other parties was achieved by
ensuring the ascendancy of the Bolsheviks via infiltration of
governmental agencies and their all-important executive committees,
and the use of decrees and wholesale arrests. The sole party status was
reached soon after Kronstadt.

The severe treatment meted out to external opposition compares
unfavourably to that directed towards critical discussion within the
Party. In this period various important opposition groups did exist
within the Party — for example the Left, Military, Democratic
Centralist and, more interesting, Workers' Oppositions. The last
mentioned fostered the increased influence of trade unions which, if it
had been allowed to develop, could have had a most important effect.
However, due to such disasters as the Civil War and Lenin's overriding
belief in the need for unity, the activities of all the opposition groups
were distinctly circumscribed, but nothing more drastic than warnings
as to future behaviour were received by their individual members.

As to the economic situation, the term usually applied to this period
is 'war communism', which is identified by Nove[4] as

1) an attempt to ban private manufacture, the nationalisation of
nearly all industry, the allocation of nearly all material stocks, and
of what little output there was, by the state, especially for war
purposes; 2) a ban on private trade, never quite effective anywhere,
but spasmodically enforced; 3) seizure of peasant surpluses

(*prodrazverstka*); 4) the partial elimination of money from the state's dealings with its own organisations and the citizens. Free rations, when there was anything to ration; 5) all these factors combined with terror and arbitrariness, expropriations, requisitions. Efforts to discipline, with party control over trade unions. A seige economy with a communist ideology. A partly organised chaos.

However, if this policy was only partly organised, it may be considered some improvement on the total chaos that reigned before its introduction, which had been in significant part due to the interventionalists and the upheavals of the Civil War. As regards the actual revolution, the main effect in agriculture was on the large estates which suffered expropriations, usually of an undirected and disorganised kind. The upheavals, grain requisitions and collapse of the rouble led to a drastic fall in the level of agricultural production. The inhabitants of cities and towns left for the country, believing food would be more readily available. Westwood[5] includes some statistics relating to Petrograd which illustrate this, which are reproduced in Table 3.1.

Overall, 10 million people died in the Civil War years, the number of workers falling from 2.5 to 1.25 million; industrial production in 1921 was one-fifth of that in 1913.

The policy included attempts at organisation, but many decrees had the opposite effect — for example, the nationalisation of industry was greatly disorganised by the Decree on Workers Control which had the practical effect of enabling the workers to do whatever they wished regardless of what was in their best interests, or regarded as such, in the long run.

Table 3.1: Population of Petrograd, 1914-20

Year	Pop. (millions)	Births per 1,000	Deaths per 1,000
1914	2.2	25	21
1917	2.5	18	25
1918	1.5	15	44
1919	0.8	15.5	81.5
1920	0.6	12	90-120 (est.)

Theory in the 1919 Party Programme

This Programme, adopted at the Eighth Party Conference held in Moscow on 13-23 March 1919, does not contain many surprising details. Importance is attached to the use of the dictatorship of the proletariat; the assistance of the peasantry is acknowledged; and many statements in the previous programme (that of 1903) on various aspects of Marxism were reaccepted. The withering away can be interpreted in class terms – 'until the division of society into classes has been abolished and all government disappears'.[6] Not unexpectedly, the Soviet government is seen as truly democratic, having the interests of the majority at heart, and 'guaranteeing to the working masses incomparably more opportunities to vote and to recall their delegates'.

In the *ABC of Communism*,[7] written by Bukharin and Preobrazhensky as a commentary on this programme, Bukharin, who wrote the theoretical part of the book, included a section on the dictatorship of the proletariat, which takes a very orthodox line. The dictatorship is to be used to suppress and overcome the bourgeoisie, will be a temporary phenomenon, and will grow progressively milder only when the 'suppression of the exploiters is complete, when they have ceased to resist, when it is no longer in their power to injure the working class'.[8] It is not only an agency for suppression, but also a 'lever for effecting economic transformation'; it has both positive and negative aspects.

At the end of this section, Bukharin comments on ethics, saying in reply to criticism that the Bolsheviks are arbitrary in their moral judgements, that the 'proletariat is fighting solely on behalf of the new social order'. 'Whatever helps in the struggle is good; whatever hinders, is bad.'[9]

On the withering away, Bukharin writes, 'Meanwhile the bourgeoisie, little by little, will fuse with the proletariat; the workers' State will gradually die out; society as a whole will be transformed into a communist society in which there will be no classes.'[10] Note the parallel between the absence of class and that of state. A further treatment of this question comes under the heading 'Administration in the Communist System', which begins 'In a communist society there will be no classes. But if there will be no classes, this implies that *in communist society there will likewise be no State*.'[11] Direction is to be given by 'statistical bureaux', the workers following the directives because they will know that 'this work is necessary and that life goes easier when everything is done according to a prearranged plan and when the social order is like a well-oiled machine'.[12] Bureaucracy will not exist because no special section of the population will work permanently in the bureaux, posts will be rotated, individuals will carry out many different functions consecutively. Obviously this is referring to mass participation in the administration, one of the constituent concepts of the withering away. It is interesting to note that a bureaucracy is thought impossible because of the rotation of posts – perhaps its existence depends on the posts, not the persons occupying them.

On 12 December 1919 the 'Basic Principles for the Criminal Law of the RSFSR' were issued.[13] They began with a long preamble containing various comments on aspects of theory. Reference was made to the need to use the state and law during the transition period, and the disappearance of classes has its usual significance – 'Only when the opposition of the overthrown bourgeois and intermediate classes has been finally overcome and a communist system realised, will the proletariat abolish the state as an organisation of force and law as a function of the state.' This seems remarkably in accordance with the teachings of Marx (and Lenin).

Attitudes to Law and Crime

The 1903 Party Programme had said very little about law. Only two proposals were put forward, that of giving every person the right to sue officials in the ordinary manner via the courts, and the electing of judges by the people. Lenin had worked upon revisions of the Programme in 1917, and expanded the second of the two given above into 'Election by the people of judges and other officials, both civil and military, with the right to recall any of them at any time by decision of a majority of the electors.'[14] Due to the Revolution, changes were not made until 1919, when the new programme was adopted.

Section 11, entitled 'Jurisprudence', begins by stating that the old organs of repression – i.e. the old courts, are to be abolished, and that judges are to be elected by and from the working class. The complex system of courts is to be replaced 'by a very simplified, uniform system of people's courts' and assessors are to be used, involving the people in the administration of justice.[15] Punishments are replaced by educative measures, and on the subject of the old law:

> The soviet government, abolishing all the laws of the overthrown governments, commissioned the judges elected by the soviets to carry out the will of the proletariat in compliance with its decrees and in cases of absence or incompleteness of decrees to be guided by

socialist conscience.

The importance of the courts to the dictatorship of the proletariat is fully recognised.

In *The ABC of Communism*, Preobrazhensky says that the old courts concealed their class basis but the new do not, being 'places where the working majority passes judgement upon the exploiting minority' (one assumes 'previously exploiting' is meant).[16] To this effect the judges are elected by and from the working class. The judges must decide matters in accordance with 'proletarian ideology', as opposed to bourgeois, when considering matters arising from the 'break-up of the old relationships'. When dealing with the 'vast number of cases which occur independently of the peculiar conditions of the revolutionary era — minor criminal cases of a petty-bourgeois character', the courts must apply the new attitudes and penal measures adopted by the revolutionary proletariat.[17]

When considering the future, Preobrazhensky says the Cheka and revolutionary tribunals are transient and will not be needed 'when the counter-revolution has been successfully crushed'. However, because of 'vestiges of bourgeois society in its manifold manifestations', the courts may be needed for a long time, as the abolition of class, which itself can take some time, does not immediately lead to the abolition of class ideology. Peasant ideology will be slow to change and 'anti-social offences arising out of personal egoism' will long provide work for the courts. They will change in character, becoming expressions of public opinion and giving decisions of a purely moral significance.[18]

The first statute to act as a guide to the courts on crime generally was the Basic Principles, but before this, there were some other guides of a non-comprehensive nature available, such as the *Sudebnoe Nastolnoe Rukovodstvo*,[19] brought out by the Commissariat for Military Affairs in Petrograd. This was primarily for the use of various military courts and tribunals, but contained a general section on the principles of criminal law under the heading 'Fundamental Concepts of Substantive Criminal Law'. This commences by saying that

a crime is any act forbidden by law on pain of punishment. . . However, the presence of the fact of a crime is not enough for the application of punishment: essential, first and foremost, is personal guilt. The criminal must be conscious of that committed by him.[20]

Mental incapacity is to free from punishment, and there are degrees of guilt with corresponding degrees of punishment. A list of mitigating and aggravating factors follows. Social danger is not mentioned here, but may be an overriding factor to be applied to any case. The more conservative attitude may be due in part to the purposes and origins of the book, for it was to be a comprehensive, easy to follow guide for the layman, and the old ways may have offered an easier pattern to follow than the unsettled new. As to the Basic Principles themselves, they were concerned with law and criminal law in some detail. The preamble speaks of the past use made of law:

> In the course of the struggle with their class enemies, the proletariat applies. . .measures of force, but applies them at first without a particular system, from case to case, without organisation. The experience of the struggle, however, accustomed the proletariat to uniform measures, resulting in a system giving birth to new law.

The first section after the preamble gave various pertinent definitions:

> Law — this is a system (order) of social relations, corresponding to the interests of the ruling class and the protection of its organised force;. . .Criminal law consists of legal rules and other legal measures by which the system of social relations of a given class society is protected from offences (crimes) by means of repression (punishment);. . .Soviet criminal law has the task of guarding by means of repression, the system of social relations corresponding to the interests of the toiling masses who are being organised into the ruling class under the dictatorship of the proletariat during the period of transition from capitalism to communism.

These definitions are orthodox, the class nature of law, law as the will of the ruling class (as determined by the mode of production), the dictatorship of the proletariat and transition period, all being considered in the usual accepted way.

Articles 5-16 inclusive make up the largest section of the Principles, entitled 'On Offences and Punishments'. An offence is defined as 'the infringement of the order of social relations being guarded by the criminal law', and 'provokes the necessary struggle of the state power against persons (criminals) committing such activity or tolerating such inaction.' (Arts. 5 and 6). Punishment, as defined by Article 7, is 'those measures of compulsory pressure by means of which the authority guarantees a given order of social relations from the violations of the latter (criminals)', and its purpose is 'the protection of the social order from an offence which was committed, or such attempted perpetrations, and from future possible offences both by the person in question and other persons' (Art. 8). This is to be done by adopting him into the new social order or, if that is impossible, to isolate him, and for 'exceptional cases', 'physical destruction' is mentioned.

Articles 11 and 12 concern themselves with the character of the criminal and the offence. As well as the normal inquiries as to why the offence was committed, the 'mode of his former life' is to be considered, and

> whether the crime is committed by a person who belongs to the propertied class, with the object of the restoration, preservation or acquisition of any privilege linked with the right of ownership; or by the poor, in a state of starvation or need.

Also, 'whether the act is committed in the interests of the restoration of the power of the oppressing classes, or for self-interest'. Realisation of harm done, public security, whether it is a first offence, are all specifically mentioned.

This section continues with comments on minors (under 14), mental incapacity, extreme necessity and necessary defence, ending with Article 16 which says, 'With the disappearance of the conditions in which a certain act, or the person having committed it, appeared to be dangerous for a given system, whoever committed it is not subject to punishment.' This is a logical deduction from the proposition that the purpose of punishment (and criminal law) is to protect the social order: if there is no need of protection then there is no need of punishment. Naturally, this degrades any retributive approaches and social defence becomes an important criterion.

After sections devoted to the stages of implementation of a crime and participation, Article 25 lists the possible punishments. This list is characterised by many socially orientated punishments such as reprimands, censure, instructional courses, boycotts, expulsion from organisations, deprivation of political rights, and declaration that the person is an enemy of the people or of the revolution. The 'nominal' nature of many of these could be countered by the additional application of forced labour, deprivation of liberty, suspension from office, and even execution, as the final part of the article says a combination of the punishments could be used.

One can see that in many respects, these principles are very 'Marxist'

in their orientation — witness the definitions of law and crime. That of
Soviet criminal law assumes that the dictatorship of the proletariat is
in being, which it is not. Equally, the inclusion of various class factors
in the aggravating and mitigating circumstances mirrors a transition
period situation, when this is more one of readjustments. The
Principles have a material approach, speaking of the protection of the
'system of social relations' as a basis for law, and the social danger of
Article 16. However, they also have many things in common with
Western European laws of a similar type, and include many definitions
of pertinent concepts.

Early Development of the Courts and Other Agencies

An important landmark in early Soviet legislation is the Decree No. 1
on the Courts,[21] which had many theoretical and practical implications,
but the events that took place before this decree are thought to be
significant by many Soviet authors. Ushakov[22] says the experience of
the organisation and operation of the temporary revolutionary courts
that had grown up before this decree on the basis of the 'creative
initiative of the revolutionary masses' was used to form the principles
of the new system. Mal'kevich[23] sums up his survey of this early period
by saying that it does not begin with the Decree but with 'the moment
of the beginning of Soviet power', the initial stage before the Decree
being 'characterised by the destruction of the old court and by the
predominance of the spontaneous law-making of the masses', which
must be realised before the true nature of the creation of the courts is
understood. Gringauz[24] divides this period into two stages, that up to
the publication of the Decree — or its receipt in a locality, which was a
'period of free law-making, on the basis of the system of decrees of
Soviet power, of appeals to the population, and so on'; and after the
publication of the Decree, when the situation underwent 'a gradual
narrowing due to the developing socialist legality'. Kozhevnikov[25] says
various institutions of a judicial nature, although not always called
'courts', were set up on the 'initiative of the masses' acting through
local soviets in Petrograd, Kronstadt, Moscow, etc., while Stuchka[26]
says that revolutionary tribunals were functioning in some way before
the Decree. Polianskii[27] agrees, saying, 'At first, there was the
spontaneous appearance of the revolutionary tribunals which were
charged with fighting the counterrevolution alongside the military
formations.'

Scott[28] mentions the Special Committee for Fighting Pogroms, set up in September 1917, which issued a proclamation – printed in *Izvestiia* of 6 (17) December 1917 – saying 'attempts to break into wine cellars, warehouses, factories, stalls, shops, private apartments, and so on and so forth, will be broken up by machine gun fire without any kind of warning.' This Committee was not a court agency or a definite forerunner of the Cheka, but shows that agencies of some kind functioned from the very early stages to deal with particular types of situation, usually by using severe measures. There are parallel developments between court and other agencies in this period. Both were mainly concerned with crime, because they were primarily interested in actions detrimental to the regime, and that is how such actions were classified; and the importance of civil actions may not be so apparent in the revolutionary situation.

Decree No. 1 'On the Courts'[29]

This is an important enactment affecting many areas of legal development. Its first article abolished 'the hitherto existing general judicial institutions', 'hitherto' perhaps making some reference to an abolition by the revolutionary conscience or revolutionary legal consciousness? The following two articles abolished the justices of the peace, investigators, the bar and the procurator's supervision. Under the post-1864 Tsarist system, there had been three levels of general courts, hearing all but relatively minor offences and disputes; commercial courts in Petrograd, Moscow, Odessa (and Warsaw); and two systems of inferior courts, volost and justice of the peace courts. Hazard[30] asks us to remember that there were two court systems (disregarding the commercial), and this had an effect on the 1917 and 1918 decrees.

The abolished courts are to be replaced 'by courts formed on the basis of democratic elections' and universal suffrage when this could be arranged. Until that time, the judges were to be elected by the local soviets – a practice which actually continued to 1948. Article 8 of the decree says:

For the struggle against the counter-revolutionary forces in the form of the adoption of measures of protection from them for the revolution and its achievements, and equally for the trying of acts in the struggle with marauders, plunderers, saboteurs and other abuses of merchants, industrialists, officials and other persons, worker-peasant revolutionary tribunals are introduced.

Clearly, these 'courts' are to be class orientated, the cases they are to hear involving crimes supposedly committed by members of the bourgeoisie, although the inclusion of 'and other persons' means that anyone could be involved. The revolution, the existing order, is to be protected from 'marauders, plunderers and saboteurs', and these and phrases such as 'other abuses', introduce the wide definitions that are so typical of this period. Hazard[31] sums up by saying they dealt with 'political crimes', which, as we shall see, are always the most difficult to pin down.

The abolition of the procuracy, bar, investigators, etc. meant that these functions had to be reallocated. The judges were to be their own investigators, and any citizen of good character could be a prosecutor or defender. The Procuracy as set up by Peter the Great had been the 'eyes of the Tsar' and would have been of use in the new situation, not so much in its capacity to enforce legality, which was somewhat relative at this time, but as an information gatherer and unifying factor. In the new situation, the ruling power was not to be alienated from the masses as they were to rule, but a 'vanguard' had to keep a close watch on 'backward elements' and vestiges of the old ruling class. In this, the masses themselves were supposed to keep the authorities informed, and in so doing, became closer to the authorities via participation in the administration. In practice, these arrangements were not found to work well, with separate colleges of accusers and defenders considered by later legislation, but the problem of the procuracy remained, becoming of particular importance on the advent of the NEP when steps were taken.

On the subject of the prerevolutionary law, Article 5 said:

> The local courts decide cases in the name of the Russian Republic and are directed in their decisions and verdicts by the laws of the overthrown governments only to the extent that these have not been abolished by the revolution and are not contradicted by revolutionary conscience and revolutionary legal consciousness. Note: All laws are considered cancelled which are contradicted by the decrees of the TsIK of the Soviets of worker, soldier and peasant deputies and of the Worker-Peasant Government, and also the minimum programmes of the R.S.D.L. party and the S.R. party.

It is interesting to note that the first draft of the decree had said the old codes were not to be used and the courts had to rely on the new decrees and revolutionary conscience and legal consciousness only.

Mal'kevich[32] says that the change was due to the view that the people's conscience had to be brought nearer to that of the government, even though the government did not want to thrust its will on the people. This follows Lenin's belief that class consciousness had to be 'injected' into the masses by the *déclassé* leaders, but one should realise that the leaders, having faith in their beliefs, are thrusting them upon the masses.

The decree was not very detailed on the subject of revolutionary tribunals, so Shteinberg issued an instruction 'On the Revolutionary Tribunals', dated 19 December 1917 (o.s.). Their jurisdiction was to include cases of organising uprisings against, or actively opposing the government and disturbing the work of institutions; unnecessary reductions in the production of consumer goods — if a decree gave the relevant jurisdiction; and the misuse of a social or administrative position. There was to be a special revolutionary tribunal for the Press.[33] Punishments were to consist of fines, deprivation of liberty exile, public censure, being declared a public enemy, total or partial deprivation of political rights or property, and compulsory public work. In deciding upon a punishment appropriate to a particular case, 'the circumstances of the case, and dictates of revolutionary conscience' were to guide the tribunal.

Some parts of the jurisdiction are defined in rather general terms, and all parts are concerned with acts important to the regime rather than interpersonal offences. With the ordinary courts, we can see the beginning of two systems of courts, one for anti-state or especially dangerous crimes, and one for the more usual offences. Shteinberg attempted to de-emphasise this by having the assessors chosen by lot, not political reliability, and by having a Department of Cassation at the People's Commissariat of Justice, but this was stopped later on the grounds that the instruction was 'irregular'. After the collapse of the coalition, the tribunals become more severe in their actions; for example on 16 June 1918 they are freed from the maximum limits on their powers of punishing — so allowing the use of the death penalty. Lenin strongly supported this, as he greatly appreciated the coercive use of the tribunals and said that reforms were not so necessary as the setting up of 'a really revolutionary court that is rapid and mercilessly severe in dealing with counter-revolutionaries, hooligans, idlers and disorganisers'.[34]

'Counter-revolutionaries' are a necessary target for any regime trying to establish itself, but this and the other category mentioned are obviously indefinite and one can only conclude that jointly they constitute a general class of people that do not support the new order and positively or negatively undermine it in a way that is not, or cannot, be closely defined.

Subsequent Developments

Early in 1918, the Decree No. 2 'On the Courts' was issued.[35] It introduced a multi-tiered court structure with jurisdiction dependent on the punishment involved. Lengthy discussions over the many objections — mainly directed at Shteinberg, who thought the new court system should be a final realisation of the 1864 reforms — had their effect on the decree. There were many links with the old system, as the district courts had to hear cases left over from the previous regime, the 1864 Court Rules were to be used unless they had been abolished, and officials of the old system could be used in the new. However, new elements had been introduced, such as the election of officials, the elimination of many formal procedural rules, and the introduction of the concept of social danger — in Article 17 (juveniles).

Article 36 says formal rules are not to stand in the way of justice, and the old laws are to be followed 'only in so far as they have not been abrogated by decrees of the Central Executive Committee and the Council of People's Commissars and do not contradict socialist legal consciousness'. This formula is simpler than before, with the references to party programmes eliminated. As this was the result of a compromise, one may find it easy to connect this 'legally-bound decree' with the Left SRs, but Zelitch[36] discovered that Stuchka signed the Instruction implementing the decree and concludes that the Bolsheviks may have had a change of heart. As many things were uncertain and unplanned in this period, it is difficult to decide on this point, but if there had been a change of heart, it was rather out of character and some external influence is suggested.

Contemporaneously with the introduction of the more complex court system, that of the revolutionary tribunals was simplified. Many special tribunals, and all local and military ones except those in major centres, were abolished by the decree of 4 May 1918.[37] Kucherov[38] adds that jurisdiction was 'on the one hand curtailed by the transferring of all general crimes to the competence of the local courts, but on the other hand, enlarged by cases of pogroms, bribery, forgery, illegal use of Soviet documents, hooliganism and espionage', which seems an odd mixture of offences closely related to the safety of the state and more ordinary crimes. The aim was to make the tribunals more efficient and more centralised — this latter was effected by the establishment of a tribunal at the VTsIK. Their use was undenied.

Stuchka[39] has their task as 'the infliction of severe and relentless punishment by the working class and the poorer peasants on the countless enemies of the revolution'. Kurskii refers to them as 'organs of struggle with counter-revolution and sabotage', saying the purpose of the May decree was to 'concentrate the struggle with counter-revolution'.[40] More normal crimes were stressed, or at least included, by Denisov,[41] who says, 'they wrestled with marauders and thieves, saboteurs and other crimes.' He refers to them as 'special courts', while some say they were not courts at all. The Decree No. 3, 'On the Courts,'[42] enacted in July 1918, to some extent reverted to the concept of a single people's court by increasing the jurisdiction of the local over the district courts. Serious crimes such as rape, robbery, etc., were to stay with the district courts, however. There were no direct references to prerevolutionary law in this decree, but Article 3, in specifically mentioning the 'decrees of the. . .Government and socialist conscience' would seem to imply that it was not to be used.

The Decree on the People's Courts of 30 November 1918[43] reflected Kurskii's ideas, as had Decree No. 2 Shteinberg's. There was a clear move back to the single court structure with the circuit, cassation and district courts being abolished. These latter, Kurskii says,[44] had been found to be mechanical and slow, and he suggested that any necessary specialisation could be organised within the single court structure, with certain courts specialising in particular types of case. This decree specifically said that there were to be no references made to the prerevolutionary law. If a decree did not deal with a particular area then the 'socialist legal consciousness' had to supply the answer. This had the important side-effect of freeing the regime from any dependence on prerevolutionary lawyers, so a new start was possible. Military Revolutionary Tribunals had been established as a system by a decree of 4 February 1919, and were separate from the PCJ. Although they were primarily designed to deal with crimes committed by military personnel, they also considered counter-revolutionary offences and those committed by civilians in office, and Kucherov[45] points out that at the Front, 'In reality, they sat in justice over all other criminal offences, since there were no regular courts.'

The court reference aid produced by the PCJ in 1918 says these tribunals are to be guided in their judgements and decisions

> by the interests of the Soviet Republic, of its defence from the enemies of the Socialist Revolution and by the interests of the class war for the triumph of the proletariat, being guided by its

revolutionary communist legal consciousness and revolutionary conscience.[46]

The revolutionary tribunal system continued to develop until by mid-1920[47] it consisted of provincial, military, military-railroad tribunals, with a Supreme tribunal overviewing. A decree[48] of 23 June 1921 supposedly united the tribunals into one system, but Berman[49] says that little reduction occurred in reality, and after the failure of Krylenko's scheme at the Fourth Congress (see later), the revolutionary tribunals were abolished at the end of 1922, with their jurisdiction taken over by the intermediate courts of the People's Court System, and a new set of 'military tribunals', responsible to the Supreme Court, were set up to hear military cases.

The Procuracy Re-emerges

Late in 1921, discussion commenced on the need for a strong independent procuracy, in an article by Krylenko published in *Izvestiia.*[50] The first issue of *Ezhenedel'nik Sovetskoi Iustitsii* (1 Jan. 1922), a draft decree, was published with a preamble saying its aim would be to intensify supervision over the legality of all agencies to improve the struggle against crime. There was to be a Department of the Procuracy of the PCJ, headed by the Procurator of the Republic. Morgan[51] says this 'combined once again in the procuracy the function of supervision over governmental agencies and prosecution of crimes, with challenge of judicial sentences, which it possessed under the Tsars before 1864'. However, note that decrees of the Sovnarkom and Council of Labour and Defence were not subject to this appeal – the highest levels of the regime were not to be scrutinised. General supervision had existed before this; the PCJ had overviewed local government decrees, and the Commissariat of State Control (later, Workers' and Peasants' Inspection) had checked officials, but a well organised body specifically devoted to such work would obviously be more efficient. After the publication of the decree, discussion centred on the question of centralisation, for the decree had suggested a decentralised system with local agencies attached to departments of justice in the executive committees of provincial soviets, while a minority of centralists, led by Krylenko, proposed the abolition of the local departments of justice with the procurator choosing his own staff, sending reports directly to the central control. The Procurator of the Republic would be the Commissar for Justice, to avoid conflicts, and would have access to the CEC. The most persuasive reason for centralisation was the freedom from local control, but Estrin, the majority spokesman, felt that this independence would be there in any case, and if the local departments of justice were abolished someone else would have to carry out their functions. The Fourth Congress, and Lenin, were to decide.

The Fourth Congress

This Congress, held from 26 January 1922, was of 'Persons Engaged in the Administration of Justice' and its decisions affected all three agencies so far discussed. The unification of the court structure was an important question. Kurskii, although basically favouring a single court structure, opposed it at the present time, as he thought it would be impossible to establish a court effective against counter-revolution, and yet intimate with the people. The opposing view was put forward by Krylenko, Kurskii's eventual successor (in 1928), who visualised a three-tiered structure with the criminal cases being heard by professional, politically aware judges – a system involving increased centralisation and politicisation of the People's Courts in return for amalgamation with the revolutionary tribunals. Note that the use of 'politically aware' judges for certain cases had been discussed at the previous congress (25 June 1920), as it had been considered that certain categories of crime sent from the revolutionary tribunals and Cheka to the People's Courts, notably illegal traffic in alcohol and exemption from military duty due to religious convictions, had been treated with undue leniency. To deal with them, Special Sessions of the People's Courts with politically dependent judges were to be used.[52] At this congress, Krylenko's approach was not accepted, a fact which may have been used against him in 1937, as a supposed sign of leniency toward counter-revolutionaries, but he had some effect, as the outcome was a proposal for two systems of courts, one for politically orientated cases, and one for all others. The jurisdiction of the revolutionary tribunals was to be narrowed, and the People's Court would be reaffirmed as an organ of the dictatorship of the proletariat, and the masses drawn into its work. It is worth restating here that Krylenko's aims were in some way achieved with the reorganisation of the court system at the end of 1922, when the tribunals were abolished and their jurisdiction taken over by the People's Courts[53] (see above).

In the debate on the procuracy, Kurskii supported the localised approach, considering it premature to abolish local agencies, but the Congress supported Krylenko and a draft was sent to the CEC, where there was inconclusive debate. This resulted in Lenin's famous letter of

22 May 1922, which rejects dual subordination as 'law cannot be
Kaluga or Kazan law, but that it must be uniform all-Russia law,'[54]
and dual subordination is only important where local variations are
necessary, for example in agriculture. This letter had its desired effect,
as the CEC adopted the decree[55] and a centralised system, with the
Commissar of Justice as Public Procurator and Chief of the Office of
Procurator. This is similar to Alexander I's usage, and the offices were
not separated until 1933. On the membership of this formidable
control and information gathering system, a survey of 1923 showed
only 2.4 per cent of provincial procurators, and 21.1 per cent of their
staffs, were not members of the Party. Only 17.5 per cent were of
worker origin and 22.1 per cent peasant, indicating that the majority
were drawn from the prerevolutionary professional classes, who would
of course tend to be better educated.[56] The Cheka was also discussed
at this Congress, but this will be detailed with consideration of the
Cheka as a whole.

The Cheka

This agency is treated separately because, as its full name would
indicate, it is exceptional in many ways, and does not fit into the
normal scheme of dealing with offences — a fact understood by its
contemporary critics and emphasised by its official designation as an
agency of investigation. It was set up in December 1917, not by statute
but by hasty and incomplete notes of a meeting of the Sovnarkom.[57]
Its tasks were to be

> 1) to stop and liquidate all attempts at, and acts of, counter-
> revolution and sabotage throughout Russia on the part of any
> person whatsoever; 2) to bring before the court of the revolutionary
> tribunal all saboteurs and counter-revolutionaries, and to work out
> measures for the struggle against them; 3) the commission conducts
> only the preliminary investigation, in so far as that is needed to stop
> such acts.

Its attention was directed towards 'the press, sabotage, etc., of the
right-wing SRs, saboteurs and strikers'.[58] There are similarities of
purpose between the revolutionary tribunals and the Cheka, the
essential difference being that the latter is only investigatory. However,
relying on decrees such as 'The Fatherland is in Danger,'[59] it begins to
assume 'judicial' functions and acts with great ruthlessness. 'It will
suppress with a pitiless hand all attempts at uprising and will choke all

appeals for the overthrow of the Soviet authority,'[60] and another aim is the 'pitiless destruction at the place of the crime' of offenders.[61] Dzerzhinsky, its first head, speaks of being 'on the firing line' and of 'tearing the enemy apart', and supports the victory of the revolution at the expense of the innocent, for 'the Cheka is not a court of law'.[62] From March 1918, considerable functional and territorial development takes place, and an increase in the severity, frequency and range of the Cheka's actions,when the Terror formally commenced with the decree 'On the Red Terror,'[63] which spoke of the need to strengthen the Cheka (and of isolating class enemies in concentration camps).

Lenin was a staunch supporter of the Cheka, as was Trotsky, both of whom emphasised the need to crush the old ruling classes and to establish the dictatorship of the proletariat. Mistakes were admitted, but support continued. However, the Cheka did have its critics, such as Shteinberg, other Left SRs, and more lethally, Krylenko, who, using the theoretically unnecessary overlap in functions between the Cheka and the revolutionary tribunals, emphasised the latter at the expense of the former. These criticisms did have some effect, even if only making necessary Lenin's apologia. Attempts to exercise control via the PCJ failed,[64] but the Statute of the Vecheka[65] of 2 November 1918 attempted some form of organisation and clarification, applying dual subordination to the Cheka system, and saying it was to work 'in close contact' with the Commissariats of Justice and of Internal Affairs – a perhaps deliberately vague phrase. At the Fourth Congress of Judicial Workers, the Cheka was discussed and some changes were recommended, such as the abolition of the special chambers dealing with 'parasitic elements' in society, who appeared to be dangerous even though it was impossible to find evidence of actions justifying a criminal prosecution.

The abolition of the Cheka came with the decree of 6 February 1922,[66] following a resolution at the Ninth Congress of Soviets which had spoken of 'heroic work', but added that the more stable situation (not to say the NEP) called for a curtailment of powers. Its investigatory functions were to be exercised by the newly created State Political Police – the GPU.

Other Early Legislation

As well as issuing the important decrees on the machinery and agencies of the legal system, the government promulgated decrees and orders on a wide variety of topics. Feldbrugge[67] gives a comprehensive list of law-issuing authorities which includes the All-Russian Congress of Soviets, the CEC, the Sovnarkom and Lenin as its Chairman, other individual commissars, the Council of Workers' and Peasants' Defence, the Revolutionary Military Council of the Republic, and the Cheka. The *Sobranie Uzakonenii* for 1917-18 has 1,033 entries, that for 1919, 596, and as this is not the only publicatory vehicle for decrees, one can see that the situation is complicated due to the number of sources and the amount of material.

Lapenna[68] analyses these decrees into four categories.

(i) Decrees without any legal meaning, being more like political proclamations, such as 'To the People', 'On Peace', and 'The Socialist Fatherland is in Danger'. Note that these were sometimes used as a pretext for action – the last of the above-mentioned was used in this manner by the Cheka (see above). In a speech to the Eighth Congress of the RCP(B), Lenin replied to the criticism that there were too many decrees by saying, 'These decrees, while in practice they could not be carried into effect fully and immediately, played an important part as propaganda.'[69]

(ii) Decrees issued mainly for propaganda but with legal sections that were not intended to be acted upon, or were impossible to perform because of the practical circumstances, for example the decree 'On Workers' Control'.

(iii) Decrees that amount to the legalisation of arbitrariness and terror, for example 'On the Red Terror', 'On the Arrest of the Leaders of the Civil War against the Revolution'.

(iv) Decrees aiming at the construction of a new system of law in the accepted Western sense, such as the decrees on courts and specific crimes.

Note that Lenin himself plays a key role here, for as Lapenna says, 'During the six years of Lenin's rule nothing important was ever enacted without his direct participation, approval or at least tacit consent.'[70] The few exceptions, such as the repeal of the death penalty, did not remain so for long. It will be instructive to consider in detail some of the decrees of the early period to see the type of action that concerned the government and the language used by the decrees.

Desertion was dealt with by several decrees at this time, the first detailed treatment being in that dated 25 December 1918.[71] Its preamble, a common feature of decrees at this time, said that persons were 'wilfully absenting themselves from their units' and leaving the front line, 'one of the most serious and disgraceful crimes', to combat which, inquiries into desertion were to be organised. Deserters who gave themselves up within two weeks of the publication of the decree were to incur no penalty, but this was not to apply to cases arising after the publication of the decree. The possible penalties ranged from monetary deductions from pay to execution, with no further indications as to the requisite degrees of guilt for each penalty. Art. 8(a) said the People's Commissariats of Justice and of Military Affairs were to elaborate upon this. Harbourers of deserters were liable to forced labour for up to five years. This decree is typical in many ways of those of this period: the use of a preamble to outline, sometimes at length, the aims of the decree, often carrying a propaganda message; the allowance for a period of grace to encourage offenders to give themselves up; and a lack of detail in the decree with provision for an outside body to elaborate (it would be more usual still to be too general and not allow for further elaboration). Certainty is helped a little in this decree by the fact that desertion is a relatively precise term, somewhat self-defining, and the word 'wilfully' is used, which would indicate, at least on the face of it, a requirement that the act be done intentionally.

On 3 March 1919 'On measures of struggle with desertion'[72] was issued, saying that officials and official bodies are to observe strictly, and 'strictly and immediately put into practice' all decrees and resolutions about desertion and conscription. Infringements are to be heard by the People's Court, with the penalty for concealment increased to five years' confinement with or without compulsory forced labour. Negligence was made sufficient grounds for the offence, with the responsible officials 'subject to punishment in accordance with the circumstances of the case'.

On 3 June of that year 'On measures towards the eradication of desertion'[73] was issued, referring in its preamble to the Tsarist generals and foreign bourgeoisie wanting to restore the old order, and to 'cowards' and 'people who look after number one' deserting the ranks and so necessitating more call-ups and taking the 'last worker' from families. 'The Soviet power and all workers must be merciless towards such traitors,' but a seven-day period is allowed for persons to give themselves up and so avoid punishment. Article 3 states that those who do not surrender themselves are to be 'considered as enemies of the working people and are condemned to severe punishment, right up to shooting'. Article 4 mentions confiscation of property, in whole or in part, and permanent or temporary deprivation of agricultural allotments, which are to be used by Red Army men, but these are not the only punishments possible, as the revolutionary tribunals are 'authorised to apply the following amongst other measures of punishment'. Families of deserters guilty of concealment could be sentenced to do a variety of work for the families of Red Army men if these families need help. Note that the worsened situation is reflected in the shorter period of grace and the attempt to blame the need for the increased conscription on Tsarist generals and the foreign bourgeoisie and 'cowards'.

Sabotage is another recurrent theme in Soviet legislation of this period, and even in 1917 there were at least three decrees directly dealing with the subject. The first was that of 9 November (OS)[74] and concerned itself with sabotage by 'higher postal-telegraphic officials' which made impossible the efficient working of all enterprises and institutions. The groups of saboteurs in the postal-telegraphic departments had to be eliminated. No precise definitions are used and the decree is careful to attach blame to 'higher officials', not ordinary workers, adding that the latter's welfare is 'closer and dearer' to the government than to the saboteurs.

The decree of 11 November (OS),[75] exhaustively entitled 'On the struggle with the bourgeoisie and their agents, who sabotage the foodstuff-supply for the army and impede the conclusion of the peace,' was entirely polemical and general, with no precise formulae whatsoever. All that it says about penalties is that the saboteurs must be eliminated, and if there is any resistance, they are to be arrested. The decree is aimed at 'all speculators, marauders, embezzlers of public funds, and counter-revolutionary officials, who are holding up the foodstuffs work'. No further definitions are given. Finally, on 18 December, 'On sabotage of the officials of the Ministry of Food'[76] was published, very similar to the above in its use of polemics and lack of precise definitions. It ended with an appeal by the Sovnarkom to 'guard the revolution and closely rally the ranks'.

The Death Penalty

Russia has a very long history of hostility to the use of this penalty, dating back to the Russkaia Pravda and the reign of Iaroslav the Wise in the eleventh century. Even before this, the testament of Vladimir Monomakh, drawn up in 1125, had said, 'Do not kill anyone, either guilty or not, nor do you order to kill.'[77] The use of the penalty gradually became widespread, but Catherine II and Elisabeth I limited its use to sporadic executions. It reappeared in ordinary law after Speransky's codification in 1833. The Provisional Government abolished it in March 1917, only to reinstate it four months later as the military situation deteriorated.

For political reasons, Lenin had called for the abolition of the death penalty, and one of the first actions of the Second Congress of Soviets had complied with this call.[78] Lenin was absent, but on hearing of the action is reported to have said, 'Nonsense. How can one make a revolution without firing squads? Do you think you will be able to deal with all your enemies by laying down your arms? What other means of repression do you have?'[79]

In any case, it was restored in 1918, not by any particular decree but by the use of it by the Cheka and the revolutionary tribunals, only to be abolished yet again on 17 January 1920.[80] Under this decree, the military tribunals retained the right to execute, but a general reintroduction was to take place only in the event of a further armed intervention by the foreign powers, or if they gave material support for insurrectionists. This condition was fulfilled by Wrangel's activities in the Crimea, and the Poles advancing into the Ukraine, so the death penalty was restored on 4 May 1920[81] and no further abolitions occurred until the 1940s.

A Note on Criminology and Sentencing Policy

The upheavals of this period had an effect on criminology as they had on law generally. Research on crime was interrupted and did not get under way systematically once more until the NEP. Few statistics were gathered, and those that were usually concerned themselves with juveniles, an important problem of the time. Revolution and civil war had disrupted family life, producing the *besprizornye* by the million. As migration to the cities increased, the criminal population – both juvenile and adult – became increasingly significant. The *besprizornye* were to institute two stages of criminal activity, one when they were juvenile offenders, and another, not altogether temporally separate of course, when they had matured in age and, one assumes, in criminal technique. The accepted causes of crime were given a distinctly ideological aspect, with Preobrazhensky, in *The ABC of Communism*, when discussing crime generally, saying that in bourgeois society it mainly involved property, the punishments being 'various expressions of the vengeful sentiments of the infuriated owner'. However, the proletarian court had to deal with offences caused by 'vestiges of the bourgeois society' and 'cannot take vengeance upon people simply because these happen to have lived in bourgeois society'.[82]

Article 10 of the Basic Principles had said:

> In the selection of punishment one should have in view that crime
> is caused by the structure of the social relations in which the
> criminal lives. Therefore the punishment is not retribution for 'guilt',
> is not the expiation of guilt. It serves as a defensive measure, a
> punishment should be expedient and at the same time be totally
> lacking in cruelty and should not cause useless and unnecessary
> suffering to the offender.

Kriminologiia[83] says of this time that 'there was the problem of
working out concrete measures in the struggle with criminality in the
country – a serious legacy of tsarism.'[84] It goes on to say that at first
any study of crime took place at the investigation stage, and then
carried out by the militia as a whole, with the Vecheka, scientific
workers and trained students playing a part. Analysis of official data
and selective inquiries into particular areas were the normal work
pattern.[85] Consideration of some of the pertinent statistics of the
period can be rewarding. Schlesinger,[86] referring to information in
Kurskii's book *Soviet Justice* (Moscow, 1919), says that in a sample
of 61,128 judgments in the courts, 35 per cent involved imprisonment,
and four-fifths of these were under conditions of probation; 8 per cent
involved socially necessary work; 4 per cent fines; with 10 per cent for
other punishments; the rest were acquitted (43 per cent).

Kurskii gave another set of statistics in his article 'Novoe Ugolovnoe
Pravo',[87] in which 44,899 criminal cases from the Moscow People's
Court were considered. Of those convicted, 56.9 per cent were fined,
35.6 per cent had some form of deprivation of liberty, social labour
accounted for 2.2 per cent, and other punishments 5.3 per cent. As the
deprivation of liberty figures include those under probation, the
sentences are lenient. Note the wide variation in court practice, 4 per
cent being fined in the first set of figures, 56.9 per cent in the second.

An interesting comparison between the courts and the revolutionary
tribunals is afforded by figures given by Juviler.[88] It is interesting to
see that the revolutionary tribunals deal with a relatively small
percentage of cases compared with the ordinary courts, an obviously
normal state of affairs, but one not so apparent when considering these
fearsomely powerful tribunals. The proportion of those exonerated is
much lower at the tribunals (14.8 per cent) than the courts (33.9 per
cent), perhaps a reflection of the wide definitions of counter-revolution

Table 3.2: Actions of People's Courts (46 Gubernias) and Revolutionary Tribunals (45 Gubernias), RSFSR, 1920

| | People's Courts | | Revolutionary Tribunals | |
	No.	Percentage	No.	Percentage
Persons brought to trial	881,933	–	26,738	–
Exonerated	299,362	35	3,960	14.8
Convicted	582,571	65	22,778	85.2
Including:				
Shot	–	–	776	3.4
Confinement (inc. suspended)	199,182	34.2	16,107	70.7
Compulsory work (no confinement)	132,835	22.8	1,421	6.2
Fines	172,656	29.6	638	2.8
Public Censure	37,678	6.5	623	2.7
Other	40,220	6.9	3,223	14.2

used, or the extra scrutiny applied to such cases. Any liberal tendencies introduced into the courts by the assessors would not apply to the tribunals. Shooting could only be awarded by the tribunals (and the Cheka), hence the zero statistic for the courts. The fact that suspended sentences are included in the figure for confinement generally makes it more difficult to draw firm conclusions, but the higher percentage of this penalty used by the tribunals is of no surprise considering the greater importance attached to counter-revolutionary crime. This is reflected in the greater use made of the less severe penalties by the courts. In terms of social danger, that of an enemy of the regime is intrinsically greater than that of the ordinary criminal, and will lead to more severe measures, as

> it is assumed that it is much easier to re-educate a person who has violated social standards generally recognised in his own milieu than to induce a person to drop activities which his situation has accustomed him to regard as legitimate.[89]

The Role of Legal Consciousness

There is a most noticeable lack of precise definitions in the laws of this period. If the laws are directed against 'social danger' (itself not fully

defined), how are judges to decide whether or not a particular act
falls within this concept? The answer lies in the use of 'revolutionary
legal consciousness' or some similarly named concept. It is mentioned
many times in the early decrees on the courts with reference to the use
of prerevolutionary law. Decree No. 1 said that such law may be used
as long as it did not contradict the newly promulgated laws, party
programmes, revolutionary conscience (*sovest'*) and revolutionary legal
consciousness (*pravosoznanie*). Different terminology is used in other
decrees — 'socialist legal consciousness' (Decree No. 2); and 'socialist
conscience' (Decree No. 3).

Despite these slight differences, these are of course similar concepts.
Do they have different emphases? It is doubtful as to whether 'socialist
legal consciousness' stresses law in a way that 'socialist conscience'
does not. There may, however, be more significant differences between
'revolutionary' and 'socialist', as the former could be of a more
primitive nature and occur chronologically before the latter. In later
usage, 'socialist' was the normal term, but to begin with, they were
interchangeable. Regardless of the exact wording, the term certainly
refers to an important concept.

Traynin, in 'On Revolutionary Legality',[90] says that in the first five
years,

> the place of law and legality. . .was occupied by revolutionary legal
> consciousness. As in previous years every court decision was based
> on law, so in the first five years of the revolution, the reference to
> the revolutionary law consciousness was a sufficient ground for any
> sentence. It was true of legal improvisation when revolutionary
> instinct served both as a criterion and a source of judicial truth.

The greater degree of freedom of action allowed by this approach is
defended by Kurskii, who says the judge is not so much an 'interpreter'
as a 'legislator', who undertakes 'creative work'. Although bourgeois
legal systems allow the judge some discretion, 'The limits of this
operation of the proletarian people's court are incomparably greater. . .
in this function: in its main operation — criminal repression — the
people's court is absolutely free and is guided above all by its sense of
justice.'[91]

Reisner[92] thought that 'This revolutionary legal consciousness was
nothing other than an intuition which lay at the foundation of the
Soviet legal order'; and Stuchka[93] believed its antecedents lay in
Petrazhitsky's Intuitive Theory of Law. E.H. Carr[94] agrees with this and

adds that 'the epithet "revolutionary" was introduced in order to guard against any suspicion that an idealist conception of right was being smuggled into Soviet legal theory.' He quotes Stuchka as saying, 'We have taken our stand on the point of view [of the Petrazhitsky school] about intuitive right but we differ profoundly from it about the basis of that point of view;' it was added to the November 1917 Decree 'by necessity', and 'we never declared the consciousness of right to be some mystical source of truth and justice.'[95] One should note that social consciousness has a class character, for as Wetter summarises, 'The opinions, inclinations, feelings, and customs of a class are evoked by its conditions of life and correspond to its class-interests.'[96]

Stuchka's reference to its addition by necessity to the November decree is of course related to the use of the old law. That law had reflected the will of the old ruling class, and would be unsuitable as a whole in the new situation unless the interests of the ruling class of the transition period were coincidental, which they were not. However, to supply some means of guidance the prerevolutionary law was not immediately discarded, but referrals to it were forbidden by the end of 1918. Obviously a comprehensive system could not have developed by then, and the role of legal consciousness was to fill in the gaps, as it had previously been to decide upon which of the old laws still applied in the new situation. The period before the Decree No. 1 was often extolled as an important stage of legal development, a stage in which spontaneity was emphasised. At this time, 'revolutionary legal consciousness' was given maximum scope primarily because there was nothing else to rely on except the old law, which if it did apply would be recognised as needing some modifications.

The importance of the concept was gradually cut down by the passing of new decrees, giving the judge something more concrete than his own consciousness on which to base his decisions. Hazard[97] draws one's attention to Kurskii's list of decrees passed by the regime specifically defining crime. The list is mostly concerned with anti-state acts, but there is a section entitled 'Crimes against the individual' containing decrees concerned with attempts on life, rape, robbery, and causing serious bodily harm, with the People's Court Act of 1918 given as authority for their inclusion. As this act only included them for procedural purposes, and did not define them, Hazard suggests that the Commissar was 'no longer prepared at this point to follow established policy in leaving to individual initiative at the local level the determination of what should become the initiative of the new Russia'. He accuses Kurskii of natural law tendencies for 'declaring that certain acts were assuredly violation of the social consciousness of law, and by doing so he was equating social consciousness with the law of nature'.[98] As Kurskii was only trying to clarify the concept, saying that it was law in a real sense, although imprecisely formulated, one considers this to be an unusual view: to say that theft is a violation of a criminal code does not equate that code with natural law. Hazard[99] believes that Kurskii had already evidenced a willingness to limit the concept, in '*Iz Praktiki Narodnogo Suda*', when he described what he considered to be good work in the People's Courts. Four of the examples concerned criminal law: intoxication and the admission of guilt had resulted in leniency in a murder case; six months' deprivation of freedom was awarded to an attempted robber, even though he was supposedly an anarchist and had a bomb and a revolver, as there had been no threat to life; the embezzlement of 21,953 roubles by one of previously good character resulted in one year's imprisonment rather than a conditional sentence, to act as a deterrent to others in a similar position; and sexual relations between a landlord and a girl of thirteen, where, although not covered by prerevolutionary law (it had happened in 1916), the former was publicly censured and made to pay the court costs, as the revolutionary legal consciousness of the public considered the act a crime as society had lost a useful worker.

If the use of revolutionary legal consciousness was limited by the issuing of new codes and decrees, and by guidance such as this above, another method would have been to use the prerevolutionary law. Strogovich, in his article 'At the Sources of Soviet Legal Science',[100] suggested that 'in a very insignificant measure and for a very short time — a number of old laws could have been kept in force until corresponding new laws had been passed, since there were not sufficient new Soviet laws for the regulation of many important social relations,' implying that legal consciousness did not work totally satisfactorily.

Conclusions

If Marxist theory is applied to this period and its events, the conclusions one reaches are fundamental to the consideration of future developments as they are built upon those that took place in this first period.

A totally basic question arises over the nature of the revolution, in that the events of October had an insular, limited action, and were more like a palace revolution than that envisaged by Marx. For Marxist socialist revolution to occur, the economic infrastructure has to be suitably developed. If it is not so developed, the revolution cannot be made to occur. Lenin's views on this matter, his change of mind on the nature of the revolution, have already been considered, and one believes that he indulged in a great deal of wishful thinking: he wanted the coming revolution to be the socialist one, and so argued to that conclusion. In reality this was certainly not so, and the whole basis of the Party's approach is therefore fixed on a most important, fundamental and far-reaching fallacy. The economic situation of the country had, not surprisingly, been adversely affected by the First World War, the Revolution, and then the Civil War. Production had fallen, the economy disjointed, and the situation was one of weakness rather than fully developed productive forces that are to lead to the socialist revolution. One has to ask the question, 'Would not the revolution in itself disrupt society?' This well may be the case, but in 1917 the situation was one of decay before the political events occurred: in fact the state of collapse and disintegration was important in enabling the political events to occur. Further problems were caused by the Civil War and the policies adopted by the Bolsheviks, but one can distinguish these events from those envisaged by Marx. The actual process whereby the Party took power reflects the disparities between practice and theory. The vote electing the Constituent Assembly is often seen as an extremely embarrassing event for the Bolsheviks, as they did not receive a majority of votes. However, the significance of this is debatable. Marx's picture of the development and advance of society had a distinctly deterministic aspect, and it is easy to conclude, if not inevitable, that the changes would happen whether or not the population voted for them, or wanted them to occur. On the last point, the bourgeoisie would supposedly not want them to happen, as they would signal the end of their domination as a class; and the proletariat as a whole may not have a developed consciousness to appreciate the significance of the event – and they would be misled by the propaganda of the bourgeoisie. Although Marxist theory does allow a certain degree of freedom of action, and events can be accelerated or slowed down within limits, one has to conclude that the vote is not such a problem when one considers the above. Unfortunately, this particular situation is not quite so easy to resolve, as the changes wrought by Lenin have to be taken into account. The main questions centre on the role of the Party, as Marx was always suspicious of political parties, and the subsequent development of the concept was a distinctly Leninist event. When Lenin argues over the nature of the

Constituent Assembly and why the Bolsheviks did not gain a majority, he is considering the Party, not the proletariat. Therefore, all the special pleading is much more suspect from a Marxist viewpoint: Lenin has added a concept and is then having to explain its non-acceptance.

The relationship between the government and the Party is highly important. Initially they were separate entities, the latter having pressure groups in the former. However, the infiltration of the government by the Party is so efficiently carried out that after an initial paralleling of structures, the two fused to form one hierarchy. This was discussed and rejected as dangerous at the Eighth Congress, but as the Party's aim was total control, it was inevitable. The disastrous effects of this event were magnified by the cessation of opposition within the Party. Many of the criticisms voiced by opposition groups were verified by later events, and even if this had not been the case, it is obviously safer to have a single party in power that allows serious discussion within its ranks than one that does not. The effect on the trade union movement is once again worth mentioning in particular, as those organisations may well have been the best way of protecting the rights of workers from an encroaching government.

As any political party is separate from the people it represents, it may be wrong to emphasise any such differentiation here, but the Party's own philosophy makes this particularly important. As the Party supposedly embodied the consciousness of the proletariat and guided it towards the fulfilment of its aims, towards achieving its historically determined position, it is obviously most important that the Party actually does reflect the wishes and aspirations of the class it has practically superseded. One immediate problem would seem to lie in its social composition, which shows far fewer peasant members than

Table 3.3: Official Class Analysis of the Party, 1917-21 (per cent)

Year	Workers	Peasants	White-collar and others
1917	60.2	7.5	32.2
1918	56.9	14.5	28.6
1919	47.8	21.8	30.4
1920	43.8	25.1	31.1
1921	41.0	28.2	30.8

Source: T.H. Rigby, *Communist Party Membership in the U.S.S.R. 1917-1967* (Princeton, 1968), p. 85.

one would suppose in such an overwhelmingly rural country as Russia. The usual preoccupations concerned worker members, and regular recruitment drives were carried out to strengthen their representation, but with the advent of the NEP, the particular relevance of having peasant members — or at least some influence over the peasantry — was to become the cause of increased recruitment and propaganda activity by the Party in the countryside. The higher educational levels that prevailed in the Party, although these were in absolute terms rather low, gives rise to little surprise, but together with the other somewhat naturally occurring event of the tendency of Party members to administrate rather than work in their original positions, would be the cause of further separation of the representors from the represented. The fact that the Party was alerted to the problem of becoming too separated from the people, as it was over the convergence of its own and governmental functions, only strengthens one's belief that the outcome was determined by the aims, organisation and methods of the Party.

The problem was one that became worse. In this period, any leaders of opposition groups inside the Party were not treated harshly, although they did suffer reallocation of work, which was a very effective method of dealing with dissent. Even some leaders outside the Party, particularly Mensheviks and SRs had their moments of favour. However, at the end of this period, the first general purge of the Party occurred, with what was to become a well known and feared method, the checking of Party documents.

On the economic front, much was said about the nature of war communism. Whether it was actively imposed, or forced on the regime by events, is difficult to decide, but one believes the true picture may be that of external events precipitating 'communist' measures in a non-communist situation. In trying to deal with the great problems they had to face, the leaders attempted to impose unsuitable policies. The effect of these on both industry and agriculture was so disastrous that Lenin had to withdraw and begin on a completely new track to keep the Bolsheviks in power. The peasant uprisings, and particularly Kronstadt, emphasised the differences between the Party and the people, but these violent criticisms were not directed at Marx. It was not Marxist to impose 'communist' measures on a society not ready for them.

Any developments in officially accepted theory during this period obtain a mantle of orthodoxy, being directly, or impliedly, approved by Lenin. Lenin's theories on the state, dictatorship of the proletariat, transition period and the withering away have already been considered in some detail, and any comments noted in this chapter have not departed from the previously discerned pattern.

Similarly, what has been said about law has not been contradicted, and if anything, the practical uses made of law closely reflected the predictions of theory. Great use was to be made, and was made, of law in this period of the 'dictatorship of the proletariat' – one may say 'this' period, as the immediate post-revolutionary years are in many ways the quintessence of the dictatorship, when the new ruling class has to establish itself.

The explanation of crime was painfully simple: 'vestiges of bourgeois society' were to blame. This led to a lenient attitude to offenders and the use of comparatively mild penalties. However, those who committed counter-revolutionary offences were not treated in this way, and had to suffer shooting and imprisonment in many cases, as well as wide definitions in the decrees dealing with their activities. This dual approach reflects Marx's in that ordinary offenders can be (i) 'forgiven', because the old society had produced them; and (ii) re-educated and rehabilitated, as they would readjust to the new order of things, an order which favoured their class. Certain difficulties arise if one remembers the lumpenproletariat, who did not seem particularly good material for re-education. The only answer, whether suitable or not, has to be that Marx was considering the political nature of that group. The bourgeois offenders, who were also a product of the previous economic system, were given severe treatment for three reasons. First, they were considered as blameworthy, which is a problematic proposition to analyse, as they were products of the system too. Answers may lie in the belief that they had a certain freedom of action not open to others, or simply in their political character, for we have seen that ethics seemed to rest on the supposition that anything furthering the revolution was good, and anything against was bad.

Secondly, they were considered as beyond reform, not susceptible to re-education because of their class – social upbringing – inherent beliefs. They would 'infect' other members of the society and should therefore be eliminated or isolated.

Thirdly, the type of offence committed by bourgeois offenders, i.e. counter-revolutionary offences, were of a more serious nature. There is some confusion over this type of offender and this type of offence, for not all counter-revolutionary offences were committed by bourgeois offenders, and similarly, not all offences committed by bourgeois offenders were counter-revolutionary.

There is not a great deal of structure in the substantive criminal law of this period, with the early decrees unsystematised, dealing with laws on an *ad hoc* basis, and allowing the relevant Commissariat to elaborate the detailed rules. The agencies and institutions of the law were more organised, with any uncertainties caused by a superabundance of agencies rather than any lack of them. The concept of the single people's court, striven for as tangible symbol of an uncomplicated legal system that could be easily administered by the public at a later date, had an unfortunate beginning, in that it had to deal with counter-revolutionary crimes, and all they entailed, and ordinary crimes. Due to a supposed inability to deal with the former, there was the parallel development of the revolutionary tribunal system and the Cheka. Although this latter was to begin with being purely investigative, it was such an effective, easily directed and less scrutinised force, that despite some protests, it gained power and became a very powerful administrative agency with both investigative and judicial powers. The changes that eventually came to this dual system were, unfortunately, more of form than substance, as the GPU and military tribunals carried on a great deal of the work of the revolutionary tribunals and Cheka, so preserving old methods and attitudes. These modifications to the administration of justice were part of a movement towards greater centralisation. The rebirth of the procuracy was part of it, as was the increased guidance given in the decrees, which initially left the local agencies a great deal of discretion, partly due perhaps to a worthy lack of faith in equivalence, but the cause of an extraordinary degree of unpredictability in the legal system. One should note here the limiting of revolutionary legal consciousness which, together with the new decrees and the minimum programmes of the two coalition parties, qualified the force of the old, prerevolutionary law that was still otherwise in force. The use of 'special sessions' of the people's court, and the methods of selection and election of judges, were an early sign of the lack of trust in the legal consciousness. That concept has in any case an obscure make-up, and was certainly affected by prerevolutionary legal traditions. In not allowing the masses to exercise their legal consciousness, whether it was socialist, revolutionary or otherwise, is entirely in line with the belief that the Party must lead the masses, and its leaders are the repository of true proletarian class consciousness. In any case, it was a haphazard way of dealing with cases because of the inherent variations and uncertainties, but one should remember that it is used on a lesser scale in Western legal systems in the interpretation of 'justice' in a particular case; in the United States

Supreme Court decisions on the Constitution, and Schlesinger gives the examples of the Swiss Code with its references to 'the rule he [the judge] would establish if called upon to legislate', and the Weimar Constitution, which was much more imprecise with its enumerations and explanations of 'fundamental rights'.[101] Soviet writers have said that the difference is one of quantity, not quality, but obviously the 'quantity' was thought to be too great and an emphasis on socialist legality comes to replace it. Stuchka wrote (in the *Entsiklopediia*) that

> the revolutionary law consciousness was replaced by revolutionary legality during our retreat [i.e. the NEP], because then, the individual class consciousness was not sufficient any more. It became necessary to establish its limits, i.e. the maximum and minimum of the retreat in an organised form, in laws and their fulfilment.[102]

What he did not say was that this process had begun before the advent of the NEP.

In this period, a great deal of attention is paid to law and the legal system, and its full importance is recognised. Law is to be part of the dictatorship of the proletariat, but not a fetter on the actions of the dictatorship – the Party and the leaders. Centralisation, increased certainty and organisation play an increasingly important role, while any attempts to involve the masses in the administration of affairs, at least in a simple sense, seems to become more distant. Perhaps any shortcomings could be explained by the extraordinary situation, but it was a somewhat inauspicious, if not a totally unpredictable, beginning.

Notes

1. M. Kozlovskii in M. Jaworskyj, *Soviet Political Thought* (Baltimore, 1967), p. 70.

2. L. Schapiro, *The Communist Party of the Soviet Union* (London, 1970), p. 183.

3. 'Theses on the Constituent Assembly', *Selected Works*, vol. II, p. 459.

4. A. Nove, *An Economic History of the U.S.S.R.* (revised edition) (London, 1976), p. 74.

5. J.N. Westwood, *Endurance and Endeavour: Russian History 1812-1971* (1973), p. 277.

6. The Programme is translated in L. Schapiro (ed.), *The U.S.S.R. and the Future* (New York and London, 1963), pp. 314-24.

7. Penguin Books, London, 1969.

8. Ibid., p. 125.

9. Ibid., p. 127.

10. Ibid., p. 125.

11. Ibid., pp. 117-18.

12. Ibid., p. 118.

13. *Sobranie Uzakonenii i Rasporiazhenii Rabochego i Krest'ianskogo Pravitel'stva*, henceforth *SU*, (1919), no. 66, item 590.

14. J.N. Hazard, *Settling Disputes in Soviet Society* (New York, 1960), p. 62.

15. Schapiro, *U.S.S.R. and the Future*, pp. 318-19.

16. Ibid., p. 272.

17. Ibid., p. 274.

18. Ibid., pp. 276-7.

19. Second edition, Petrograd, 1919.

20. This and the following is taken from ibid., pp. 17 *et seq.*

21. 24 November (some say 22) 1917. Old Style.

22. 'Sozdanie Pervogo Narodnogo Suda v Petrograde', *Sovetskoe Gosudarstvo i Pravo*, henceforth *SGiP* (1957), p. 3.

23. 'K Istorii Pervye Decretov o Sovetskom Sude', *SGiP* (1940), pp. 164 *et seq.*

24. 'K Voprosu ob Ugolovnom Prave i Prabotvorchestve Mass v 1917 i 1918', *SGiP* (1940), p. 80.

25. *Istoriia Sovetskogo Suda* (Moscow, 1957), p. 15.

26. 'Otchet Narodnogo Komissaria Iustitsii' in Hazard, *Settling Disputes in Soviet Society*, p. 8.

27. 'Revoliutsionnye Tribunaly', *Pravo i Zhizn* (1927), no. 8, in Z.L. Zile, *Ideas and Forces in Soviet Legal History* (Madison, USA, 1970), p. 42.

28. 'The Cheka', *St Anthony's Papers* (1956), p. 6.

29. *SU* (1917-18), no. 4, item 50.

30. *Settling Disputes*, p. 6.

31. Ibid., p. 47.

32. Ibid., p. 172.

33. M. Matthews, *Soviet Government* (London, 1974), pp. 233-4.

34. *Coll. W*, vol. 27, p. 219.

35. There is some confusion over publication dates; see Hazard, *Settling Disputes*, p. 9.

36. *Soviet Administration of Criminal Law* (Philadelphia, 1931), p. 23.

37. *SU* (1918), item 471.

38. S. Kucherov, *The Organs of Soviet Administration of Justice: Their History and Operation* (Leiden, 1970), p. 49.

39. See Polianskii, 'Revoliutsionnye Tribunaly' (at p. 44).

40. *Izbrannye Stat'i i Rechi* (Moscow, 1958), pp. 32 and 89.

41. A.I. Denisov, *Istoriia Gosudarstva i Prava SSSR* (Moscow, 1948), Part II, p. 17.

42. *SU* (1918), no. 52, item 589.

43. *SU* (1918), no. 85, item 889.

44. *Izbrannye*, p. 54.

45. Kucherov, *Organs*, p. 52.

46. *Sudebnoe Nastol'noe Rukovodstvo,* 2nd edn. (Moscow, 1919), p. 43.

47. See *SU* (1920), items 112 and 236.

48. *SU* (1921), item 294.

49. Ia. L. Berman in Hazard, *Settling Disputes*, p. 173.

50. 29 December 1921.

51. G.G. Morgan, 'Lenin's Letter on the Soviet Procuracy', *Am. Slav. and E.E. Rev.*, vol. 19, p. 14.

52. Not established until 16 Sept. 1920, *SU* 100, item 541. For further

details of standing sessions used to speed cases, but using ordinary judges, see
Hazard, *Settling Disputes*, p. 115.

53. *SU* (1922), no. 69, item 902.
54. *Coll. W*, vol. 33, p. 364.
55. 26 May 1922, *SU* 36, item 424.
56. *Ezh. Sov. Iust.*, 31 Dec. 1923, in Hazard, *Settling Disputes*, p. 243.
57. 7 December (OS), but see Kucherov, *Organs*, p. 56, for Dzerzhinsky's
resolution of 21 December 1917 (OS).
58. Matthews, *Soviet Government*, p. 237.
59. 21 Feb. 1918. Y. Akhapkin (ed.), *First Decrees of Soviet Power* (London,
1970), p. 109. Offenders to be 'shot on the spot'.
60. *Izvestiia*, 2 Apr. 1919. International Conciliation, 1920, p. 81.
61. Proclamation of 22 Feb. 1918: see ibid.
62. Newspaper interviews quoted by I.N. S(h)teinberg, *In the Workshop of the
Revolution* (London, 1955), pp. 224-6.
63. *SU* (1917), 65, item 710.
64. See Kucherov, *Organs*, pp. 60-1.
65. *SU* (1918), item 842.
66. *SU* (1922), item 42.
67. *Soviet Criminal Law: General Part* (Leiden, 1964), pp. 28-9.
68. L. Shapiro and P. Keddaway (eds.), *Lenin: the Man, the Theorist, the Leader*
(London, 1967), p. 250 *et seq.*
69. *Coll. W*, vol. 29, p. 209.
70. *Lenin: the Man, the Theorist, the Leader*, p. 249
71. *SU* (1918), no. 99, item 1015.
72. *SU* (1919), no. 9, item 94.
73. *SU* (1919), no. 25, item 287.
74. *SU* (1917), no. 3, item 30.
75. *SU* (1917), no. 3, item 29.
76. *SU* (1917), no. 5, item 88.
77. From W. Adams, 'Capital Punishment in Imperial and Soviet Criminal
Law', *Am. J. Comp. Law* (1970), p. 575.
78. *SU* (1917), no. 1, item 10.
79. L. Trotsky, *On Lenin* (London, 1971), p. 115.
80. *SU* (1920), nos. 4-5, item 22.
81. Ibid., no. 54, item 236.
82. Ibid., see pp. 275-6.
83. 2nd edn. (Moscow, 1968) (Gertsenzon/Collective authorship).
84. Ibid., p. 71.
85. Ibid., p. 72.
86. R. Schlesinger, *Soviet Legal Theory* (London, 1945), p. 72.
87. See *Izbrannye*, pp. 74 *et seq.*
88. P.H. Juviler, *Revolutionary Law and Order* (New York, 1976), p. 27
(from M.N. Gernet, 'Prestupnost' za granitsei i v SSSR' (Moscow: '*Sovetskoe
zakonodatel'stvo*', (1931), p. 74.)
89. Schlesinger, *Soviet Legal Theory*, p. 76.
90. *Pravo i Zhizn* (June 1922). See Kucherov, *Organs*, p. 593.
91. *Izbrannye*, p. 74.
92. See p. xxvi of Hazard's introduction to W. Babb, *Soviet Legal Philosophy*
(Cambridge, Mass., 1951).
93. *Entsiklopedicheskiy slovar' gosudarstva i prava* (Moscow, 1925-7), vol. III,
p. 330. In Kucherov, *Organs*, p. 593.
94. *Socialism in One Country* (London, 1970), vol. I, p. 80.
95. 13 Let Bor'by za Revoliutsionno-Marksistskuiu Teoriiu Prava, 1931, p. 10.
in ibid., pp. 80-1.

96. *Soviet Ideology Today* (London, 1966), p. 237.

97. *Settling Disputes*, pp. 64-7.

98. By this, Hazard means 'socialist'; the word is from 'sotsialisticheskii', not 'sotsial'nyi'.

99. *Settling Disputes*, pp. 68-70.

100. *Sots. Zak.* (1957), no. 10, pp. 20-1. In Kucherov, *Organs,* p. 668.

101. *Soviet Legal Theory*, p. 73.

102. See Kucherov, *Organs*, p. 595.

4   THE NEW ECONOMIC POLICY, 1922-1929

The requirements of the NEP affected all areas of life in the country, involving economics, law, criminology, etc., in what often amounted to intense debate and activity. This period is generally considered innovative, allowing considerable freedom in intellectual life. Genuine efforts were made in many areas to develop theories that would follow in, and extend, the traditions of Marxism. This was theoretically and practically possible because 'Marxism' had not become so dogmatic and restricted; it was still possible to have differences of opinion — even in theory, debate had not become so dangerous an occupation. This was basically because of the nature of the NEP itself. Control by the regime, although not relinquished, was to some extent relaxed, and ushered in a period of fruitful and constructive debate.

There were many important developments in law, with some distinctive work in legal theory, and codes and principles in substantive law. Many trends that were visible in the immediate post-revolutionary period continue into this one, including the further limitation on individual discretion — on the part of judges, etc., in legal affairs. This may be an actively pursued policy, but could be simply an inherent part of the development of a newly established system.

Interventions by central authority did not go unopposed, but one should not conclude that the Party lost control in any serious way. Lenin and the other leaders were careful to watch for any signs of this, which would have seemed more likely at this time, for the NEP, whether a step forward or back, had given the bourgeoisie an extension of life.

Politically the dominant person may appear to be Lenin, but he was actually inactive from the end of 1922, and Stalin was important in those years. His actions, especially interesting at, and in, the ending of the NEP, will be considered in the next chapter.

The Introduction of the NEP

In February 1921, Lenin submitted to the Party Central Committee a project for a new economic policy which was to be gradually developed into the NEP. The basic reason for its introduction was peasant appeasement, for without the support of this group the Bolsheviks would have had great difficulty in retaining power, yet the grain requisitions under 'war communism' were causing great hardship and unrest. Kronstadt was a clear indication that groups with more predictably socialist leanings were also disaffected, and the Resolution issued by the sailors on 1 March 1921 called for more freedom in society and new elections. Heavy industry was stagnant — any spending power the peasants had favoured light industry — with more than half a million unemployed and real wages less than half 1913 levels.[1] On reviewing the situation, Lenin concluded that things had gone too far under the previous policy — 'Was that a mistake? It certainly was.'[2]

The policy introduced a degree of private enterprise into the economy: the 'commanding heights' were to be under state control, but individual factories were handed over to trusts or individuals, foreign credit was sought, and the profit motive introduced. In agriculture, the major change was from requisitions of surpluses to the 'tax-in-kind', which took a fixed proportion of the produce, so giving the peasant a profit incentive. A free market, at first locally organised but then nationally so, dealt with the peasants' surpluses.

The NEP is sometimes referred to as a retreat, sometimes as a step forward, a dichotomy paralleled in the attitude to war communism which was sometimes a hasty but genuine step towards socialism, and sometimes a deviation from the true path caused by the necessities of the Civil War and revolutionary situation. This confusion is due to the apparent lack of understanding — or perhaps plethora of wishful thinking — over the application of 'Marxism' to the Russian situation.

Legal Theory in the 1920s

Kelsen[3] describes the work of Stuchka as the first attempt to develop a specifically Soviet theory of law that was not a product of state theory. The 1919 Basic Principles were greatly influenced by Stuchka, and he speaks of them in his work *A General Doctrine of Law*, saying that the definition of law in those Principles — 'Law is a system (order) of social relations which corresponds to the interests of the ruling class and which protects the ruling class by means of its organised force' — was not perfect, but 'by and large I consider this formula perfectly applicable even now since it comprises the chief indicia incorporated in the concept of law of every sort in general (and not of Soviet law alone).'[4] Stuchka's ideas, as set out in the Principles, are remarkably faithful to orthodox Marxism, with references to law withering away when communism has been achieved, and the class nature of law. Bodenheimer[5] says the main point of Stuchka's definition is the emphasis on the social basis of law, with the conception of law as a system of social relations rather than an aggregate of state-imposed norms. The rules of normal human social intercourse are given a 'sociological precedence' over governmental decrees, which are termed 'artificial' – Stuchka regards statute law as a reflection of the social and economic activities of human beings. The definition has a class aspect as the social relations 'correspond to the interests of the dominant class' and the system is 'safeguarded by the organised force of that class'. Bodenheimer asks whether the view of law as a mirror of spontaneous social relations and yet a compulsive order instituted by the ruling class is not self-contradictory, and concludes that if it is, it is a dialectical contradiction. However, there is a link in that the social order is permeated by class control.

Commodity exchange was an important aspect of Stuchka's approach, but he limited himself to civil law, restricting it 'in the Soviet society to the regulation of the surviving private property relations'. The internal economic relations of the socialist sector of economics were to be excluded, as not needing judicial regulation. On the other hand, within the realm of Soviet civil law, Stuchka consistently recognised the principle of the 'equivalent': being based on commodity exchange, the real object of any right was a certain value. 'Compensation for this value ought to be paid if, by a change of policy, the Soviet State abolished the original right, without the bearer of the right having infringed the conditions under which it had been granted.'[6]

Pashukanis developed this approach and applied it to all aspects of law. He set out his theory in 'The General Theory of Law and Marxism', written in 1924. Fuller[7] says this theory, usually termed the Commodity Exchange Theory of Law, was founded on two main principles, the first being that law and state were superstructural, reflecting the basic economic organisation of society: and the second that in the communist economy of the future, both law and state would wither away. The premiss is that the basic institution of capitalism is exchange: all goods are commodities for exchange. Law emerged in the market place when production for the market and exchange of commodities appeared, and reaches its zenith under bourgeois capitalism. Law was intrinsically bourgeois and of little interest in a socialist society. Pashukanis' theory can be attacked on two grounds: (i) that it was not Marxist, and most critics consider it so; and (ii) that it was unsuitable for a period in which the strengthening of state and law was of growing importance. On the first of these criticisms, there are two particular points to note, the first being that Pashukanis believed law to be an instrument of oppression, but only indirectly, as the domination of one class over another can exist without law — for example, based on military power or religious superstition. Note that in these given examples, law could, and probably would, play at least an organisational or institutional part in such societies. The other particular doubt about the orthodoxy of the theory concerns its view of the birth of the state:

> The state emerges because the classes would otherwise mutually put an end to each other in savage conflict and would thereby destroy society. Accordingly, the state emerges at a time when no single one of the conflicting classes can achieve a decisive victory. In that event, one of two things happens: either the state makes this relationship secure (and in that case it is a supra-class force, which we cannot admit), or the state is the result of the victory of some class, but if this is so, society's need of a state is gone since the decisive victory of a class re-establishes equilibrium and society is saved.[8]

Lapenna[9] says this means the break-up of society into classes does not automatically lead to the birth of the state, and a compromise would mean it was a supra-class phenomenon, at least at its birth, which would seem to be non-Marxist. The possibility of 'states' existing that are not working solely for a particular class has been mentioned above. The preservation of common interests could be its aim, which may include the existence of society. However, it was concluded that this could only occur when there was no ruling class, or no classes at all. It is, therefore, a supra-class force, and as 'states' are class entities, it was termed an 'organisation'. One suspects that Pashukanis is confusing these concepts in that he terms the entity that would amount to an 'organisation', a 'state', which would indeed be non-Marxist.

Pashukanis' theory was also considered to be unsuitable for this particular period in Soviet development, due to its attitude to withering away. Based as it was on economic exchange, law was to die out as economic exchange died out. The law was considered to be implicitly bourgeois, reflecting its origins:

> It must, therefore, be borne in mind that morality, law, and state

are forms of bourgeois society. The fact that the proletariat may be compelled to use them by no means signifies that they can develop further in the direction of being filled with a socialist content. They have no capacity adequate to hold a socialist content and are bound to die out to the extent that it is brought into being.[10]

In the NEP period it was convenient to link the existence and flourishing development of law to bourgeois causes, as the NEP itself was recognised as a less socialist stage; but as law did not die out, and it became important to give it a socialist content, Pashukanis' theory gave rise to embarrassment. The theory applied to both civil and criminal law, and in the latter, for example, punishment was considered to be the price paid for the crime. His influence was such that civil law courses were abandoned at law schools, and replaced by the administrative law of planning, termed 'economic law' by Pashukanis. Precise codes in criminal law were to be replaced by guiding principles. As we shall see, these aspects of the theory were not accepted, and he was subjected to attacks in 1930, and finally in 1936-7.

As well as the pronouncements made by these two leading theorists, Stuchka and Pashukanis, the prevailing attitudes can be derived from other sources, not by any means the least of which is Lenin. On 22 February 1922 he wrote a letter to Kurskii which was circulated to certain other high-ranking Party officials. In it Lenin says that the PCJ has not adapted itself to the NEP, and it should have an '*especially militant role*' in the field of education, repression of enemies, influence on judges and revolutionary tribunals, etc. He warns that 'any kind of capitalism that goes beyond the framework of state capitalism in our meaning of the concept and tasks of the state' must be restricted. Abuses of the NEP are to be countered 'with every means, including the firing squad', with triple penalties for communists as opposed to non-communists, that is, those who were not Party members. State intervention is to be extended into areas considered 'private', and in civil legal relations, to apply 'not the *corpus juris romani* but *our revolutionary concept of law*'.[11]

Not surprisingly, the withering away of law (together with that of the state) was given a great deal of consideration. Krylenko, in *Besedy o Prave i Gosudarstve*,[12] said:

> law, as a class law, will disappear at the moment of the disappearance of classes. It will disappear as an instrument of exploitation and coercion at the moment when exploitation and coercion disappear.

It will be replaced by something else, with new social relationships, with new experiences, which we will designate by a name other than law.

Stuchka[13] referred to the 'state, as well as the law in its class meaning' withering away. Both of these are using the special terminology approach to withering away, which when used is always implied, never, of course, admitted. Statements such as:

> after the revolution, the process of the transformation of society into communism will *not* be accompanied by the transformation of the proletarian state and proletarian law into the state and law of the future society or into the 'socialist law'. On the contrary, both will gradually wither away,[14]

can be understood to mean that state and law like entities may exist in the future society.

Class and Law

This interesting relationship is considered in some detail by Carr in his *Socialism in One Country.*[15] In most of the early legislation and the 1922 Code, there is no particularly easily recognised class aspect, but the 1919 Principles had said it should be taken into account when deciding upon the penalty. In the NEP it was a somewhat awkward matter, but was supported by some Party factions and therefore remained (in theory). A 1924 Commission appointed by the Party said it should remain, but some, for example Dzerzhinsky, in a surprising change of heart, say it was now an incorrect approach.

Krylenko supported special treatment for proletarians, putting this forward at the Fifth Congress of judicial workers in 1924. Critics pointed out that as long as there was no definition of 'proletarian', the approach would be difficult, if not impossible, to operate meaningfully.

In July 1924, the RSFSR Supreme Court said that courts should remember that they were class courts and should draw a distinct line between proletarians and others. The Rapporteur of the Draft Labour Code of 1924 wrote, 'The sharpness of our criminal repression is directed mainly against persons not belonging to the working class; the introduction of the class element corresponds to the general policy of the Soviet power.'[16] From this one should not be surprised that the

1924 Principles included class in the aggravating and mitigating factors. However, in the era of the Nepmen this was obviously unsuitable so, despite some adverse comment, change occurred.

On 29 June 1925, the RSFSR Supreme Court reversed its earlier decision and said that courts must remember that the application of a class approach to penal policy consisted not in bringing to justice the nepman or kulak, or in exonerating the toiler or poor or middle peasant, but in a distinct and clear understanding of the social danger of the actions of the citizen on trial, judged from the standpoint of the proletariat as a whole. First and foremost, a firm line must be drawn between actions punishable as crimes and actions which are indifferent from the point of view of criminal law, independently of who it is that commits them. It is completely inadmissible that, other conditions being identical, one citizen should be held responsible in criminal law and the other not.[17] Solts, president of the Central Control Commission of the Party believed all opposition required firm handling: 'We must not say that workers and peasants may commit offences because a worker-peasant government is in power. We should not soften their punishment in the light of their class origin. That is harmful.'[18] However, Vyshinsky, when writing about the importance of socialist legal consciousness in deciding how to act in conformity with state requirements, says:

> when an offender from the working class appears before the Soviet Court, the socialist legal consciousness should suggest to the judge both the proper approach and the right decision. For example, the law states that theft is punishable by five years of imprisonment. But, in conformity with the socialist legal consciousness, instead of sentencing the offender to prison, the judge will send him to work in a factory, giving him a suspended sentence.[19]

Ensuing discussions, partly in *Pravda* and *Izvestiia*, continued on the lines that if the class element was erased, the revolutionary aspect of revolutionary legal consciousness would be meaningless.

Regardless of this and other opposition, the class element became less important and the Decree of 6 June 1927 introduced the corresponding modifications to the Code.

The Court System

After the changes that took place in 1922 and 1924, the Republican court system basically consisted of three tiers: a Supreme Court, Provincial Courts and People's Courts. There were also certain special courts such as military tribunals, which could try civilians accused of such crimes as espionage; and the labour sessions of the People's Courts. The USSR Supreme Court overviewed these courts and also heard cases of All-Union importance.

The Statute on the Court Structure[20] set up a four-tiered structure — District, Department, Region and Supreme. The Regional Courts acted as appeal courts from the lower levels, the Supreme Court only being involved in major cases. When departments were abolished in 1930, a three-tiered structure was reinstated. The USSR Supreme Court may have been a centralising tactic, but did not have very much influence until later.

The Comrades' Courts, which had informally existed soon after the Revolution and were directed at labour discipline and work efficiency, did not at first have their jurisdiction defined — any work-related offence seemed to fall within their scope. On 5 April 1921[21] their jurisdiction was elaborated into two basic parts, that concerned with production, and covering lateness, laziness, etc.; and that relating to general behaviour, e.g. hooliganism. The available penalties, originally of a minor nature, now extended from 'remarks' to concentration camps. During the 1920s, these courts lost their disciplinary character and moved towards general offences, with the decree of 30 December 1929 a landmark, moving them away from trade unions and towards enterprises.[22] Further reorganisation was undertaken on 20 February 1931,[23] when they were termed 'productional', increased their jurisdiction over theft and property disputes, but limited the available penalties. Probably due to doubts over their true function, little more was done with them until 1961.

The 1922 Criminal Code

This was the first criminal code for the RSFSR, although Feldbrugge mentions the existence of earlier local codes, such as that issued by the local Soviet authorities to the revolutionary tribunals and people's courts of the partisan troops on the North Kan Front in Central Siberia.[24] The meeting of judiciary workers in June 1920 had passed a resolution on the need for a code, and at the end of that year the PCJ brought out a draft general part followed by a special part in early 1921.[25] This special part was influenced by the 1903 *Ugolovnoe Ulozenie* to some extent, had no maximum or minimum penalties, no sanctions for those guilty of specific offences, and used loose descriptions rather than precise definitions — the emphasis was supposedly on guidance rather than hindrance. Timasheff would have them rejected for not conforming to 'the exigencies of the law of a socialist society', and any suspicion of the lack of specific guidance would not be surprising at this particular stage.[26] Later in 1921, the Soviet Institute of Law published a Draft Code, but it was rejected because of too close links with the sociological school of criminology. It was none the less an influential force at this time.[27]

The PCJ then issued another draft which after changes in the Sovnark became the 1922 Code. Kurskii said it was the synthesis of all precedents, norms derived from revolutionary consciousness, and the most progressive trends in science.[28] Prerevolutionary law was not an acknowledged source, but we shall see that it had an influence, and Feldbrugge says that the Instructions issued by the Supreme Tribunal attached to the VTsIK for the use of Guberniia Revolutionary Tribunals, which contained a list of crimes compiled from previous experience, appear to be one of the chief sources of the special part.[29]

The General Part of the 1922 Code

In accordance with normal usage, the Code consists of a general and a special part, the former consisting of

> (i) statements about the applicability of the Code, especially in time and space;
> (ii) statements about the general elements of criminal offences and their modalities, such as criminal attempt and complicity;
> (iii) general rules about punishment; and
> (iv) rules about the application of these principles to various offences.[30]

Article 5 says the Code

> has as its task the lawful defence of the toilers' state from crimes and from socially dangerous elements, and accomplishes this defence by means of the use of punishments or other measures of social defence against violators of revolutionary legal order.

Note the emphasis on the protection of the state and society and the reference to 'socially dangerous elements' as a separate category from 'crimes'. This has practical importance, as Article 49 states that

> Persons, declared by the court as socially dangerous on account of their criminal activities or their connection with the criminal environment of a given locality, can be deprived by sentence of the court of the right to reside in the defined locality for a period of not more than three years.

This enables action to be taken before the commission of a criminal offence, and amounts to a logical extension of the use made of social danger as the basis of legal action rather than some more formal concept. Perhaps it is a genuine belief that justice will prevail despite the opportunity for abuse afforded by this article that allows a Commentary to depreciate the importance of it by saying:

> The enactment of our Criminal Code on participation (Article 16) is sufficiently broad to encompass all kinds of criminal connection between offenders, so that it would seem that the requirement of this term (Article 49) side by side with that stated above is practically superfluous.[31]

Article 6 defines crime as 'any socially dangerous act or omission. . . threatening the foundation of Soviet authority and legal order established by the Worker-Peasant power for the time of transition to a communist system'. Here the importance of the state, the regime, is stated, and closely identified with the system of law, itself said to be established for a particular period.

The concept of social danger plays an important role in this Code. Article 7 says, 'The danger of a person is shown by the commission of acts harmful to society, or if his activities exhibit a grave threat to the social legal order.' This has one standard directly referring to law, and one referring to society in general, paralleling Article 5. Article 36 allows conditional release when 'the degree of danger of the convicted to the community does not demand his compulsory isolation.' However, social danger, despite its undoubted importance, is not defined with any greater precision: perhaps such a concept has to be defined thus. Normally there is a reference to 'society' or the 'community', but one cannot assume a total separation of these concepts from that of the regime.

Article 25 lists the mitigating and aggravating factors, and includes

a) if the crime was committed in the interests of the restoration of
the power of the bourgeoisie, or in the merely personal interests of
the committor of the crime; b) the crime was directed against the
interests of the state or individual interests.

Social danger is not just measured in political terms, as this article goes
on to mention gangs, violence, etc.

The purposes of punishment are set out by Article 8 – to prevent
the commission of crimes by the offender himself, and other members
of society; to adapt the offender to social life by the use of corrective
labour, and to deprive the individual of any further possibilities for
committing offences. The aim is to reform, not punish *per se*, so
punishment 'must be expedient, and at the same time completely free
of signs of torture and must not cause useless and unnecessary suffering
to the criminal' (Art. 26), and signs of 'improvement' can lead to
conditional release from imprisonment or compulsory labour (Art. 52).

There is some confusion over the question of retroactivity, for
although Article 23 says the Code applies 'in respect of all acts not
examined by the courts up to its introduction into force', i.e. total
retroactivity, the 1923 Code of Criminal Procedure says that
criminality and punishability are determined by the law in force at the
time of performance, except that laws depriving actions of their
criminality and punishability were to be retroactive – a notably liberal
provision.

The by now familiar reference to legal consciousness comes in
Article 9, which has judicial bodies determining punishment in
accordance with their 'socialist legal consciousness' and the
fundamental principles of the Code. Note that this concerns the
application of punishment only, not the assessment of criminality,
which must be derived from the Code – and the use of analogy.

One of the fundamental attitudes of this Code is clearly
demonstrated by Article 27, which reads:

In prescribing the measure of punishment, the Criminal Code
distinguishes between two categories of crime: a) that directed
against, or recognised as the most dangerous to, the basis of the legal
order established by the worker-peasant authority: for which the
lowest penalty set down by the Code cannot be reduced by the
court; and b) all other crimes, for which maximum limits of

punishments awardable by the court were established.

On the ability to reduce sentences, Article 28 says that 'exceptional circumstances' allow the application of a lesser penalty if the court sets out the reasons. Does this apply to both types of offence? The Commentary would suggest that it could, as it says the division is a 'general evaluation' and not to be used in 'concrete cases'. One suspects that in serious cases it could apply, but never would in practice.

The Concept of Analogy

This has a most interesting history. It was included in the 1845 Code, itself a revision from the Incorporated Laws of 1832 — drawn up by a committee led by Speransky. Article 151 of the Code read, 'If the law does not contain a definite provision about the crime which is being tried, the court sentences the offender to the punishment applicable to a crime most similar to the one committed, as to kind and gravity.'[32] Rulings continually cut down this provision's applicability until it only covered situations where the law had provided for a crime but had omitted the penalty, which was of course rare.

The 1903 Code commenced with the statement that 'An act must be prohibited at the time of its commission by law on pain of punishment, to be criminal.'[33] This was aimed at preventing the use of analogy and retroactivity, and gave considerable satisfaction to those with progressive views.

On Soviet usage, Starosolskyj[34] says:

The dogma of analogy as known to the Soviet system of criminal law, presupposes a certain view on law and legality: that justice is based not only on law; that there is a material concept of crime (and law itself); that the judge has a law-creative power,

and adds that all these prerequisites existed before the 1922 Code. Where a crime is considered to be such because, for example, of danger caused to society, the question of whether or not the act has been included in a Code is not paramount. In a situation where there are relatively few legal rules, reliance on analogy could become very important. This was the case in the early Soviet period and, moreover, the use of legal consciousness indicates that sources of law other than decrees and codes are to be used, which is not surprising in the circumstances. There is a difference between the use of legal consciousness and the use of analogy, in that the latter requires the existence of a standard — usually a Special Part, with which to make the analogy. As there was no such standard at that time, analogy was not mentioned in the 1919 Principles.

The PCJ's Draft Code of 1920 was strongly influenced by Kurskii, who, together with Krylenko, emphasised the need for guidelines rather than strict definitions, so the draft gave the courts a considerable role in deciding upon questions of social danger. The 1921 Institute of Soviet Law Draft Code kept the material concept of crime and the revolutionary consciousness of law, but had no specific reference to analogy, and used 'equivalence', degrees of punishment, etc. The 'Little Sovnarkom' Draft included the principle of *nullum crimen*, but had little influence.

The 1922 Code, derived as it was from the PCJ Draft, clearly came down in favour of the use of analogy. Article 10 reads:

> In cases of the absence in the criminal code of direct instructions on an individual type of crime, the punishment or measure of social defence to be used is that in accordance with the article of the criminal code dealing with the crime most similar in importance and type, and with the regulations of the General Part of the code.

Kurskii, in a speech explaining the Draft to the VTsIK said, pragmatically, 'One Criminal Code cannot include all the varied criminal actions. . .we must have an article. . .[on] analogy.'[35] Analogy is a well known concept in Soviet criminal law, and as we shall see, much has been written about it. However, it is as well to realise that some of the practical value of its inclusion in the Code was negated by the use of the wide definitions in the Special Part, which would make unnecessary any resort to analogy, especially in counter-revolutionary cases. Gernet and Trainin, in their commentary, give the impression that its presence is in no way 'sinister', but simply there to fill any gaps in the Special Part. Checks on the use of the article consist of (i) the view that it must not be used if there is a definite provision covering the situation, and (ii) if the law clearly indicates that a particular action is not to be considered criminal, then analogy must not be used. The example given is of a person helping in the suicide of another adult, there being no specific article, 148 covering cases involving helping a minor only. The commentary concludes that it would probably be incorrect to use analogy, as by limiting the offence in such a specific way, the intention must be not to punish in cases involving the suicide of adults — it is not a situation that has been overlooked accidentally.[36]

Elsewhere, Trainin[37] says analogy is to be used to fill gaps in the Special Part of the code, so drawing one's attention to the fact that the Special Part is really a selection of offences, not a definitive list. He quotes Professor Chel'tsov-Bebutov as saying that 'the legislator considers the special part of the code as an approximate, but not exhaustive, list of punishable acts'.[38]

Counter-revolutionary Crime

The Special Part of the 1922 Code consists of eight sections, altogether subdivided into 170 articles. The first of these sections – that setting out the law on State Crimes – can be of special interest, indicating as it does the prevalent attitudes to those considered as not upholding the political system. This section is further divided into two parts, the first of which is headed 'counter-revolutionary crime'. Article 57 says:

Any act is deemed counter-revolutionary when it is directed towards the overthrow of the proletarian revolutionary authority of the worker-peasant Soviets existing on the basis of the Constitution of the RSFSR Workers'-Peasants' Government, and also actions aimed at assisting that section of the international bourgeoisie which does not recognise the equal rights of the communist system of ownership, which is coming to replace capitalism, and seeks its overthrow by means of intervention or blockade, espionage, finance of the press and so forth.

The most striking aspect of this lengthy definition, the terminology of which reflects the Civil War and Interventionalist period, is its extraordinary breadth. There have only to be actions 'directed' towards the overthrow of authority – itself a concept with many ramifications. Both internal and external activity is covered by the definition and moreover, in the second part of the definition, the activity need not actually assist but needs only to be aimed at assisting.

Throughout this section, the penalties are very heavy. If there has been intent, then it can be death and confiscation of all property to five years' imprisonment with strict isolation plus confiscation. If there is no intent, then a minimum of three years' imprisonment is allowed.

Lenin's letter to Kurskii, written on 17 May 1922, is pertinent here. It concerned a 'supplementary article' to the Code (No. 57), of which Lenin gives two variants, both of which use wide definitions. He says:

The main idea will be clear, I hope, in spite of the faulty drafting –

to put forward publicly a thesis that is correct in principle and
politically (not strictly juridical), which explains the *substance* of
terror, its necessity and limits, and provides *justification* for it. The
courts must not ban terror — to promise that would be deception
of self-deception — but must formulate the motives underlying it,
legalise it as a principle, plainly without any make-believe or
embellishment. It must be formulated in the broadest possible
manner, for only revolutionary law[39] and revolutionary conscience
can more or less widely determine the limits within which it should
be applied.[40]

The Notes to this letter say that Lenin's recommendations were used
for Articles 57, 58, 61 and 70, and certainly his emphasis on the need
for formulations in 'the broadest possible manner' had an effect. If
revolutionary legal consciousness can determine the limits of terror,
then if it were free, it could act as a limiting factor on the dictatorship
of the proletariat. However, as it is directed and interpreted by the
Party, which in any case is the dictatorship, then no conflict can occur,
and Lenin's belief in a dictatorship unfettered by law exists. Trainin[41]
has an informative section on counter-revolutionary activity,
commencing with the general point that 'traitorous crimes' are directed
against the outer or external security of the state, while counter-
revolutionary ones attack the internal structure:

> The complex economic and social processes — the development of
> the productive forces, the alignment of classes, *et al.* — find
> expression and agreement in the corresponding legal organisation —
> the state. But the social forces never find themselves in a condition
> of rest. That is why within the state continual changes are going on,
> and sometimes real encroachments to the developed political system.
> The distinctive peculiarity of political crimes is that they are
> knowingly directed not against individual features of the existing
> system, at the separate organs of power or separate functions of
> authority, but against the very foundation of law and order, against
> the constitution of authority.

Estrin, the author of a popular textbook used in Party schools, by law
workers, and by those studying privately, says in it, 'Our code is the
Code of the proletarian revolution. By this very fact, the most serious
crime the Criminal Code of the RSFSR recognises is that directed and
aimed against the proletarian revolution — i.e. counter-revolutionary

activity.' He defines this as having 'as its aim the overthrow of the victorious proletarian revolutionary power of the worker-peasant soviets, the abolition of the soviet regime'.[42] Estrin then goes on to speak of counter-revolutionaries wanting to 'take the bull by the horns' and 'wring the neck of Soviet power' in that extraordinary mixture of picturesque and technical language typical of a certain type of Soviet writing — one should remember the popular nature of the book.

While agreeing with the basic definitions of counter-revolutionary activity given by these authors, one is not so sure that Trainin's differentiation between 'traitorous' and 'counter-revolutionary' has a parallel in substantive law, or that it is an implicit aspect of the latter activity that it is directed against the regime as a whole. On the first of these points, Article 61 relates to helping the international bourgeoisie, which could be directed against the external security of the state and yet be against the continued existence of the regime. On the question of whether the activity has to be directed against the regime as a whole, rather than a particular aspect of it, to be termed counter-revolutionary, Article 63 punishes the stopping of 'the normal operation of soviet institutions and enterprises' which could be considered separately as well as a whole.

In conclusion to this section, one can say that a 'line by line' analysis of the individual articles would not be a particularly useful approach. The outstanding feature of this part of the Code is the breadth of the definitions, and practically any action could be classified as counter-revolutionary if it were so wished. The section sets out to protect the existence of the 'system' — by which one should theoretically mean the dictatorship of the proletariat. However, in practice the emphasis is now on protecting the rule of the Party and its leaders, a protection afforded by this very comprehensive section of the Code, where safeguards against misuse do not lie in the definitions themselves.

Other Aspects of the Code

Parallels with counter-revolutionary crime can be seen in the second part of Chapter 1, dealing with crimes against public administration. Definitions are, again, wide — 'provoking the weakening of the power and authority of the Government (*vlast*')'. Punishments range from the supreme penalty to small fines. Usually the punishment is less if there is a lack of a specified intent.

Article 125 to some extent protects religious freedom by awarding up to six months' compulsory labour for 'hindering the performance of religious ceremonies', but adds the stipulation 'in so far as they do not infringe public order and are not accompanied by encroachments on the rights of citizens' – a very Soviet approach.

The greater concern felt in all areas where the action may affect the state is evidenced by Article 126, where normal labour desertion is punishable with compulsory labour from one week, while that 'prejudicing the defence of the country' leads to imprisonment or compulsory labour for not less than six months, or confiscation of property in whole or in part, or a substantial fine. Nepmen, predictably treated with a certain suspicion, are to follow the various labour regulations or suffer a fine of from 100 roubles, forced labour for not more than three months, or deprivation of liberty for up to one year (Article 132).

Article 142 shows the attitude of the Code to a standard area, murder, and awards not less than eight years' deprivation of liberty for premeditated murder, which is lowered to three years' maximum if there are mitigating circumstances such as 'strong mental agitation' (Article 144). Generally, one may say that the Code treats 'ordinary' crimes in a reasonably predictable and acceptable manner. One particular article worth noting is No. 176 on hooliganism, which has an interesting history in Soviet criminal law, and can be considered as a useful indication of the 'hardness' or 'softness' of the regime's attitude to antisocial acts. The Code defines it as the 'rowdy, pointless actions attended by an overt display of disrespect towards individual citizens or society', and is punishable with compulsory labour or deprivation of liberty for a period of up to one year.

A final point could be Article 180, which says amongst other things that simple theft from a private person leads to forced labour for a period up to six months, or deprivation of liberty for the same; while simple theft from State or public stores or institutions warrants imprisonment or compulsory labour for up to one year. This again illustrates a clear characteristic of the Code.

Subsequent Changes to the 1922 Code

The 1922 Code had a short life – from 1922 to 1926, yet underwent many changes in the form of additions and deletions, both partial and whole. This was due to the rapid changes of circumstances, and the hurried composition of the Code which led to the need for technical changes. The alterations occurred in practically all parts of the Code.

Article 57, the important definition of counter-revolution, was changed on 10 July 1923, by Decree of the VTsIK.[43] The original version had been comprehensive – 'any act. . .directed towards the overthrow of the proletarian revolutionary authority of the worker-peasant Soviets', but the new version was even more so, as 'overthrowing' now becomes 'overthrowing, undermining or weakening'. Also, 'an act is also held to be counter-revolutionary which, though not directly aimed at attaining the above objects, nevertheless, to the knowledge of the person committing it, endangers the fundamental political or economic achievements of the proletarian revolution' was added.[44] This may have made little practical difference as the original definition was so wide in any case, so perhaps one has to view it as a theoretical widening of the definition.

Some of the changes were more specific in their action and usually involved an increase in penalty or decrease in the necessary intent. Generally, one may say the trend was to make the law more severe.

Conclusions on the 1922 Code

In this Code, there is great emphasis on the protection of the state and society, an emphasis reflected in the principles of the General Part and the penalties of the Special Part. A twofold attitude to offences, i.e. those aimed at the political system and all other offences, is openly stated, and is explicable in terms of enemies of the regime and new order trying to overthrow it, and erring individuals committing offences under the influences of the old society. Schlesinger describes the effect of this approach as the

> explicit enumeration of the ordinary offences subject to punishment, whilst as to counter-revolutionary attempts the mere fact of proven counter-revolutionary intention was regarded as a sufficient basis to render an action liable to punishment, independent of whether or not it had been explicitly provided for in the Code.[45]

He adds that this latter point is supported by Lenin's references to the legislation, not abolition, of terror. The question of analogy is closely related to this approach because of its effect on the nature of the Special Part, making it a collection of examples, not a definitive list. Schlesinger concludes that

> a) in dealing with counter-revolutionary crimes, analogy is accepted as an expedient to determine the sanctions to be applied against acts regarded as criminal independent of their explicit description in the Criminal Code; and b) in dealing with ordinary crimes, it merely serves to fill gaps left unwittingly by the legislator in shaping the

Code.[46]

This would seem to be a sensible suggestion and would apply in nearly all cases. It explains the great importance attached to counter-revolutionary crime and the accompanying wide, imprecise definitions.

The relationship between analogy and revolutionary legal consciousness is of interest, the latter concept being mentioned in Article 9 of the Code under the name of 'socialistic conception of law', to be used in the determination of punishment. Carr says the introduction of analogy amounted to 'the abandonment of "revolutionary consciousness" as a method of filling gaps in the legislative code and the substitution of what was, at any rate in form, a legal criterion'.[47] As such, this was part of the trend, apparent from 1917, that placed increasingly less emphasis on the use of legal consciousness. This was certain to happen as the legal system developed, and even with analogy its application would be influenced by this revolutionary legal consciousness — perhaps it would delineate the acceptable limits within which normal discretion could operate, for example.

The Code was noteworthy for its great number of necessary alterations, for which one of the main reasons was poor drafting. Berman believes this Code (and the 1926 one for that matter) is 'replete with vague, sweeping definitions of crimes in which technical legal terms are used in a popular sense, and popular terms in a technical legal sense', and 'is full of unintended inconsistencies and ambiguities'. Many revolutionary terms were used but in reality the draftsmen had taken 'the prerevolutionary codes as models, together with Western codes, and attempted to give them a Bolshevik cast'.[48]

This relationship between the Code and prerevolutionary law was considered in some depth by Timasheff. An initial problem is the confused state of the prerevolutionary law, based as it was on three codes: that of 1845, consisting of 2,224 articles and revised in 1885 (and it had been a revision of Volume 15 of the 1832 Incorporated Laws to begin with); the Statute of 1864, which was a list of articles from the 1845 Code that could be applied by Justices of the Peace; and that of 1903, the product of a great deal of research but piecemeal enactment. All of the Codes had numerous amendments and additions.

There are definite similarities between pre- and post-revolutionary law. The most noticeable influence is the 1903 Code, as it was highly respected in legal circles and the discussion surrounding it left an imprint on the minds of the drafters. An example is the fourfold division of guilt used by the 1903 Code and followed in the 1922 (and 1926) Code. The words used in the definitions were very alike: Article 48 of the earlier said 'A criminal act is considered to be intentional not only when the guilty one wished (zhelal") for its commission, but when he consciously permitted (soznatel'no dopuskal") the consequences to occur';[49] while Article 11 of the 1922 Code says acting intentionally is 'foreseeing the consequences of their actions and wished (zhelal") or consciously permitted (soznatel'no dopuskal") them'. Necessary defence was influenced by Article 45 of the 1903 Code, saying, 'An act is not considered as criminal when committed under necessary defence against an illegal infringement to the person or property rights of the one protecting himself or another.' The concepts of preparation and attempt were separate in the 1903 Code with the former only punishable if specifically stated to be so, and the latter only in non-petty cases. The 1922 Code kept them separate (the 1926 did not) but the punishment for attempt was modified to that for the completed crime in cases where the attempt failed, and if the attemptor decided not to carry out his aim, then what has been done is punished as it stands (if punishable at all): a twofold distinction that was in the 1845 Code.

In the Special Part, some of the sections of the 1922 Code were completely new, notably that on counter-revolutionary crime. Timasheff[50] says that the 1903 Code 'penalised precisely circumscribed actions', and compares it favourably in this respect with the Soviet codes. One is not so sure that this is the case, as Article 108 of the 1903 Code, for example, punishes 'Russian nationals, guilty in the furtherance or favouring of the enemy in their military or other hostile acts against Russia', which seems a wide approach. Two pertinent points can be made: (i) this type of crime may have to be worded in this manner as the concept itself is general, and (ii) if this is so, then justice will depend on the fair application of the law rather than on the definitions themselves, and Soviet practice was not always just in these cases. The 1903 Code's treatment of homicide, personal injury – with some changes – and property law, were basically followed by the 1922 Code; but sexual offences, considered one of the more unfortunate parts of the 1903 Code, were somewhat simplified by the 1922 Code – although not enough.

One concludes that there are definite interconnections between pre- and post-revolutionary law, when the codes are compared. This should not seem practically surprising, as the draftsmen of the Soviet codes would be trained in prerevolutionary law, and as the 1903 Code was an advanced, carefully considered law, some borrowings would take place. This did not happen in political areas, and one should not think that there were no new ideas in the Soviet codes: the concept of social danger and the material definition of crime, the rules on the application of punishments and the lowering of penalties for 'ordinary' crimes were innovations. If there is such a connection, is it acceptable or defensible? Yes, one believes it is, as there is certain to be a continuity between the old and new in this sort of situation, and from a theoretical viewpoint the definitions used are not so important in deciding the nature of law as the mode of application. To be proletarian law (which in a Marxist sense this is not), the new system does not have to completely reject the old − although one would expect some modifications.

The 1923 USSR Constitution and its Outcome

During this period, the dismemberment of the country ceased and a movement to reunify was instigated by the Bolsheviks, who recognised that counter-revolution would have less chance of success after unification had been achieved. An important factor was the Red Army, now victorious and, generally, the most pressing arguments were military. After much debate, various treaties were signed and led to the formation of four basic units: Ukraine, Transcaucasus, White Russia and Russia itself. They all passed resolutions favouring the formation of a federation, and delegates from all four constituted themselves the First Congress of Soviets of the USSR on 30 December 1922. Further debates and discussions led to the USSR Constitution, adopted by the VTsIK on 6 July 1923.

   Article 1(o) gave the USSR's supreme authorities power to establish 'the bases of judicial administration (*sudoustroistvo*) and legal proceedings, and also the civil and criminal legislation of the Union'; 1(p) gave the power to enact basic labour laws; and 1(v) the right of amnesty for the USSR.

   The relationship between the Union and the Union Republics on the matter of legislation could sometimes be problematic − or at least there is speculation over this − because of its ill-defined nature, and there is the special difficulty over the lack of separation in some areas of the RSFSR from the USSR and their 'special' relationship. Due to the importance of the Party, it is difficult to quantify the importance of this matter, but it has often been the practice that the RSFSR led in various policy matters and the other Union Republics followed.

Chapter VII concerned itself with the Supreme Court of the Union, which was to enforce 'revolutionary legality' within the USSR. The Procurator (created by Article 46) was attached to this body, and the two were very interdependent until the end of the 1920s. Interestingly enough, one organ the Procurator could check was the OGPU. Article 61 said it was created with 'the aim of the unification of the revolutionary efforts of the union republics in the struggle with political and economic counter-revolution, espionage and banditry'. An important result of these stipulations was the issuing on 31 October 1924[51] of the Fundamental Principles. These were in several respects similar to the General Part of the 1922 Code, but there were changes of order and emphasis, as well as an interesting attitude to punishment.

The introduction sets out the purpose of criminal legislation, saying its task is 'the judicial-legal protection of the state of the workers from socially dangerous acts which undermine the authority of the workers or which violate the established legal order', this being done 'by means of the use of measures of social defence'. Throughout these principles, the terms 'socially dangerous act' and 'measures of social defence' rather than 'crime' and 'punishment' are used. Many of the previously accepted attitudes – two types of crime, the use of minimum penalties, etc., continue here. One change to the Principles which should be particularly noted was the removal of the direct reference to class membership in the list of aggravating circumstances.[52]

The 1926 Criminal Code of the RSFSR

It may seem odd to issue a new code only four years after the first, but the 1924 Guiding Principles presented the possibility of a new code due to the number of changes found necessary in respect of the 1922 Code. After initial disputes with the Union authorities, mainly over the new concept of state crimes – in so far as who had authority to decide upon crimes against the administration – the VTsIK of the RSFSR issued the Code on 22 November 1926.[53] It was to come into force on the first day of the following year, and although it had the rather misleading title of 'Criminal Code of the RSFSR 1926 Edition', suggesting it was an amendment of the earlier code, it was in fact a new code.

Schlesinger[54] says the correlation between the Principles and this code was complicated by the greater emphasis placed by the former on fighting potential dangers rather than actual breaches, by, for example, regarding the class of the offender as an aggravating or mitigating factor, and by the use of protective banishment. The RSFSR authorities were against this approach, and although the Code complied with it, the Principles were later changed (on 27 February 1927) to correspond with the views held in the RSFSR, and its code underwent a corresponding change on 6 June 1927. This is sometimes thought to be an example of a 'special relationship' between the two, but as the same experts would advise both authorities, and considering the nature of the Soviet system, one has to treat this with a certain degree of doubt.

The General Part

The aim of the code is 'the protection of the socialist state of the Workers and peasants and of its established legal order from socially-dangerous acts (crimes) by means of the use of measures of social defence to persons who commit them' (Art. 1).

Three elements of this statement typify the Code, the first being the reference to the protection of the state, which occurs in direct and oblique forms throughout the Code, and has played an important part in Soviet legislation up to this point. The second element is that the protection is against 'socially dangerous acts (crimes)', which it would seem are interchangeable terms, and this, together with the analogy provision, makes the Code open-ended — as indeed do the wide definitions. The Code prefers to use the term 'socially dangerous act' rather than 'crime'. Finally, offences are not 'punished', but have 'measures of social defence' applied to the perpetrator. This is part of the dominant materialism of the Code, the lack of emphasis attached to formal elements — if an act is socially dangerous, then it is a crime. The 1922 Code had demonstrated similar aims, but the terms 'crime' and 'punishment' had coexisted with those above. The 1926 Code's credence in crime as social danger is further illustrated by Article 6, which defines the latter as 'directed against the Soviet system or violates the legal order established by the Worker-Peasant authority for the period of transition to a communist system'. It concludes in a Note attached to the article that

An action is not a crime although it falls under the formal definition of any article of the Special Part of this Code, if by virtue of its obvious minor importance and of the absence of harmful consequences, its character is deprived of social danger.

We have, therefore, a situation where the question of whether or not the criminal law is to apply depends on whether the act is 'directed at the Soviet system or violates the legal order'. If it does either of these, then it is termed 'socially dangerous' and the criminal law will apply. Even if one considers the new stipulation as in some way formal, then its effect can be removed if the act is of 'obvious minor importance' or has no 'harmful consequences'.

Article 7, in saying that measures can be applied to persons 'who constitute a danger on account of their connection with a criminal environment or on account of their former activities', shows the supposed influence of the USSR Principles on the fighting of potential dangers rather than actual breaches. Article 8 says penal measures do not apply to an act which has subsequently lost its socially dangerous nature by 'reason of a change in the penal law or because of the mere fact of an alteration in the social-political situation', or if the person has ceased to be socially dangerous in the opinion of the court. The reference to penal laws gives them a certain retroactive effect; while that regarding the social-political situation restates the connection between it and social danger.

Analogy is dealt with in Article 16, with the statement that if an act is not precisely covered by the Code, 'then the basis and limits of responsibility are determined in conformity with those articles of the Code which make provision for the most similar type of crime'. Two points to note are that the use of analogy is in the spirit of the Code: it is the social danger of the act that is considered, not the breach of a formal rule; and the wide definitions of the Code make any great reliance on analogy unnecessary, as an act could relatively easily be made to come within the ambit of one or other of the articles in the Special Part. From the above, one sees the materialist, non-formal approach of the Code, but more formal elements were included in it, such as Article 10, which said that measures of a judicial-correctional nature only apply if the person acted 'intentionally' or 'carelessly', and then goes on to define these terms.

Measures of Social Defence

Their purpose is said by Article 9 to be (i) the prevention of new crimes by those who have committed them, (ii) to influence other unstable members of society, and (iii) the adaption of those 'who have committed criminal acts to the conditions of the community life of the toilers' state'. Retribution, physical suffering and personal humiliation are all specifically excluded. The actual measures are comprehensive

and fall into three categories – medical, medical-educational (for those
under 14), and judicial-correctional. Shooting, still termed an
'exceptional measure', is reserved for the 'more serious forms of crime
that threaten the foundations of Soviet power and the Soviet system'.
It has to be used only in articles where it is specially indicated (Art. 21),
which indicates a special control over its use. However, it is uncertain
as to whether this in itself would strictly control it. The remaining
articles in this part of the Code describe in more detail the various
measures that can be used, a point of particular interest being that
deprivation of liberty can be from 1 day to ten years, limits which
undergo considerable changes when later practicalities come to have
their effect. In Part V, there are some noteworthy policy statements
on the application of punishment. Article 45 says that the application
of judicial-correctional measures depends on the General Part of the
Code, the relevant Article(s) of the Special Part, and from the court's
'socialist legal consciousness, derived from taking into account the
social danger of the committed crime, the circumstances of the act and
the personality of the perpetrator of the crime'. The last factor
indicates that non-social aspects have to be taken into account, but as
we shall see, the explanations of crime acceptable to the regime have to
be based on social causes, so one cannot read too much into this.
Articles 46 and 47 restate the view that there are two types of crime,
those 'directed against the foundations of the Soviet system. . .and are
consequently deemed the most dangerous', and 'all other crimes'. The
application of upper and lower limits is as before. As aiming to restore
the power of the bourgeoisie, or membership in the past or present –
nepmen? – of the class of persons who exploited the work of others,
are aggravating factors, and being a 'worker or toiling peasant' is
mitigating, class is a pertinent factor. Article 51 allows a court to lower
penalties outside the given limits if reasons are given, and the final
section of the General Part is concerned with conditional release and
conditional sentences, which depend for their application on a lack of
social danger, either at the time of sentence or, as regards conditional
release, a change brought about by reform.

The Special Part of the Code

The arrangement of the chapters in this Code was very similar to that
in the 1922 Code, except that Chapter 1(2) in the old code was
renamed 'Crimes against the administration which are particularly
dangerous to the USSR', and a new Chapter 2 was added, 'Other crimes
against the administration'. The former constituted the newly used

concept of a state crime. Apart from the ensuing change in number, but not order, the only other changes were an exchange in order of Military Crimes and Infringements of the regulations for the protection of public health, etc., and the addition of a new chapter on 'Crimes constituting a survival of the tribal manner of life', which came at the end of the Code. The chapter order can indicate some sort of order of importance attached to the different types of crime, but the position of Military Crimes, although more logical at the very end of the Code, is probably due to the fact that they could have constituted a separate code in themselves, rather than any lack of importance. The final chapter is as such because it was added later, on 6 April 1928.

Counter-revolutionary Crime

This is contained in Article 58, which, having 18 subdivisions, is sufficiently complex to form a chapter in itself. The initial version of Chapter 1 had a short life of only six months, as it was greatly amended on 6 June 1927[55] by an All-Union law. This was due to above-mentioned differences between RSFSR and USSR authorities.

The definition of counter-revolutionary crime was considerably modified by the change. In the original code, an act was considered counter-revolutionary if

> directed towards the overthrow, undermining or weakening of the authority of the Worker-Peasant Soviets and which exists on the basis of the Constitution of the RSFSR Worker-Peasant's Government, and also actions directed at that part of the international bourgeoisie which does not recognise the equal rights of the communist system,

or is aimed at 'the foundation of the political and economic achievements of the proletarian revolution'. This is the usual type of wide definition that in cases of necessity could cover practically any act. When the definition was changed, the references to the international bourgeoisie went into a separate article and 'or towards the undermining or weakening of the internal security of the USSR or of the basic economic, political and national conquests of the proletarian revolution' was added to the first element. Constituent and autonomous republican governments were also specifically protected, so reflecting the constitutional change since the 1922 Code. Moreover, due to 'international solidarity', acts against other 'workers' states' were to be considered as counter-revolutionary under this Code, even

if the state did not belong to the USSR, so identifying this government
with proletarian interests throughout the world. The ultimate   ate
effect of these changes was to make the article wider, if that were
possible, than before, with some evidence on the practical effects given
by Solzhenitsyn. In the *Gulag Archipelago*[56] he lists some amazing
cases: a factory director receiving ten years as he was the first to stop
applauding Stalin; non-political cases being reclassified to fill 'quotas';
and gypsies camping in a city square seized under Article 58 to fulfil
the plan of arrests. There are many more. The remaining 17 parts of
Article 58 cover a very wide range of behaviour, such as the organisation
of insurrection or invasion (58-2); dealing with foreign governments
(58-3); and participating in an organisation with counter-revolutionary
aims (58-4); and wide terms such as 'active operation or struggle against
the working class and revolutionary movement' were included. As is
usual with counter-revolutionary crime, there are a number of very
general definitions, and some reasonably detailed descriptions of
particular actions. The former allow the application of the Code if an
act does not readily fall into one of the definitions. Due to the degree
of choice available in Article 58, one is drawn to the conclusion that
detailed consideration of both the original and later versions of Article
58 is unnecessary and unprofitable. Even the penalties have lower
limits only, and little can be deduced about its practical effect.
However, one can certainly conclude that both versions of Article 58
could cover any action they were called upon so to do.

Other Aspects of the Code

Just as the first part of Chapter 1 consisted of a single article, the
second — 'Crimes against the Administration that are particularly
dangerous to the USSR' — is constituted by Article 59. The basic
definition says that these acts are

> not directly aimed at the overthrow of the Soviet power and the
> Worker-Peasant Government, nevertheless result in a breach of the
> correct operation of the organs of administration or national
> economy, linked with resistance to the organs of power and a
> hindering of their operation, disobedience to the laws, or with other
> actions challenging the power and authority of the regime (*vlast'*).

The following eleven subsections set out the different types of this
offence. The overall impression of this chapter is similar to the previous
one, with wide definitions and heavy penalties — although these are not

quite as severe as the social danger of the offences is considered to be less.

Chapter 2 concerned itself with other actions against the administration, such as non-payment of taxes, failure to perform a duty, concealing inherited property and evading military service. As would be expected, the penalties are less severe, for example up to one year for wilful damage to state property if a first offence (otherwise, five years). Hooliganism falls within this section of the Code and is defined as 'any rowdy acts, attended by overt disrespect towards society' and carries a penalty of deprivation of liberty for up to three months, provided that no administrative penalty has been applied. A heavier penalty is involved — up to two years deprivation of liberty, if 'the aforesaid acts amount to riotous or excessive behaviour, or were committed repeatedly or persistently notwithstanding a warning by the organs guarding public order, or if the acts were distinguished by exceptional cynicism or insolence' (Art. 74). As one can see, the penalties have been increased and show the concern with this type of act.

Chapter 3, dealing with official crimes, starts with a definition of abuse of authority that is very similar to that used in the 1922 Code, but the minimum penalty is less than before — six months rather than one year with strict isolation. Following Chapter 4, which is on church matters and is generally anti-clerical in nature, except for Article 127, which gives some protection to the celebration of religious rites, comes the chapter on Economic Crime, consisting of eight articles, Nos. 128-35. Article 128 applies deprivation of liberty for up to two years or forced labour for up to one year (and a disciplinary penalty if loss is insignificant) for 'mismanagement' by any person in control of a state or public enterprise. This was less severe than the 1922 Code, where there had been a basic minimum of one year's imprisonment. Other articles deal with delivery of bad quality goods, misappropriation of state or public property, etc., and were in many respects more limited than the 1922 Code which tended to be more detailed in matters involving contracts. As in the earlier code, this chapter is followed by that on offences against life, health, etc., and it is instructive to compare penalties. Premeditated murder with aggravating circumstances carries deprivation of liberty for not more than ten years (under the 1922 Code not less than eight years with strict isolation); other premeditated murders, not exceeding eight years (before, not less than three years with strict isolation); infliction of grievous bodily harm, not exceeding eight years (before, not less than three years).

From these examples, one can see that a major difference in approach
is shown by the 1922 Code's use of minimum penalty limits, while the
later code relies on maximum ones, which would indicate a more
liberal approach. However, the wide disparity of limits would make
predictions in individual cases difficult.

The chapter on Crimes against Property has the usual tendency to
award heavier penalties for theft of state property than for private, the
former usually involving up to two years' deprivation of liberty, or one
of forced labour, while the latter carries both for three or six months.
The 1922 Code tended to use minimum penalties. The remaining
chapters of the Code deal with public health, security and order
regulations and military crimes.

Chapter 10, on 'Crimes constituting a Survival of the Tribal Manner
of Life', it will be remembered, was added later, on 6 April 1928[57]
(see later).

Subsequent Changes to the 1926 Code

The important changes to Article 58 have already been considered.
On 6 June 1927, a decree[58] changed many articles in the Code, notably
the lists of aggravating and mitigating circumstances contained in
Articles 47 and 48. It was no longer an aggravating factor that the
offender was a member of the 'class which exploits the labour of
others'; and no longer mitigating that he was a 'worker or toiling
peasant'. This de-emphasis of class was due to a more stable situation,
and the needs of the nepmen, as economic developments needed more
freedom for entrepreneurs and technicians. A decree[59] of 31 October
1927 affected the law on official crimes. Article 110 had the penalty
applicable if a weapon or force was involved in exceeding authority,
from in exceptional cases, shooting, to deprivation of liberty for not
less than two years. The sections in Article 112 (misuse of authority
resulting in administrative disorganisation) and 114 (unjust sentencing
by judges) applying shooting in exceptional circumstances were
removed.

The production of spirits at home, often a target of legislation, was
dealt with by a decree[60] of 16 January 1928. The penalty was as before,
with the additional possibility of a 500-rouble fine instead of
deprivation of liberty, but the possibility of a reduction in sentence if
committed 'on account of necessity, unemployment, or lack of
awareness with the aim of satisfying their or their families' minimum
requirements' ceased to apply.

In April 1928, the already mentioned additional chapter was added to the Code as part of the campaign to eliminate customary tribal and religious-based legal practices that had become particularly noted after the creation of the Turkmen and Bashkir autonomous republics. The new chapter did not mention any specific areas, and was mainly concerned with feuds and matrimonial questions. Sometimes the method was to apply the ordinary criminal law, as in cases of rape, but for bigamy, forced labour up to one year or up to 1,000-rouble fine replaces the ordinary law, and the article in question, No. 199, says the law does not apply to 'unions concluded before the promulgation of these laws'. Sociological, rather than legislative, forces were to lead to the abandonment of these local practices. Article 112 underwent further changes on 28 May 1928,[61] which expanded the meaning of a 'disciplinary penalty', used for minor offences, to 'forced labour for a period not exceeding one month, or discharge from office, or deprivation for a period not exceeding two years of the right to hold executive or responsible office, or the obligation to make good the damage done, or a public reprimand', which can only be described as a significant increase in guidance.

Robbery penalties were changed in 1929.[62] Previously, people of 'special social danger' who carry out a robbery that results in death or severe mutilation were to be shot. Now, the death penalty was still to apply, but to armed robbery with 'aggravating circumstances of a particularly serious nature'.

Conclusions on the 1926 Code

Many aspects of this Code do not conflict with the previous practice. Acts are not to be considered criminal because they involve the breaking of a formal rule; the social danger involved in the person and the act are the deciding factors. The question is really one of applying sanctions rather than criminality. This Code follows the earlier one in the rejection of *nullem crimen*, as illustrated by the wide definitions, analogy and general social danger approach. Justice is not to be achieved by the application of formal rules, but by an appreciation of the 'true situation'. The area of counter-revolutionary crime was still of special interest, and was part of a wider concept, but with 'state crime' definitions are such that practically any act can come within its ambit. In theory, the act has to be socially dangerous, Article 6 saying that an act is not a crime if there is no social danger, and Article 8 stating that penalties do not apply if the social danger is later removed.

Other individual items worthy of note include Article 6, referring to the 'transition to a Communist regime', and so limiting the lifetime of the law; Article 45, saying the 'socialist conception of justice' is to help decide on matters of punishment (but not criminality); and the class references in Articles 47 and 48, which were later removed.

The special part contains the usual heavier penalties for counter-revolutionary and anti-state actions, which corresponds to their social danger. Comparing the other chapters with the 1922 Code, one concludes that although there were certain changes of emphasis, the Codes are not of a different substance, but show a progression of attitudes that sometimes involves the use of heavier penalties and sometimes lighter.

Other Republican Codes

Ginsburgs and Mason[63] drew very informative conclusions from a study of the RSFSR and Uzbek Codes, the latter being chosen as it was issued in 1926, before the uniformity and centralisation drives began in earnest, and because that republic was one of stature and widely different from the RSFSR. The original codes had not been similar — although the ground covered was often the same. In their General Parts, the RSFSR had six sections, the Uzbek four, which is contrary to the tendency in the Special Parts for the Uzbek to have many more articles, 385 to 298 as of 1 November 1954. This was the result of the policy of splitting what were single articles in the RSFSR Code into two or three parts, supposedly to clarify the law. The Uzbek Code includes a chapter on water crimes, and the chapter sequence is altered by military crimes coming second. In the Special Part, the number of identical articles may have been small to begin with, but as time progresses, the situation changes (see Table 4.1). One can see that no or little copying took place during the initial draftings, but as the campaigns for uniformity grow, central decrees are followed by the Republics. In fact, this comes to happen to such an extent, that these Republican codes become somewhat defunct, not being kept up to date as the central decrees change the law. Also, the distribution of these identical articles varies significantly by chapter, viz. that on counter-revolutionary crimes is all the same, as is that on military crimes. Local customary crimes have only 2 out of 17 articles identical.

A comparison of the Codes draws one to conclude that in many respects they reflect the requirements of their areas, the uniformity being applied at definite stages. The Uzbek Code contains many articles with more severe penalties than the Russian, and its definitions generally widen the scope of the law, although there are instances when the reverse is true. There are signs of enforced similarities, but also of

Table 4.1: Distribution of Identical Articles by Years

Year	Total	Complete Articles	Paragraphs
1926	5	3	2
1927	26	24	2
1928	29	26	3
1929	30	23	7
1930	6	2	4
1931	9	7	2
1932	1	1	0
1933	1	1	0
1934	12	11	1
1935	10	9	1
1936	4	2	2
1937	1	1	0
1941	1	1	0
1947	4	4	0

Source: G. Ginsbergs and G. Mason, 'Soviet Criminal Law Reform' in
    G.O.W. Mueller (ed.), *Essays in Criminal Science* (London, 1961), p. 416.

necessary local variations.

The Study of Crime during the NEP

From the statistics of convictions, it would appear that crime was increasing during this period. This led to a renewed interest in the study of crime which produced research, statistics and journals. On the Union level, the State Institute for the Study of Crime and the Criminal was established in 1925, with four divisions: socio-economic, biopsychological, penitentiary and criminalistic. The first two of these indicate the main criminological areas of speculation in this period, although one should remember the general point that in this period there was a pluralist approach. The Communist Academy had a section devoted to law and state, which carried out work in this field, but the establishment of the Institute, incidentally subordinated to the Russian NKVD, was more significant. Local offices for the study of crime were established at Moscow, Leningrad, Saratov, Odessa, Kiev, Karkov, Rostov-on-Don, Baku and Minsk, in which both theoreticians and practitioners worked, but they were not centrally co-ordinated.

Biopsychological theories are very typical of this period, and based criminal behaviour in organically and genetically conditioned individual disorders. E.K. Krasnushkin, who headed this section of the Institute, believed that once the environmental and economic defects had acted upon the person during his upbringing, the resulting defects in personality made him a member of the criminal group made up of social derelicts. The social conditions had to be studied to understand how they affected the personality, before social reforms could be effective. One can see that this theory is a synthesis of sociological and biopsychological approaches, which is a little unusual, as these often conflicted with each other. Those such as A.A. Gertsenzon and D.I. Kurskii, who emphasised socially orientated factors and were against biological determinism, were more suited to future needs. With the end of the NEP, the 'biologists' came under attack, on the basis that they ascribed to criminals personalities that were not amenable to socially based modifications. Lombroso was brought into it, and as would be expected, the 'biologists' lost the argument. The conclusion was that 'Social phenomena, to which crime belongs, cannot be explained by the methods of the natural sciences, in particular psychiatry. Therefore any attempts to show that crime is explained by the biological constitution of the individual are doomed to failure.'[64] Vyshinsky[65] was at least orthodox, when he decided that

> Each Communist knows what generates crime in contemporary society and who [i.e. which class] supplies the offenders. Crime is generated by misery; by capitalist oppression; by corruption and oppression by the capitalist society. The working class also supplies offenders, because it has been plundered and corrupted by capitalism.

If a pluralist approach prevailed in criminology, one area of agreement was punishment. Penal servitude, the old prison system and exile to Siberia were opposed by the Bolsheviks, no doubt partly due to their first-hand knowledge of them. While Shirvindt directed the Institute, forced labour was banned, and prisons became 'places of detention' or 'corrective labour colonies'. However, any enlightened changes in the situation were defeated by the overcrowding in the 'places of confinement' that took place.

The increase in the prison population had been partly caused by the impossibility of organising the use of forced labour without

Table 4.2: Total Convictions: USSR and RSFSR

Year	Per 100,000 Inhabitants	Convictions RSFSR	Index 1928 = 100	Convictions USSR (est.)
1925	1,000	974,000	88	1,420,000
1926		1,030,000	93.5	1,510,000
1927	1,073	1,100,000	99.5	1,602,000
1928		1,106,000	100	1,610,000
1929	1,363	1,450,000	131	2,110,000

Source: Peter H. Juviler, *Revolutionary Law and Order* (New York, 1976), p. 31.

Table 4.3: Prisoners in Places of Detention

Year	No. in USSR 1 January	Average Length of Sentence (RSFSR)	Prison Population as Percentage Prison Capacity (RSFSR)
1924	87,800	1.25 years	120
1925	148,000	0.89 years	132
1926	155,000	0.72 years	177
1927	198,000	–	–

Source: Adapted from Juviler, *Revolutionary Law and Order*.

confinement, one of the original good ideas of the regime. As there was considerable unemployment, it was found difficult to place those who had been sentenced in work, and it became necessary to allow them to be employed at enterprises attached to places of confinement.[66] This was found to be unsuitable on the large scale, and in the country, 75 per cent of the official rate for the job was often more than that actually received by normal workers. In the urban situation, the offender often stayed at his usual place of work, making the penalty amount to a fine. Concern over the overcrowding, and for that matter, cases of premature release – often serious offenders were released to help with the harvest – grew, until a resolution of the TsIK and the Sovnarkom of the RSFSR was issued on 26 March 1923.[67] This said that severe measures were to be taken in cases involving great social danger, but in lesser offences deprivation of liberty should be replaced by other measures. Due to the alarmist atmosphere prevailing at this time (Shakhty was coming into the news), the part of this resolution

referring to the need for severe measures for serious offenders came
to be emphasised, and the corrective labour code was tightened up on
21 May 1928.[68] Short-term sentences were again attacked, and for
professional criminals exile was thought appropriate. In November
1928, it was decided that a person who had been sentenced to forced
labour without detention for more than six months, could, if there
were no suitable establishments near his place of residence, serve his
sentence in labour establishments elsewhere. In the beginning of 1929,
a PCJ circular said that no more sentences of deprivation of liberty for
less than one year were to be pronounced, and any at the moment were
to be transferred to forced labour.[69]

At the Sixth Congress of judicial workers, held in February 1929,
the calls for the reduced use of short sentences continued, and
Krylenko was criticised for his ideas in his draft code (see later). A new
system of corrective labour institutions was outlined, made up of many
different types of institution, such as forced labour camps, isolators,
etc. The OGPU extended its powers over places of confinement, as
there was little delineation between those for major state crimes and
those for more ordinary offences. The overall picture shows that a
remedial approach to penology was being replaced by calls from
'realists' demanding more severe measures in the name of security.

Conclusions

Obviously, the most important feature of this period is the New
Economic Policy which, regardless of whether it was an orthodox
progression or a retrogressive deviation, had a profound effect on many
aspects of both theory and practice.

If the teachings of Marx are applied to this situation, is there
supposed to be a dictatorship of the proletariat, and are state and law,
which while existing further that dictatorship, withering away? A good
beginning is afforded by asking whether there was a dictatorship of the
proletariat. The Party had an ideology which supplied strong reasons
why it should play a leading role in the dictatorship. It was the
'vanguard of the proletariat' and the repository of its 'true'
consciousness. It was openly supposed that if the proletariat had not
had the Party, they would not achieve their destiny as quickly, as they
had but 'trade union consciousness', which would centre them on
short-term immediate improvements, and they would not develop or
adopt the correct long-term strategy. In its conspiratorial days, i.e.

before 1917, it would have been difficult for the Party to be influenced
by the proletariat because of the Party's nature and that of Tsarism,
and in any case, its Marxist heritage had to be adapted to the Russian
situation, with its preponderance of peasants. With the arrival of more
stable conditions, the composition of the Party, in both quantitative
and qualitative terms, received considerable attention. Available figures
say that at the beginning of 1922 (on 1 January) Party membership
totalled 528,354, of which 77.7 per cent — 410,430 — were full
members, the rest being candidate members.[70] In this 'proletarian'
party, 44.4 per cent of members were of worker origin, 26.7 per cent
peasant, and 28.9 per cent white-collar.[71] The Lenin and October
Enrolments boosted intake, so by 1 January 1929 there were 1,090,508
full members, and 444,854 candidates, of which 61.4 per cent were of
worker origin and 21.7 per cent peasant.[72] However, when occupation
rather than origin was considered, these last figures became 44.0 per
cent workers, 13.0 per cent collective and individual farmers, and 43.0
per cent white-collar, etc.[73] The decrease in peasant membership on
the eve of collectivisation caused concern, and methods of increasing
their intake were instigated. With the huge increase in membership, the
percentage of members who had joined before the Party had come to
power necessarily fell sharply, but as would be expected, they were
concentrated in the higher ranks of the Party apparatus and so had an
influence out of all proportion to their absolute numbers, especially as
those newly enrolled had little experience, were young, and not as well
educated.[74]

One can see that the Party has features that distinguish it from the
general population and make it highly susceptible to leadership from
above. This in itself would have remained the concern of the Party
rather than the country if the government had been independent of the
Party, but it was not. All the boards in the people's commissariats were
'almost exclusively staffed by party members', as were the directorates
in finance and industry.[75] Other areas so affected include the trade
unions and army. This leads one to the seemingly inevitable conclusion
that the dictatorship of the proletariat did not exist. The Party had a
dominant theoretical relationship with the proletariat to begin with,
and the seizure of power by the 'proletariat' had been done by the
Party. This in itself could cause no surprise in so far as a class as such
could hardly seize power in any literal sense, but once power had been
achieved, opposition was silenced and one-party rule established.
Forces, perhaps inevitable, more probably due to the personalities
involved, caused the spiritual death of the Party, and all criticism

and opposition within it stopped. It ceased to be an active, constructive force (in fact it is doubtful as to whether it ever was so) and took on an administrative face. The Leninist legacy, and Stalin's activities, made it easily controllable from above, and its pre-eminent position in the state made this latter entity susceptible to what followed.

What can be deduced from the importance of class at this stage? If this is a society moving towards communism, then according to Marx, the classes should be withering away. Quite apart from the position of the Party, was this the case, was class becoming less important? The 1922 Code was remarkably free from formal comment on the subject. There were references to the 'international bourgeoisie' in the definition of counter-revolutionary crime, and it was an aggravating factor if a crime had been committed with the aim of restoring the power of the bourgeoisie, but these refer to the protection afforded to the state (i.e. the regime), and not to class *per se*. However, one cannot say that class was of no importance to this code as, for example, on a most general level, part of the aims of punishment was the adaptation of the offender to the new social norms, and workers and peasants would be considered as more easily corrected than members of the bourgeoisie. The 1924 Principles in introducing membership of the exploiting class as an aggravating factor, and being a worker or toiling peasant as a mitigating one, were the high-water mark of class influence. After this the opposite view became prevalent, and the 1926 Code had its references removed in 1927.

The economy of this period was not of the type that one would have assumed would be adopted in the building of communism. Lenin was not consistent in his revealed attitudes towards it, sometimes saying it was a retreat, sometimes an advance from the over-enthusiasm of war communism. One concludes that on strictly ideological grounds it was a retreat to capitalism, but taking the long-term view, it was an advance, as without it the regime may well have lost power. It was certainly an effective step, as conditions in agriculture and industry improved. However, one must not overlook the fact that many thought the NEP to be a retrogressive unwanted step, a betrayal of former practices, and unemployment and inflation existed. Taking these things into consideration, one must conclude that even if the NEP was a tactical necessity, which it almost certainly was, it was not on the orthodox road to communism. One must immediately qualify this by saying that it happened because of the Russian situation, and in one way was in total agreement with Marx's teaching. The economy of Russia was not sufficiently developed for the advent of a pre-communist stage, and in

Table 4.4: Agriculture

	1922	1925
Sown area (hectares)	77.7	104.3
Grain harvest (tons)	50.3	72.5
Horses (head)	24.1	27.1
Cattle (head)	45.8	62.1
Pigs (head)	12.0	21.8
(all in millions)		

Source: Adapted from *Sotsialisticheskoe stroitel'stvo* (Moscow, 1934), p. 4.
In A. Nove, *An Economic History of the U.S.S.R.* (London, 1976).

Table 4.5: Industry

Average monthly wage in constant roubles

1913	30.49
1920-1	10.15
1921-2	12.15
1922-3	15.88
1923-4	20.75
1924-5	25.18
1925-6	28.57

Source: Adapted from I.A. Gladkov, *Sovetskoe Narodnoe Khozyaistvo (1921-5)*
(Moscow, 1960), p. 536.

so far as the NEP developed the economy, it was following Marx. Of
course the particulars of the local conditions cannot be overlooked.
Although Marx envisaged a revolution, it would not be, perhaps, of
such a destructive kind: the most advanced economy may have needed
a recovery. All this special pleading does not alter the basic fact that
Marx's theory could not be applied validly in the manner attempted.

The state was primarily supposed to be withering away. One has to
make the qualification of 'primarily' for two reasons. The first is that
the theory of socialism in one country existed, with its inherent
concepts of a strong state and law; and secondly, even if one disregards
this theory, the more orthodox approach would allow the NEP had an
effect on state theory: the state would not be withering at whatever
its usual rate could be expected to be because if a superstructural
concept such as the state had to reflect the economic base (and of

course it had to), then the capitalist revival of the NEP would
strengthen the state, even though the state could be considered as a
special type. By 'special type' one is referring to the qualifications made
about the state of the transition period, one that has the interests of
the majority at heart, but if this approach was postulated by the
Bolsheviks, one has to reply that this was not the transition period and
the state did not have the interests of the majority at heart. Was the
state given any great eminence or protection during this time? Yes: it
most definitely was. The 1922 Code had as its aim the 'lawful defence
of the toilers' state' and defined crime as actions 'threatening the
foundation of Soviet authority'; the 1924 Constitution was a clear sign
that state, or more correctly constitutional, matters were to be given
careful consideration; the 1926 Code was similar to that of 1922 in
this respect. Although one cannot assume that there will be no
organisatory force in the future society to take the place of the state,
one cannot consider these developments as a move in that direction.

It is most important to note that as the Party was the government,
in the sense that its members filled the great majority of the posts in
the government and administration, an aim to overthrow the social and
political structure was one aimed at the existence of the rule of the
Party. If the Party had reflected the true interests of the proletariat,
whose dictatorship this supposedly was, then there would be some
grounds for saying that the protection of this rule was the protection
of the dictatorship of the proletariat. However, (i) the Party was not
synonymous with the interests of the proletariat; (ii) the Party as a
whole did not exercise power, only the upper reaches of it — and this
was to become increasingly the case; and (iii) in terms of Marx's theory,
this was not the dictatorship of the proletariat.

The change in theory that allowed for the continued existence of
the state (and law) at least reflected reality to this extent. Were some
of the special qualities of the state, or the difficulties surrounding it,
explained by it being a transition period state? Although certain
parallels can be drawn, they are of no help in the final analysis, as this
was not the transition period. Law, its role, and legal theory all
underwent change in this period. A main influence was the belief that
law was to be of importance in the immediate and medium-term future.
In many ways this new stance gained support from theory — law was a
bourgeois phenomenon and the NEP was a return to capitalism which
gave the bourgeoisie and bourgeois values a lease of life; the capitalist
elements were to be closely scrutinised, a process that, together with
the increase in legally regulated relationships that took place, would

expand the role of law.

Legal theory found it easy to explain the existence of law, but Stuchka, and more especially Pashukanis, linked law too closely with bourgeois elements. Statements such as 'The withering away of bourgois Law can under no circumstances mean its replacement by some categories of proletarian Law, but only the withering away of law in general'[76] were distinctly inconvenient. When the NEP ended, the new theories rejected this approach, but one should understand that during the NEP they were eminently suitable, for

> The essential point of the theories of Stuchka and Pashukanis was that, by explicitly associating the survival of law with the practices of the NEP, they provided it with a temporary sanction, while leaving the way open for its eventual disappearance with the advent of socialism. The conception of law had the same ambivalent character as the general conception of the NEP, which was simultaneously interpreted as a retreat from socialism and a necessary stage in the advance towards it.[77]

Institutional aspects of law, such as the court system, were further developed and then resimplified. The Comrades' Courts were still used, but their primary aim involved control and discipline rather than the involvement of the public in the legal process, and cannot be considered as anything very significant in the withering away. The Supreme Court of the USSR was part of the centralising and strengthening of the state, and its Procurator was not a particularly powerful figure until later.

In substantive law, the major features were the Codes. Many of their provisions were influenced by prerevolutionary law, but the law had a definite Soviet stamp, with protection of the system and social danger emphasised. The concept protected or threatened in the definitions was not, of course, society pure and simple, but the particular political system. However, an analysis of the concept of social danger should deduce that apart from the political aspects, there was also an interesting attempt to define wrong in terms of harm done to society, that is the community and its members, rather than by reference to the breach of a formal rule. This introduces one to the idea that many aspects and developments of law were perfectly 'normal' and comparable with accepted Western ideas. Apart from the section on counter-revolutionary crime, the 1922 Code contained many liberal provisions: it is only when the existence or workings of the political structure are threatened that the Code is very severe. The subsequent

changes to the Code that were not caused by faults in the drafting
tended to make the law more severe, by increasing the penalty or
decreasing the required intent. The 1924 Principles were more social
defence orientated, with the purpose of legislation still the protection
of the state. The supposed Union influence is shown by the inclusion
of protective banishment, but Article 6 indicated a need for the
commission of an actual offence and reminds one of the RSFSR
approach. However, over this and the aforementioned changes that
occurred to the RSFSR 1926 Code and these Principles, one should
not overestimate any suspected differences between the Union and
the Republican authorities, as many of the same experts would advise
both, and the connections between the two were such that serious
differences were highly unlikely to occur, although there do seem to
have been some doubts and resentments on the part of the separate
Republican authorities on the whole question of centralisation.

The 1926 Code was a new code, but there was a degree of truth in
terming it the '1926 Edition', as in many respects it agrees with the
earlier Code. There is the usual lack of concern with formal elements,
to the extent that the Code can be considered open-ended, the Special
Part not being a definitive list but a series of guiding examples. Social
defence and danger still play an important part, as they are used to
define many other concepts. As was the case with the earlier Code,
later changes tended to increase penalties, but the removal of class
membership as an aggravating or mitigating factor in itself is of
particular note, not so much in its effect on the nepmen and experts
(who were of course favoured by it), but because it removes the shield
of class membership from worker and peasant offenders. This in itself
has interesting implications. It may, more simply, be due to the rising
crime rate, as offences were committed by workers and peasants and
practical necessities can be as important as those of theory. On this
latter point, various questions are raised, not the least of which
concerns the crime rate. Was this supposed to be falling or not? When
communism had been achieved, there was to be no crime (although
one has to keep in mind the possible modifications that may apply to
this basic premiss), and in the move towards that position, crime would
be withering away; but for Marx, this was not a transition period, and
even for Lenin, the re-emergence of bourgeois influences in the NEP
gave a reason, if not for a rising crime rate, at least for doubts over its
decline. The application of harsher measures against workers and
peasants must be considered pragmatically: the increased numbers of
offenders had to be dealt with, and the measures taken were not

considered to be retributive, but reformatory.

Practical difficulties adversely affected the system of punishment used, as the more adventurous and constructive kind involving work rather than imprisonment were found to be unworkable when great numbers were considered. Then, even though the list of possible measures included reprimands, censure, banishment, exile, loss of civil and political rights, etc., the increased use of the more usual penalties made the 'measures of social defence' seem more like 'punishments' (and 'socially dangersous acts' seem like 'crimes'), even though the Soviet authorities would have said the basic orientations of the state and social system invalidated this criticism. The growth in the crime rate, and the generally more open society of the NEP, resulted in a considerable interest in the causes of crime, with a pluralist approach being followed. However, it became imperative that (i) the offenders could be reformed, and (ii) the contemporary society did not have any inherent causes of crime. Any biological approach was rejected on these grounds, and sociological theories supported at their expense until they too came to be considered as inconvenient, whereupon criminological research was effectively halted. In some respects this is in agreement with Marx, whose basic approach was one of economic determinism, for although he mentioned other factors (only in a fragmentary manner), the causes of crime were seen as in society, not the individual. When one considers that the contemporary society was supposedly of the transition period, one realises that too great an emphasis on the defects of that society would be unwelcome, although in theory it should have some: it was after all in transition from the imperfect to the perfect!

From all this one can see that law was not withering away, and neither, according to Marx, should it have been. On the contrary, it became more developed and organised, and the trend away from the use of the revolutionary consciousness or socialist consciousness as a guide to the application of law was continued. This is a point to remember as the law became more and more imposed upon the members of society as time went on, reaching new levels in the 1930s. The peculiar characteristic of law in the NEP — the protection and non-protection of rights — was perhaps most clearly illustrated by Article 1 of the Civil Code: 'Civil rights shall be protected in law except in cases where they are exercised in contradiction with their social-economic purpose.' Unfortunately, it was the Party that decided on this last point, and the leadership of the Party at that: it was not the transition period, it was not the dictatorship of the proletariat, and law and state were not withering away.

Notes

1. S.N. Prokopovich, *Narodoe Khoziastvo SSSR* (New York, 1952), vol. II, pp. 97-8 (24.3 to 11.5 in 1913 roubles).

2. *SW*, vol. III, p. 511.

3. *The Communist Theory of Law* (London, 1955), p. 64.

4. *Soviet Legal Philosophy*, trans. H.W. Babb (Mass., 1951), p. 20.

5. 'Soviet Legal Philosophy', *Cornell L.R.* (1952), at pp. 54-5.

6. R. Schlesinger, *Soviet Legal Theory* (London, 1946), p. 154.

7. 'Pashukanis and Vyshinsky: A Study in the Development of Marxist Legal Theory', *Mich. L.R.*, vol. 47, pp. 1157-66.

8. 'The General Theory' in H. Babb, *Soviet Legal Philosophy* (Cambridge, Mass., 1951), pp. 184-5.

9. I. Lapenna, *State and Law: Soviet and Yugoslav Theory* (London, 1964), p. 21.

10. Babb, *Soviet Legal Philosophy*, p. 201.

11. See Lenin, *Coll. Works*, vol. 36, pp. 560-4.

12. Moscow, 1924. Here from M. Jaworskyj (ed.), *Soviet Political Thought* (Baltimore, 1967), p. 155.

13. *Uchenie O Gosudarstve Proletariata i Krestianstva i Ego Konstitutii,* 5th edn. (Moscow-Leningrad, 1926). Here from ibid., p. 243.

14. Podvolotskii, *Marksistskaia Teoriia Prava* (Moscow-Petrograd, 1923). Here from ibid., p. 114.

15. Details will be found in vol. 2, pp. 461 *et seq.*

16. Ibid., p. 464.

17. Ibid., p. 465.

18. Ibid., p. 466.

19. 'Eshcho Raz o Sotsialisticheskom Provosozanii', *Rabochii Sud*, nos. 5-6, (1925), pp. 196-200, In Jaworskyj, *Soviet Political Thought,* p. 202.

20. *SU* (1926), no. 85, item 624.

21. *SU*, no. 23/4, item 142.

22. *SU* (1930), no. 4, item 52.

23. *SU*, no. 14, item 160.

24. *Soviet Criminal Law: General Part* (Leyden, 1964), p. 30.

25. See *Materialy Narodnogo Kommissariata Iusticii*, vols. VII and X, for this.

26. 'The Impact of the Penal Law of Imperial Russia on Soviet Penal Law', *Am. Slav. & E. Eur. Rev.* (1953), p. 441.

27. Code published in *Prol. Rev. i Pravo* (1921), no. 15.

28. In Timasheff, 'Impact of the Penal Law', p. 446 (from *ESJ* (1922), no. 18).

29. Feldbrugge, *Soviet Criminal Law*, p. 30.

30. Timasheff, 'Impact of the Penal Law', p. 448.

31. M.N. Gernet and A.N. Trainin (eds.), *Ugolovnie Kodeks: Prakticheskii Kommentarii* (Moscow, 1925), pp. 68-9.

32. Timasheff, 'Impact of the Penal Law', p. 449.

33. *Ugolovnoe Ulozhenie* (St Petersburg, 1912).

34. *The Principle of Analogy in Criminal Law* (New York, 1954), p. 7.

35. *Izbrannye Stati'i i Rechi* (Moscow, 1958), p. 132.

36. *Ugolovnie Kodeks*, p. 17.

37. A.N. Trainin, *Ugolovnoe Pravo RSFSR* (Leningrad, 1925), p. 6.

38. Originally in *Vestnik Sov. Iust.* (1923), no. 2.

39. I.e. legal consciousness – *pravosoznanie*.

40. *Coll. Works*, vol. 33, p. 358 (5th Russ. edn., vol. 45, pp. 190-1).

41. *Ugolovnoe Pravo*, p. 26.

42. A.YA. Estrin, *Ugolovnoe Pravo RSFSR* (Moscow, 1923).

43. *SU*, no. 48, item 479.

44. Ibid.

45. *Soviet Legal Theory*, p. 106.

46. Ibid., p. 108.

47. *Socialism in One Country* (London, 1970), vol. I, p. 90.

48. *Soviet Criminal Law and Procedure*, 2nd edn. (Harvard, 1972), p. 114.

49. All references are to *Ugolovnoe Ulozhenie* (St Petersburg), 1912.

50. Timasheff, 'Impact of Penal Law', p. 460.

51. *Sobranie Zakonov i Rasporiazhenii Raboche-Krest'ianskogo Pravitel'stra SSSR* (henceforth *SZ*), no.24, item 205.

52. 13 October 1929: *SZ*, no. 67, item 627.

53. *SU*, no. 80, item 60.

54. *Soviet Legal Theory*, p. 105.

55. *SU*, no. 49, item 330.

56. Collins/Fontana, 1974, pp. 70-1.

57. *SU*, no. 47, item 356.

58. *SU*, no. 49, item 330.

59. *SU*, no. 110, item 737.

60. *SU*, no. 10, item 92.

61. *SU*, no. 139, item 907.

62. On 26 August, *SU*, no. 65, item 642.

63. 'Soviet Criminal Law Reform' in G.O.W. Mueller, *Essays in Criminal Science* (London, 1961), pp. 409-44.

64. A.A. Gertsenzon *et al.* (eds.), *Kriminologiia*, 2nd edn. (Moscow, 1968), pp. 78-9.

65. 'Eshcho Raz o Sotsialisticheskom Pravosozanii', *Rabochii Sud*, nos. 5-6 (1925), pp. 196-200; from Jaworskyj, *Soviet Political Thought*, pp. 201-2.

66. Decree of February 1923, see E.H. Carr, *Foundations of a Planned Economy 1926-1929* (London, 1974), vol. 2, p. 360.

67. See ibid., pp. 364-5.

68. *SU*, no. 57, item 426.

69. *Ezhen. Sov. Iust.* (17 Jan. 1929), no. 2, p. 48.

70. T.H. Rigby, *Communist Party Membership in the U.S.S.R. 1917-1967* (Princeton, 1968), p. 52.

71. Ibid., p. 116.

72. Rigby, *Communist Party Membership*, p. 52.

73. Ibid., p. 116.

74. 1927 census returns indicated that less than 1 per cent of the members had undergone higher education, less than 8 per cent secondary education. L. Schapiro, *The Communist Party of the Soviet Union* (London, 1970), p. 315.

75. Molotov, at the Fourteenth Congress, December 1925; Gregor (ed.), *The Early Soviet Period, 1917-1929*, vol. 2 of R.H. McNeal (ed.) *Resolutions and Decisions of the Communist Party of the Soviet Union* (Toronto, 1974), pp. 21-2.

76. Schlesinger, *Soviet Legal Theory*, p. 156 (from 'The General Theory').

77. Carr, *Socialism in One Country*, vol. I, p. 99.

5   THE 1930s

This chapter deals with the period from the end of the NEP in 1928/9 to the Second World War. The starting point is apt because the NEP was not so much abandoned as war communism had had to be, but ended via conscious decisions made by the regime. This change of policy was definite, and affected many areas of politics, law and economics.

The changes were far-reaching, and did amount to a 'revolution from above' in agriculture as well as in legal theory, criminology, and the Party itself. Many trends of the NEP were reversed and some developments were stopped altogether: the whole basis of society altered.

Although the NEP on its introduction had been considered by some to be a retrogressive step, a move away from a 'revolutionary' approach, the changes in this period that accompanied its rejection were themselves conservative, moving further away from the ideals of the revolution. State and law became more accepted and continued to be used as ordering influences in society. Many new serious offences were introduced and penalties increased, and there was a hardening of attitudes to offenders.

In many ways this is a very interesting period, for the many innovations in legal theory that in the previous decade had been worthy of the closest attention were now rejected. This was of considerable importance. In rejecting previous practices, this period can appear somewhat negative, but the positive side includes two examples of what must be the most blatant abuse of law to achieve particular ends: the purges and collectivisation.

Generally, this must be considered a repressive period in which Stalin did achieve certain difficult goals — even if they were self-imposed.

Policy Changes and Party Manoeuvres

By the end of the Civil War, Stalin was Commissar of Nationalities, and of the Workers' and Peasants' Inspectorate, and a member of the Politbureau. He had often been considered a 'middle' candidate by

differing factions and had become very well entrenched. The first
mentioned of his offices gave him great power when, after the
revolution had died down, the outlying provinces became increasingly
important; the second gave him power over the Party apparatus, as
that Commissariat was to check on inefficiency and corruption within
the Party. The power wielded by him in this area was consolidated
when he was appointed General Secretary of the Central Committee —
a post created to co-ordinate the many branches of the Party apparatus.

Socialism in One Country

This theory was Stalin's most important theoretical construct. Its
success was partly due to the comfort it gave to a Party in a difficult
quandary. It is linked to Trotsky's theory of 'permanent revolution',
which had two important aspects: that the anti-feudal revolution would
be extended into an anti-capitalist phase, and that the revolution would
pass from a national to an international phase. Lenin's attitude to this
theory changed, for at first he rebuked Trotsky for thinking that the
country could begin to construct socialism before other Western
countries, but in 1917 he supported the view that advances towards
socialism could be made. When no supporting revolutions materialised
abroad the great problem arose head on: could Russia by herself build
a socialist economy?

Stalin began by saying that Trotsky had underestimated the role of
the peasantry, and drew attention to certain passages in Lenin's writings
that would seem to support the importance of socialism in one country
to the dictatorship of the proletariat.[1] Lenin is made to appear as a
supporter of the theory, Trotsky as advocating a passive role. In 'The
Problems of Leninism' (1926), Stalin differentiated between the
possibility of 'building up socialism by the efforts of one country' and
whether any one country could consider itself 'fully guaranteed against
counter-revolution without a victorious revolution in a number of
other countries'.[2] Hindsight will not allow one to be surprised by the
fact that the answer to the former point was 'yes', to the latter 'no'.
With debates in the Politbureau periodically taking place, the theory
gains in stature with that of the chief protagonist. Its usefulness cannot
be denied.

The End of the NEP

The elimination of opponents by Stalin in the 1920s and 1930s is
closely connected with the economic problems of the country and the
various solutions put forward. Stalin, Zinoviev, Kamenev and Bukharin

were for a prospering of the peasantry, their resulting capital then directed towards industry, while the left of the Party emphasised the needs of industry at the expense of those of the peasants. With extraordinary skill and judgement, Stalin defeated both left and right in the Party – partly by playing one off against the other. Various ominous events occurred: the Shakhty trial, which indicated that the alliance between regime and experts, once considered as so necessary, was ending; and plans produced for the expansion of industry worked on the premiss that agriculture would have to be collectivised. Intense debate in the 4-12 July 1928 meeting of the Central Committee resulted in the acceptance of the need for collectivisation, and in April of the following year, the Sixteenth Congress approved it. The four main features of the policy – industrialisation, collectivisation, planning and socialism in one country – were partly borrowed, and partly a new synthesis. The success of its acceptance was to some extent due to its convenience in both theoretical and practical terms, for it allowed for economic development other than by means of the NEP, which was ideologically suspect. Unfortunately the new approach was equally suspect from a Marxist viewpoint.

The Party

Over the period as a whole, Party membership increased from 1,535,362 candidates and full members in 1929 to 2,306,973 in 1939, and 3,399,975 in 1940.[3] Proletarianisation occurred, with 43.5 per cent of total membership in 1932 being of worker occupation. Note that only 18.3 per cent were collective farmers and individual peasants.[4] White-collar workers – the 'best and foremost people' – were enrolled at a much greater rate, but the countryside remained poorly represented. As to the internal functioning of the Party, the most important development was the increased decision-making by Stalin and the Politbureau at the expense of the Central Committee and Party Conferences and Congresses, which were held more infrequently. The Party becomes less important in decision-making, so testing even further the theory that it represented the proletariat.

The Purges: An Outline

Popular belief centres the purge on the years 1936-8, the time of the great show trials, but actually the purge was a process that had been used several times over the preceding years against different types of people, and these trials were only a part, albeit a spectacular one, of a long process.

During the NEP the secret police, normally used to implement the purges, concentrated on any kind of 'counter-revolutionary' — often members of former political parties, especially those of the right, whereas those of the left received better treatment until the end of the NEP. On this event, the major targets become nepmen; the old intelligentsia, who were blamed for the failures that had taken place; and the kulaks. An early event in the process was the Shakhty trial, already mentioned, and the prevailing policy was clearly evidenced by a speech made by Stalin to the Central Committee in April 1929.

'Shakhtyites' are now in all branches of our industry. Many of them have been caught but as yet, far from all of them have been caught. Wrecking by the bourgeois intelligentsia is one of the most dangerous forms of resistance against developing socialism. Wrecking is all the more dangerous as it is connected with international capital. Bourgeois wrecking undoubtedly shows that the capitalist elements are as yet far from putting down their arms, and are building up their forces for a new offensive against the Soviet power.[5]

This amounts to re-establishing the same reason used to excuse the use of severe measures immediately after the revolution — imminent danger to the regime's existence.

Other notable trials of this period include those of the Union for Liberating the Ukraine (1929), the Toiling Peasant Party (1930), the Industrial Party (1930), and the Union Bureau of the Central Committee of the Menshevik Party (1931). That of the Industrial Party had the unusual feature of directly involving the French president, Poincaré, who had been supposedly bribed. The quality of the evidence offered by the prosecution at these trials was not of the highest, and often there were obvious fabrications as to the personal background of the accused, or the existence of the illegal organisation itself.

After these trials, there was a period of calm up to the winter of 1932-3, and various reinstatements took place, the removal of large numbers of technicians having caused considerable problems. The fall in living standards in the winter of 1932 necessitated more prosecutions to allocate blame. In January 1933, the Metro-Vickers trial took place, implicating six British engineers and eleven Russians on charges of sabotage in power stations and espionage. In March, a large-scale conspiracy was unearthed by the OGPU in the People's Commissariat

of Agriculture and State Farming, with the result that 35 people were
shot. Victims were said to be descended from 'bourgeois and
landowning classes'.[6]

Kirov's Murder

This took place on 1 December 1934, and was committed by
L. Nikolaev, a young communist. The evidence as to whether Stalin was
implicated in this assassination of a powerful rival is not clear, but
there were suspicious contemporary circumstances — the security
officers who had failed to guard Kirov were given light sentences, etc.,
and Khrushchev was to hint at suspicious circumstances in the 'secret
speech':

> It must be asserted that to this day the circumstances surrounding
> Kirov's murder hide many things which are inexplicable and
> mysterious. . .After the murder of Kirov top functionaries of the
> NKVD were given very light sentences but in 1937 they were shot.
> We can assume that they were shot in order to cover the traces of
> the organisers of Kirov's killing.[7]

However, at the time, it was said that Nikolaev was part of a 'Leningrad
Centre' and on 30 December, he and accomplices were executed.
Zinoviev was implicated in this, and there were many re-expulsions
from the Party.

On the same day as Kirov's death, an 'Amendment of the Criminal
Procedural Codes of the Union Republics' was issued by the CEC.[8]
This changed the procedure on 'the investigation and consideration of
cases relating to terrorist organisations and terrorist acts against agents
of the Soviet government', limiting investigation to ten days, saying the
indictment must be presented to the accused 24 hours before the trial,
and there were to be no defence counsel or appeal. 'Sentence to the
highest degree of punishment must be carried out immediately after
the passing of the sentence.' Krylenko says, colourfully, that the decree
was introduced because 'We cannot let the scum, the double dealing
scoundrels and traitors, the class enemy no matter how disguised,
direct their poisoned weapons against those. . .who give their life and
blood. . .to the cause of building socialism.'[9]

In the spring of 1935, Stalin sent Zhdanov to purge Leningrad, and
thousands of people were sent to Siberia. Later in that year, the purge
continued, but in the lower ranks of the Party, and was still restricted.
Another screening of Party documents took place in accordance with

a secret letter addressed to all Party organisations – 'On Disorders in
the Registration, Issuance, and Custody of Party Cards, and On
Measures for Regulating the Matter' (13 May 1933).[10]

On 25 May 1935 the Society of Old Bolsheviks was 'voluntarily'
wound up, a sign of things to come – but debate at that time centred
on the new constitution.

The Climax of the Purges

The first of the great show trials took place on 19-24 August 1936, and
was termed the Cases of the Trotskyite-Zinovievite Terrorist Centre.
The main figures were Zinoviev and Kamenev, Trotsky not being
available, who were accused of, amongst other things, setting up a
terrorist group and carrying out Kirov's murder. They were primarily
charged under Article 58.8 of the Code – acts of terrorism against
Soviet leaders – and Article 58.11 – organised activity for the
commission of any counter-revolutionary crime. When one considers
the careers of these two, one cannot be surprised that they were among
the first to go, as they had undergone more than their fair share of
expulsions, recantations, readmittances and re-expulsions. Zinoviev
realised his strategy had failed and said his greatest political mistake
had been to desert Trotsky in 1927. Already sentenced to 10 years by
their first trial in January 1935, they were now sentenced, with their
co-defendants, to death with confiscation of personal property.

The second of the trials took place on 23-30 January 1937, but was
the least important for Stalin, as the other two were aimed at defeating
important rivals. Pyataksov and Radek were the most illustrious figures
in this trial of the 'Anti-Soviet Trotskyite Centre', and were accused of
setting up terrorist and sabotage groups, and having the renunciation of
industrialisation and collectivisation in their political platform. This
last point was included to foster unpopularity, and had played a part
in the earlier trial, as after their execution, the press said that Zinoviev
and Kamenev had the restoration of capitalism as a partial aim.
However, they had been accused of trying to seize power from Stalin,
which was not repeated in the second trial, as it may have seemed a
little obvious. The charges against Pyataksov and Radek fell under
Articles 58.1a, 58.8, 58.9 and 58.11, amongst others, with the evidence
both opaque and voluminous. The outcome was that Radek got 10
years, as he was not classed as directly responsible, and the others were
sentenced to be shot. Personal property of all the accused was
confiscated.

In the interval before the last of these trials, there was a virulent and important purge in the army that took place in June 1937. The most famous victim was Marshall Tukhachevskii, but generally the upper ranks were decimated, with 90 per cent of the generals and half the entire officer corps purged. The great majority of the Civil War veterans, who tended to be in the upper ranks, went, and this had a considerable effect in the war years to follow.

The last of the trials took place on 2-13 March 1938, with the accused including three members of Lenin's Politbureau – Bukharin, Rykov and Krestinsky; Rabovsky, the legendary leader of the Ukrainian and Balkan revolutionary movements; and Yagoda, formerly Head of the Secret Police. A very comprehensive series of charges was alleged, and many loose ends of previous trials were linked together. Articles 58.1a, 58.2, 58.7, 58.8, 58.9 and 58.11 were invoked for the charges. Rabovsky, 'not having taken a direct part in the organisation of terrorist, diversive and wrecking activities'[11] received twenty years' imprisonment, plus five years' deprivation of political rights after expiry of sentence, and confiscation of all personal property. The others mentioned above, 'being irreconcilable enemies of the Soviet power',[12] were sentenced to be shot, with confiscation of all personal property.

It will be noted that in all three trials, the last being the Anti-Soviet Block of Rights and Trotskyites, Trotsky is implicated. He was not, of course, forgiven or forgotten by Stalin, who perhaps saw a parallel between the *Bulletin* and *Iskra*.

The Ending of the Purge

The final stage of the Great Purge involved a wave of arrests throughout the NKVD. It is not totally clear why this signal that the purges were to be mitigated occurred, but the web of accusations, counter-accusations, confessions and recantations had threatened the total collapse of the Party, with initiative completely stifled for fear of the consequences. A decree of the Central Committee issued on 19 January 1938[13] was the first public comment on the change. In it Stalin blamed lower officials for excesses, and

drew attention of party organisations to the fact that while doing much to clear the Trotskyite and rightist agents of fascism from their ranks, they commit, in the course of this work, serious mistakes and distortions which hinder the removal of double-dealers, spies and wreckers from the Party. Despite numerous instructions and warnings. . .party organisations in many instances approach the exclusions of Communists from the Party in a completely incorrect and criminally irresponsible manner.

The decree continued, calling for reviews of exclusions, and for cases to be heard individually, etc. After this, a series of changes began to occur. The lack of Party members was to some extent alleviated by recruitment,[14] and non-members were allowed into the higher ranks of the administration.[15] In July, Beria became Ezhov's deputy, and on 8 December, replaced him as Head of the NKVD. Mass arrests were stopped, as were many cases under investigation, and prison conditions were substantially ameliorated.[16] Stalin now appeared as the dispenser of justice, and having admitted that mistakes had been made, he, and to some extent the Party in general, took the credit for putting them right. He therefore had the convenience of the elimination of opponents, and the credit for stopping actions that he himself had initiated.

Collectivisation and its Consequences

Collectivisation was the most significant force affecting law in the 1930s. To be more precise, one should say 'rapid' collectivisation, for up to 1929 there had been a policy involving gradual collectivisation, but the growth of collective farming had been very slow, dependent as it was on voluntary membership, and by October 1929, only 4.1 per cent of the total number of peasant holdings were collectivised.[17]

The reasons underlying the change are complex. Schapiro[18] says Stalin had probably adopted this approach in late 1927, but concealed it until later. Schapiro offers some reasons for the change that are personally linked to Stalin – a change would allow rivals to be eliminated; it would lay the foundations of a defence industry (this reason, mooted after the beginning of the war is thought unlikely by Schapiro); the peasants, relatively free under the NEP, would undergo more Party control; and by causing divisions within society, Stalin himself would be safe. Nove,[19] emphasising the economic element, gives three possible reasons for the change, the most basic being the inconsistency between the nepmen and the ambitious investment programmes and concentration of resources in the state, competing as they did for resources and diverting them from priority needs. The prices policy was in trouble, as price cuts had been the response to the 'scissors' crisis, and the continuation of such a policy had caused distribution problems, with the towns, being nearest to the factories, receiving a more than equitable share, and the villages having to pay more. The government had lowered procurement prices, so the peasants were more unwilling to sell. These policies, which by themselves would have ended the NEP, were accompanied by a lack of support for the NEP in many quarters where it had been considered a retrograde step in the first place.

The procurement crisis at the end of 1927 was a prelude to collectivisation, as grain was extracted from recalcitrant peasants, not by increasing prices as Bukharin had suggested, but by forced extractions using the power of Article 107 of the criminal code – covering speculation in grain. Stalin had personally led some of these forays, but weakened when Bukharin, Rykov and Tomskii protested. However, this was a portent, and rather inconsistent behaviour from the man who at the Fifteenth Party Congress (December 1927) had said that the way out of a slow development in agriculture was 'to go over to collective cultivation of the land. . .to unite the small and dwarf peasant farms gradually but surely, not by pressure but by example and persuasion'.[20]

Although there may have been small-scale collectivisations as an experiment, generally the campaign began without preparation and experience, and there was therefore considerable confusion. However, any confusion did not seem to affect adversely the speed of the policy's implementation, with the majority of the peasant holdings being collectivised in a short time. On this timing, Schapiro[21] says 'the percentage of collectives rose from 4.1% of households in October 1929, to 21% on 20 January, 1930. By 10 March 1930, 58% of all farms were collective.'

In these early stages of collectivisation, some decrees and pronouncements of the government set the tone and pattern for future action. The 'Decree Regarding the Spring Sowing Campaign of 1930' of 23 December 1929[22] partly directed itself to encouraging the poor and middle peasants to join the collective farms, but also 'to fully approve the measures of social influence which the collective farms have taken up against those peasants who, before joining the kolkhozes, sold off their livestock, equipment and seed'. The peasants were not to have the best of both worlds. Another significant reference in this decree is 'to draw the attention of all kolkhozes to the enormous tasks which lie before them in the spring sowing campaign and which cannot be completed without a resolute raising of labour discipline'. This is an early reference to a concept that was to receive a great deal of attention in the coming legislation.

The following month saw the issuing of a decree 'on measures of struggle against the destructive slaughter of cattle'[23] – a major problem at the time, caused by the peasants' desire to sell, kill or eat their stock rather than have them collectivised. Significantly, the decree begins:

> In a number of places a destructive slaughter of cattle is taking place. This is one of the methods of sabotage on the part of kulaks which they adopt in order to undermine collectivisation and to impede the development of agriculture.

Raion executive committees were empowered to deprive 'the right to use the land and also to confiscate cattle and agricultural equipment, of those kulaks who destructively destroy their cattle or instigate others to do so'. They were also to be subject to criminal prosecution and the courts were to sentence them to a maximum of two years' detention with or without deportation from their places of normal habitation. This decree resulted in the RSFSR decree of 20 January 1930 that added article 79.1 to the Code.[24] A decree of 1 February 1930[25] is a good example to show both methods of attack used against the kulak. The first of its provisions acted economically, as it repudiated 'in the districts of complete collectivisation the provisions of law allowing the rent of land and the use of hired labour in individual peasant households'; and the second, in granting to local authorities the right to take 'all the essential measures for combatting the kulaks, up to complete confiscation of the property of the kulaks and their eviction from the raions and oblasts in which they live'.

The aim was to destroy the kulak as kulak, to destroy them as a class. This was a predictable step for the regime to take because of the economic and political power of the kulak, so their destruction went hand in hand with collectivisation: the latter precluded the former. Initially, heated debate ensued on the matter, with some in the Party not supporting such drastic action. However, as large-scale collectivisation itself portended their doom, defending them amounted to defending the NEP and was sure to fail. Fainsod[26] points out that they had their defenders in the villages, and all sections of the peasantry closed ranks against collectivisation. A district soviet executive committee chairman is quoted as saying, 'Why such pressure on the kulak? We will turn him and the population against us. This will be fatal for the NEP.'[27]

At this early stage of the campaign, the kulaks did not act passively and the number of terrorist acts increased dramatically. The Procurator of the Western Oblast reported that

> During the two-month period July-August 1929 there were thirty-
> four such cases; in September their number reached twenty-five, and
> during October mounted to forty-seven. Of the forty-seven victims
> of attack in October, ten were chairmen and eight secretaries of
> village soviets, eight were grain delivery officials, and the rest a
> variety of 'activists' who participated in the campaign.[28]

The report continues to say that half the persons arrested for terrorist
acts in October were kulak or 'well to do' and the rest had family links
with this or still had a 'petty-bourgeois mentality'.

Notwithstanding any support for the kulaks in the localities and
elsewhere, their elimination proceeded. A decree, in the form of a
secret letter sent on 12 February to the dekulakisation commissions,
ordered the kulaks to be divided into three groups: the counter-
revolutionary, who were to be arrested by the OGPU; the richer, to
be deported outside their own region; and the rest, who were not to be
deported, but given land of the worst sort. Red Army men were exempt
from this. Most of their property was to be confiscated and they were
not to sell it beforehand. Originally, it was planned to give some of this
property to the poor and middle peasants, but Stalin decided against
this for the eminently practical reason that they might become more
difficult to persuade if they had something to lose.

This first phase of rapid collectivisation ended with Stalin's article
'Dizzy from Success', issued on 2 March 1930, in which he blames the
excessive zeal of the officials carrying out the collectivisation for the
chaos and extravagant behaviour, and specifically mentions the
disastrous effect of the wholesale slaughter of livestock that this had
produced. This article was taken as authority to leave the kolkhozes,
and peasants did this on a huge scale. In the USSR as a whole, the
percentage of peasant households collectivised fell from 57.6 on 10
March to 37.3 on 1 April, and 23.6 on 1 June.[29]

The Second Stage of the Campaign

This easing of the rate of collectivisation did not last for long, as at the
Sixteenth Party Congress in June-July 1930, the importance of
collectivisation, albeit on a voluntary basis, was emphasised, and by
July 1931, for the USSR as a whole, 52.7 per cent of peasant
households had been collectivised. This proportion was to rise steadily
in successive years. The figures, as percentages calculated in July of

each year, were 61.5, 64.4, 71.4, 83.2, 89.6.[30]

The campaign had been resumed by use of more subtle measures
than before, such as discriminatory taxes and special privileges. A
decree of 2 April 1930[31] had lifted the tax on certain animals 'in the
kolkhozes as well as those still in the individual possession of members
of the kolkhozes', and freed the kolkhozes from repayments on
outstanding debts based on the confiscated property of kulaks. Later
in the same month, a decree[32] gave 60 million roubles supplementary
credit to assist the spring sowing, and various taxes were lowered or
abolished. This applied only to the collectivised sector. An example of
the discriminatory tax method of attack is the decree 'Regarding the
assessment for the single agricultural tax of 1931'[33] issued on 6 April
1931, in which the non-socialised incomes of members of the kolkhozes
were on lower rates than individual peasant households — for example
17 per cent as compared with 25 per cent. Kulaks were assessed on
actual rather than average income — which favours the lower earners,
and the highest rate of tax was 70 per cent as compared with 30 per
cent for others. Deliberately evading taxes was of course a criminal
offence.

The serious problem of the wholesale destruction of cattle was still
a cause for concern, and a decree of 1 November 1930,[34] after speaking
of the measures taken by the government to improve the situation,
introduced regulations limiting the lawful slaughter of cattle of certain
types, such as pedigree or young animals, rams and bulls. Kulaks who
maliciously violated the law or instigated others to do so were subject
to partial or whole confiscation of the animals belonging to them, and
deprivation of liberty for up to two years with or without banishment.

It was recognised that the kulaks had already been dealt heavy blows,
but they had still not to be forgotten or overlooked.

> The principal instrument of exploitation, the means of production,
> has been seized from the kulak for the middle and poor peasant
> masses in the country. He was deprived of the means of upkeep for
> the conditions of his former existence and the means to exploit the
> work of the farm labourer. This clearly was the case for most kulaks.
> However, does this mean that the class struggle in the countryside
> where there is complete collectivisation loses its sharpness?[35]

The answer is no, and examples are given of the continuing struggle.

In a decree of 21 December 1931,[36] published in *Izvestiia* the
following day, and concerning a report of the Kolkhoztsentr, there was

a general survey, not surprisingly showing affairs in a favourable light, that included the official reasons for any progress and successes made. They were

> achieved owing to strict adherence to the general policy of the Party, to the successful progress of the industrialisation of the U.S.S.R. and to the liberal assistance rendered to the kolkhoz peasantry by the Soviet State. Together with this, the strengthening of the kolkhozes has been assisted by the adoption of piecework remuneration by the overwhelming majority of the kolkhozes, by a steady struggle for wholesale collectivisation, by liquidation of the kulaks as a class, and by the activity of the kolkhoz peasantry for the economic strengthening of the kolkhozes.

The use of such non-socialist measures as piecework remuneration had been found necessary to boost production in agriculture. Increasing production in industry is a more difficult problem, as large amounts of capital are needed to supply the investment − in agriculture so much depends on individual effort. With the demoralisation of the peasants, destruction of livestock and great upheavals, the harvests were poor. The food situation in the countryside was worsened by the increasingly heavy procurements made by the government on behalf of the towns, which had to be fed if the regime was to survive, and by the fact that grain exports increased each year in this period. The peasants had to supply the government with large amounts of grain at low prices, with the sanctions of fines and imprisonment if there was any failure to deliver. In order to alleviate the famine situation, these methods of procurement, based as they were on practically arbitrary assessments, were replaced in January 1933 by another method, based on acreage sown (or supposed to be sown). The surplus left after the payment of these fixed amounts could be disposed of by the peasant who had, therefore, an incentive, and production increased. The criminal law played an important part in this situation, for even before the change in the procurement policy, there had been a private grain market, only partly official, with much higher prices. On 22 August 1932, it was decreed that 'speculation' was to carry the increased penalty of from five to ten years' deprivation of liberty without any right of amnesty.[37] Previously it had been deprivation up to one year, with or without confiscation of property in whole or in part. This Union legislation was introduced into the RSFSR Code on 10 November 1932[38] with no upper limit − 'not less than five years deprivation of liberty with whole or part confiscation of property'. A line was drawn in that the sale of private stocks of grain was allowed, but if this was the sole or major means of support, then it was a crime, and invoked heavy penalties.

Lawlessness in this Period

A degree of lawlessness was inevitable with the nature of the collectivisation policy. When Schapiro considered the Smolensk Archive he drew two conclusions:

> First, that in spite of occasional attempts to restrain excesses, a vast disorganised campaign of arrests, deportations and confiscation was unleashed against rich, middle and poor peasants alike who resisted the attempt to force them into the new collectiveness. . .Secondly, that what was perhaps originally intended as an orderly reform, at any rate by some of the more responsible party officials, very soon turned into an orgy of wholesale looting.[39]

The first warning that a change of attitude was necessary came, again, from Stalin himself, in the Stalin-Molotov letter, sent secretly to all Party workers, the Procuracy and OGPU, etc., on 8 May 1933.

> The Central Committee and the Sovnarkom are informed that disorderly mass arrests in the countryside are still a part of the practice of our officials. Such arrests are made by chairmen of kolkhozes and members of kolkhoz administrations, by chairmen of village soviets and secretaries of Party cells, by raion and krai officials; arrests are made by all who desire to, and who, strictly speaking, have no right to make arrests. It is not surprising that in such a saturnalia of arrests, organs which do have the right to arrest, including the organs of the O.G.P.U. and especially the militia, lose all feeling of moderation and often perpetrate arrest without any basis, according to the rule 'First arrest, and then investigate'.[40]

Soon after this, on 25 May 1933, a secret circular from the Central Control Commission and the Commissariat of Workers' and Peasants' Inspection referred to the fact that 'mass arrests continue, that there is legal repression on an extraordinary scale' and often the result was 'extremely misdirected legal repression'.[41]

One outcome of this was a strengthening of the Procuracy over the other agencies. The Procuracy was also to organise the release of large numbers of prisoners from the overcrowded places of confinement, and to have various duties in overviewing arrests, including those of the OGPU.

Various Other Decrees

At the end of 1932, a number of important decrees were issued that tightened labour discipline, but before these decrees there was a noticeable tendency towards severity. A harsh law of 1929,[42] which was retroactive in effect, declared that officials who had defected were punishable by death and were 'outside the law'. In that year, places of confinement had been reorganised, with correctional labour colonies used for persons sentenced to less than three years' deprivation of liberty, while for cases involving longer periods 'correctional labour camps in remote regions of the USSR' were to be utilised.[43] On 20 May 1930 the minimum period for deprivation of liberty was raised from 1 day to 1 year, but this should be seen as an attempt to reduce the prison population rather than a repressive measure.[44] The 23 January 1931 saw All-Union legislation to strengthen the law 'On responsibility for crimes disorganising the workers' transport',[45] which led to the adoption of Article 59.3(c) to the RSFSR Code on 15 February 1931.[46] This article says that a breach, by transport workers, of labour discipline that adversely affects the running of the enterprise, poor-quality maintenance of the rolling stock or track, etc., and results in an accident, will entail deprivation of liberty for a period of up to ten years, and 'In such cases when the acts have an obviously malicious character, the supreme measure of social defence with confiscation of property applies.'

Labour Discipline and Other Repressive Laws

An All-Union decree of 13 February 1931[47] had led to the addition of Article 79.2 to the RSFSR Code.[48] The Union decree had stated that 'The Soviet state directs huge resources for the acquisition of tractors and agricultural machinery for the socialised sector of the rural economy.' For this machinery 'careful treatment was particularly necessary. All the same, on account of the criminally negligent handling of the tractors and agricultural machinery, numerous cases of damage and breakage have occurred.' The outcome in the RSFSR Code was 'The spoiling or breaking of tractors and agricultural machinery belonging to any state farms, machine-tractor stations, and collective farms, if caused by criminally careless treatment, leads to forced labour for up to six months,' and three years for repeated offences or serious damage.

Behind this decree lies the considerable problem of what to do when an unskilled labour force has been subjected to rapid changes of conditions and to some extent supplied with complex equipment it is not trained to use. Mistakes and damage were sure to occur, as well as faults in the machinery itself, so the legislation must be considered as unduly repressive.

Kulaks were not forgotten, with legislation applying to work and otherwise. On 20 November 1930, a decree[49] widened the types of property able to be confiscated from them, and one of 15 February 1931[50] applied a penalty of two years' deprivation of liberty with or without exile and confiscation of property, in whole or in part, for refusal to perform any 'duty, state task or work of state importance'. This could apply to non-kulaks if there were any aggravating circumstances — an official extension of liability often unofficially granted. Generally, the penalty for this latter category was a fine or up to one year's deprivation of liberty or forced labour. This anti-kulak, pro-collectivisation attitude is reflected in other legislation; for example, the protection of livestock continued to be of great importance, and further decrees on the subject included the All-Union one of 7 December 1931.[51] This led to the addition of Articles 79.3 and 79.4 to the RSFSR Code,[52] applying deprivation of liberty for a period not exceeding two years, with or without banishment, for kulaks caught killing or maiming horses, but forced labour for half that time if it was done by a worker or member of a collective farm. Criminally negligent treatment leading to loss carries the penalty of forced labour for a period not exceeding six months, but this is increased to three years' deprivation of liberty if done 'systematically'. As regards industry, 20 March 1931[53] saw an addition to the Code of Articles 128(a) and (b), applying a penalty of up to five years' deprivation of liberty, or up to one year of forced labour, for large-scale or systematic delivery of poor-quality goods, and up to two years' deprivation of liberty or one of forced labour for failure to comply with compulsory standards. At the beginning of 1932, there was a call from All-Union legislation to intensify the struggle with theft and loss in the postal system.[54] On 20 February 1932, Article 73.1 of the RSFSR Code was amended and applied deprivation of liberty for a period not exceeding five years for attacks upon 'executive social workers in connection with their social or productive work, in cases where the act cannot by reason of its nature, of the circumstances, or of its consequences, be considered an act of terrorism'[55] — a rather fine distinction.

The Decree of 7 August 1932[56]

This very important decree was concerned with the 'Protection of the Property of State Enterprises, Collective Farms, and Co-operatives, and the Strengthening of Social (Socialist) Property', according to its title. Its preamble refers to theft of goods in transit by rail or water, and the theft of collective farm property 'by hooligan and generally anti-social elements', and the 'violence and threats of kulak elements to collective farm workers'. Social property, in the form of state, collective farm, or co-operative, is termed the 'basis of the Soviet system' and is 'sacred and inviolable'. Persons offending against it are to be considered as 'enemies of the people'. The theft of goods in transit leads to death by shooting or, if there are extenuating circumstances, deprivation of liberty for not less than ten years, both with confiscation of property, and both not able to be amnestied. The same sentences are to apply to cases involving collective and co-operative property. The final section of the decree says there must be

> a resolute struggle with those anti-social kulak-capitalist elements who use force and threats or advocate the use of force and threats against members of the kolkhozes with the aim of compelling the latter to leave the kolkhozes aiming at their forcible destruction. Such crimes are considered as state crimes.

The penalty for any such offence is imprisonment in a concentration camp from five to ten years without the possibility of amnesty. *Forty Years of Soviet Law* says that this law, published in a period of 'spirited class struggle', 'for the first time in Soviet legislation proclaimed the principle set out in the subsequent constitution, that public property (state, kolkhoz and co-operative) is the basis of the Soviet system, sacred and inviolable'.[57] Although there were earlier laws affording greater protection to state or public property as compared with that for private property, this law adds a degree of sanctity and protection not previously given.

Berman[58] says this law 'introduced for the first time into Soviet criminal law the theoretical distinction between the stealing of socialist property and the theft of property of individual citizens'. This must refer to the point that it is now the 'basis of the Soviet regime' and acting against it amounts to acting against the regime. This parallels counter-revolutionary acts, hence the heavy penalties. Note that the practice of having heavier penalties to protect public property still applied during this period; for example, a decree of 28 February 1930 awards up to five years' deprivation of liberty for causing loss to a public institution by misuse of a cheque, and only two years for private loss.[59]

Krylenko, in 'Safeguarding Public (Socialist) Property',[60] written soon after the introduction of this decree, includes a typical reference to kulaks, for after saying, 'Robbery and pilfering of socialist property constitutes at the present time, a form of the class struggle on the part of the conquered, but not yet annihilated class enemy,' divides the offenders into four main categories. 'The conscious class-enemy — the counter-revolutionary', against which capital punishment is the 'most proper measure'; 'the former private trader, speculator or merchant, who has succeeded in sneaking into our co-operative and supply organisations';[61] 'dekulakised kulaks'; and 'ordinary peasants'. Rather interestingly, Krylenko goes on to ask why such crimes are committed, and concludes that it is 'not only a lack of understanding which results from certain traditional views that were formed during the course of hundreds and thousands of years, but also the *absence of any desire to understand*' the different class nature now existing. 'It is not sufficient to apply merely educational measures in the case of such actions. We say that at the present stage of the revolution these sections of the population should be threatened.' Here, then, factors of a more subjective nature are being introduced, and by juxtaposing the 'traditional views' with the 'absence of any desire to understand', a degree of personal blameworthiness is indicated. This is unusual, and more so when one considers that it applies to all four of the above-mentioned categories, including 'ordinary peasants'. One could note that the law seems to apply only to state property in transit, but it was actually applied to theft to state property in all situations, which is in any case implied by the title and preamble. Berman[62] adds that the destruction of state property, and the failure to protect it, were dealt with by later legislation,[63] and not, as one might have thought, by analogy.

As this law is connected with collectivisation, its primary effect would be expected in agriculture, and this is upheld by figures given by Shlyapochnikov.[64] Of the convictions under the law from its promulgation to 1 April 1933, 73.3 per cent were agricultural, 7.9 per cent industrial, 12.9 per cent trade and 3.4 per cent transport offences. He concludes that the figures 'strikingly reflect the great acuteness of the class struggle in the countryside', and mentions the 'embittered resistance of the embittered kulaks to collective farm construction and their attempt to break up the collective and state farms'. Figures are also given breaking down into social groups all those convicted in the RSFSR (under this law) from 1 January to 1 May 1933: kulaks 5.9 per cent, merchants and other socially alien elements 1.1 per cent, persons without a definite occupation 3.2 per cent, the 'well-to-do' 3.9 per cent, middle peasants 15.1 per cent, poor peasants 6.0 per cent, kolkhozniki 33.6 per cent, workers 13.4 per cent, officials 14.7 per cent.[65] The motive behind the thefts is most likely hunger – out of 2,856 cases of theft considered in the Urals region, 2,319 concerned the theft of bread, 21 fodder and 77 cattle.[66]

One may think that the percentage of offences committed by the favoured social groups – poor and middle peasants, workers and kolkhozniki – rather high at 68.1 per cent. This would no doubt be 'explained' by the decimation of the kulaks and 'well-to-do' and their subsequent adoption into the collective farms after dekulakisation, but there is no reason to explain why 'ordinary' people did not commit these offences, and in any case the confiscations and deportations, although directed primarily at kulaks, had fallen on all social groups, so producing a reaction against the system from all sections of society.

Further Restrictions

In this generally repressive period, there were yet further restrictions on movement, at work, etc. An introduction to the first mentioned is offered by the Decree of 7 August, which referred to kulaks and other elements 'compelling' kolkhozniki to leave the collective farms – implying that if left to themselves the workers would not have departed. This was not the case, and during the winter of 1932-3 large numbers of peasants were moving from the country into the towns. This movement was no doubt intensified by the famine conditions prevalent in the countryside, incidentally evidenced by the large numbers of crimes concerned with the acquisition of food. The entry of these people into the towns had resulted in a fall in the standard of living there, and it was felt necessary to take steps so that the countryside would not be denuded of workers, or the towns suffered either directly, by having to cater for more people, or indirectly from lack of future supplies of food, the suppliers having become consumers. An important step in implementing controls was the introduction of a passport system on 27 December 1932.[67] The reason given was

with the aim of better registration of the population of towns, workers' settlements, and newly-erected 'reliefs' in these populous

places of persons not attached to a factory or who do not work in
the establishments or schools, and do not perform socially-useful
work (excepting the infirm and pensioners) and also with the aim of
freeing these places from concealed kulak, criminal, and other antisocial elements.

Passports were to be issued to all those over 16 years of age, and were
to be the sole means of identification, with changes of address noted
and fines for not carrying them at all times. If a move was
contemplated, a passport had to be obtained for the new area. If this
was not done, deportation back to the original area would take place.
Forgery of passports was to be treated as a state crime under Article 22
of the Law on State Crimes.[68] This system was at first only to apply to
Moscow, Leningrad and Kharkov, but a decree of 28 April 1933[69] made
it apply to most other towns and settlements, and the frontier zone
with Western Europe.

Other regulatory decrees of this period include that of 15 November
1932,[70] which ordered that 'in cases of only one day's absence from
work without a valid cause' a worker would be dismissed from the
services of a factory or institution and deprived of his food card and
also of the lodgings attached to the factory. This was a further
repression of the worker, as dismissal had previously applied to cases
of absenteeism without a sufficient reason for a total period of three
days during a month.

Concern was also expressed over sabotage in, and the general
undermining of, the kolkhozes. A resolution of 11 January 1933[71]
set up political departments at machine and tractor stations and
sovkhozi and spoke of anti-Soviet elements amongst the peasants
making use of the 'non-conscious portion of the kolkhoz peasantry'
and taking positions of responsibility within the institutions. They had
to be resisted and destroyed. A decree of 14 March 1933[72] informs us
that 'some state employees have been committing counter-revolutionary
wrecking activities', and that it was intended to try at 'judicial sessions
of the Collegium of the OGPU, acts of sabotage, arsons, explosions, the
damaging of industrial installations of the state institutions and for
other types of sabotage' with 'special severity' for cases involving
employees at state institutions and organisations.

Further limitations on the movement of the individual were imposed
by a decree of 17 March 1933[73] limiting the possibilities of leaving
kolkhozes, by saying that in future permission had to be obtained or
the person in question would be expelled from kolkhoz membership

and he and his family would receive no share of the assets.

At the end of 1933, the delivery of poor-quality goods from state factories resulted in a decree suggesting that managers maintained a 'criminally careless attitude towards the quality of the goods produced'. The delivery of such goods caused 'considerable harm to the State', especially if defence was involved, and is thought to be a 'grave political crime' with terms of imprisonment of not less than five years' applicable.[74]

The Decree of 8 June 1934[75]

This decree, together with that of 7 August 1932, is considered to be one of the most distinctive features of the law in this period. It is drafted in the form of a supplement to the decree on Crimes against the State, that became Articles 58 and 59 of the RSFSR Code.[76] A major feature of the new decree was the introduction of the concept of 'betrayal of the motherland' or 'treason' into Soviet law. This was defined as

> an action committed by a citizen of the USSR to the detriment of the military might of the USSR, of its state sovereignty, or of the inviolability of its territory, such as espionage, the giving of any military or state secret, passing over to the side of the enemy, fleeing or flying across the frontier.

The punishment was, not surprisingly, severe — death by shooting plus confiscation of all property, or if there were extenuating circumstances, which in any case could not apply to those 'in military employ', then deprivation of freedom for ten years with confiscation of property applied. If the case involved the defection of a person 'in military employ' which can mean more than a serviceman, then any member of his family who is of full age and helps him or does not inform the authorities is subject to deprivation of liberty for from five to ten years and confiscation of all property. The final paragraph of this section says:

> Any other member of the traitor's family who is of full age, jointly living with him or maintained by him at the time when the crime was committed, is liable to deprivation of electoral rights and exile to remote raions of Siberia for five years.

Two particular points to note are that the flight across the frontier is termed traitorous *per se* — there need be no divulging of information, etc.; and the use of collective responsibility in the last-mentioned paragraph, the use of which bears no relation to those punished, its sole function being a deterrent to defectors. Krylenko[77] reports that this decree was adopted 'on the direct initiative of the greatest leader of toilers, comrade Stalin', not because of any great number of betrayals but due to the 'deepest feeling of indignation, resentment', etc., directed towards any traitor. Collective responsibility was dismissed with 'Well and what of it?' supported by the obligatory quotation from Lenin — this time, 'Personal responsibility of all former capitalists or former owners of enterprises in all committees and arrest).' (imprisonment, former capitalists by shooting, their families by arrest)'. (*Coll. Works*, vol. XXI, p. 183). Krylenko says the principle is carried out without any constraint, and rigid repression is applied if there is any provocation.

On 10 July 1934[78] the OGPU was incorporated into the MVD, the first duties of which were the 'guaranteeing of revolutionary order and state security' and the 'protection of social (socialist) property'. On the same day, Yagoda was appointed Commissar for Home Affairs; he was also the nominal vice-chairman of the OGPU, but as the chairman, Menzhinsky, was ill, he actually headed that body. This change was part of the build-up to the purges, Yagoda being instrumental in their early stages.

The unremittingly repressive nature of the legislation in this period continues with increased penalties for infringements of the passport regulations,[79] the adoption of shooting as punishment for murder,[80] and a recommencement of interest in the problem of hooliganism. In the early stages of the collectivisation campaign hooligan acts had often taken the form of kulak, or supposedly kulak, elements acting against the collectivists. For example, Bulatov[81] cites cases that include those of three kolkhozniki from the First Furrow Collective Farm who 'unmercifully beat kolkhoz activists in the woods' because of a decision to expel kulak elements from the farm. In the Tulsk raion

three prosperous peasants burst into the flat of the chairman of the village soviet, dissatisfied by the rates (set up by him) of agricultural taxes, insulted him by vulgar language and threatened to kill him. The peasants, having arrived at the meeting of the agricultural soviet with activists, broke up the meeting. The People's Court sentenced two of the defendants to one and a half years deprivation of liberty, and the third — to compulsory labour.

Not all the cases concern 'prosperous peasants'. One involves an attack by hooligans on one Alekese'ev and his son while they were in a narrow lane at midnight on 15 January 1932. They were beaten up, but a yardman and a relation of his who ran out to help received a number of serious knife wounds. The hooligan group was made up of 8 students, 2 of school age, 1 worker, 1 carter and 2 *déclassés* without a definite occupation.

An increase in this type of behaviour would be expected in this period, especially in the rural regions, due to the general upheaval and the actions of the dekulakisation squads, so more legislation was forthcoming. The All-Union decree of 29 March 1935[82] directed itself against hooliganism utilising firearms and sidearms, and prohibited the manufacture, storage, sale and wearing of daggers, Finnish knives, etc. For the more serious hooligan acts the penalties were increased from a maximum of 2 years to one of 5. This increase has been considered as severe, but theorists in the Soviet Union took the opposite view — 'Why are we not applying a harsher form of punishment? We consider that some differentiation should be made between hooligans and hooligans. It is impossible to treat them alike.'[83]

This concern over hooliganism was not unconnected with one over minors in general. The age of criminal responsibility was lowered from 16 to 12 years for certain crimes — thefts, assaults, injuries, mutilations, murder or attempted murder.[84] Berman[85] says the death penalty would not apply, as the only crime listed that could invoke it was via the decree of 7 August 1932 which allowed mitigating circumstances to lower the penalty, and in the Code minority was a mitigating factor. The decree, the aim of which was 'a most rapid elimination of crime amongst minors' included the clauses:

> Persons who have been found guilty of instigating or attracting minors to the participation in various crimes, and also of compelling minors to occupations of speculation, prostitution, begging, and so on — to be subject to imprisonment for not less than 5 years.

Krylenko says the decree was passed because 'Life has shown that a great number of the gravest crimes — murders, criminal attack, robbery — are committed by such juveniles', i.e. those under 16, the previous minimum age. Society has to take more care in dealing with the problem, but fault is attached to the 'declassed adolescents whose consciousness — to use the usual expression — is burdened with the gravest of crimes'.[86]

On 1 June 1935, *Izvestiia* published a decree 'On the liquidation of homelessness and neglect of children',[87] which concluded that the homes and institutions that existed to deal with the problem were not adequate. 'The organised struggle against child hooliganism and against criminal elements among children and young people is entirely insufficient and in many places is totally absent,' and parents who 'do not take proper care of their children and allow them to engage in hooliganism, theft, vice and vagabondage, are not reprimanded or prosecuted'. The entire system was to be overhauled, with the local soviets taking initiatives in this field. Parents were to be fined up to 200 roubles for the acts of their children.

On 25 November 1935 the lowering of the age of responsibility for certain crimes mentioned above was introduced into the RSFSR Code.[88] Legislation in 1936 was as multifarious as usual, with regulations covering abortions,[89] the non-employment of pregnant women, or lowering their wages,[90] and an increase in the penalty for leaving the USSR without a valid passport — from up to one year of forced labour or a fine, to confinement in a camp from one to three years.[91]

At the end of the year, on 5 December, the new Constitution was ratified by the Extraordinary Eighth Congress of Soviets of the USSR. It was felt at the time that this may have indicated a degree of liberalisation within the regime, but events were to show otherwise.

The 1936 Constitution

On 1 February 1935, the Plenum of the Central Committee of the Party instructed Molotov to draw up a list of suggested changes to the Constitution aimed at furthering the democratisation of the electoral system and

> making more precise the social-economic bases of the Constitution — in the sense of bringing the Constitution into conformity with the present correlation of class forces in the U.S.S.R. (the creation of new socialist industry, the liquidation of the kulaks, the confirmation of socialist property as the basis of Soviet society, etc.).[92]

As a result, the CEC set up a Constitutional Commission, headed by Stalin and including Bukharin and Rykov.

After the publication of a Draft Constitution on 12 June 1936 a considerable amount of debate took place, partly due no doubt to a desire to have a debate 'free within limits' to affect the USSR and the outside world. Inside the USSR, hopes were raised in expectation of a liberalisation of the regime, and outside, Stalin wanted to project a picture of a democratic society discussing its constitutional basis openly and freely. Some suggestions were incorporated, and the final draft was presented to the Extraordinary Eighth Congress on 25 November 1936. In his speech, Stalin introduced certain important points. He said that there were no antagonistic classes in the society, which now consisted of the two friendly classes of workers and peasants, therefore there was no need to have disfranchised classes. The elections were to be direct, with no differences between workers and peasants. The position of the Party was to remain unchanged. The reason behind the changes was Stalin's aim of collective security with the Western countries against Fascism and its allies. The Constitution was to allay fears amongst Western countries as to the democratic nature of the Soviet regime. The Constitution was approved by the Congress on 5 December 1936.

Pertinent aspects of the Constitution include Article 4, saying that the economic foundation of the USSR is

> the socialist system of economy and the socialist ownership of the implements and means of production firmly established as a result of the liquidation of the capitalist system of economy, the abolition of private property in the implements and means of production and the abolition of the exploitation of man by man.[93]

The following article has socialist property consisting of state, co-operative and collective property, a distinction we have seen in the decrees of the period. Article 14 has the Union taking responsibility for safeguarding the security of the state and producing 'legislation governing the judicial system and judicial procedure; criminal and civil codes'. The Union law is to prevail if there are discrepancies between it and Republican law (Art. 20). Cases are to be heard in public 'unless otherwise provided for by law', and the accused are guaranteed a right of defence, a stipulation not always in force in the subsequent purges. Article 112 says, 'Judges are independent and subject only to the law.' Polyansky informs us that this does not mean

> their independence of politics. The judges are subject only to law –

this provision expresses the subordination of the judges to the policy
of the Soviet regime, which finds its expression in the law. The
demand that the work of the judge be subject to law and the demand
that it be subject to the policy of the Communist Party cannot be in
contradiction in our country.[94]

One assumes that this would also apply to Article 113, in which the
Procuracy is given the duty of strictly enforcing the law; and affects the
exercise of the civil liberties given in Chapter X, such as freedom of
speech, the press, rights of assembly, etc. 'The guarantees of civil
freedoms which the constitution offered raised some interesting
problems in a state in which the monopoly of political power had long
been the preserve of the communist party, itself above the law,' and
'Official comment, when the draft was first published for discussion
stressed that the rights were accorded only to those who submitted to
party leadership, and not to those who wished to criticise it.'[95] The
freedoms are, therefore, strictly qualified and limited.

Article 131 said it was the duty of citizens to 'safeguard and fortify
social, socialist property as the sacred and inviolable foundation of the
Soviet system, as the source of the wealth and might of the country;
as the source of the prosperous and cultural life of all the toilers'.
Persons encroaching on this property were 'enemies of the people'.
This emphasis on the protection of socialist property is typical of this
period; here the reference to it being the basis of the 'prosperous and
cultural life' may be an extension of its importance, but in any case the
tenor of the Article agrees with that of the law in general on this
subject.

The concept of treason, introduced by the 1934 decree, is
mentioned in Article 133. Defending the fatherland is a sacred duty,
'Treason to the country — violation of the oath, desertion to the
enemy, impairing the military power of the state, or espionage — is
punishable with all the severity of the law as the worst of crimes.'
Treason can be considered as external counter-revolution, and the
increased importance of the former, together with the more subdued
approach to the latter, is symptomatic of a regime that feels secure at
home, but threatened by external enemies.

Summarising the Constitution, one sees that law and property are
given considerable importance, and that this conservative approach is
matched by the further entrenchment of the Party and the emphasis on
the defence of the state. The various rights guaranteed by the
Constitution have to be exercised in certain ways, and although Stalin

wished to project a more democratic image for the regime, Party authoritarianism still prevails.

Developments after the Constitution

A decree[96] of 20 September 1936 gave the courts the right to decide upon the type of regime applicable to persons guilty of dangerous crimes when they were confined to prison, supposedly making the law more responsive to individual needs. On 14 March 1937, a decree[97] abolished the deprivation of franchise because of 'social origin, property status and former activities', which relates to Stalin's statements on the existence of two friendly classes mentioned above.

The year 1938 was of greater interest, and commenced with an amnesty commemorating the twenty years' existence of the Red Army.[98] It applied to first offenders who were servicemen and sentenced to deprivation of liberty for periods of up to three years, to conditional sentences, and to crimes in the investigatory stage involving penalties of not more than three years. It does not apply to those condemned for state crimes.

The unflagging interest of the regime in any action felt to threaten its control is further evidenced by regulations of 20 May 1938[99] concerning Article 28.1 of the Code, which said that

> Deprivation of liberty is applied for a period of 1 to 10 years, but for acts of espionage, wrecking, and acts of sabotage (Arts. 58.1(a), 58.6, 58.7, and 58.9 of the present code) — for longer periods, but not more than 25 years,

which is a distinctly significant increase. The sections of Article 58 refer to espionage, the undermining of state industry, transport, trade, currency, etc.

The decree of 16 August 1938[100] — on Court Organisation — had introductory sections of some interest here. Article 2 said that justice in the USSR aims at defending 'as established by the Constitution of the USSR and constituent republics and autonomous republics, the social and state structure of the USSR, the socialist economic system and socialist property', as well as certain individual rights and rights and interests of state institutions. 'Justice in the USSR has as its task the guaranteeing of the precise and undeviating execution of Soviet laws by all institutions, organisations, officials and citizens of the

USSR.' The term 'punishment' is used, but reform and re-education are aims as well as chastisement. The ultimate goal is to have educated citizens

> in the spirit of devotion to the motherland and the cause of socialism, in the spirit of a precise and undeviating execution of Soviet laws, of a careful attitude towards socialist property, labour discipline, an honest attitude towards State and social duties, and a respect for the rules of a socialist community.

This is remarkably reminiscent of predicted behaviour under communism, but is here referring to a 'socialist' situation. Statements as to the independence of the courts (Art. 6) must be viewed in the light of comments made about similar stipulations in the Constitution (see above). Finally, Article 4, in saying the courts are to carry out their functions by 'the examining in judicial session of criminal acts and the application of legally established measures of punishment', may be taken as settling that a crime is the only grounds for court proceedings, and punishment the only outcome – except for civil matters of course. The decree continues, giving detailed rules of the organisation of the court system.

Reforms in Legal Theory

Pashukanis is the most important figure in this area, and having based law on the existence of the free exchange of goods in the market place, committed the personally disastrous error of thinking that, as socialism was to be achieved at the end of the Second Five-Year Plan, and the Stalin Constitution spoke of the Soviet Union as being a socialist state, law should have begun to wither away. A practical result of this attitude, not held by Pashukanis alone, was the production in the early 1930s of various Draft Codes, the most famous of which had been produced by Krylenko. It was published on 10 July 1930[101] with an introduction by Krylenko which called for a return to the spirit of the 1919 Basic Principles with their Marxist creativity. The earlier codes were attacked over their use of equivalence, their 'precise' definitions, and their too great emphasis on deprivation of freedom as a penalty. The Draft Code divided crime into two categories – the especially dangerous, which correlated to counter-revolutionary crime; and the less dangerous, which consisted of all the rest. Offenders under the first category were to be treated as class enemies and subjected to class measures, which involved isolation and constructive work, if not death. Measures used against less serious offenders were to aim at re-education and reform, not punishment *per se.* These general provisions were contained in Part I, followed by Part II, which outlined examples of crimes and appropriate measures, but in a non-specific way: there was no use of equivalence. Part II having dealt with the especially serious crimes, Part III did the same for the less serious. Although Krylenko was against the use of specific definitions, many of the articles were comparable to those of the earlier codes. Hazard[102] quotes Article 16.5 as saying, 'Espionage, i.e. theft, transmission or gathering for the purpose of transmission of information, constituting because of its contents state secrets, to foreign states, counter-revolutionary organisations or private persons'.

At the same time as Krylenko was producing and refining this Draft, Shirvindt, heading a committee at the State Institute for the Study of Crime and the Criminal, produced a Draft for new Fundamentals,[103] which would, if accepted, have governed Republican Codes – including Krylenko's. This Draft, which had been produced under the collaboration of Piontkovskii, Trainin and Utevskii, amongst others, in some ways did not conflict with Krylenko's attitudes. It also mistrusted a dosage system and tariff approach, but was generally more conservative, with a General and Special Part, and more precise definitions. Krylenko condemned it as rightist and reactionary, and made what may have been a quantitative difference one of quality. In any event, the debates were theoretical as none of the Drafts were accepted and acted upon.

Forty Years of Soviet Law[104] says that two trends appeared at this time. One gave a minimum of guidance, leaving it to the court to determine how and what to punish, but the other gave 'detailed, precisely circumscribed law', leaving the court with little discretion. Krylenko is said to have led the former group, with support from Pashukanis, Berman, Bulatov, Estrin, *et al.*, but 'never was predominant in the theory of Soviet criminal law and never achieved its expression in the legislation'. This tendency had a 'negative influence on the condition of socialist legislation in the sphere of the struggle with crime' Pashukanis had always been in danger of falling into heresy with his attitude to the class nature of law, as he could not see how that alone could explain law's 'sanctifying' effect, and he had unorthodox theories as to the birth of law. The emphasis at this time lay fully on the class nature of law and crime as, for example, set out by Roginskii and

Karnitskii.[105] They stated categorically that crime was a 'class conception' and 'an historical phenomenon, caused by the class structure of society'. 'Before the appearance of classes and the development of the state. . .there was no crime.' The concept of crime changes historically, for

> Those acts which are dangerous at a given time for a ruling class are considered as criminal. The very same act committed when one class is in power may be criminal and yet it will not be considered criminal when another class is in power. A crime is that which is harmful to a class, that which infringes upon its rule, that which threatens the order of social relations which it has established.

However, having placed law and crime firmly on a class basis, the jurists were in danger of conflicting with Stalin's views as indicated when he said the new Constitution 'proceeds from the fact that there are no longer any antagonistic classes in society; that society consists of two friendly classes, of workers and peasants'.[106] If there are no antagonistic classes, why was law so important and crime so prevalent? If one decides to answer this non-Marxist situation in Marxist terms, pertinent points include: (i) there are still remnants of former classes; (ii) this is a class situation, even if the classes are 'friendly'; and (iii) as regards crime, it could be due to vestiges of the past, and for law, one has to consider the international situation.

As Pashukanis' theory was closely bound to the NEP, a decline in the fortunes of the latter would precipitate trouble for the former, but in 1929-30, Stalin instituted a change of course that in itself would have been fatal for Pashukanis. At the Plenum of the Party Central Committee in April 1929, Stalin attacked Bukharin's approach to the withering away and the class nature of the state, because, he said, it fostered antagonism by the working class to the state in general, including the state of the transition period, and as this was supposedly what existed at the time, this was a very unwelcome development. In the following year, in his Report to the Sixteenth Congress, he made his famous remark,

> We stand for the withering away of the state. At the same time we stand for the strengthening of the dictatorship of the proletariat, which is the mightiest and strongest state power that has ever existed. The highest possible development of the state power, with the object of preparing the conditions *for* the withering away of the state

power – such is the Marxist formula. Is this 'contradictory'? Yes, it is 'contradictory'. But this contradiction is bound up with life, and fully reflects Marx's dialectics.[107]

This approach was further developed in his 7 January 1933 Report on the Results of the First Five Year Plan.

> The abolition of classes is not achieved by the extinction of the Class struggle, but by its intensification. The state will wither away, not as a result of weakening the state power, but as a result of strengthening it to the utmost, which is necessary for finally crushing the remnants of the dying classes and for organising defence against capitalist encirclement, which is far from having been done away with as yet, and will not soon be done away with.[108]

Of course these changes result in a recantation by Pashukanis who, in 'The Soviet State and the Revolution in Law',[109] says his theory on the origins of the state is incorrect as he had failed to understand that

> the victory of the class of exploiters can never lead to the annihilation of the exploited. This very simple consideration refutes in its entirety all my argument to the effect that the need of a state disappears in the event that one class were victorious,

and speaks of preserving 'the state throughout the entire transition period as the most important instrumentality for the building of socialism'.

In 1936, when commenting on the existence of the state in the first phase of development, he says, 'It is then a matter of preparing the conditions for the withering away of the state. The withering away itself will be possible only in the second phase of communism.'[110] However, these recantations did not save Pashukanis, and both Krylenko and he were removed from their posts and disappeared in the early months of 1937. These attacks were chiefly directed by Vyshinsky, who, in an address, 'The Fundamental Tasks of the Science of Soviet Socialist Law' in 1938, accused them of radically distorting the Marxist-Leninist theory of state and law. 'Every sort of attempt to construct a theory of socialist law they declared to be an attempt to proclaim the form of law and law itself immortal.' They had confused the dying out of bourgeois law with the dying out of law in general, and 'generally excluded any necessity for building a theory of law',[111] and argued that it was the destiny of Soviet law to undergo no further development.

Lon L. Fuller[112] summarised differences between the old and new approach as exemplified by Pashukanis and Vyshinsky by saying that both think law and state will wither away, but the former links this with the disappearance of the capitalist economic system, while the latter emphasises the need for men to obey the rules of social order without needing coercion; Pashukanis denies that socialist law has any special nature, that law was bourgeois, which Vyshinsky certainly disagreed with, for he believed socialist law to have this special nature that differentiated it from bourgeois; and Pashukanis believed that morality, in the sense of a 'standard regulating the relation of man to man' would also wither, while Vyshinsky says morality must be very strong before state and law would wither, so allocating it an important role; finally, Vyshinsky firmly restated a belief in the class nature of law, from which Pashukanis had seemed to deviate.

Hazard[113] points out that underlying the new interpretations is a different analysis of the early stages of the historical development of the criminal law. Punishment was thought to have paralleled the rise of exchange, but not evolved from it, with protection from further injury more important than equivalence in the primitive stage. With the advent of class rule it becomes a tool of repression with changes brought about not by changes in exchange value, but in the ruling class's evaluation of the inherent danger.

With the aspects considered above and his emphasis on social danger rather than fault and the subsequent disregarding of the formal elements of crime, together with his lack of belief in the re-educatory powers of punishment and his use of measures of social defence, his downfall was easy to predict. Man's reasoning powers were now considered important, punishment was to have a deterrent effect, and the Draft Codes with their guidelines were now out of favour. Perhaps the most damaging factor for Pashukanis was the effect of his teaching, which had resulted in the abandoning of the ordinary law courses for students, and the courts treating the Codes as discretionary. This was totally unacceptable when Stalin began to stress the importance of state and 'law', an event of a more theoretical than practical value.

The Fate of Criminology

We have seen that in the period of the NEP research on crime had been carried on diligently, with the emphasis on a pluralist approach to crime causation. With the changes in law and politics, crime had now to be explained in terms of a survival from the past, and although this had been part of the approach, it now had to be pre-eminent, and the pluralism of the NEP would have to end. Attacks had already been made by Pashukanis, Krylenko and Stuchka, who reaffirmed that law and crime were class-based and should wither with the progression to communism. Further criticisms of biopsychological theories were made at the end of 1928, and soon after, the Section of State and Law at the Communist Academy launched an all-out attack on contemporary criminological research, many aspects of which were typified by work at the Institute for the Study of Crime and the Criminal. Researchers were criticised for biopsychological, and particularly genetic, approaches, for being too theoretical, and for reducing crime to a series of sociological factors that did not reflect the true unified social picture. When the RSFSR NKVD had been abolished on 1 January 1931, the Institute was renamed and reorganised, with research on biopsychology and personality terminated. Shirvindt, its director, had related crime to vestiges of the past, revolutionary upheavals and 'growing pains of development'.[114] These explanations, especially the last mentioned, were not now satisfactory, and on 20 April 1932, Shlyapochnikov, Shirvindt's eventual successor, postulated what were in future to be the only acceptable explanations for crime, at the renamed Institute for the Study of Crime.

The new explanation totally rejected the premiss that there were any active causes for crime in the Soviet system. Vestiges of the past were the only acceptable explanation, but even they were not to be seen only in passive terms, but also in a positive reaction made by certain elements such as kulaks, wreckers and even ordinary workers in some instances, to the advancements made in society. What were often termed 'ordinary' crimes, by which we mean those without an obvious anti-state aspect, were now considered to be of the same quality as counter-revolutionary crimes, in that they too disrupted society, although not to the same individual extent.

The emphasis moves from the study of the causes of crime and penal policy to the law itself, and sentencing; prediction was obviously becoming too dangerous and uncertain. Criminological research ceases, and the last national statistics on crime appear in 1935. There were various calls for its recommencement, but serious work does not restart until after the death of Stalin.

Trends in Sentencing Policy

Generally, penalties used against most sorts of crime increase as this period progresses, which is of course paralleled by the change in the explanations of crime. Criminals were becoming more individually blameworthy, and the withering away itself was receding. Statistics of this period show a decrease in the incidence of crime with improvements in the economic conditions of life — a suitable orthodox correlation.

Table 5.1: Reduction in the Number of Crimes Committed in the USSR in 1937, as compared with 1935 (per cent)

Convictions in general (for all crimes)	28.0
Under the Law of 7 August 1932	89.3
For crimes against the administration	36.8
For official crimes	49.9
For property crimes	26.2

The respective figures for the RSFSR over 1935-7 are 52.1 per cent, 98.7 per cent, 52.0 per cent, 62.9 per cent and 60.3 per cent.[115] The particularly large drop in the number of offences relating to the law of 7 August 1932 is of course due to the stabilised agricultural situation, and is therefore prima facie acceptable. Juviler includes some interesting statistics on the convictions in this period that shed light on the level of crime (see Table 5.2).

Collectivisation was the obvious cause for the increase in the number of convictions after the first half of 1929. This continues until the end of 1933, but it is interesting to see that the ending of the initial stage in the collectivisation campaign in March/April of 1930 is reflected in the lower figures for the second half of that year.

It is also interesting to see the relative occurrence of individual types of crime (Table 5.4).

From the various tables, one can deduce that significant changes took place in the pattern of crime over this period. Counter-revolutionary crimes remained a small proportion of the whole — under 1 per cent, but when one sees the absolute figures there has actually been an eightfold increase in the period from 1928 to 1933. The preliminary build-up to the purges may provide an explanation. The effect of the Law of 7 August 1932 and part of the offences against property must be linked with the collectivisation campaign, and while

Table 5.2: Trends in Convictions, 1928-34

		Indices: 1928 (I) = 100 1928 Year = 100 RSFSR	Court Convictions USSR (est.)	Court Convictions RSFSR
1928	I	100		
	II	104.9		
	Year	100	1,610,000	1,106,000
1929	I	124		
	II	143.9		
	Year	131	2,110,000	1,450,000
1930	I	141		
	II	118		
	Year	126	2,020,000	1,392,000
1931	I	152.7		
	II	138.3		
	Year	142	2,280,000	1,570,000
1933	I	152.2		
	II	143.3		
	Year	144	2,320,000	1,590,000
1934	I	116.8		
	II	101.4		
	Year	107	1,710,000	1,182,000

I = first half, II = second half. No available figures for 1932.
Source: R.H. Juviler, *Revolutionary Law and Order* (New York, 1976), p. 50.

Table 5.3: Numbers of Convictions in RSFSR

	1928	1933
Total	1,106,000	1,590,000
Counter-revolutionary	1,100	8,000
7 August 1932	–	102,000
Administrative	500,000	524,000
Misconduct in office	86,000	398,000
Against property	227,000	508,000
Against persons	292,000	53,000

Source: Juviler, *Revolutionary Law and Order*, p. 52.

Table 5.4: Proportions of Types of Convicted Crime (percentages), RSFSR 1928-34

Offence	1928	1929	1932	1933	1934
Counter-revolutionary	0.1	0.4	0.7	0.5	0.2
7 August 1932	–	–	0.5	6.3	2.6
Administrative[a]	45.3	42.5	42.3	32.7	30.9
Misconduct in office	7.7	11.2	21.4	25.1	30.9
Property	20.4	24.1	29.2	32.0	30.1
Against the person	26.4	21.5	5.5	3.3	4.5

Note: a. Mainly hooliganism and illicit alcohol.
Source: Juviler, *Revolutionary Law and Order*, p. 52.

the former are of relatively limited importance, the latter undergo a very large increase in absolute numbers, from 227,000 in 1928 to 508,000 in 1933, and as a proportion of the total convictions, 20.4 per cent to 32.0 per cent respectively, clearly showing the increased importance attached to property, or at least social and state property, in this period. Offences of hooliganism and moonshining, often subject to legislation, increase slightly, and fall as a proportion by 12.6 per cent. The most startling changes occur to offences involving misconduct in office, which rise from 86,000 in 1928 to 398,000 in 1933; and offences against the person, which undergo a comparative fall, from 292,000 to 53,000. The former is most extraordinary, and seemingly difficult to explain, until one sees that Juviler[116] says:

Courts in some districts were sentencing between a quarter and a half of all chairmen of kolkhozes and village soviets. . .for this category of offense. In Moscow Province, 8,847 ordinary kolkhoz. . .peasants were convicted of misconduct in office during 1933 for real or imagined lapses as petty as failing to salt the dinner.

If this was the case, and this type of offence was being used here, then it indicates that the increase in the incidence of this crime is due to the greater emphasis placed upon labour discipline in these years, and illuminates the effect of this trend in practice. The great fall in the offences against the person may be due to the increased control of society and checks on movement, but such an extraordinary fall is difficult to explain adequately in these terms. Gertsenzon gives an interesting table of the social composition of those convicted in the

Table 5.5: Convictions in USSR, 1931-4

	1931	1932	1933	1934
Workers	19.0	20.4	17.5	19.2
Farm workers	0.7	0.6	0.4	0.2
White-collar workers	13.7	12.6	12.6	18.4
Handicraftsmen[a]	0.9	0.5	0.4	0.4
Merchants and businessmen	0.5	0.3	0.2	0.2
Kulaks	11.9	5.9	5.2	2.9
Individual peasant farmer-workers	32.7	30.9	28.1	19.6
Kolkhozniki	11.4	20.9	27.8	31.0
Déclassés	3.7	3.7	4.8	4.8

Note: a. *Kustari.*
Source: A.A. Gertsenzon, *Sovetskaia Ugolovniia Statistika*, 2nd edn. (Moscow),
    p. 205.

RSFSR (see Table 5.5). Naturally, this table reflects the importance of the social groups within the country, not merely their criminality. For example, it is not that members of collective farms are becoming more criminal, but they are becoming more numerous, hence they commit more crimes as a group. The fall in the numbers of kulaks and individual peasant farmers is directly related to this. The level of workers remains steady, and that of white-collar workers rises, both of which are predictable if one considers the state of society at the time.

It is interesting to see that criminality does not seem to be falling – this is disregarding the relative weighting of different types of offence. As the social composition of society changes, the convictions are moved around rather than lowered. On the forms of penalty applied, Gertsenzon includes a table for the RSFSR (Table 5.6). The most dramatic change is in the use of short terms of deprivation of freedom, from 25.6 to 1.4 per cent. This was caused by the gross overcrowding of the prisons which meant that alternative sentences had to be used, and prison reserved for more serious cases. As the prisons were full of the purged, many of whom had done little of any consequence, this seems a little ironic. For more serious crimes attracting heavier sentences, deprivation of freedom was increasingly applied, while corrective labour became the norm for the less serious, and the use of this penalty was eventually to supply a significant proportion of the cheap labour force – particularly used on prestige projects.

The peak use of banishment and exile coincides with dekulakisation,

Table 5.6: Measures of Punishment in the RSFSR (percentages)

Type	1928	1929	1930	1931	1932	1933	1934
Suspended sentence	7.3	3.4	2.7	4.1	1.1	1.2	1.4
Deprivation of freedom:							
To 1 year	25.6	3.8	1.8	1.9	1.5	0.7	1.4
1 to 3 years	3.9	5.9	6.2	9.1	10.9	11.5	12.7
3 to 5 years	1.0	1.1	1.0	1.0	2.7	4.5	4.6
Over 5 years	0.7	0.9	0.6	0.6	3.8	12.3	7.0
Total	31.2	11.7	9.6	12.6	18.9	29.0	25.7
Corrective labour	22.0	50.8	56.9	57.5	54.2	49.7	56.9
Banishment and exile	–	1.6	4.5	7.3	3.9	4.3	0.5
Fines	31.0	26.7	17.1	13.1	12.2	7.2	5.3
Public reprimand	2.6	4.4	6.0	4.2	3.7	2.2	2.2
Dismissal[a]	0.1	0.3	0.5	0.2	0.1	0.08	0.06
Other	0.1	0.4	2.5	0.9	5.84	6.3	7.9
None applied	5.6	0.7	0.2	0.1	0.06	0.04	0.02

Note: a. This includes disfranchisement, dismissal from office, prohibition from an occupation.

Source: Gertsenzon, *Sovietskaiia Ugolovniia Statistika*, pp. 211-12.

as kulaks of certain categories were resettled, so affecting the figures. The use of other penalties either remains of minor importance — reprimands and dismissals, or declines — suspended sentences and fines. Overall, sentencing policy is firmly based on deprivation of liberty for serious cases and corrective labour for the others.

Summarising, one can say that criminology undergoes a definite decline in this period. The pluralist approach that existed before was now considered unsuitable, and the only acceptable explanations were unconvincing and obviously tailored to the needs of theory. However, even this is a rather doubtful basis, as theory may not actually require it. If this were a state of the transition period, which of course it is not, then according to Marxist theory, society is imperfect, and cannot be expected to be totally free of causes of crime. In so far as vestiges of the past were seen as causes of crime, and were in the contemporary society, the practice of the time was not being un-Marxist, but in saying that they were the only causes, the position was too exclusive. It was not necessary to rule out all other causes.

Evidence that other causes were active in society is offered by the

continuing occurrence of crime. Over the whole period, crime, as
reflected by convictions, was supposed to have fallen. However, until
the end of 1933, it rises — making the collectivisation campaign an
active cause? There were great variations in the levels of specific types
of crime, some more explicable than others, and the change in social
composition of society is reproduced in the relevant proportion tables.
Crime did not seem to be withering away; in fact, changes in sentencing
policy had to occur to deal with the number of cases, with corrective
labour supplying a useful work-force.

Conclusions

Two main features of this period are collectivisation and the series of
purges, the former affecting the majority of the population, while the
latter, although widespread, centred on the Party.

Stalin was a very astute political strategist, as his dealings with the
right and left of the Party show, and the purge was a useful and
devastating method of dealing with opponents. However, this method
of dealing with opponents could be an expected outcome of any highly
charged political situation where opposing views and personalities exist,
and should not be linked solely with Stalin. The necessary prerequisite,
or at least important facilitating factor, that existed to make the
Russian experience so classical, and Stalin such a master of the purge
technique, was an ideology awarded great pre-eminence. The stature of
Marxism-Leninism-Stalinism, for that was what it now was, in Russian
politics and society enabled it to be used, with a degree of credibility,
as the factor to decide between right and wrong, mainly in politics, but
also in other areas such as economics. Such a standard was especially
useful in the trial situation, as it supplied the example with which to
contrast the defendant's behaviour and beliefs.

To begin with, the political trial was directed at members of anti-
Stalinist political groups, and was no more or less reprehensible than
previous manipulations of the concept of counter-revolution. The
Shakhty period was the beginning of its use to excuse failure by
allocating blame to individuals for the shortcomings produced by policy;
and, as experts of various types were the defendants, a definite step
towards ending the relationship between them and the regime, that had
been a significant part of the NEP. Various smaller-scale political
eliminations led up to the intensive purging that occurred after Kirov's
murder, an intensity that reached its political climax in the Great Purge

Trial of 1938.

The use of the criminal law in the purges is in one respect the most clear example of its utilisation for political, non-judicial reasons. However, this may be true to the extent that this use of 'law' is not an extreme but legitimate use, but is illegitimate. Is a trial where the evidence is so obviously and knowingly falsified a trial in any real sense, or a mere travesty?

One concludes that this aspect of the history of the period at best indicates a ruthless use of legal forms and concepts to suppress opposition, either of a group or an individual, and at worst, a complete disregard of justice and the content of legal forms that would be laughable if it were not so disturbing. It is not possible to award precise degrees of blame to Stalin and his much discussed personality, the exact motives of whom are as complex as those of his opponents who did little to save themselves, but one should not look solely to personal motives as the cause, for too strict an adherence to an ideology, coupled with a seeming inability on the part of the regime to confess mistakes, is a highly dangerous situation.

Collectivisation saw equally ruthless uses made of law. Although there were political reasons for ending the NEP, economics also played a part, so here the use made of law is not as political as with the purges. Perhaps a distinction should be made between using the law against kulaks and well-to-do peasants, and against ordinary peasants, as the former were more political, the latter more regulatory. Many types of law were used against kulaks, including tax and credit privileges, with criminal law acting when the kulaks reacted to the collectivisors – this tended to happen more in the early stages of the campaign – and ended up before the courts. Kulaks, having more to lose, would be expected to be strongly anti-collective, but there is evidence to show that other sections of the peasantry were similarly opinionated. In any case, there was no clear definition of 'kulak', and measures nominally directed against them were highly indiscriminate in their effect.

Analyses of crimes committed at this time show that members of all classes and groups perpetrated significant numbers of crimes, and from the type of crime committed, it is obvious that all strata of society were resentful. This is not at all surprising if one considers that the collectivisation squads were committing acts of looting and destruction against all categories of peasant, not just those who were better off financially. Many of the crimes can be connected to the circumstances prevailing at the time, for example the widespread slaughter of cattle and the thefts of food.

Generally, the legislation in this period can be described as oppressive, in that heavy penalties are introduced for a wide range of behaviour. This includes the defection of officials; damage to railway property; the slaughter of livestock; an interest in increasing labour discipline; restrictions on movement – this was particularly directed at stopping an increase in the town population, and holding kolkhozniki to the collective farms; and a concern over minors and hooliganism. Special mention should be made of the glorification of state property, particularly by the Decree of 7 August 1932, which, being directed primarily at collective farms, produced its main effect in agriculturally based crimes.

Part of Stalin's achievement was the glorification of the state, which began with its rehabilitation in the theory of socialism in one country. The Decree of 8 June 1934 introduced the concept of treason, part of the change from 'counter-revolutionary' to 'anti-state'. The Constitution attempts to make the regime more respectable to the West, and offers certain civil freedoms to this effect. However, it is made clear that legality cannot conflict with the wishes of the Party, which is in accord with the Leninist concept of a dictatorship unfettered by law. An important statement in the Constitution relates to the Soviet Union being a socialist state, composed of two friendly classes. State property was again stated to be of great importance, which in itself reflects the importance of the state in an indirect way.

The supposed fact that antagonistic classes no longer existed and socialism had been achieved was fatal to Pashukanis' approach to law, as he had incontrovertibly linked its existence with that of the bourgeois capitalist economic system. For him, law could not have a socialist nature or content, it was essentially bourgeois. To be acceptable, a theory of law (and state) had to encompass the Marxist tenet that withering away would occur by the advent of communism, and Stalin's view that state and law would grow stronger – for the expressed purpose of stamping out the last remnants of the former society – and then wither.

Krylenko[117] had said that the court and law were

the main regulating factors, with the help of which the proletariat and the communist party will direct the future progress of socialist construction, the struggle against the final remnants of the class enemies and the eradication of the remaining vestiges of capitalist attitudes in the consciousness of the socialist toilers.

These aims are not at variance with those expressed at the 1932 Party
Conference, when it was said that:

> The chief political idea of the Second Five Year Plan is to do away
> with the capitalist elements and with classes in general; to destroy
> fully the causes giving rise to class distinctions and exploitation; to
> abolish the survivals of capitalism in the economy and the
> consciousness of the people; to transform the whole working
> population of the country into conscious and active builders of a
> classless society.[118]

Any differences between workers and peasants would be abolished.

Similar sentiments in the Constitution are balanced by the
postponement of communism and the withering away: they are now
not considered possible in the immediate future. It is this conservative
force that defeats Pashukanis and Krylenko, for law and socialism have
become compatible.

Criminology was affected by this change, with the pluralist approach
of the NEP giving way to an emphasis of the effects of the past society,
which now were considered to have active and passive aspects. There
was a rejection of non-social causes of criminality, but contemporary
Soviet society was to contain none of these causes. More personal blame
was attached to offenders, with re-education a partial aim, and
'punishment' and 'crime' again in use. Restrictions become such that
criminological research ceases. Sentencing policy changes but is not
liberalised. The great number of cases strain the prison system, so
deprivation of freedom is used in a smaller proportion of cases,
especially those involving sentences of short duration, with correctional
labour playing a more important part. Generally, crime seems to be
increasing, so perhaps it is convenient that the withering away has been
deferred.

What are the theoretical implications of this deferral? If Marx's
theory had applied, then this was to be the transition period, in which
withering away of state and law were to take place. Stalin altered this,
saying a strengthening of state and law had to happen before the
withering away, linking the change to the differences of the Russian
situation from that envisaged by Marx. If one considers the legislation
of the period, Stalin's contention seems at least to have some base in
reality, as the law was certainly showing no signs of withering away. In
both the purges and collectivisation the use, or more correctly misuse,
of law played an instrumental part. In fact, it has often been said that

the former displayed a certain legalistic attitude on the part of the regime or should one say Stalin, in that trials were used at all – why bother when the outcome was so obvious? Apart from the advantages of 'justice' being seen to be done, the pre-eminence of the ideology, already mentioned above, was also important. The way it was exercised in the Soviet Union made it necessary to treat oppositionists seriously and severely, for there could be only one approach and one answer that was 'correct'.

The state and its protection were emphasised in this period. The Law of 8 June 1934 treated infractions with great severity, and state property received an almost continuous stream of protective decrees, no doubt supposedly explained by the fiction that such property belonged to the whole people and was therefore particularly sacrosanct. In reality, the harsh measures were a method of protecting the *status quo* from infringements that would be all the more frequent because the owner of the property was not an individual. In the future society under communism, this type of property may well be of a particularly high order, but now it was not, and considering how it had been accumulated under collectivisation, the number of offences in the countryside should not be surprising.

This divergence between theory and reality is of course central to this study, and has other aspects in this period that should be illuminated, as they are so blatant. Labour discipline legislation placed extreme limitations on the freedom of workers and peasants, and movement became more restricted, which must at any time be considered as reprehensible – and surely particularly inapposite where the government was supposedly so definitely of the people. In practice it acted against the people whenever this was felt necessary, and this would be often when such widespread changes as were introduced happened. Collectivisation itself, which involved the most extensive upheavals in the lives of so many, must be considered as the prime example of this despite the later attempts to gloss over the force used,[119] and at the same time, various measures were trying to limit the worst excesses, for example, the strengthening of the procuracy, but the overall picture remained unchanged.

The most important force over the people was the Party. It did make attempts to reflect more closely the society it ruled, mainly by attempts to recruit more workers into its ranks, but the peasantry was not overlooked, and extensive, if not over-successful, attempts were made to increase the peasant/collective farm membership. In some ways this became a less important task as the Party as a whole became less involved in decision-making. However, it was administrative and bureaucratic — this being partly due, no doubt, to its governing function, and Stalin's strengthening of his hold changed its nature, making it less democratic and representative.

The 'dictatorship of the proletariat', which had become the dictatorship over the proletariat by the Party, was now the dictatorship over the proletariat by the Party leadership.

Notes

1. For more details, see E.H. Carr, *Socialism in One Country* (London, 1970), vol. II, pp. 49-50.
2. See R.N. Carew Hunt, *The Theory and Practice of Communism* (London, 1963), p. 222.
3. T.H. Rigby, *Communist Party Membership in the U.S.S.R. 1917-1967* (Princeton, 1968), p. 52.
4. Ibid., p. 199.
5. J. Stalin, *Sochineniia* (Gosudarstvennoe Izdatel'stvo Politicheskoi Literatury, Moscow, 1946 onwards), vol. XII, p. 14.
6. *Izvestiia*, 12 March 1933, p. 2; see M. Fainsod, *How Russia is Ruled* (Cambridge, Mass., 1970), p. 432.
7. H.M. Christman, *Communism in Action: A Documentary History* (New York, 1969), p. 177.
8. *SZ*, no. 64, item 459; often termed the 'Kirov decree'.
9. Report to the Second Session of the All-Russia CEC of the XVI Congress, in W.E. Rappard *et al.* (eds.), *Source Book on European Governments* (New York, 1937), p. V-173.
10. For a detailed examination of the effect of these purges in the Western Oblast, see M. Fainsod, *Smolensk Under Soviet Rule* (New York, 1963).
11. R.C. Tucker and S.F. Cohen, *The Great Purge Trial* (New York, 1965), p. 689.
12. Ibid., p. 682.
13. Published that day in *Pravda*; translated in M. Matthews, *Soviet Government* (London, 1974).
14. Resolution of the Central Committee of 14 July 1938; see L. Schapiro, *The Communist Party of the Soviet Union* (London, 1970), p. 436.
15. Resolution of the Central Committee of 4 March 1938, in ibid.
16. See Fainsod, *How Russia is Ruled*, pp. 442-3.
17. Ibid., p. 531.
18. Schapiro, *CPSU*, p. 365
19. A. Nove, *An Economic History of the USSR* (London, 1976), pp. 138 *et seq.*
20. J. Stalin, *Collected Works* (Moscow, 1952-5), vol. X, p. 313.
21. *CPSU*, p. 388.
22. *SZ* (1930), no. 1, item 4.
23. *SZ*, no. 6, item 66.
24. *SU*, no. 3, item 26.
25. *SZ*, no. 9, item 105.
26. See *Smolensk*, 'The Story of Collectivisation'.
27. Ibid., p. 240.

28. Ibid., p. 241.

29. Nove, *Economic History of the U.S.S.R.*, p. 172.

30. Ibid., p. 174.

31. *SZ*, no. 21, item 230.

32. *SZ*, no. 24, item 261.

33. *SZ*, no. 19, item 171.

34. *SZ*, no. 57, item 598.

35. Chortkov, 'Novye formy klassovoi bor'by kulachestva', *Sov. Iust.* (1931), no. 30, p. 14.

36. In *Slavonic Review* (1932), vol. XI, pp. 200 *et seq.*

37. *SZ*, no. 65, item 375.

38. *SU*, no. 87, item 385.

39. *CPSU*, p. 390.

40. Fainsod, *Smolensk*, p. 185.

41. Ibid., p. 186.

42. *SZ*, no. 76, item 732.

43. *SZ*, no. 72, item 686 (cf. *SZ* (1930), 22/248, and 26/344).

44. *SU*, no. 26, item 344.

45. *SZ*, no. 4, item 44.

46. *SU*, no. 9, item 103.

47. *SZ*, no. 9, item 104.

48. *SU*, no. 15, item 162.

49. *SU*, no. 62, item 763.

50. *SU*, no. 9, item 102.

51. *SZ*, no. 71, item 474.

52. *SU*, no. 68, item 304.

53. *SU*, no. 15, item 162.

54. On 7 February, *SZ*, no. 9, item 49.

55. *SU*, no. 21, item 103.

56. *SU*, no. 62, item 360.

57. *Sorok Let Sovetskogo Prava* (Leningrad, 1957), vol. I, p. 557.

58. *Soviet Criminal Law and Procedure: The RSFSR Codes* (Cambridge, Mass., 1972), p. 29.

59. *SU*, no. 11, item 131.

60. Moscow-Leningrad, 1933, pp. 31 *et seq.*

61. There were a small number of decrees on this point, e.g. 23 November 1930 (*SZ*, no. 57), dealing with 'false co-operatives', that is those with kulaks and other prohibited members.

62. *Soviet Criminal Law*, p. 29.

63. See, for example, *SZ*, 6/41.

64. 'Zakon 7 Avgusta ob Okrane Obshchestvennoi Sobstvennosti i Praktika ego Primeneniia v RSFSR', *SGiP* (1933), no. 5.

65. As with many early statistics, this does not total to 100.

66. Shlyapochnikov, 'Zakon 7 Avgusta', p. 26.

67. *SZ*, no. 84, item 516.

68. *SZ* (1929), no. 72, item 687.

69. *SZ*, no. 28, item 168.

70. *SZ*, no. 78, item 475.

71. *Izvestiia*, 13 January 1933.

72. *SZ*, no. 9, item 108.

73. *Izvestiia*, 18 March 1933.

74. *SZ*, no. 73, item 442. This leads to the change of Article 128(a) of the RSFSR Code – *SU* (1934), no. 9, item 51.

75. *SZ*, no. 33, item 255.

76. 25 February 1927, *SZ*, no. 12, item 123.

77. Report to All-Russian CEC of XVI Congress. *Izvestiia*, 12 February 1936. See Rappard, *Source Book*, pp. V-166 *et seq.*

78. *SZ*, no. 36, item 283.

79. 1 July 1934, *SU*, no. 27, item 157 − residing in an area without appropriate passport − 2 years' imprisonment.

80. 1 Sept. 1934. *SU*, no. 34, item 206.

81. 'Khuliganstvo i mepy bor'by s nim v rekonstruktivnom periode', *SGiP*, (1933), no. 4, pp. 66-7.

82. *SZ*, no. 18, item 141. The change in RSFSR Code takes place on 10 May 1935, by *SU*, no. 14, item 146.

83. Krylenko in Rappard, *Source Book*, at pp. V-174/5.

84. On 7 April 1935, *SZ*, no. 19, item 155.

85. *Soviet Criminal Law*, p. 30.

86. In Rappard, *Source Book*, p. V-175.

87. Trans. in *Slavonic Review* (1936), vol. XIV, pp. 444 *et seq.*

88. *SU* (1936), no. 1, item 1.

89. 27 June 1936, *SZ*, no. 34, item 309.

90. 5 October 1936, *SZ*, no. 51, item 419.

91. 5 October 1936, *SZ*, no. 52, item 423.

92. See Fainsod, *How Russia is Ruled*, pp. 370-1.

93. Translation is that of the Co-operative Publishing Society of Foreign Workers in the USSR (Moscow, 1937).

94. 'The Soviet Criminal Court as a Conductor of the Policy of the Party and the Soviet Regime', *Vestnik Moskovskogo Universiteta* (Nov. 1950) in Fainsod, *How Russia is Ruled*, p. 375.

95. Schapiro, *CPSU*, pp. 410 and 411.

96. *SU*, no. 20, item 131.

97. *SZ*, no. 20, item 75.

98. 24 January 1938. *Vedomosti* (1938), no. 1.

99. See *Ugolovnye Kodeks RSFSR* (Moscow, 1953), p. 9.

100. *Vedomosti*, no. 11.

101. *Esh. Sov. Iust.*, no. 19.

102. 'The Abortive Codes of the Pashukanis School' in F.J. Feldbrugge, *Codification in the Communist World* (Leyden, 1975), pp. 145-75; at p. 161.

103. *Proekt osnovnykh nachal ugolovnogo zakonodatel'stva soiuznykh respublik i ugolovnogo kodeksa RSFSR* (Moscow, 1930).

104. Vol. I, pp. 558 *et seq.*

105. *Ugolovnyi Kodeks R.S.F.S.R.*, 9th edn (Moscow, 1936), p. 31, here from J. Hazard and M.L. Weisberg, *Cases and Readings in Soviet Law* (New York, 1950), p. 43.

106. 'On the New Constitution', here from Fainsod, *How Russia is Ruled*, pp. 371-2.

107. *Collected Works*, vol. XII, p. 381.

108. Ibid., vol. XIII, p. 215.

109. See H.W. Babb, *Soviet Legal Philosophy* (Cambridge, Mass., 1951), at p. 264.

110. 'Gosudarstvo i Pravo Pri Sotsializme', *Sov. Gos.* (1936), no. 3; here from Lapenna, p. 35.

111. Babb, *Soviet Legal Philosophy*, p. 325.

112. 'Pashukanis and Vyshinsky: A Study in the Development of Marxian Legal Theory', *Mich. L.R.*, vol. 47, pp. 1157-66.

113. 'Reforming Soviet Criminal Law', *Jour. Crim. Law* (1938), vol. 29, pp. 157-69.

114. See P.H. Juviler, *Revolutionary Law and Order* (New York, 1976), p. 45.

115. Man'kovskii, 'Voprosy Ugolovnogo Prava v Period Perekhoda ot Sotsializma k Kommunizmu', *SGiP* (1939), no. 3, p. 88.

116. Juviler, *Revolutionary Law and Order*, p. 52.

117. 'O Sude i Prave v Epokhy Sotsializma', *Sov. Iust.* (1936), no. 19, p. 8.

118. H.J. Berman, *Justice in the U.S.S.R.*, 2nd edn. (Cambridge, 1966), p. 38.

119. For example, I.V. Pavlov speaks of collective management having started to 'arise' after the revolution (in *Voprosy Sovetskogo Gosudarstva i Prava*, p. 305); and *Istoriia Gosudarstva i Prava SSSR* says, 'the peasants began to express the wish to join kolkhozes,' p. 155.

6   FROM THE PURGES TO THE DEATH OF STALIN

After the 1920s and 1930s, this may appear to be a rather uninteresting period. The repressive nature of the society precluded the possibility of a pluralist approach in many areas of discussion, and others — notably criminology — were static. Theory developed in a predictable fashion, with the need for state and law becoming more emphasised: both were to be strengthened to prepare for the withering away.

If the control of the regime — rather than the Party — could be extended, it was, and certainly underwent no decline, but tactics changed in the war years when calls upon nationalism were, understandably, found to be useful. Legal restraints were non-existent: the dictatorship was to use law but not be limited by it.

In substantive law many decrees relating to labour discipline were issued and adversely affected the standard of life of ordinary people. Socialist property was further protected, as was personal, another sign of increasing conservatism.

The war brought many necessary decrees of a regulatory and organisational character, and predictably interrupted normal development.

Amnesties were a frequently occurring feature of the post-war years, with the ordinary offender, rather than the political, obtaining the benefits. Liberal measures, usually in the form of court directives, were forthcoming but were outnumbered by those of a repressive nature — for example those on state secrets and the protection of state property.

The prevailing picture is one of continued suppression, and the actions of the NKVD and the 1930-like developments in the years leading up to Stalin's death show that the old methods had not been forgotten, and perhaps that they were about to be extended once more in full.

Changes in Theory

On 10 March 1939, Stalin delivered a Report to the Eighteenth Congress of the Communist Party which included an interesting and informative summary of the official policy on the theory of the state, contained in the final section of the report, and entitled 'Some

Questions of Theory'.

The question, clearly set forth, was why had the state not withered, or begun to do so, if the exploiting classes had been abolished in the USSR and the country was advancing towards communism, socialism having been achieved? Stalin replied, perhaps predictably, that individuals that ask this question have not properly understood the theory, or 'the present-day international conditions, have overlooked the capitalist encirclement and the dangers it entails for the socialist country'.[1] Then, after mentioning the possibility and need to adapt theory to practical considerations, he adds that Engels' statement about the withering away (in *Anti-Duhring*)

> is correct, but only on one of two conditions: (1) *if* we study the socialist state only from the angle of the internal development of a country, abstracting ourselves in advance from the international factor, isolating, for the convenience of investigation, the country and the state from the international situation; or (2) *if* we assume that Socialism is already victorious in all countries, or in the majority of countries, that a socialist encirclement exists instead of a capitalist encirclement, that there is no more danger of foreign attack, and that there is no more need to strengthen the army and the state.[2]

A distinction has to be drawn between the development of a 'socialist state in general' and a 'specific socialist state', as the latter has to take cognisance of the actual international situation. The conclusion drawn is compatible with, not to say a necessary part of, the theory of socialism in one country, as the 'menace of foreign military attack' means that the socialist state 'must have at its disposal a well-trained army, well-organised punitive organs, and a strong intelligence service, consequently, must have its own state, strong enough to defend the conquests of Socialism'.[3] However, Stalin says that the forms and functions of the state can change, and that since the revolution, two main phases of development have occurred. The first – up to the elimination of exploiting classes – involved the state in suppressing the overthrown classes, defending the country, and restoring industry and agriculture. The second phase lasted from 'the elimination of the capitalist elements in town and country to the complete victory of the socialist economic system and the adoption of the new Constitution'. Here the functions were the establishment of the economic system, to instigate a cultural revolution, and to defend the country.[4] Note that defence is a function of both periods, but in the latter, external rather than internal elements were the major concern — although the protection of socialist property was mentioned as being of particular importance. Having considered socialism, Stalin said that under communism, the state will remain, 'unless the capitalist encirclement is liquidated, and unless the danger of foreign military attack has been eliminated, although naturally the forms of our state will again change in conformity with the change in the situation at home and abroad'.[5] This does not seem to be too far from the possibility of 'communism in one country'.

Lapenna concludes that as Stalin asserts that there is no exploitation or classes in the Soviet Union, he

> deviates from the doctrine of the class character of the state, and permits the existence of a *classless state*. If this is so, then obviously the whole structure of the Marxist theory of the state falls apart, because the principal element, the very foundation, of that theory is, that the state is an instrument for government by a single class, which effects its dictatorship over the others.[6]

Stalin is adding to previous theory, but it is more difficult to decide on the extent to which this is being done. Considering the date, the many references to defence are understandable, but in emphasising the relationship between the USSR and other countries, Stalin is drawing more attention to the inapplicability of Marxist theory in the first place. It is not a variation on a party programme, but a development occurring in society, and while an emphasis on its deterministic side can be depressing and carried too far, to go to the opposite extreme simply invalidates one's position. It would seem a somewhat perverse situation to be explaining away the non-occurrence of a particular event, i.e. the withering away, when according to the original theory, it should not, and could not, be happening anyway. The contemporary Soviet state was not moving towards communism, and to introduce further arguments and qualifying factors is misleading.

Lapenna's point about the class aspect of the state is absolutely true, with perhaps a minor qualifying factor in that the Soviet state has classes, but they are said to be non-exploiting, and 'friendly'. However, from the orthodox point of view, these classes are themselves suspect, and the Soviet situation would amount to a classless situation with a state — a Marxist impossibility. Neither does this situation correspond to that with an apolitical social organisation, as the existing entity is very much a state in the classical tradition.

Base and Superstructure

Important pronouncements on the nature of these concepts were made
by Stalin in 'Marxism and Linguistics' — incidentally, an example of the
typically Soviet approach of directing general ideological changes via
seemingly unrelated problems. He commences by stating the accepted
Marxist view of the dependence of the superstructure on the base, with
changes in the latter leading to changes in the former; but then states:

> the superstructure is a product of the base; but this does not mean
> that it merely reflects the base, that it is passive, neutral, indifferent
> to the fate of its base, to the fate of the classes, to the character of
> the system. On the contrary, no sooner does it arise than it becomes
> an exceedingly active force, actively assisting its base to take shape
> and consolidate itself, and doing everything it can to help the new
> system finish off and eliminate the old base and the old classes.[7]

The degree of the independence of the superstructure has given rise to
much discussion, and it was certainly possible to imply some degree of
independence from what Marx, and more especially Engels, actually
wrote, but here Stalin goes further. He says, 'language cannot be ranked
either among bases or among superstructures. Neither can it be ranked
among "intermediate" phenomena between the base and the
superstructure, as such "intermediate" phenomena do not exist.'[8] This
statement has two important effects: (i) Stalin 'hereby dissociates the
categories of base-superstructure from the categories of matter-mind,
on which they had previously been modeled';[9] and (ii) in freeing
linguistics from the superstructure, it implies that other disciplines may
not have to be a part of it either.

Could law be one of these disciplines? In coming to his conclusions
on linguistics, Stalin had explained that language was a product of many
different epochs, of many different base-superstructure relationships,
and was of too general or universal character to be significantly attached
to one period or one class. This approach would not apply readily to
law, as it is so completely different in action and nature. Law can be
changed to fit particular conditions relatively easily, but language cannot
be so altered as its function is not so specific. Law is much more closely
related to a particular period and is more political in its action.

What does emerge from 'Marxism and Linguistics' as regards law is
the relative freedom enjoyed by the superstructure — a freedom

previously implied, but never stated so clearly or widely. Law being part of the superstructure must enjoy this freedom, and although different parts of the superstructure could be independent in varying degrees, theory now recognises a significantly greater freedom of action for law.

Summarising what has been said so far, one has further delay and more qualifying factors applying to the withering away, with state and law having another extension to their importance and existence. Along with other aspects of the superstructure, they are recognised as having a considerable degree of freedom, which will allow for greater disparity between Marxism and practice — explained in terms of superstructural influence. One concludes that theory has moved further away from its original position and nearer to the contemporary practice.

Attitudes to Law

The chief spokesman in this area is Vyshinsky, who paralleled the growing emphasis on the importance of the state in the transition to communism by stressing the value of law in this period. His views on law and state are set out in *The Law of the Soviet State*:[10]

> The state of the transition period from capitalism to communism is one which itself effectuates the political power of the proletariat, the dictatorship of the proletariat. It is differentiated sharply and fundamentally from the bourgeois state. . .[11] Marxism-Leninism, as distinguished from anarchism, starts by admitting the necessity of proletarian utilisation of the state for its purposes of emancipation.[12]

He restates that the dictatorship of the proletariat is not limited by laws, but in 'creating its own laws, makes use of them, demands that they be observed, and punishes breach of them'.[13] The alliance of workers and peasants, with the importance of the guiding role of the former, is upheld, but Vyshinsky also says that, 'The political basis of the USSR comprises — as the most important principle of the worker class dictatorship — the leading and directing role of the Communist Party in all fields of economic, social and cultural activity.'[14] Law and state will only wither away in

> the highest phase of communism, with the annihilation of the capitalist encirclement; when all will learn to get along without special rules defining the conduct of people under the threat of punishment and with the aid of constraint; when people are so

accustomed to observe the fundamental rules of community life that
they will fulfil them without constraint of any sort.[15]

The external situation is considered to be a vital factor in the future
development of law and state, and in the meantime, 'Constantly by
reinforcing the socialist state and law by every means. . .the toilers of
our country will guarantee the building of the communist society and
the triumph of communism.'[16] On the strengthening of the law, 'it
reinforces the stability of the state order and of the state discipline, and
multiplies tenfold the powers of socialism, mobilising and directing
them against forces hostile to them.'[17] From these statements, one can
conclude that, not surprisingly, Vyshinsky is not in conflict with Stalin
over this matter. The law is to be of great use in the transition period,
and will be used by the dictatorship but will not bind the dictatorship.
These points are orthodox and do not give rise to any special problems.
The new factor is that of capitalist encirclement, which supposedly has
the effect of extending the life of law, and offers a plausible reason for
strengthening state and law. Vyshinsky attacked anyone not believing
in the importance of law and in the special character of Soviet law. Just
as the state was to be special, in that it did not suppress the majority,
the law too was special, as it was the will of the proletariat and had
approved functions. Pashukanis was an obvious target, but Stuchka,
Reisner and others were also attacked.[18]

Other writers of this period supported these theses. Iodkovsky says
that the Stalin Constitution 'ended the period marked by such changes
in legislation as to preclude final codification'. The strengthening of the
law and state, the stability of law, 'must be interpreted by us as pointing
to the necessity for large-scale codification.'[19] Despite these and similar
comments, codification did not progress because of historical events and
Stalin's duality of attitude towards law and legality.

Chkhvikvadze[20] attacked Strogovich for not upholding the
essentially different nature of Soviet law, saying he 'does not point out
the contrast between Soviet and bourgeois law. For him the Soviet
criminal trial is nothing other than the bourgeois criminal trial revised
and adapted to the circumstances of socialist justice.' Formalism,
considered to be an important part of bourgeois justice, is entirely
rejected, as

one of the most dangerous manifestations of the bourgeois juridical
approach in our literature. It is equivalent to emasculation of the
political and class essence of juridical institutions, departure from

reality, neglect of the practical, preoccupation with 'juridical
technique', and creation of high-flown, unrealistic juridical
inventions and schemes.[21]

This materialistic tendency is supported by the belief that law must
play a positive role in policy implementation. Polyansky says the
Communist Party influences law by direct rulings and by conclusions
of a more general nature:

> Legislation is the first and foremost form in which the policy of the
> Soviet regime finds reflection. 'The political tasks set by the
> Communist Party and the Soviet regime are met with the aid of
> Soviet law' (*Theory of State and Law*, 1949, p. 125). Hence correct
> application of a correctly comprehended Soviet law is
> implementation of the policy of the Soviet regime.[22]

Saying judges are independent does not mean that they are independent
of politics, as they are subordinate to law, which is an expression of
politics. Any suspected antagonisms in this arrangement are false, for

> The demand that the work of the judge be subject to the law and
> the demand that it be subject to the policy of the Communist Party
> cannot be in contradistinction in our country, if only for the reason
> that the policy of the Soviet regime and the Communist Party as a
> matter of fact demands of the judge strict observance of the
> principles of legality.[23]

Polyansky then adds, 'However, the demand that the judges be guided
by the policy of the Communist Party is considerably broader than the
demand for strict observance of the principle of legality.'[24] The exact
nature of this independence is difficult to discover, as the judge has the
'right and responsibility to decide each individual case in accordance
with his own inner conviction in strict accord with the circumstances of
the case and with the prescription of the law',[25] but in

> deciding the concrete case before him the judge is guided not only
> by his inner convictions in assessing the evidence and in establishing
> whether or not there are mitigating circumstances, but in selecting
> the measure of punishment is obliged to follow the general
> instructions of the executive Soviet and Party organs concerning the
> significance of this or that crime or the circumstances under which

it is committed.[26]

One can, therefore, assume that policy will have an important effect on many aspects of judicial decision-making, and the 'independence' of the judiciary has to be understood in a specialised sense, in that the judges are free to act within the system or the guidelines. In Western countries this happens, as policy does play an important part in such decision-making, and the question is really one of degree, with the Soviet judges being controlled to a much greater extent. Both situations are entirely different, each based on its own suppositions. Summarising, one has law awarded an important role in the period, with formal elements decried, and the importance of policy, of the Party, recognised. The situation is that of a dictatorship applying and using law, but not bound by it, with the political nature of that law being admitted.

This policy, of greater stability in law linked with a rejection of formalism, is reflected in the better status awarded to the legal profession, which commented that its role was to seek the truth and help the court in individual cases, not to mislead for the sake of a client.[27]

The Party in the War and Post-war Period

The lack of importance in the decision-making process increased in this period, Stalin and his personal secretariat dealing with a great many matters. The prime motive force on recruitment and distribution of members was the winning of the war. The majority of the recruits were in the armed forces, and were in some ways considered to be less careerist and more trustworthy, as the dangers and responsibilities that Party membership involved would deter undesirables. The pre-war membership of 3,399,975 on 1 January 1940, and 3,872,465 for 1941 (same date), fell to 3,063,876 by the beginning of 1942, with the following three years becoming 3,854,701, 4,918,561 and 5,760,369 respectively.[28]

At the end of the war, the Party was very different from what it had been before: approximately 3.5 million members had been killed and 18.3 per cent of all members were under 25 and 63.6 per cent were under 35. There was a general air of inexperience, and after the war, it was indoctrination and training, rather than recruitment, that were emphasised, which led to problems for some, as Party membership was an important personal asset. The Party was still stronger in the urban areas, and relatively weak on the collective farms.

Economic Development

Obviously the war centred the economy on military needs. Great destruction and upheaval throughout the economy had resulted, and any growth afterwards was of the nature of rebuilding and consolidation rather than growth in absolute terms. Agriculture was the cause of particular concern, as it remained in a weak state. Procurement prices had not risen between 1940 and 1947, and peasant income was too low. Even the all-important private plots were not as sound as they could have been because of high taxes and a limit on pasture facilities. The kolkhozes were reformed into larger units and the labour system changed, but the life of the kolkhoz peasant remained highly unsatisfactory, and did not improve until after Stalin's death.

Labour Discipline

Decrees concerned with strengthening labour discipline are one of the most typical aspects of legislative practice at this time. Their aim was to increase productivity by striking at absenteeism, unpunctuality and slackness at work, but contrary to the zeal exercised in their implementation, they had a highly repressive effect on society generally, by threatening a specific vital need, the right to work.

Initially, the use of traditional measures such as administrative penalties, together with the use of labour books to record the personal work history and performance, were used — the latter being connected with the internal passport system, which also controlled movement and discipline. However, in 1940 a new series of decrees introduced further restrictions and penalties. On 26 June 1940[29] the Supreme Soviet of the USSR decreed that the basic work day was to increase by one hour — normally from seven to eight, except for certain categories of dangerous work and for 'clerks in offices', where it was from six to eight. The six-day week was changed to seven, with Sunday as the rest day. Article 3 said, 'Voluntary withdrawal of a worker or clerk from government, co-operative and social enterprises and offices, as well as voluntary transfer from one enterprise or office to another, is forbidden.' Only 'directors and chiefs' could give the necessary permission, and then only for serious illness, age, educational purposes or pregnancy. A workman or clerk offending against the decree was to be penalised by corrective labour at their place of work for terms of up to six months with up to 25 per cent wage reduction, for absenteeism 'without satisfactory reason'. Two to four months' imprisonment could be applied for voluntarily leaving a job without permission. The directors or chiefs that did not instigate prosecution, or rehired offenders – which often happened due to labour shortages – were to be 'held responsible before a court'. This threatening of officials if they did not act within the spirit of the law became more widespread, eventually covering the judiciary.

The PCJ and the Procurator of the USSR issued regulations on 22 July to the effect that being twenty minutes late for work, returning late from, or leaving early for, lunch or at the end of the day, were all to be classed as absenteeism and treated accordingly.[30] Schwarz[31] says that although this was in agreement with the original decree and some[32] supported a hard line, 'In actual practice, the "milder" interpretation prevailed at that time; only those who were more than twenty minutes late at the beginning of the work period were considered truants.' The Supreme Court of the USSR ruled the following month that any 'loafing on the job' for more than twenty minutes would constitute an offence under the decree, and it came to cover overtime work and work done on days off.[33] Any sentence of corrective labour was considered as an interruption of employment, with sickness payments inapplicable until six months after the commencement – some thought termination, of the corrective labour.[34] Other related decrees of the period include that of 10 August 1940,[35] which punished petty theft from enterprises or institutions with imprisonment for a period of up to one year; and hooliganism in enterprises, institutions or public places, had the penalty raised from three months to up to one year. To emphasise the serious view taken of these offences, an attached statement said these punishments were to apply unless the actions fell under other articles of the code – with heavier penalties involved in most cases if this occurred.

In October, regulations imposing direction of labour on specialists – 'engineers, technicians, foremen, employees, qualified workers' – and instigating a compulsory call-up of 1 million young school-leavers for training at 'reserve labour schools' to counteract the falling numbers of trainees, were introduced.[36] These regulations for employees had their counterpart for managers in the Edict of 16 November 1940,[37] which was concerned with the issuance of poor-quality goods. Previously dealt with by Articles 128(a) and (b) of the Code, the new law made the 'directors, chief engineers and heads of technical control' liable for 'the output of poor quality or substandard industrial production'. The crime was considered to be the equivalent of sabotage and punished with five to eight years' imprisonment – it had previously attracted five years if systematic or on a large scale, and two if otherwise.

Schwarz gives some interesting data on the effect of this type of legislation. The earlier law of 28 December 1939 had usually led to eight to twelve months' imprisonment for managerial violations, and, afraid of being accused of leniency, the managers began to dismiss people on the slightest pretext. Two cases mentioned concern a woman who had not heard of a change of work schedule because she had gone home (rightfully), and one who was late because of crowded buses and locker rooms. Referring to reports in *Trud* and *Industria* of 2 February 1939, Schwarz says 129 workers were discharged from one Moscow factory in January 1939 alone, and 500 from the Petrovsky Works in Dnepropetrovsk. There are cases of 15- to 22-minute lunch breaks, and no lunch at all, due to a constant fear of dismissal. There was also a great decline in the number of sick notes issued.[38]

After the introduction of the 1940 legislation, judges and managers accused of leniency were tried — for example Butskaia[39] was removed from office and indicted because she had 'sentenced 76 per cent of defendants accused of "truancy" to corrective labour terms of less than three months, with wage cuts of only 10 per cent in most cases'. Not surprisingly, sentences became heavier after this. On 29 July 1940, the Supreme Soviet issued a decree 'On the disciplining responsibility of judges',[40] which further reduced their independence by applying administrative penalties to them. A decree of 10 August 1940[41] said that people's assessors were not to sit in work discipline cases, that only professional judges were to be used.

These measures caused the judges to become harsher still, but the situation became so unpredictable that Goliakov, in an article in *Sovetskaia Iustitsiia* of December 1940, denounced both the over-lenient and over-severe, in an attempt to stop the more obvious discrepancies that were affecting the prestige of the courts.[42] However, the basic trend continued and the system of heavy penalties for the violation of labour discipline was incorporated into the 'Standard Rules of the International Labour Organisation' issued by the Sovnarkom in 1941.

One must realise that these labour regulations and decrees, although interesting from a theoretical viewpoint, had a very real effect throughout society. Due to a fear of losing their jobs, the normal behaviour of employees was distorted until it involved the whole life-style. If ever the dictatorship of the proletariat became a dictatorship over the proletariat, this is a clear example.

The Second World War

'The invasion of Soviet territory by the Germans on 22 June 1941 found the country quite unprepared, both militarily and industrially.'[43] Anti-Stalinists blamed this lack of preparation on him personally, and the failure of his non-aggression policy with Germany, but this does not take into account the nature of the totalitarian regime and the position in which the Party had placed itself. Both of these are relevant, as the former did not allow the pro-German policy to coexist easily with preparations for war; and as to the latter, the conduct of the Party in allowing Stalin to become so omnipotent to some extent precluded complaint on that very same matter. Despite the unpreparedness, one factor greatly in favour of the Soviet Union was that the nature of the state meant that a change-over to war conditions could be achieved relatively easily — one has already noted that in economic planning significant changes could be effected by simple administrative decision.

On 30 June 1941,[44] a State Committee of Defence was instituted, consisting of Stalin, Molotov, Voroshilov, Malenkov and Beria. It had wide powers and amounted to a War Cabinet. Its use at this time affected the governing methods in the post-war years after its disbandment.

Preparation for drastic action soon began in law. A decree[45] declared European Russia to be a theatre of war, and so passed jurisdiction from the ordinary courts to the military, with their lack of assessors. Soon after the outbreak of war, various predictable measures were taken, such as extended military service — all males from 16 to 50 were to have military training in available time outside work hours;[46] and various restrictions affecting personal liberty, such as a tax on the childless, designed to increase the population.[47]

A decree of 6 June 1941[48] punished the 'spreading in wartime of false rumours that cause alarm amongst the population' by two to five years' imprisonment. On 20 July 1941,[49] the Commissariats of the Interior and of State Security were amalgamated under Beria as Commissar of the former, and so restored the unified police force that had existed before the war. On 19 October 1941[50] the Committee of State Defence ordered the 'shooting on sight' of spies, provocateurs and other enemy agents, but Hazard[51] says, 'This order was issued. . .when the enemy was 100 kilometers from Moscow, and apparently applied only in the Moscow area and during the period of crisis.' The self-explanatory entitled decree 'On the responsibility of workers and employees of enterprises in the war industry for unauthorised departures from works' was issued on 26 December 1941,[52] and said the workers were to consider themselves mobilised and had to stay in their jobs, with unauthorised departures 'considered as desertion and the guilty persons. . .punished with imprisonment for 5 to 8 years'. This approach was used by a decree of 29 September 1942,[53] which awarded workers in raions near the front a change of status, which meant that they were now considered as mobilised personnel, with the penalties above applying if they left their job without authorisation, and subject to evacuation, with managers criminally liable for not providing for total evacuation, to imprisonment from five to ten years.

The protection of socialist property, always close to the heart of the regime, was of obvious importance now. Chkhikvadze[54] says that

> In the period of the Great Patriotic War, the criminal-legal struggle with infringements of socialist property was intensified even more, in particular that involving military property, state property, the needs of the front, the defence industry, the supplying of the heroic toilers in the interior.

The social danger of this type of crime was increased by the wartime conditions, and, generally, the criminal law was 'subordinate to one problem — the intensification of the struggle with crimes that infringe on the defence of the country'. N.D. Durmanov[55] says that the war changed the nature or importance of certain acts, making them socially dangerous if they were not already considered to be so, or increasing their social danger if they were. Particular acts mentioned by him include non-fulfilment of various wartime duties, the spreading of false rumours, not partaking in the mobilisation of production or construction work, insubordination to relevant military orders, and not participating in necessary military instruction. He then quotes I.T. Golyakov on the precise point of theft of socialist property:

> The struggle with thefts and embezzlement has special important significance in wartime conditions, when the Soviet people are struggling for every rouble, for every pood of bread, for the careful accurate allocation of grain, raw materials, finished products, remembering the instructions of Comrade Stalin on universal support for the front by all necessary means for the successful struggle with the occupying forces.[56]

Decrees on the protection of socialist property include that of 23 June

1942, establishing that 'persons guilty of theft (of motor fuel) from the agricultural machinery pool and the state farms, must be handed over to the court and sentenced by the People's Court to imprisonment for from 3 to 5 years'. Hazard gives an example of a case of theft of socialist property in which three out of six defendants received the death penalty, and the others ten years' imprisonment.[57]

Further manipulations of the labour system were undertaken by a decree of 29 December 1941,[58] which introduced an income tax assessed both on size of income and classification of the recipient, with those who worked in private practice in the professions paying twice as much as those working directly for the state. On 2 November 1942, the Supreme Soviet issued an interesting decree 'On the formation of an Extraordinary State Commission for the examination and investigation of the crimes of the German-Fascist aggressors and their confederates',[59] and instigates the formation of a new Cheka-like organisation. The preamble says the Germans,

> having treacherously attacked the Soviet Union. . .are committing in their temporary occupation of Soviet territory, monstrous crimes – beatings, tortures and murders of the peaceful inhabitants; the violent taking into foreign servitude of a hundred thousand Soviet citizens; the general robbing of the town and rural population and the removal to Germany of the personal property of Soviet citizens, of the accumulation of their honest work, and also of kolkhoz and state property; the destruction of monuments of the art and culture of the people of the Soviet Union and the plundering of the artistic and historical heritage; the destruction of the buildings and the looting of the equipment of religious culture.

This comprehensive list – the inclusion of religious objects reminding one that the Orthodox Church received more lenient treatment in the war, indicates the seriousness of the situation, and the Commission was to collect evidence and 'to instruct the appropriate organs to carry out investigations, to interrogate victims, to collect corroborating testimony and other documentary facts'. The powers of the Commission are somewhat ambiguous, and one wonders how judicial its investigatory functions would have become. Feldbrugge[60] mentions a decree of 19 April 1943[61] that introduced the death penalty for enemy personnel found guilty of torturing or murdering prisoners of war or civilians. The penalty applied also to espionage or treason committed by Soviet citizens. Co-operation with the Germans led to 15 to 20 years' forced labour. The practice of 'mobilising' certain categories of worker continued into 1943, with the railways[62] and sea and river transportations systems[63] affected, so extending military criminal law and procedure into these areas.

On 15 November 1943, a decree[64] was issued punishing the disclosure of state secrets with officials receiving deprivation of liberty for up to five years for 'disclosure of information constituting a state secret and equally, for the loss of documents containing such information'. If 'serious consequences' ensued, then the upper limit was ten years. If it was a private person rather than an official, then deprivation of liberty for up to three years applied. Previously, this type of action had been considered as treason or espionage, even if there had been no counter-revolutionary intent; now it is a lesser offence, with the necessary degree of intent left rather ambiguous. In cases involving officials, accidental loss would seem to be covered, but 'knowingly' is used with regard to private individuals, so negligent behaviour would supposedly be excluded.

A Note on Sentencing Policy

Feldbrugge[65] says that a conspicuous trait of court practice in the war years was the use of the second part of Article 28 of the Code. This says that servicemen sent to military correctional units are instead to be sent to the front and their sentences postponed, or in cases involving 'steadfast defenders of the USSR' to be cancelled or commuted. The 1960 Textbook on the General Part is quoted as saying that this policy was found to be very effective as the number of second offenders among these soldiers was very small. One assumes that the death rate of soldiers in wartime, which tends to be high, was not overlooked. *Forty Years of Soviet Law*[66] includes an interesting table of sentences used in this period, after saying that:

> In the first years of the war, the particular importance of repression led to a considerable increase in the role of deprivation of liberty among the other measures of punishment, and a significantly decreased use of conditional sentences and correctional-labour, but by the end of the war, the normal usage was beginning to be noticed again.

One can see that the use of fines and 'other' forms play a proportionally

Table 6.1: **Measures of Punishment, 1941-4**

Year		D. of L.	Cond.	Corr. L.	Fine	Other
			Measure of Punishment			
2nd 6 months	1941	67.4	3.4	19.1	7.5	2.6
1st 6 months	1942	69.3	4.2	17.9	6.8	1.8
2nd 6 months	1942	65.9	6.6	19.9	6.5	1.1
1st 6 months	1943	60.3	10.3	23.5	5.5	0.8
2nd 6 months	1943	47.7	16.0	29.4	5.9	2.0
1st 6 months	1944	48.9	15.1	30.1	4.9	1.0
2nd 6 months	1944	52.1	14.0	28.1	5.0	0.8

Source: F.J. Feldbrugge, *Soviet Criminal Law: General Part* (Leyden, 1975),
  vol. II, p. 491. Originally from Iakubovich, 'O pravovoi priroge instituta
  uslovnogo osuzhdeniia', *Sovetskoe Gosudarstvo* (1946), nos. 11-12, p. 55.

unimportant part, and deprivation of liberty is becoming less used – so
returning to the more normal pattern, with conditional release, and
especially correctional labour, more frequently used.

Some General Developments in the Law

One of the more interesting of these was the move away from what had
been classified once as distinctly Soviet concepts in previous years, such
as the increasing use of the terms 'crime' and 'punishment' at the
expense of 'socially dangerous acts' and 'measures of social defence'.
This was a continuation of past practice and is paralleled by the
increasing emphasis on freedom of will and moral guilt.[67] There was not
a great deal of criminological research in this period, due to Stalin's
repression of it and the war, but this attitude to guilt was in line with
earlier trends. Moreover, in some of the laws considered here, the
penalties have been severe and seem to be retributive and deterrent
rather than re-educative.

The hardening of attitudes did not mean that the law was to be more
widely applied, and the more formal approach had its effect. Many
articles of the codes were narrowed in their operation by an insistence
on the need for intent rather than negligence or intent. At the very
beginning of this period, the Supreme Court had overruled an earlier
decision which had allowed conviction for counter-revolutionary
offences even though there had been no desire to undermine Soviet
power.[68] By 1951, the need for intent in this area seems secure, with a

leading textbook[69] saying that 'the object of counter-revolutionary crime is the dictatorship of the ruling class' and counter-revolutionary intent, as evidenced by a desire to bring about the 'overthrow, undermining or weakening of the power of the workers and peasants' being necessary.

Other restrictive judgements concerned speculation — that resale at a higher price was speculation only if the goods had been originally bought with that intention;[70] and for theft of state property, the accused had to know that the property was socialist property, and intend to steal it.[71]

Analogy

During this period, intense discussions had taken place over analogy with many criticisms made. In and around 1938, interest grew in the possibility of a new code, with Vyshinsky, leading the forces of the Law Institute, believing analogy was necessary as statutes could not foresee every eventuality, and that it was a necessary weapon in the battle with enemies, and last, but by no means least, that Lenin and Stalin had supported its use. Conversely, the All-Union Institute of Juridical Science tended to emphasise the stability of law, which was now after all a Stalinist notion, and was against analogy. However, a fundamental point to understand is that it was not necessary to have analogy to achieve the stated goals, as the material definition of crime and the extremely wide definitions used by the decrees and codes meant that any particular law could cover a wide range of behaviour. This tends to be overlooked by many writers.

Earlier thought had placed limits upon analogy; for example Shargorodshii says that a judgement based on analogy should not become a precedent for 'analogy cannot and should not establish a new body of crimes with binding force'.[72] The subject side of the sostav, covering who could commit a particular crime, was not to be widened by the use of analogy, so only servicemen could commit military crimes, only officials official, unless the law was changed. This was expressed by the Plenum of the Supreme Court on 6 January 1944 in Re Tsybina:

> Art. 121 of the Criminal Code deals with an act committed by a public official; since, therefore, the law itself limits the kind of person to whom it pertains, it is not proper to extend the law by analogy to those persons not directly provided by law.[73]

It is also understood that analogy could not be used to widen the subjective characteristics of a crime, so if intent was needed, negligence would not do; but the evidence is conflicting.[74] The approach of the Yugoslav Code, for example, is to be preferred, Article 7.4 saying, 'The perpetrator shall be criminally responsible for a criminal offence committed by negligence only when so provided by statute,' avoiding any uncertainties.[75] Neither the general or special objects can have analogy applied to them, and if the first does not apply, as outlined in Article 6 of the RSFSR Code, the act is not a crime at all.

Analogy can be applied to the objective characteristics if they are considered as non-essential, or not listed in the definition. For example, on 6 May 1943, a Plenary Session of the Supreme Court of the USSR said that courts were often too restrictive in their interpretation of the list of places in Article 162 of the Code, providing liability for theft in places of public use – 'railway station, on a landing stage, on a steamer, in a railway carriage or in a hotel'. The Court said, 'theft of private property of citizens, committed in *any* place of public use. . .should be made subject by analogy to Art. 162 of the Criminal Code.'[76]

As the objective characteristics have many practical applications, limiting analogy to their extension is not so restrictive. Any limitation must come from a willingness not to misuse the doctrine, rather than from such technicalities. In any case, it was still considered to be an important aspect of law, Men'shagin (in 1948) still saying that analogy aims at filling gaps, and socially dangerous acts should be punishable even if not covered by a particular rule of law.[77] Notwithstanding the complaints expressed about its use, 'all Soviet learned criminologists are unanimous in the appraisal of analogy in the working of criminal legislation.' Man'kovskii[78] says that 'one of the most important points debated in the doctrine of law was the question of analogy' and 'in the conditions of war the practical role of the principle of analogy in the reinforcement of socialist legality appears fully. In wartime, the application of analogy is increased considerably.'   An example of this is given by Ginsburgs and Rusis.[79] The law relating to the protection of state secrets punished the disclosure of confidential material by certain classes of person, and was either objectively or subjectively qualified to exclude 'an act of mere public or private indiscretion involving secret information without anti-regime motivation, or for carelessness leading to loss of documents containing such information'. By using analogy, the disclosure without counter-revolutionary intent was punished, not by applying Article 121 of the RSFSR Code, which originally applied to officials passing on unauthorised information, but only carried a penalty of up to three years' deprivation of liberty; but by applying

Article 193.25, covering disclosure by members of the armed forces, and carrying as a maximum the death penalty, or Article 58.6, espionage, with similar penalties. This approach prevailed until the middle of the war.

As has been stated before, the use of analogy does not seem so surprising in a system so materialist as the Soviet, and the extended use during wartime would not be unusual. As more conservative trends developed in Soviet legal practice, perhaps one could have expected analogy to lose favour, and to some extent it did, but its practical use was advantageous, so it had its opponents, but also its defenders.

Legislation in the Period after the War

Just as one cannot express any real surprise at the severity of many laws issued during wartime, one could reasonably expect to see a more liberal trend emerge with the conclusion of hostilities, and this was partly expressed by a series of amnesties in the post-war years. Amnesties themselves pose interesting questions on the nature of rule-breaking, and their use is more easily explained in systems where the danger of the offender is of prime importance. If a person is to be punished for the breaking of a particular rule *per se*, the use of amnesties seems incongruous, but if any prerequisite social danger is no longer present, then release would seem an obvious move. An earlier amnesty, that of 16 July 1940,[80] did not apply these approaches rigidly, as it freed from punishment 'citizens convicted by the courts to correctional labour and milder measures of punishment if they, after conviction, participate in the fight against the Finnish Whiteguards'. Here, questions of social danger do not seem to be involved, as recruitment would appear to be the driving force. Fighting in the army could be viewed as a type of punishment, or the social danger of persons willing to do it may be considered as less than others, but these considerations do not change the real nature of the amnesty.

An amnesty of 30 December 1944[81] dealt with persons who had left their jobs without authorisation. Offenders had to give themselves up to the authorities by 15 February 1945.

The major amnesty of 7 July 1948[82] freed those sentenced to less than three years' deprivation of liberty, those who had left their jobs without authorisation, servicemen convicted for a variety of crimes such as not returning to the army from military correctional units; and to shorten by half the period remaining to sentences of over three years.

This did not apply to counter-revolutionary crimes, theft of socialist property under the law of 7 August 1932, banditry, counterfeiting, robbery and intentional murder. Article 6 also singled out 'persons repeatedly convicted for embezzlement, burglary, robbery and hooliganism' as being unsuitable for amnesty, and is perhaps important in that the earlier list would hardly include many sentences of under three years. This amnesty was later extended to cover workers on the railways and water transport systems[83] and to persons convicted by the Zakarpatskoe Ukraine Court.[84]

Other features of this period include the 12 July 1946[85] ruling by the Plenum of the Supreme Court that the 1938 Law on Court Organisation had, by saying that courts had the power to apply punishment to criminals (and therefore only to criminals), repealed the reference in the Code to criminal environment being a ground for the application of measures in itself (Art. 7). Berman[86] says that in not applying this to Article 58.1(c) of the Code, which made relatives of deserters from the armed forces liable to punishment, the court showed its basic weakness in what might otherwise appear to be a position of strength.

On 26 May 1947[87] the death penalty was abolished in peacetime, and replaced by sentences of 25 years in correctional labour camps. This was due to the 'grown might of the Soviet State' and 'the exceptional loyalty of the entire population'.

On 4 June 1947, two decrees were issued on the protection of private and public property.[88] That protecting private property[89] punishes 'theft, that is covert or open appropriation of the private property of citizens' by 5 to 6 years in a corrective labour camp – which is a large increase, as previously it had been 3 months' forced labour or deprivation of liberty. If committed by a gang or for a second time, then it was to be 6 to 10 years in a corrective labour camp. The penalty for robbery was increased from not more than 5 years to 10-15 years, with confiscation of property. If life or health had been threatened, or a gang was involved, or it was for a second time, then it was to be 15 to 20 years, while previously it had been up to 10 years.

These heavy sentences were used in practice, as cases show. In 1951, the two ringleaders of a gang of robbers who attacked several people were given 25 years' imprisonment, and the other members got 20, 15 and 10 years.[90] Cases in 1953 show the same approach, with murdering a taxicab driver with intent to steal carrying 25 years plus 5 years' loss of rights, and 20 years;[91] a gang tried for various attacks and woundings received 25 years plus loss of electoral rights for 5 years, and 20 years;[92]

and the same sentences applied to a gang specialising in datcha robberies.[93] Earlier attempts to mitigate the law failed.[94] The decree[95] concerned with the protection of state property, and issued on the same day, repealed the law of 7 August 1932, and replaced the death penalty for the stealing of socialist property with 7 to 10 years in a corrective labour camp, with or without confiscation of property. This is increased to 10 to 25 years if a gang is involved, it is done on a large scale, or for a second time. For 'collective farm, co-operative or other public property' the penalties are 5 to 8 and 8 to 20 years respectively. Reflecting these levels, one Timofeyev received 25 years in corrective labour camp plus confiscation of property and loss of electoral rights for 5 years, under Article 2 of this decree, for obtaining money from books by false pretences.[96] The heaviest sentence possible seems to have been used frequently in this period, as shown by the cases of Davydov,[97] Bogomolov,[98] and that concerning 'Plunderers of Socialist Property' in *Pravda*, 14 October 1953, where a sentence of 25 years was given for the stealing of watches and various gold articles from a watch factory.[99] In both of these decrees, the failure to report the commission of an offence was an offence in itself. On 9 June 1947, a new decree was issued on the liability for the disclosure of state secrets.[100] Officials were to receive from eight to twelve years in a corrective labour camp, servicemen from ten to twenty years, and private individuals five to ten years. Loss of relevant documents by officials or servicemen led to four to six years, and five to eight years, respectively. If serious consequences were forthcoming, then it was six to ten years and eight to twelve years. 'Registration or transmittal abroad of inventions, discoveries and technical improvements constituting a state secret' could result in a sentence from ten to fifteen years. In all cases, it is mentioned that treason and espionage may be the relevant concept, each with its own penalties. The day before the publication of this decree, a list of items classified as state secrets was issued by the USSR Council of Ministers.[101] It included practically any information about the armed forces and the defence of country, information of an economic character – either involving industry generally or any specific part of it, 'information on discoveries, inventions and improvements of a non-military character', and other information such as state ciphers, treaties, etc. Most of these categories refer to obviously highly sensitive information and cause no surprise, but perhaps the discoveries, etc., of a non-military character are an unusual state secret.

A decree of 7 April 1948[102] on the preparation and sale of illegally manufactured alcoholic spirit reminds one that this subject has often been the subject of legislation. The penalty for manufacture is increased from up to one year, to deprivation of liberty for one to two years with confiscation of the alcohol and instruments of manufacture; and if there is an intention to resell, then six to seven years in a correctional labour camp with confiscation of property in whole or in part (this had been up to one year or a fine). On 4 January 1948, the Praesidium issued a decree[103] on 'Increasing the Liability for Rape', which did exactly this, from one to five years, to from ten to fifteen years in a corrective labour camp. Further,

> the rape of minors, as well as rape carried out by a group of persons, or rape which involves particularly grave consequences, is punishable by confinement in a corrective labour camp for a term of from 15 to 20 years.

Previously, eight years had been usual. The death penalty, recently abolished (see above), was reintroduced for traitors and spies on 12 January 1950.[104] This was supposedly done 'in view of petitions received from national republics, trade unions, peasant organisations and cultural representatives' and was to apply to 'traitors to the motherland, spies and subversive diversionists'.

In 1953 another amnesty was issued,[105] partly due to the fact that 'Law observance and socialist order have grown stronger and the incidence of crime has considerably decreased,' and is to apply to 'persons who have committed offences representing no great danger to the state and who have shown by their conscientious attitude to work that they are fit to return to honest working life and become useful members of society'. Basically it applies to sentences of up to five years, but it applies to all crimes committed in an official capacity, all economic offences and to various military crimes. Other sentences are reduced by half. Section 7 says that it is not to apply to persons sentenced to more than five years for counter-revolutionary crimes, major thefts of socialist property, banditry and premeditated murder. In the unlikely event of one of these offences resulting in a sentence of less than five years, the amnesty does apply, which is somewhat unusual as the normal practice had been to exclude these crimes – especially counter-revolutionary – entirely.

Summarising, one can see that many heavy penalties were introduced in this period, with theft of public and private property, the protection of state secrets (which were defined in wide terms), and rape receiving particular attention. The possible heavy sentences were used, as cases show. The death penalty was reinstated after a short time, but in any case 25 years in a corrective labour camp was a severe, if not equivalent, sentence. However, amnesties were issued that covered a wide variety of cases, but usually did not cover anti-state offences, whether they be counter-revolutionary or theft of state property; and the clearing up of the question of the effect of the criminal environment in enabling punishment to be applied was useful, if not totally comprehensive. The overall impression is one of severity and repression, with some alleviating factors.

Conclusions

Berman[106] says that beginning in the mid-1930s, there is a move towards social stability which involved the acceptance of many concepts that would seem to be non-revolutionary. Examples given by him include the emphasis on Russian history, a move away from internationalism, the Red Army becoming the Soviet Army, Commissars becoming Ministers, a liberalisation over the Church, many NEP concepts reintroduced within the planned economy, and personal ownership being more important. This is in conformity with the developments in theory, where the most noticeable concept is 'stability'. Stalin taught that the state would not wither away until capitalist encirclement had ceased — a view that integrates naturally with the theory of socialism in one country. Vyshinsky, in agreement with Stalin, says the law will not wither away either, and a strengthening of both state and law become a prerequisite of withering away. As Marx and Engels had visualised a revolution on a larger scale before the movement towards communism could begin, can one assume that this change complies with classical Marxism? What Berman says of Vyshinsky's work seems appropriate.

> Vyshinsky faced the necessity of developing a theory which, in the interests of stability, would put socialist law on its feet, give it a life of its own, apart from economics and politics in the narrow sense of those words, and which at the same time, in the interests of the fiction of the continuity of the Revolution, would appear Marxist-Leninist.[107]

The theory has changed so much from what Marx actually wrote that discussing whether a particular aspect is or is not Marxist can be entirely pointless, unless the many qualifying factors are kept in mind. One of the commendable actions taken by the Soviet regime was the change in the nomenclature used in philosophy, for Marxism became Marxism-Leninism, so recognising the importance of Lenin's alterations. Stalin added -Stalinism which is exactly as the name suggests, a theory connected with those coming earlier, but with its own additions and changes, and amounting to a new theory. Are these innovations truly qualitative, and not merely quantitative? This author believes that they should be considered as the former, because although they were often made or caused by good reasons, effort and wishful thinking cannot make a theory fit a situation to which it cannot apply.

Regarding the Party, a particularly important point to consider is its relationship to the decision-making process. Did it, or did it not, play a considerable role? During the war, decisions would have to be made quickly, and the Party — at least in the form of Congresses and Conferences — was of little everyday use. However, when the Defence Committee had been disbanded, Stalin tended to govern in the same small-group manner, so the Party did not recover its importance. This could be described as a typically Stalinist development, as it so clearly reflects his own personal predelictions. This situation should therefore be kept in mind when one evaluates 'Party' influence. For example, the discussion on the independence of judges indicated quite clearly that the 'will of the Party' permeates their judicial decisions, and is emphasised as one of the materialist, anti-formal aspects of Soviet law. The will of the Party, and law, are not considered as being able to conflict, because of the supposed class connections. Law is the will of the ruling class, that class is the proletariat, and the Party is its vanguard and the repository of its consciousness, therefore law and the Party cannot be in conflict. From former experience, a more likely explanation would seem to lie in the total power of the Party and its ability to influence the law, both its formulation and application. The moot point over whether the Party itself really did exercise control, or some part of it did so, is now accentuated by the more personal rule of the leader. The guiding forces within large groups often necessarily consist of small circles. If the large group is supposed to reflect the wishes of society as a whole in some particular way — and here they are, via consciousness — any doubts one may have on the veracity of this relationship are emphasised by the small ruling group or clique existing within the larger. Is it really possible to accept that a group of, say, twenty or thirty people has any special connection with the consciousness of the mass of society? As in the Soviet situation, where one man to a considerable extent exercised the power personally, the question is couched in its most extreme form. Is the relationship between the masses and one man based on an acceptable if special form of leadership, or on dictatorship?

Viewed in this light, perhaps the composition of the Party is not so important, for if leadership has developed to one person, the role of the Party may be minimised. However, the Party is still a very influential and important force within society in that decision-making at lower levels and policy implementation were part of its functions, and must be very carefully considered. Recruitment in this period was based on specific objectives. During the war years, it was primarily aimed at the armed forces, to the extent that the members of which were at one point a majority of all party members. This in itself meant that workers, and more especially peasants, increased their representation, as they constituted the largest group within the army. The level of white-collar and intelligentsia members remained high, however, and after the war more particularly so. With the increase in peasant members via the armed forces, Party representation in rural areas improved, but was still poor enough to warrant the reorganisations felt necessary later.

Another feature of Party membership worth noting is that it had suffered a great upheaval and turnover. The intake had been higher, and many members had been killed in the fighting. This led to the situation where a majority of the Party were inexperienced and undisciplined, so making consolidation, rather than expansion, the major issue. A further turnover in members was caused by the ejection of undesirables. To the differentiation between the highest leadership and the Party must be added that of the delegate level and ordinary member, the former being older and of different experience. This results in a multi-tiered structure; at the top one has the leader, Stalin, and his immediate entourage, then the upper Party leadership, then ordinary members, and finally the masses — which are themselves a mixture of power and interest groups. The overall conclusion to be drawn from this is, as it has been so many times before, that this is hardly the dictatorship of the proletariat as envisaged by Marx.

Conclusions of a similarly general sort are best drawn from any consideration of the economic situation. War would have a far-reaching effect on any economy, and retard advancement. They would not take place in a society moving closely to communism, and do not fit into a Marxist 'scheme'. Certain features of the Russian situation influenced the effect, such as the poor showing of agriculture throughout the entire period. The antipathy of the peasantry has always been a problematic and embarrassing feature of the regime, as was the reaction of some of the population to the arrival of the Germans. The system did not reflect their aspirations.

One of the most important concerns of pre-war legislation was with labour discipline. The working day was lengthened; absenteeism closely scrutinised and widely defined, with dismissal as a possible penalty; petty theft and hooliganism were treated more severely; managers were punished for the production of poor-quality goods, judges for leniency. Production was increased by these measures, but the intensified control over individuals that the legislation necessarily entailed cannot be overlooked. The lives of ordinary citizens were affected in many ways, and they were not even represented in the court, as assessors were not used.

The initial unpreparedness for war could be more easily overcome in the Soviet Union because of the nature of the regime. Many necessary decrees on providing training, against the spreading of rumours, etc. were introduced, the theft of socialist property yet more severely condemned, and there were more controls on labour. Military law and procedure were more widespread in their use, and some of the explanations of the heavier sentences were in terms of the change brought about by the wartime conditions. The Extraordinary Commission used against the Germans was reminiscent of that earlier Extraordinary Commission, the Cheka, but this one did not have a similar development, primarily because there was no need for it so to do; suitable forces with suitable powers already existed. Sentencing policy in this period involved the use of heavy penalties, but the deprivation of liberty becomes less used, and undoubtedly useful measures, such as sending offenders who were servicemen to the front, prevailed. Analogy was the cause of much debate. In many ways it became more restricted in its application, with facets of the sostav excluded. It was still used, the change affecting its standing – it was now not quite so respectable, but one should not overlook the fact that the regime did not have to depend on it, as the wide definitions and material definition of crime made it, in a fundamental way, totally unnecessary. However, the greater control exercised over analogy was accompanied by restrictive readings of some of the definitions. Direct intent only would do for certain offences – speculation was reconsidered, as was counter-revolutionary crime itself.

After the war a series of amnesties released many categories of offender, but counter-revolutionaries, offenders against the sanctity of socialist property and serious crimes such as banditry and intentional

murder were excluded. Liberal measures included the decision of the
Supreme Court on the effect of a criminal environment on the
applicability of punishment, and the repeal of the death penalty,
although this latter act was short-lived, as it was reintroduced for traitors
and spies, and state secrets were heavily protected and widely defined.
More protection was provided for private and public property. Perhaps
the introduction of these new repressive measures were the foundation
of a trend? The old forces were still very much alive. After the purges
the NKVD had concentrated on persons likely to be unreliable if there
was a war, and were active in the newly occupied territories of Poland
and the Baltic states. Once war broke out, suspected groups such as the
Volga-Germans were 'scrutinised', and then later, persons in the
reoccupied areas who were thought to be spies or agents, or infected
with capitalist, anti-Soviet ideals. Many national minorities were severely
penalised because of alleged disloyalty. These included the Crimean
Tartars, the Kalmyks and the Chechens and Ingush. Soviet citizens who,
after the war, found themselves in Austria or Germany, or who had fled
to those countries — and many had, as the Germans were initially often
welcomed as liberators — were investigated, and large-scale deportations
occurred in the border regions.

Fainsod[108] reports Khrushchev as saying in the later anti-Stalin
campaign that at this time, Stalin had become more suspicious. The
Leningrad case and that involving the Georgian Nationalist Party did not
bode well, neither did the anti-Jewish campaign. This culminated in the
Doctor's Plot, a supposed conspiracy to destroy the health of certain
military personnel, and according to Khruschchev, had no foundation
in truth. The complaints made about the lack of works produced by
scholars, Korovin and Training being mentioned by name, were most
probably caused by a fear of incurring official displeasure.[109]

Fainsod[110] mentions Khrushchev's belief that Stalin was about to
'finish off the old members of the Politburo' and that Voroshilov,
Molotov and Mikoyan were under suspicion. He concludes that 'If
Khrushchev's testimony is to be credited, only Stalin's fatal illness
averted a blood bath in the very highest Kremlin circles.' The thought
that these circles could have had some inkling of this has given rise to
the uncorroborated speculations on the circumstances of Stalin's death
on 5 March 1953, which if nothing else was opportune.

It is particularly appropriate that this period should end with the
death of Stalin, as his personal actions and qualities are fundamental to
the theoretical and practical events. In the former, the original theory
of Marx was left further behind, with the state and law becoming not

accepted but emphasised. The usual explanation given related to external affairs, which were far from those envisaged by Marx and so offered a convenient excuse. Perhaps the 'practical' approach reached its apogee in the treaty with Germany, the greatest Fascist power, which incidentally illustrates the considerable use of the theory of socialism in one country in 'explaining' actions. On the practical level, the country underwent terrible privations in the war, and these, together with more internally imposed restrictions, must have made communism seem very far away.

Notes

1. *The Essential Stalin*, edited by B. Franklin (London, 1973), at p. 380.
2. Ibid., p. 382.
3. Ibid., p. 383.
4. Ibid., pp. 385-6.
5. Ibid., p. 387.
6. I. Lapenna, *State and Law: Soviet and Yugoslav Theory* (London, 1964), pp. 38-9.
7. *Essential Stalin*, p. 408.
8. Ibid., p, 431.
9. R.T. De George, *Patterns of Soviet Thought* (Ann Arbor, 1970), p. 196.
10. New York, 1948. Translated by H.W. Babb.
11. Ibid., p. 40.
12. Ibid., p. 41.
13. Ibid., p. 48.
14. Ibid., p. 159.
15. Ibid., p. 52.
16. Ibid., p. 62.
17. Ibid., p. 51.
18. See previous chapter, and Lapenna, *State and Law*, pp. 90 *et seq.*
19. 'On the Codification of Soviet Laws', *SGiP* (April 1949). Trans. in *Current Digest of the Soviet Press* (henceforth *CDSP*), 1949-28-14.
20. 'On Major Shortcomings in Juridical Science', *Lit. Gaz.* (1949), no. 72. Trans. , 1949-39-16.
21. Ibid., p. 17.
22. 'The Soviet Criminal Court as a Conductor of the Policy of the Party and the Soviet Regime', *Vestnik Moskovskogo Universiteta* (Nov. 1950), no. 11. Trans. *CDSP*, 1952-6-8.
23. Ibid., p. 10.
24. Ibid.
25. Ibid.
26. Ibid.
27. See *CDSP*, 1951-22, pp. 10 *et seq.* for pertinent letters.
28. T.H. Rigby, *Communist Party Membership in the U.S.S.R. 1917-1967* (Princeton, 1968), p. 52.
29. *Vedomosti Verkhovnogo Soveta SSSR* (1940), no. 20. Trans. in M. Matthews (ed.), *Soviet Government* (London, 1974), pp. 431-2. One should note that contradicted the Constitution – and this was a mere 'law', not an amendment proper.

30. *Sovetskaia Iustitsiia* (1940), no. 13, p. 5.

31. S. Schwarz, *Labour in the Soviet Union* (London, 1953), p. 108.

32. E.g. D. Shveitser would have being late for lunch an offence, see ibid.

33. *Sov. Zak.* (December 1940), p. 7 (see ibid.).

34. *Pravda*, 22 September 1940.

35. *Vedomosti* (1940), no. 28 (if unqualified, then 'SSSR' is implied).

36. See A. Nove, *An Economic History of the U.S.S.R.* (London, 1976), p. 260.

37. Sbornik Dokumentov, p. 413.

38. Schwarz, *Labour in the Soviet Union*, pp. 104 *et seq.*

39. *Sov. Iust.* (1940), no. 14. See Schwarz, *Labour in the Soviet Union*, p. 111.

40. *Sov. Iust.* (1940), nos. 17-18. See ibid., p. 112.

41. *Izvestiia*, 11 August 1940. See ibid.

42. See Schwarz, *Labour in the Soviet Union*, pp. 114-15.

43. L. Schapiro, *The Communist Party of the Soviet Union* (London, 1970), p. 495.

44. *Vedomosti*, no. 31, 6 July 1941.

45. *Izvestiia*, 24 June 1941. This and many other decrees are considered in Hazard's 'Soviet Wartime Legislation' in *Russian Review* (1942), pp. 22-30.

46. *Izvestiia*, 18 September 1941.

47. *Pravda*, 24 November 1941.

48. *Vedomosti* (1941), no. 32.

49. *Pravda*, 21 July 1941.

50. *Izvestiia*, 21 October 1941.

51. 'Soviet Wartime Legislation', p. 41.

52. *Vedomosti* (1942), no. 2.

53. *Vedomosti* (1942), no. 38.

54. *Sovetskoe Ugolovnoe Pravo, Chast' Obshchaia* (Moscow, 1952), p. 86.

55. *Poniatie Prestupleniia* (Moscow-Leningrad, 1948), p. 150.

56. Ibid., pp. 151-2.

57. 'Soviet Wartime Legislation', p. 24.

58. *Izvestiia*, 30 December 1941.

59. *Vedomosti* (1942), no. 40.

60. F.J. Feldbrugge, *Soviet Criminal Law: General Part* (Leyden, 1975), p. 36.

61. From V.M. Chkhikvadze, *Sovetskoe Voenno-ugolovnoe Pravo* (Moscow, 1948), p. 114.

62. *Vedomosti* (1943), no. 15.

63. *Vedomosti* (1943), no. 18.

64. *Vedomosti* (1943), no. 49.

65. *Soviet Criminal Law*, p. 36.

66. Vol. II, p. 490.

67. V.D. Men'shagin, *Ugolovnoe Pravo: Obshchaia Chast'* (Moscow, 1948), p. 305.

68. 31 December 1938. H.J. Berman and J.W. Spindler, *Soviet Criminal Law and Procedure: The RSFSR Codes* (Cambridge, Mass., 1972), p. 33.

69. A.A. Gertzenson *et al.*, *Sovetskoe Ugolovnoe Pravo: Chast' Osobennaia* (Moscow, 1951), p. 54.

70. See Berman, *Soviet Criminal Law.*

71. Ibid.

72. *Sots. Zak.* (1938), no. 7. J. Starosolskyj, *The Principle of Analogy in Criminal Law* (New York, 1954), p. 67.

73. Ibid., p. 68.

74. For details, see ibid.

75. *Collection of Yugoslav Laws*: vol. XI (the Criminal Code) (Beograd, 1964),

p. 21.
    76. Starosolskyj, *Principle of Analogy*, p. 73.
    77. Ibid., pp. 244 *et seq.*
    78. *Sovetskoe Ugolovnoe Pravo v Period Otechestvennoi Voiny, Ucheniye Zapiski* (Leningrad University, 1948), no. 106.
    79. *Soviet Criminal Law and the Protection of State Secrets*, Law in Eastern Europe, no. 7 (Leyden, 1963), p. 22.
    80. *Vedomosti* (1940), no. 25.
    81. *Vedomosti* (1945), no. 1.
    82. *Vedomosti* (1945), no. 39.
    83. *Vedomosti* (1945), no. 39.
    84. *Vedomosti* (1946), no. 24.
    85. In Berman, *Soviet Criminal Law*, p. 34.
    86. Ibid.
    87. *Vedomosti* (1947), no. 17.
    88. P.H. Solomon, in *Soviet Criminologists and Criminal Policy* (London, 1978), says they represent 'the most important criminal legislation of the post-World War II period, and they constituted the most repressive legislation relating to ordinary criminals promulgated under Stalin's rule' (p. 27).
    89. *Vedomosti* (1947), no. 19.
    90. *Vecherniaia Moskva*, 15 August 1951. *CDSP*, 1951-33-36.
    91. *Pravda*, 16 Nov. 1953. *CDSP*, 1953-46-17.
    92. *Moskovskaia Pravda*, 18 Nov. 1953. Ibid.
    93. *Pravda*, 4 Dec. 1953. *CDSP*, 1953-49-45.
    94. The judges were brought into line, and scholars such as Durmanov and Vyshinskaia were criticised or ignored. See Solomon, *Soviet Criminologists*, p. 31.
    95. *Vedomosti* (1947), no. 19.
    96. *Pravda*, 16 May 1952. *CDSP*, 20-26.
    97. *Izvestiia*, 15 Nov. 1952. *CDSP*, 1952-46-26.
    98. *Sovetskaia Belorussia*, 22 Mar. 1953. *CDSP*, 1953-12-21.
    99. *CDSP*, 1953-41-29.
    100. *Vedomosti* (1947), no. 20.
    101. *Izvestiia*, 10 June 1947.
    102. *Vedomosti* (1948), no. 14.
    103. Sbornik Dokumentov, p. 434.
    104. *Vedomosti* (1950), no. 3.
    105. *Pravda* and *Izvestiia*, 28 March. *CDSP*, 1953-10-3.
    106. *Justice in the USSR* (Cambridge, Mass., 1966), pp. 47 *et seq.*
    107. Ibid., p. 54.
    108. *How Russia is Ruled* (Cambridge, Mass., 1970), pp. 445-6.
    109. See 'Certain Questions in the Scholarly Work of the Law Institutes', *Kulture i Zhizn*, 21 Sept. 1950. *CDSP*, 1950-11-41.
    110. *How Russia is Ruled*, p. 447.

FROM 1953 TO THE PRESENT DAY

The death of Stalin brought many changes. The usual pattern exhibited
a move towards a more liberal approach in substantive law and
procedure, but as any rule has its exceptions, certain problem areas
attracted severity. Theory underwent change that was usually directed
towards the previously accepted goals, with superstructural freedom
and the strengthening of the state of importance. There was
considerable preoccupation with individual personal rights, as reflected
in procedural changes, with Vyshinsky's views being rejected: and
documents — the Constitution, the RSFSR Code, listing protected
interests. However, the interests of the state were not overlooked, and
personal interests were not considered to be rights if they conflicted
with those of the state.

Criminological research commences once more in this period, itself
a reflection of the new liberalism, but theories must have a strictly
social bias before they are approved. One major problem is the inability
to admit any possibility that socialist society has any inherent causes of
crime, too much emphasis being placed on 'vestiges of the past', and
prevention seems simplistic, depending on the removal of conditions
and circumstances facilitating crime, rather than an interest of why a
particular individual has committed a crime — no doubt because of the
implications. Although many previously obscure areas of law are
clarified, and their application tightened up, the introduction of the
anti-parasite legislation has an opposite effect, and in many ways is
unusual practice for this time. One believes that this legislation and that
concerned with other general behaviour, such as drunkenness and
hooliganism, reflect the increasing intolerance of the Soviet regime to
antisocial behaviour. This has a certain internal logic in a situation
where the contemporary society is believed to have no causes of crime,
and therefore the individual is in some way to blame.

Political and Social Aspects of this Period

On the death of Stalin, Malenkov may have seemed the obvious heir,
but Khrushchev was to be the successor. He rose to power through
Party connections, placing his supporters in key positions and generally

asserting the importance of the Party over the administration. He affected development with his own style and preferences – sometimes the result was commendable, sometimes not. Hodnett[1] says:

> The essence of khrushchevism was not its liberalism, as some have thought, but its radicalism. What the new doctrine said, in effect, was that the basic social and political problems of the Soviet Union (i.e., those associated with the divergent interests of the white-collar and blue-collar workers, city dwellers and farmers, young and old, and Russians and non-Russians) had already been eliminated.

This is an extension of the view that socialism had been achieved, which was at best an overstatement. It was realised that consumer goods, housing, services and agriculture all required immediate attention. Procurement prices were considerably raised, and quotas greatly reduced, which improved the income on kolkhozes. The Virgin Lands Campaign and reorganisation of state and collective farms significantly increased agricultural production, but, as with so many of the campaigns, success was limited by failure to take into account local conditions and requirements, and a somewhat hasty implementation.

However, it would be misleading to think that conditions had not improved for average income and production in general have all increased up to the present time. The collective farm workers have improved the most, but started from the weakest position. When compared to the state farm workers, they seem in a very favourable position, as their private plots are larger in size.

After the death of Stalin, the Party was expanded, with the emphasis on workers and peasants. Total membership in 1953 was 6,897,224, and by 1956 had reached 7,173,521.[2] The tendency to recruit from workers and peasants made the Party more representative of society as a whole, but this change should be seen as one of quantity rather than quality, and in any case, it was not the Party as a whole that exercised power. The position of the Party (in theory) remained the same, with the 1961 Party rules saying it is 'the guiding and directing force of Soviet society', and going on to mention the need for Party discipline and 'ideological and organizational unity'.

The Party was far from being Lenin's elitist conspiratorial group, and Frank[3] makes the telling point that continuous recruitment, even at a low rate, 'means that the party is reinforcing an existing expectation in many socio-occupational groups that party membership is virtually an adjunct of their jobs'.

State and Law

After the death of Stalin, the reaction to his policies, which did not emphasise personal rights, might be thought to encompass aspects of state and legal theory, and to some extent this is true. Until Khrushchev's famous speech, however, prolonged direct attacks on Stalin were not in order, and articles supporting his theories were written.

Many basic important aspects remained the same. For example, Konstantinov,[4] while saying the base is the ultimate moulding force, writes of the independence of the superstructure:

> It is the most important feature of the superstructure that being a product and a reflection of the definite basis of a given historical period, it exerts a retroactive influence on the basis that created it. . . The superstructure is not passive or neutral to the fate of its basis, to the fate of the classes and the social system. Once begotten, the superstructure becomes a powerful active force that assists its basis to take shape and consolidate. The superstructure helps the new system, the progressive forces of society, to finish off the old basis, the old classes and reactionary forces.

Of course this is a truly Marxist concept, doubts over its pedigree only occurring if it is over-emphasised. If the superstructure is given too great a range of freedom, then as well as affecting the pre-eminence of the base, it can offer excuses for a wide range of what may seem to be inexplicable irregularities in the state and legal systems, irregularities which critics might say appeared distinctly unsocialist, and not typical or to be expected in a society that was supposedly well on the path to communism.

Almost, it would seem, in answer to these particular questions, ten years later Kelle[5] wrote that certain social and economic mechanisms that had existed before, such as personal material incentive schemes, could be imbued with a new social content and used to further development. He also speaks of the importance of ending 'antagonisms' in society, as the 'new type of historical development' offers the opportunity to create 'a mechanism of economic and social planning for all society, in the interests of the toilers' and

> The liquidation of antagonistic attitudes is an obvious precondition for the creation of this kind of mechanism, because without

overcoming the inner antagonisms and securing the unity of aims,
interests and actions of society, the effective planning of economic
and social change is unthinkable.[6]

This introduces a recurrent train of thought in Soviet practice during
this entire period — the eradication of differences in the structure of
society. Usually this really referred to class differences and reflects the
growing number of questions asked by critics of the Soviet system
about this matter.

At present, Soviet society is supposed to consist of two friendly
classes, workers and peasants, with a 'stratum' of intellectuals or
intelligentsia. The position of the peasantry has caused considerable
problems from the very beginning, as they outnumbered the
proletarians in what was to be their state. Generally, and especially in
the period of collectivisation, the peasants received harsh treatment,
and we have seen that their living standards were lower than the rest of
society. It became a preoccupation to find ways of integrating them
into society, into the proletariat, but often this resulted in meaningless
changes, such as the automatic classification of peasants on state farms
as 'workers'.[7]

Simush[8] predictably says the

fundamental change in the character of social treatment in the
countryside began with the victory of the Great October Revolution.
The socialisation of the chief means of production in the
agricultural economy — the land, turned them from an object of
purchase and sale into the property of the whole people.

The continuation of small-scale farming enabled class differences to
remain — it was termed 'heterogeneous'; and only the 'mass
collectivisation of individual producers, under the co-operative plan of
Lenin' could begin the gradual consolidation into 'one socialist class'.
Note that here collectivisation is considered from the political rather
than economic view, and these advantages, while recognised, are not
the usual put forward. Perhaps they have become more useful since the
disastrous effect of the changes on agricultural production have been
realised — or admitted. While not subscribing to a belief in the existence
of classes within the peasantry, writers are willing to admit that the
group is not undifferentiated. However, this does not touch upon the
interesting relationship between the classes within the country as a
whole, practical considerations of which have already been noted. The

official theoretical approach to this states quite clearly that the proletariat is the main class, but qualifications — whether minor or not, do have to be introduced to match the practical situation. Baitin,[9] to quote one example, elaborates the formula by saying, 'The social-class basis of the state of the dictatorship of the proletariat is formed by the working class and the non-proletarian mass of toilers, that is, by the vast majority of the members of society.' This is necessary to give some degree of possible veracity or acceptability to the idea that the Soviet state is a dictatorship of the proletariat — i.e. it reflects the composition of society, its aims and aspirations, which we have concluded on many previous occasions it most certainly does not.

This whole problem is important, as it is directly linked to the all-important, if by now distinctly theoretical, question of the 'withering away'. In the first chapter of this study it was concluded that Marx closely connected those phenomena and that of political power, and contemporary Soviet opinion shows an acceptance of this or something similar. For example, Mamut,[10] reviewing Marx's position, says:

> The giving by the public power of regulation and stability to a certain antagonistic structure, of an attempt to restrain, to smooth out irreconcilable class conflicts at the expense of the suppression of the exploitation of the masses assists the conservation of this structure, delaying the future social development.

In the advance towards communism the classes were to die away, the future society being classless. If Soviet society is on this path, and as it has been officially 'socialist' for some considerable time, it should be not only on the path but well along it. This dying away of the classes should be in some way evidenced. Of course in any serious Marxist sense they are not doing this — although important changes in the social structure have occurred. The theoretical change is one of words — they are now 'friendly classes', not antagonistic ones. The growing importance of the intelligentsia has not gone unnoticed in Soviet thought, Simush[11] saying, 'In the development of the social class structure of the Soviet society two tendencies constantly interact — the tendency towards professional differentiation of the social organism and the tendency to its eventual social integration.' The former of the two has resulted in considerable growth in that area, Kosolapov[12] explaining

the building of a socialist and communist society necessitates a growth in the number of those working with their minds, as the volume of such work increases in the national economy, so entailing an increase in their numbers. Suffice to say that from 1926 to the present day, the number of these persons in the USSR increased approximately ten times.

When considering these inter-linked concepts, one cannot overlook that of 'political power'. Politics, in Marx's theory, is described in terms of class – the suppression of one by another involves the use of political power. The 'withering away' can be considered in these terms, for the dying out of the state could be referring to the dying out of political power, an event contemporaneous with the degeneration of classes. In his analysis of the nature of political power, Tikhomirov[13] says:

> In a class society the social power acquires the character of a political state power. The founders of Marxism emphasised the unity of political and state power, stressing the organised force of one class for the suppression of the others as a characteristic of political power.

Under socialism, this type of power is fully developed, with a true understanding of its nature only being achieved

> by means of combining the concepts 'authority' (*upravlenie*) and 'political power', integrating them in the concept of 'social administration' (*sotsial'noe upravlenie*). The core of social administration consists of political power. To be exact, the power defines the social character of the administration, its basic aims and areas of action because it expresses policy.

Under socialism, therefore, it is recognised that there is political power. It is of a special sort, or comes to be so, because the forces guiding society, symbolised by the state, have a particular nature, non-exploitive, which is more akin to social administration. In a communist society, social administration will be the state in a total sense, and then there will be no political power as that concept is now understood. Khrushchev,[14] in a speech to the Twenty-First Party Congress, spoke of the two stages of development to communism, and informed us that

> The Soviet people under the guidance of the Party have reached such heights, have accomplished such a great reform in all sections of economic and social-political life, that it gives an opportunity to our

country to enter now into a new important period of our development − a period of the large-scale construction of communist society.

Khrushchev believed communist society would be organised and classless, with administration taking the place of the state. Certain analogous functions would remain, but they would be different in character and form. At the present time the functions of the state were in the realms of economics and defence, and due to the needs of the latter, the state had to be strengthened. Stalin's views have not been totally rejected therefore, and Lapenna[15] says the difference lies in the degree of decentralisation, but that 'even if very widespread, does not affect the existence of the state as such, nor can it be understood as the "withering away" of the state in the Marxist sense of the word'.

Platkovskii[16] has an unequivocal view of the state, saying that the withering away cannot be truly understood unless it is borne in mind that the tasks and functions of the socialist state are constantly changing in the course of constructing a communist society. 'Marxism-Leninism sees in the strengthening not the weakening of the socialist state the sole true road for preparing conditions for a dying out of the state, in objective natural conformity for passing from state to non-state.' His comment that 'A complete dying away of the state is possible only under full communism, and when there is no danger of military invasion from outside'[17] seems to allow for the possibility of full-scale communism to be achieved with a state in existence. Although Marx may well have envisaged some sort of organisational entity in the future society, what Platkovskii has in mind seems entirely different, as a 'normal' state would exist in his prediction − note the reference to defence, although it would no doubt be said to have a 'different quality'. This development should be the cause of little surprise, as the state has a seemingly indefatigable hold on Soviet theory, and the use of the term 'full-scale' communism, which must compare with some lesser-scale version, warns one of future trends.

Lepeshkin[18] writes of a twofold purpose for the dictatorship of the proletariat − the suppression of the exploiting classes and the preparation of the necessary conditions for the construction of communism.

And so, if the presence of the dictatorship of the proletariat is necessarily connected with the existence of antagonistic classes or their remnants, then the existence of the socialist state is vital to the toilers after this, when all the capitalist classes are destroyed. . .The dictatorship of the proletariat is an historical, transient political institution, coupled only with the resolution of definite historically determined problems – guaranteeing not only the total but final victory of socialism; at the same time the existence of the Soviet state is determined not only by this danger but also with the construction of a complete communist society.[19]

This is an interesting point, as the previous generally accepted theories did not separate the existence of the dictatorship of the proletariat and that of the state in anything like such a forthright manner. The presence of class antagonism is an important factor, as it is an important part of the dictatorship, yet

The essential difference between the state of the dictatorship of the proletariat and the all-people's state is the liquidation of the political supremacy of the one working class and the establishment of the rule of all classes and social groups in Soviet society, that is, the political power of the people.[20]

This view can be the cause of further problems, as politics was thought to be a class-based entity, and one of the features of communist society was that it was to be classless and apolitical, these two concepts being impliedly interdependent. However, here a classless situation with 'the political power of the whole people' being exercised is offered, so severing the links between the existence of class and politics.

From the above one can conclude that the state is going to continue for the foreseeable future, primarily, it is said, for defence. The theory has undergone more contortions to support these expectations and in so doing has become more removed from Marx's original thought. Any withering away that is to take place in the meantime is going to affect the existence of the dictatorship of the proletariat (?), which having been separated from that of the state, does not affect that of the latter. There are some changes in attitudes to law, with more emphasis being placed on the rights of the individual – nominally. Piontkovskii[21] says that subjective rights do have the quality of law and previously too great an emphasis had been attached to 'imperative norm prohibitions' (*povelitel'nye normy-zaprety*). While permissive (*dozvolitel'nye*) norms' were overlooked. These have since become important in Soviet legislation and 'exactly establish the subjective rights of citizens'. One may think that such a move would be accompanied by a lessening of the importance attached to state rights, but they were still treated as of primary importance, showing the true nature of these personal 'rights'. Selektov[22] wrote that

> Under a socialist system there is a correlation between society and the state. As distinct from an exploiting state, which represents the interests of one part of society — a wealthy minority — the state under socialism conveys the wishes of all society, all the people. State interests coincide with social interests. . .and the interests of society generally as the interests of the state. . .the interests of society and the individual are the same.

As we shall see when the new Constitution is considered, the new emphasis on the rights of the individual have little appearance of reality when they are so closely identified with those of the state. A genuine right must be able to conflict with a state right under socialism; it is only under communism that the two are conceivably one. However, despite this considerable drawback, one has to recognise that law is being awarded a new degree of respect compared to what went before. The upholding of 'socialist legality' continues.

On the application of law, Kurylev[23] says it must be creative but not too flexible, as that would be against socialist legality. Concepts should be explained, at least those widely used in law, and examples given of their use in cases of omission and comission. He includes 'cynicism' (*tsinizm*) among these, so recognising the problem associated with some of these general, difficult-to-define concepts.

As with the state, law does not seem about to wither away, in fact its uses continue to be recognised, and emphasis and importance is attached to its regard. Paralleling the convergence of the state and administration of society, the rights of the state and of individuals cannot be in conflict with each other. Terms applicable to a communist situation are being used in one which is neither that nor socialist.

Vyshinsky and Law

That many theories of Vyshinsky were attacked in and after 1956 should cause little surprise, for he had provided the necessary theoretical backing to many of Stalin's actions and aims, and with the change of policy, he would be an obvious target. A leading article in *Sovetskoe Gosudarstvo i Pravo* on the Twentieth Party Congress attacked many aspects of law. Khrushchev's complaints about the state of legal science were upheld — i.e. that it had not developed to meet the situation.

Scholars were criticised for a lack of new works and theories, which would at first seem a little naïve, but it was recognised that 'the widespread diffusion of the cult of personality had played a negative role in the development of legal science',[24] as had the work of Vyshinsky, 'by blind worship of his pronouncements, by converting some of them into infallible dogma and by the inadmissible concealing of serious mistakes in his works'.[25] Now, the observance of Soviet law was paramount and the rights and interests of citizens must be upheld. A major obstacle to this was Vyshinsky's theory of evidence which denied the need for absolute truth and allowed conviction on the probability of the facts evaluated by the court.

Rakhunov[26] attacked the non-adherance to the presumption of innocence and the reliance on torture-induced evidence. In a joint article, Piontkovskii and Chkhikvadze[27] rejected the concept that it was the dangerous state of the individual that led to the use of punishment rather than the commission of a prohibited act. Vyshinsky had said that guilt did not depend on such a commission, but on the personality of the accused, and the conditions and circumstances surrounding the crime, the act itself being almost of a secondary importance. This was rejected, as confusing guilt with the causal link.

Analogy, once thought necessary to the true development of Soviet law, was now not only considered unnecessary, but thought to be actively dangerous to the campaign to strengthen socialist legality. In the following year, Piontkovskii[28] made further attacks on Vyshinsky, saying his works were 'inordinately praised', although along with correct propositions, they contained serious errors. Vyshinsky's belief that 'provocateurs and traitors' were operating on the legal front had been incorrect, and Pashukanis and Krylenko are said to have been wrongfully accused. Vyshinsky's views on economic law — i.e. that it should be liquidated, and on evidence, were attacked and rejected. Not surprisingly, 'Beria and his gang' were implicated in all this, attacks on them being prevalent at this time.[29] In attacking Vyshinsky, his critics are not attacking the existence of law. In fact, these attacks are based on the lack of certainty and acceptability engendered in law by him. The new attitude is altogether commendable on numerous counts. If there is to be law, and this seems to be both practically the case, and acceptable in theory, then that law should not be arbitrary and its application badly organised. The strengthening of the state, and an ineffective, arbitrary legal system, would have led to the 'unfettered dictatorship' that seems to have become dreaded by rulers and ruled alike. Lapenna,[30] when discussing the concept of legality, says this tendency. . .is nothing but an attempt to establish a system in which the rule of law will be paramount, in which all state and party organs will also obey its prescriptions, in which, in short, the dictatorship – contrary to Lenin's concept – will be bound by its own laws while they remain in force.

This is certainly the case, and altogether safer for everyone. The theoretical concept of socialist legality was extensively detailed by Ferimove, Professor of Law at Leningrad University[31] – although whether this reflects the practical situation is another matter. The fullness of the description indicates the importance attached.

a) The steadfast observance and fulfillment of statutes and of other legal measures based upon them and introduced for their fulfillment – by all institutions, organizations, officials and citizens;
b) The issuance of legal measures only by organizations so empowered and strictly within the competence of each of them as outlined by legislation;
c) The adoption of legal measures in a strictly defined form and in an established manner;
d) The supremacy of a statute within the system of legal measures and the conformity of legal measures of lower organs of power and control with the legal measures of superior organs which have primary juridical power in relation to the former;
e) Timeliness in the issuance of legal measures and likewise their stability and relative unchangeability;
f) The exact and uniform application of legal measures in complete conformity with their meaning and with the maintenance of organizational or procedural forms established by legislation;
g) Timely execution or application of legal measures;
h) The carrying-out of legal measures to the extent and in the sense intended by those legal measures themselves;
i) The guarantee of the carrying-out of legal measures through all necessary material and spiritual means;
j) The implementation of supervision, control and checking of the carrying out of legal measures;
k) Timely modification or more precise definition of the contents and of the addition of legal measures in force, and likewise in the case of necessity their repeal by competent organs in an established manner.

The 1961 Party Programme[32]

This programme was published in draft form at the end of July 1961
and adopted after discussions at the Twenty-Second Congress on 31
October 1961. It is divided into two parts, 'The Transition from
Capitalism to Communism is the Road of Human Progress', which is the
more general section covering many theoretical aspects; and 'The Tasks
of the Communist Party of the Soviet Union in Building a Communist
Society', which is, as the title suggests, more specifically on the Soviet
situation. Each of these sections has many subdivisions – the whole
programme is approximately four or five times longer than that of 1919.

The theoretical section of the programme contains many predictable
statements covering capitalism being the last exploiting system, about
to succumb to revolutionary forces, to be followed by a move towards
socialism and communism, with the former already having been
achieved in the USSR, and the latter under construction. The tasks of
the Party in this latter stage are important and diverse, including

> the further *promotion of socialist law and order* and the improvement
> of legal rules governing economic organisation, cultural and
> educational work and contributing to the accomplishment of the
> tasks of communist construction and to the all-round development
> of the individual are very important.
>
> *The transition to communism means the fullest extension of
> personal freedom and the rights of Soviet citizens...* The Party's
> objective is to enforce strict observance of socialist legality, eradicate
> all violations of law and order, abolish crime and remove all the
> causes of crime...it is necessary severely to punish those who
> commit crimes dangerous to the society, violate the rules of the
> socialist community and refuse to live by honest labour.[33]

'Measures of public influence and education' would be the eventually
used measures against transgressors, and allow a return to useful activity,
but they would not often be needed, as there will be 'a spirit of
voluntary and conscientious fulfilment', and 'a natural fusion of rights
and duties'.

On the point of 'survivals of the past' as a cause of crime, the
programme says, 'The Party considers it an integral part of its
communist education work to combat manifestations of bourgeois
ideology and morality, and the remnants of private-owner psychology,
superstitions, and prejudices.'[34]

These comments on law and crime do not conflict with previous attitudes, and support the view that law and crime will die out, that in the meantime violations of law and order must be treated severely. Causes of such violations are social, with 'vestiges of the past' gradually becoming less important.

The state and law aspects of the programme are discussed at length in an important and interesting article by Romashkin. He says the dictatorship of the proletariat is at an end as it has fulfilled its mission from the internal point of view. This is thought not to be in conflict with Marx, for 'It is necessary to distinguish the period up to the construction of socialism (the transition period) and the period of developed socialist society,'[35] as in the latter stage an all-people's state is in existence and the dictatorship of a class over a class is not necessary. The withering away of state and law requires the attainment of high 'consciousness and culture', so the 'principles of communist morality will be introduced into everyday life', but external requirements — the defence of the country — necessitate the continued existence of the state.[36] Law is seen as an important means of implementing policy, consolidating existing relations and facilitating the emergence and development of new ones. It is directed against antisocial elements, and 'not considering measures specially intended for the struggle against the insignificant number of malicious offenders, and of agents sent to us by the imperialist states', the nature of the penalties and coercion is changing, with public influence of growing importance.[37]

This would indicate a continued change in the nature of society, part of the move towards communism, but, taking into account the previous references to the external situation, it should come as little surprise to hear that 'the withering away of the state, and also law, is a protracted process which is only completed with full communism. Only external conditions may make it necessary to preserve the state for a certain time under communism.'[38]

The withering away is seen in terms of a growth of public organisations and a decrease in a special stratum of administrators. Society is to govern itself, 'communist public self-government', but the external situation is the deciding factor on the final disappearance of the state.

In criticising these theses, Lapenna concludes that the idea of a 'classless state' or a 'party of the whole people' is nonsense from the Marxist viewpoint; that the disappearance of the dictatorship of the proletariat before the state is equally non-Marxist, as one cannot have a state without antagonistic classes; and that legal thoery will move in the expected path of

> a) *'the dictatorship* of the working class' (1) does not exist any more, but (2) 'the guiding role of the working class' among the 'two friendly classes and social strata' is preserved until 'the full victory of communism', and (3) the role of the communist party is strengthened;
> b) *the state* (1) has been transformed into an all-people's state. . . and it is a state which is withering away, (2) nevertheless the withering away is a very long and gradual process and the state will completely disappear only in 'a developed communist society' and in conditions of 'the victory and consolidation of socialism in the world arena', (3) in the meantime it is necessary to strengthen 'our Fatherland and its glorious armed forces. . .' etc.[39]

Lapenna feels that the programme should have mentioned the role of the procuracy and the right of the defendant to counsel in criminal proceedings, and that the omission may be part of Khrushchev's concept of social organisations taking over from the state, for the 'social accusers and defenders', who were not legally trained, had their importance enhanced.[40]

From the programme, one can deduce that norms and rules of some sort will exist in the future society, but are they to be legal? This would seem to be likely in part at least, as legal concepts such as ownership are to exist. However, now that state and law have been separated, the latter can exist without the former.

Explanations of Crime

The central thesis on this matter is that crime is caused socially, not by forces in present society, but by 'vestiges of the past'. This socially orientated approach has been the permanent mainstay of Soviet criminology since its inception and is more ideologically acceptable than other explanations. Before 1930, when the study of criminology was in its earlier stage of development, this and other more suspect explanations were put forward, a situation which repeated itself in the late 1950s when research and study began once more, and at no time was the social approach seriously superseded, and was of great importance, albeit in a passive manner, in the intervening years.

As late as 1954, the strictly orthodox line is seen to prevail, with Gorshenin[41] informing us that:

Crime has radically diminished year after year in our country as a result of the tremendous gains in improving the material welfare and culture in our country, of the constant educational work which has ensured a constant growth in the awareness of the masses. And if we still do have causes of crime, of various violations of Soviet law, this is due first of all to the tenacity of vestiges of capitalism in the minds of the people, to vestiges of bourgeois ideology.

It is not that this approach becomes unacceptable in later practice, but that it becomes questioned as the sole explanation.

On the nature of these vestiges, Piontkovskii[42] explained that in the first phase of development, there were two causes of crime:

(1) the resistance of the overthrown exploiting classes, supported by the entire international bourgeoisie;
(2) the resistance of the petty-bourgeois anarchic spirit and of bourgeois ways and habits to which are still subject rather broad groups of the working people.

In the phase of development from socialism to communism, the conditions would be more propitious, and foreign agents are said to be a cause, but vestiges still play the most important part – certainly in cases involving 'ordinary' criminals. As would be expected, Gertsenzon[43] links the causes of crime to capitalist society, saying that in those societies criminologists will not be able to initiate useful reforms unless those reforms strike at capitalism itself, as that is the root cause. Vestiges of this past are the main cause of crime in socialist society. After saying they are the cause of crime, Ostroumov and Chugunov[44] add:

the vitality of these vestiges of the past is explained by the fact that the consciousness lags behind social life, by the presence of the capitalist world that is hostile to us, and by the continuing shortcomings in material and cultural services to citizens and in their education. Vestiges of the past are rooted in the mode of life and in the minds of millions of persons long after the disappearance of the economic conditions that gave rise to them.

Their nature is subjected to greater analysis as study progresses and Karpets[45] speaks of three aspects: 'the historically conditioned quality of social phenomena', 'the operation of the objective law of the lag of consciousness behind existence', and 'the presence and influence of antagonistic socio-economic systems along with socialism'. These are said to be the 'main general causes of the first order', and secondary causes such as the differences between urban and rural life, desires and possibilities in employment, the shortcomings of the economy, etc., are said to exist in Soviet society. One of the major problems with the social explanations is how to connect the general with the specific. How do they cause crime in individual cases? Why does one individual commit an offence and another not?

Alcohol is of course a major concern in the USSR, a study by Vaisberg and Taibakova of 450 juveniles in the Kazakh SSR revealing that 41 per cent had committed offences when intoxicated, and that 72 per cent of these were habitual heavy drinkers.[46] It must be one of the most important facets of the vestiges of the past. The actual explanation of how alcohol causes crime is interesting. Its basic tenet is that alcoholic behaviour is learned behaviour, and it becomes a habit as drinking continues. Deeper explanations of why certain individuals drink and others do not are avoided — the problem is seen as relatively simple. A.B. Sakharov, in his important work *O Lichnosti Prestupnika i Prichinakh Prestupnosti v SSSR*,[47] characteristically takes a more personality-oriented view, saying that

> alcohol induces the release and manifestation of the real antisocial essence of the given subject, the inherent unfavourable moral qualities in him, individualistic and egoistical motives, base feelings, etc. . . . Even in a state of intoxication, a person does not do that which is totally alien to his nature; possessing high and strong moral principles he, even under the influence of alcohol, does not commit an immoral act.[48]

Important mechanical factors, often discussed in relation to juvenile delinquency, include incorrect child-rearing, shortcomings in the work of state and public agencies, etc., with the measures to combat crime being related to these points. They include: (i) economic measures — such as the increased production of non-alcoholic drinks, the production of more consumer goods; (ii) cultural and educational measures, such as campaigns against crime; and (iii) administrative measures, such as controlling the sale of alcohol, reorganisation of freight schedules, etc.

Research has also been done on the effect of group values on
individual behaviour and the production of crime.[49] Although the social
approach was the most important in Soviet criminology, there were
others. Sakharov, in his above-mentioned work, emphasised the need to
consider the personality of the offender. This was and still is a subtle
area of research, the basic idea not being totally sound ideologically,
suggesting as it did that root causes existed in present society. Once
society had changed and achieved communism, there was to be no
crime, and if the personality of the offender, affected in some biological,
genetic, hereditary way, produced 'ordinary' crime, then the whole
explanation was unsound. No doubt realising these dangers, or believing
in the tenets of orthodoxy, Sakharov is guarded in his exposition,
saying:

> depending on the tendency of the personality, the level and breadth
> of its requirements and interests, the moral qualities, properties of
> the will and other social attributes of the individual, the aspects of
> the temperament assume a positive or negative value since they
> strengthen or weaken the characteristics and how they will be
> manifested in the individual, in his actions.[50]

He categorically states that these characteristics are not inborn, but are
a product of social influences. Such explanations as these gave rise to
much criticism and concern. Ostroumov and Chugunov wrote that these
factors were of interest, but

> one should not exaggerate the role of the personal characteristics of
> the subject in the commission of crime and seek assistance in
> biology, which is not part of Soviet criminology. But neither can one
> disregard the psychological traits of the individual. And it is
> exceedingly important to emphasise that individual personality traits
> are the result of the conditions under which the person has lived,
> been raised, and has functioned.[51]

Lashko[52] believes the personality of offenders has to be considered if
they are to be re-educated and corrected. To this end, various
circumstances had to be considered, such as the upbringing and family
background, work experience and skills, the circumstances and character
of the crime, and 'the direction of the outlook, opinions, interests,
aspirations, enthusiasms and inclinations'. Moreover, 'The positive and
negative aspects of character, physical condition and psychological

peculiarities' had to be taken into account also. This includes the expected mixture of the social and the psychological, the latter being taken into consideration, but not allowed to become free of the former.

Despite the obvious opposition to the introduction of overtly biological factors into Soviet criminology, I.S. Noi, with various collaborators, offered a distinctly biologically orientated theory that was not widely publicised, but received a great deal of criticism. His idea of 'innate programmes' of the individual's behaviour being 'coded' into instinctual reactions was too biological and was therefore condemned. Biological factors, in any variation, are totally unacceptable to Soviet criminology.

Gertsenzon[53] took a middle course, somewhat akin to Sakharov, saying the study of the 'causes and conditions leading to the commission of crimes' is of great importance in recognising that vestiges of the past are the chief cause of crime and enabling one to act accordingly. A study of the personality of the offender would be an important factor in the selection of punishment, not because crime was 'rooted in the very personality', but because 'the influence of external causes, conditions and circumstances does not occur mechanically but as refracted through the psychology, character and temperament of the person'.

Antonian,[54] in a discussion of the effects of urbanisation on crime, thought that some 'negative social consequences of urbanisation, including social-psychological ones, can be conducive to the commission of crimes'. This approach has been followed up by Iakovlev, in an article in the January 1978 issue of *Sovetskoe Gosudarstvo i Pravo.*[55] He analyses the causes of crime, or at least certain types of crime, into that resulting from the malfunctioning of economic and social institutions, which he says results in a more rational, preventable type of deviance; and that resulting from the disorganisation of social groups (family, production groups, etc.). This latter involves impulsive, emotional, violent actions, but again these can be prevented. It is interesting to see analysis of the causes occurring, but the suggested response is on the simplistic level of saying the cause must be dealt with.

Despite these modifications to the theory, the underlying problem with the approach was the lack of investigation into causal connections in individual cases, far too great an emphasis being placed on mechanics. Kudriavtsev[56] attaches importance to the accepted fact that having committed one offence, an offender is more likely to commit more, and says for example that 20 per cent of those convicted for hooliganism had already had administrative penalties applied to them, 52 per cent disciplinary, and 70 per cent had been described 'unfavourably' at work.

He had already stated that the 'functional dependence' of antisocial acts and the phenomena generating them underwent the 'most widespread investigation',[57] from which one can see that these types of approach, although certainly of some use, were over-used.

We can therefore conclude that social explanations of crime causation are of prime importance in Soviet criminology. This is based on ideological requirements as well as anything else, with other explanations — especially those of a biological nature — being thought non-Marxist. Due to doubts over the ability of social explanations to explain all aspects of crime, psychological aspects came to be considered as well. These seem to be tolerated unless they are of a biological nature, whereupon they are totally condemned.

Criminological research is still in a comparatively youthful stage, albeit its second, and thought seems directed at generalities rather than specifics. A weakness in Soviet theories is the lack of attention paid to the final links in the chain of causation. Why one individual in certain circumstances commits an offence and another in the same circumstances does not, is treated unsatisfactorily.

However, the effect of particular circumstances facilitating the commission of certain offences, such as subcultures and gangs, urbanisation and personality, are being studied.

This whole question of what causes crime is of considerable importance, as the theories of a non-social nature may cause ideological problems. Marx based his view of crime on the simple premiss that the inequalities of capitalist society produced the crime. In the future society, these were not going to exist and therefore there would be no crime. It has already been suggested that some neutral forms of crime may exist in the future society, but they will not be socially caused. If the true explanation of crime is discovered to be wholly or partly non-social, then this theory will be disproved.

Disregarding 'crimes' caused by mental disturbance, which is not crime, how do psychological and genetic theories correlate to Marx? In the case of the former, they may be indirectly caused or affected by society, but the latter are more difficult to explain. However, one believes that they are not a great proportion of offences and the basic approach of Marx — and it was only basic — still applies.

However, as Karpets says, the social approach alone 'explains the historical transient character of crime and helps to reveal the fact that criminality is not generated by socialism, that the regularities immanent in socialism do not produce criminality'.[58] To apply this to the Soviet situation is indefensible, as (i) the level of crime is not particularly low, and (ii) the society is not nearing communism — with crime about to disappear. The restrictions placed upon researchers in the Soviet Union — and one believes there are restrictions, with control coming from the centre — and specialists having little influence in policy-making at the highest level[59] — has harmed criminology. A more pluralistic approach would have been better.

Administrative Changes

The Decree on the Procuracy of 24 May 1955[60] was the first decree to comprehensively set out the duties and structure of the procuracy. Article 1 sets the tone of the decree by saying:

> In accordance with Article 113 of the Constitution of the U.S.S.R., the Procurator General of the U.S.S.R. shall be charged with the supreme supervision over the strict execution of the laws by all ministries and their subordinate institutions and by individual officials, as well as by citizens of the U.S.S.R.

Laws were to be strictly enforced in all parts of the Union, with protected interests including the rights of state institutions, collective farms, etc., the personal, political and property rights of citizens, and the social and state system of the USSR.

The legality of the agencies of inquiry and preliminary investigation, and of the judicial process in general, was to be supervised. Articles 5 and 6 say the procuracy is to be centralised and free from local control. Of particular interest is Chapter V, concerned with supervision of legality in places of deprivation of freedom. The procuracy had had powers in this area before, but they had never been defined in detail, and seem to have been usually unenforced. Now, 'agencies of the procuracy shall be charged with responsibility for observance of socialist legality in places of deprivation of freedom,' and a procurator, with freedom of access to places and documents, was to visit places of detention and question prisoners, and deal with irregularities. One can see an importance attached to individuals' rights, but it should be noted that, as usual, the forces of state and law were not in conflict with those rights. Boldyrev, the Assistant Procurator-General of the USSR, wrote that 'The Soviet regime guarantees the working people rights and freedoms that the popular masses in capitalist countries dream about.'

Bourgeois countries have constitutions that purport to protect freedoms but 'Only in a socialist state, where exploitation of man by man has been eliminated, have class and national oppression been destroyed; only where power belongs to the working people themselves are their rights fully exercised.' However, rights and law are interdependent, so an important task is the 'constant strengthening of socialist law, which protects the sacred and inalienable rights of Soviet citizens'.[61] Examples are then given of successful protests made by the procuracy against local Soviets, such as that against Omsk City Soviet Executive Committee, which had resolved to allow citizens 450 square metres on plots allocated for private housing, when 600 had to be allowed. This is an opportune moment to say that although protests could be made against local authorities, it is generally accepted that such actions against the central authorities would not be successful. Berman[62] mentions a successful protest against the decision of a Council of Ministers of an autonomous republic, but feels it would not have happened against the USSR Council of Ministers – but actually it does not have this power. Other articles attested to the change of attitude. Topuridze, after making the somewhat optimistic statement that 'throughout the whole course of the history· of our socialist state the Communist Party and the Soviet government have firmly demanded the strictest observance of socialist justice and the strengthening of law and order in the country,' went on to denounce Beria 'and his gang' for bringing law into disrepute. The procuracy is praised for its work in upholding the law and citizens' rights.[63]

Later, in the numerous attacks on Vyshinsky and his theories, Borin[64] wrote that 'Vyshinsky and his followers distorted the true meaning and tasks of Soviet administration of justice and attempted to give legal backing for mass repressions and illegality.' The theory of legal proof, the problem of truth in legal proceedings, and the theory of maximum probability were singled out as problem areas. It is admitted that some support was still to be found for Vyshinsky, hence the need for the continued attacks.

Zhogin[65] applied himself to the sensitive area of the purges, saying that prosecutors and investigators were supplied, by Vyshinsky, with incorrect interpretations of criminal law norms:

Vyshinsky declared that ordinary criminal offences did not exist, that now these offences became crimes of a political order. He proposed that ordinary criminal cases be reconsidered with the aim of imparting a political character to them. In particular, on

November 29, 1936, Vyshinsky ordered that within a month all
criminal cases of major fires, accidents and the issuing of poor-
quality products be reviewed and studied with the aim of exposing
a counterrevolutionary, saboteur aspect to them and making the
guilty parties more heavily liable. This was a policy of imparting a
political character to ordinary criminal cases and artificially creating
cases of political crimes.

This shows that what was 'respected' in this period was not law, but
the possibility that it was not going to wither away so immediately.

No doubt in order to check such abuses in the future, the 1960 Code
of Criminal Procedure, building on the 1958 Basic Principles of Criminal
Legislation, instituted change.[66] Regulations were imposed on the State
Security Agencies powers of arrest and investigation; special procedures
for anti-state acts were abolished; further safeguards were introduced
into the pre-trial proceedings, and into evidential matters the
presumption of innocence, and rights of the accused, generally and for
appeal, etc.; and, in accordance with Soviet practice, the educational
role of the court and proceedings were emphasised. A final point to
mention, of especial interest, is that of popular participation in criminal
proceedings. Social accusers and defenders, there to represent the
appropriate collective, were introduced by the 1938 Principles, and
under the Code of Criminal Procedure their rights were wide, including
presenting evidence, arguing and questioning. Article 113 allowed the
investigator to inform the Comrades' Courts and collectives of offences;
Article 140 allowed him to suggest preventive measures to these
collectives for the future; and Article 128 enlisted the public in the
uncovering of crimes and their facilitating causes. Article 7 allowed a
case to be transferred to the Comrades' Courts, on the grounds set out
in Article 51 of the RSFSR Code of Criminal Law, which listed certain
non-serious cases.

Comrades' Courts, after an initial bout of activity, remained dormant
until Khrushchev resurrected them at the Twentieth and Twenty-First
Congresses, as part of the campaign to involve the public in the
administration of justice, and as evidence of the 'withering away'. The
latter Congress passed the resolution that

In the matter of ensuring observance of the rules of the socialist
community an increasingly important role is to be played by the
people's militia, Comrades' Courts and other such autonomous
organs; together with state institutions they must perform the

functions of preserving order in society, defending the rights of citizens, and preventing acts harmful to society.[67]

The 1961 Statute on Comrades' Courts[68] describes them as 'elective social agencies' with a strongly educational role. They are to be elected and established by collectives, educational establishments, etc.; and are to consider cases of labour discipline, petty theft and hooliganism, drunkenness, vandalism, property disputes, and other acts of a like minor nature. Penalties that could be used include comradely warnings, public censure, fines and compensation. Details were given as to the procedure to be used. Butler[69] concludes on these courts that despite criticisms levelled against them, 'a speedy and less bureaucratic means of resolving disputes has a useful place in society'.

The above-mentioned People's Volunteer Militia is another aspect of public involvement in the administration of justice, and was instituted by the decree 'On Participation by the Working People in Safeguarding Public Order' to work at enterprises, construction projects, state and collective farms, educational institutions and elsewhere. Morgan,[70] after considering their later history, concludes that although they are useful in controlling disorder, their powers are such that complaints have been made about their behaviour, and as a Party-supervised agency, they could become an over-powerful regulatory force in Soviet society.

Obviously there has been a reaction to the lack of emphasis on the rights of individuals that prevailed under the previous Soviet practice. The new procedural safeguards are particularly important as regards this, and the procuracy could be of great importance if it can act freely, or if that is too much to expect, then freely within the lower levels of control.

The involvement of the public in the administration of justice has become an important consideration. This idea has a basically continuous history in the Soviet Union, and if it did become rather obscured under Stalin, it had an important influence in early legislation on the court system. Periodic emphases on this goal were usually followed by a move away from the particular innovations when practical problems were forthcoming. Although it may be said to be, and certainly is, in the right direction, it in itself, of course, cannot be considered as a significant part of the 'withering away'.

Legislation before the Fundamental Principles

Stalin having died, a manifestation of more liberal policies would have been both welcome and expected, and to a considerable extent they were forthcoming. The amnesty of 27 March 1953[71] freed people sentenced for up to five years; those involved in certain official, economic and military crimes; the young, old and ill were to be released, and other sentences reduced by a half. What was to become a growing emphasis on individual rights was prefaced at Stalin's funeral service, when Beria — a somewhat surprising choice — said the population 'could work calmly and confidently, knowing that the Soviet government will solicitously and untiringly guard their rights, which are recorded in the Stalin Constitution'.[72] Of course, apart from the fact that this offer was one which the population had little alternative but to accept, the rights mentioned were by no means absolute, and little reliance could be placed on them. However, at least the statement was made.

Previous methods, involving harsh measures of control, were discredited, or at least there was an open attempt to do this. Nikiforov[73] wrote that people seemed to imagine that the heavy sentences previously dealt out had had an advantageous effect, but if this had been so, their use would have been continued. Actually they had failed, and so were abandoned.

Some significant measures were not publicised at the time, such as the abolition of the Special Board of the Ministry of Internal Affairs, which seems to have occurred by an unpublished decree in September 1953.[74] Cases that had been tried by the Board, and there were many, as it had been a major instrument of terror, were reviewed by military tribunals and courts, and rehabilitations, where applicable, took place. Some aspects of the liberalisation are not reflected in the legislation of the period, as important changes could be implemented without the need to alter the law. Although always of relevance, the attitude behind the surface of events is of particular importance in Soviet affairs, and at this time, a 'change of climate'[75] had occurred, with, for example, a corresponding lack of prosecutions brought under Article 58.

Despite all this, there were some increases in penalties, the most important of which was perhaps the extension of the death penalty, on 30 April 1954,[76] to 'persons who have committed premeditated murder under particularly aggravating circumstances', said to be in 'response to petitions from citizens and public organisations on applying the death sentence to murderers and in order to increase protection of citizens'. Cases involving its use include those of Stepanyan, who had been previously convicted of robbery and now murdered in the furtherance of robbery;[77] and Osipov, who murdered two workmates for purposes of robbery.[78] Liberalising measures of the period include that of 5 August 1954,[79] which relieved pregnant women of liability for illegal abortions, and just over a year later, abortions were again allowed to be performed in medical institutions.[80] Liability was removed for unauthorised travel on freight trains,[81] and on 13 May 1955, the 1941 law on the sale, exchange and release of surplus equipment by directors of state economic enterprises was repealed.[82] In September of this year, an amnesty[83] was issued which applied to 'Soviet citizens who collaborated with occupiers during the Great Patriotic War. . . sentenced to up to ten years' deprivation of freedom for assisting the enemy or for other crimes committed during the period of the. . .war' under various parts of Article 58. Other sentences were halved, but it was not to apply to those convicted of the murder and torture of Soviet citizens.

On 25 April 1956, a decree[84] ended legal liability for unauthorised quitting and absences from work. This was possible, according to the decree, as 'labour discipline at enterprises and institutions has been strengthened as a result of the growth of the working people's consciousness and the rise in their living standards and cultural level', so criminal sanctions were felt to be no longer necessary, reliance being placed on disciplinary measures and public influence. Those already serving sentences were to be freed, proceedings were to be stopped, and records of conviction removed. This decree, together with that removing the liability from unauthorised travel on freight trains, can also be seen as a reduction of the controls on freedom of movement.

This same month[85] saw the abolition of the secret special procedure used for the trial of terrorist organisations and terrorist acts under Articles 58.8 and 58.11, which involved a trial 24 hours after the indictment had been presented to the accused, did not require the presence of the accused, and the death sentence was to be carried out immediately (this was linked to the Kirov Decree). Also, in future, military courts were to have no jurisdiction over political crimes committed by civilians, except espionage.

As well as repealing laws and so eliminating liability, many offences had their penalties lowered, indicating a lessening, but not total lack, of concern in some areas; for example, on 10 January 1955,[86] that for petty theft of state or social property was lowered to correctional labour for six months to one year, or three months' deprivation of freedom for a first offence, and one to two years' deprivation of freedom for subsequent offences — previously the basic penalty had been seven years, under the law of 1947.

On 28 April 1956[87] a new list of what was to be classified as state secrets was issued, less comprehensive than the earlier, and there were liberal changes to the Statute on Military Crimes.

Some authorities consider the decree on petty speculation of 12 September 1957[88] as introducing less harsh measures,[89] as it speaks of arrest from three to fifteen days or a fine of 500 roubles, when the previously applicable penalty had been five years' deprivation of freedom.[90] However, the decree's short preamble says its purpose is to 'intensify the struggle against petty speculation', and is to apply only when Article 107 of the Code does not, so one should conclude that the decree extends liability rather than liberalises the situation. The 1 November 1957 saw the 'Amnesty to Mark the 40th Anniversary of the Great October Revolution',[91] which aimed at

> striving to alleviate the lot of citizens who have committed crimes that do not represent a grave danger to the state and calling upon these citizens to redress, by participating in socialist construction and returning to an honest working life, the wrongs they have done Soviet society.

Persons sentenced for up to three years' deprivation of liberty, women with children up to the age of eight, pregnant women, women over 55, men over 50 and minors of 16 and under were to be freed. Other sentences were halved, and cases under investigation not involving penalties of more than three years were to be stopped. It was not to apply to offences under Section 1 of the Statute on State Crimes, certain serious offences such as malicious hooliganism, recidivists, difficult prisoners, and those who had committed offences when on early release. This typical amnesty is perhaps more careful than usual in delineating those still considered to be dangerous.

Other Trends in this Period

Many articles in newspapers and periodicals show a noticeable concern with the problem of juvenile delinquency. A review of letters sent to the editor of *Izvestiia*[92] blames the schools and the family for not exercising enough control and offering too little guidance:

> in the view of many readers, there is much formalism, stereotype and neglect of the demands and interests of the child in the

organisation and content of upbringing in the schools. We talk a great deal to children about 'what not to do'. But in our work of upbringing we have little that is positive, little presentation of interesting tasks and specific goals, attaining which would discipline the child.

Details are given of young people causing trouble at dances and meetings, often being met with little or no resistance from officials. Rostov-on-Don is criticised for having too many bars, some disguised as ordinary shops, which are becoming the haunt of young workers.

Usually the parents are blamed for anything that has happened. For example, *Literaturnaia gazeta* of 13 April 1954 carried a story of a boy whose parents, a teacher and a professor, had spoilt the child and so led him to criminal habits.[93] Another case involved children who rob on railways, the fathers blaming the militia, but are themselves, together with passers-by who saw the group and did nothing, blamed by the article.[94] Another preoccupation, not unconnected with juvenile delinquency, was with hooliganism. An article in *Komsomolskaia Pravda* of 8 June 1954[95] takes the usual tactical approach, calling the offender a 'wet hen' surrounded by a 'solid circle of young, healthy fellows with Young Communist badges'. It says numbers are small — 'one may count the hoodlums on one's fingers,' but they behave loudly and uninhibitedly, their behaviour resulting from idleness. The sentences given out for hooliganism at this time are usually five years' deprivation of liberty if drunkenness is involved;[96] three years if drunkenness is not mentioned in the report;[97] with appropriate sentences for serious cases, for example Vorobyov, who wounds two citizens when he is drunk and received 10 years' deprivation of liberty,[98] and 'trivial' cases, for example Kazankin, who receives 1 year imprisonment for wife-beating.[99]

On 19 December 1956 a decree 'On responsibility for petty hooliganism' was issued,[100] which says 'Petty hooliganism shall be punished by incarceration for a period of three to 15 days, if those acts by their nature are not subject to punishment under Art. 74 of the Russian Republic Criminal Code.' Berman[101] considers that this makes it easier for the courts to apply lighter sentences, and is therefore a liberal measure. This may appear strange, as the wording says the law is to apply only where Article 74 does not. The introductory sentence says the law is to 'intensify the struggle against petty hooliganism and in view of the fact that the law does not provide for responsibility'. It would seem, therefore, that Berman's views are based on the assumption that Article 74 was applied to cases not strictly covered by it before the introduction of the new law. However, Arkhangelsky, the vice-chairman of the RSFSR Supreme Soviet, said in an interview with *Komsomolskaia Pravda* on 21 December 1956:

> Art. 74 of the Russian Republic Criminal Code, under which hoodlums are punished by imprisonment for one to five years, could not always be applied. After all, not all crimes call for such punishment. Hence petty hooliganism was not punished before. Now it will be different.[102]

If this is so, then Berman is mistaken.

Two articles, one in Trud dated 15 December − i.e. before the decree, and one after, on 22 December, show the effect of the decree in dealing with minor cases before they could escalate into something more serious. For example, one Mikhail Baranov had insulted, beaten and humiliated his wife, but nothing was done (this being before the decree), and he succeeded in inflicting severe knife wounds on her before he was arrested.[103] In a case after the decree and reported in *Pravda* on 22 December, one Kusmin caused trouble for his wife and neighbours with his uproarious behaviour, and received a sentence of three days under arrest with labour − a minimum because of his remorse.[104]

Drunkenness, as well as leading to heavier sentences for hooliganism, was itself subjected to some appraisal. A campaign against drinking began in the press in July 1954. Cases were given of families which were broken up and where children suffered. It was recognised as a serious problem, and a remnant of the past − 'Drunkenness is an evil. And against it, as against any other evil, which is still among us as a remnant of the blighted past, our whole society must struggle steadfastly and with determination.'[105] Any suggestion that it is a hereditary disease is totally rejected,[106] and an article in *Komsomolskaia Pravda* of 6 July 1954[107] blames the suggestions of drinking that occur in plays, advertisements, etc. Kurashov, the USSR Deputy Minister for Health, says, 'In capitalist society alcoholism and poverty are the result of social inequality and cruel exploitation of the working people.' Obviously this cannot apply to the Soviet state, and he then makes the startling suggestion that 'It is well-known that the enemy intelligence service makes extensive use of alcohol for its crafty ends by recruiting spies and traitors from among those who are morally degenerate and drink' and 'that is why the struggle against alcoholism concerns the vital interests of the state'.

The campaign continued for a considerable length of time, another group of articles appearing in October of the following year,[108] and clearly shows the concern felt over a serious problem in Soviet society. The safeguarding of socialist property had one of its periodic emphases in and around 1955. Krylotykh[109] wrote of the 'necessity for the strictest safeguarding of socialist property from thieves and pilferers' and thought: 'those who would harm the interests of socialist society by pilfering the national wealth are enemies of the people and must be severely punished.' The law of 4 June 1947 is referred to with approval, and, in accordance with the usual practice of confusing circumstances with reasons, the lack of suitable accounting procedures and protection of state property is said to be 'the principal reason for pilfering' — surely more of a prerequisite than a reason.

Bezuglov[110] refers to the need to strengthen socialist property, as together with the socialist economic system, it is the 'economic foundation' of the USSR. A connection is again held to exist between poor accounting and theft, but 'survivals of the past' are here the accepted cause of the acts. Sentences given for theft of socialist property are proportional to the loss suffered. Rarmik, a head book-keeper, steals 27,000 roubles, and receives 10 years in a corrective labour camp and an order to restore the money.[111] Alimov, the manager of a meat warehouse, steals 20,000 roubles' worth of meat and is generally neglectful of his duties, and gets 10 years plus confiscation of property.[112] A similar sentence applies to Potysyev, in a case involving 33,721 roubles.[113] Heifetz finds himself short of 25,000 roubles of a sum given to him for the purchase of agricultural produce, and receives 12 years plus confiscation of property and five years' loss of civil rights, after covering up leads to losses of 74,000 roubles.[114] In a case involving two 'cashier accountants', the one embezzling 57,000 roubles receives 15 years, the other, embezzling 4,000 roubles, 5 years' deprivation of liberty. Both received 5 years' subsequent loss of civil rights.[115] In a serious case involving the loss of 'hundreds of thousands of roubles' from a Military Wholesale Trust at Kiev, the ringleader got 20 years, and the others 18, 15 and 10 years, all with confiscation and subsequent loss of rights.[116]

The New Fundamental Principles

Article 14(u) of the Stalin Constitution had said that 'Legislation governing the judicial system and judicial procedure; criminal and civil' were to be issued by the USSR authorities. However, on 11 February 1957, a constitutional amendment made the individual union republics responsible for the issuing of these codes, with the federal authorities drawing up Fundamental Principles that would apply to all the codes issued.[117] This decision was part of a decentralising movement which involved strengthening the rights of the republics, and placing more authority in local hands. The production of All-Union codes had been made insuperably difficult by the unusual activities that had taken place since and during the 1930s, but the 1924 Principles, which were federal, were still in force, so the new decree actually retained the *status quo*. The overall scheme of the Principles does not greatly differ from that of the earlier ones. Romashkin,[118] in a contemporary article, said that they should 'include such provisions of general criminal law. . .and the basic principles of fixing penalties and of lifting them'. They should not include 'detailed descriptions of individual types of punishment, the question of measures of a medical or medical and educational character or certain other details contained in the existing basic principles'. Romashkin thinks the material concept of crime should still be the basis of the Principles, with all the emphasis on social danger that this entails, but adds, 'It is necessary to proceed strictly from the principle that without guilt there is no crime and no punishment,' and that 'a person is criminally responsible only when he has been found guilty of committing a socially dangerous act, deliberately or through negligence'.

The Principles will, therefore, be recognisably similar to those before, but the formal additions to their material basis introduce certain safeguards which either were felt to be necessary, or were allowed to be so felt.

The Principles were adopted by the Supreme Soviet on 25 December 1958,[119] after being issued in draft form in May of that year to facilitate debate. They had been promised for the year before, but the delay, and that involved in the issuing of the RSFSR Code, may well have been due to changes that had to be made to any All-Union Codes that may have been ready, or almost so, before the decentralisation move invoked alterations. Article 1 says the task of criminal legislation is to guard 'the soviet social and state system, socialist property, the person and rights of citizens and the whole of the socialist legal order from criminal infringements'. This is very similar to previous corresponding definitions, but the article continues to say that the criminal legislation decides 'which socially dangerous acts are criminal' and on the relevant punishments to be imposed. This reference to formal matters is an early indication of the differing approach to be followed in these Principles. Article 7 contains the highly interesting definition of crime:

> By a crime is meant a socially dangerous act (action or omission) provided for by criminal law, which encroaches on the soviet social or state system, the socialist economic system, socialist property, the person, political, work, property and other rights of citizens, and also any other socially dangerous act provided for by criminal law.[120]

When one considers all that has been said about the material definition of crime by Soviet writers, one cannot but conclude that this is a most significant change. Previously, the whole basis of the criminality of an act and whether it attracted any penalty depended on whether or not it was 'socially dangerous'. This concept was by its very nature somewhat imprecise, but a guide was given in the various codes by the article(s) setting out the purposes and protected interests. These were similar to Article 1 of these Principles.

Now, social danger is still of importance as without it an act is not a crime – the final part of Article 7 says that it will not be so if because of its 'insignificance' an act is not socially dangerous. Also, it is taken into account in deciding the measure of punishment to be applied,[121] and if through a change of circumstances the person or the act has lost its socially dangerous nature by the time of its investigation or trial, then the person will be relieved of criminal responsibility.[122]

Theoretically, of course, this has been the usual previous practice, and the present change is important in that under the new Principles this is the only way in which the social danger acts. It is now no longer possible to commit a crime on the sole grounds that the particular act is socially dangerous: it must be covered by a criminal law as well. Historically, this is the antithesis of early practice when laws and codes were considered unnecessary and disparaged – an approach which reached its apogee in the Krylenko-Pashukanis codes of 1930. There the whole essence was to avoid the use of definitions and a Special Part, and rely on social danger and the revolutionary (or socialist) consciousness to decide on criminality and punishability.

Considering the development of Soviet law since the Revolution, one cannot be too surprised that this has occurred, as law has become more accepted in the ideology and supposedly the society has been moving towards becoming one governed by the rule of law. It therefore seems almost to be expected that this change would occur. The formal approach is strengthened by Article 3, which states that:

Only a person guilty of committing a crime, that is, committing
intentionally or with negligence a socially dangerous act made an
offence by criminal law, is liable to criminal responsibility and
punishment. Criminal punishment is only applied by sentence of a
court.

Three points could be noted: (i) one has to commit a crime before
punishment applies so for example banishment for being part of a
criminal environment cannot apply in future; (ii) the elements of intent
and negligence are used, unlike the draft[123] of the Principles which
referred to 'an act containing the elements of a crime'; and (iii) only
courts can apply criminal punishment (but not administrative penalties).
Retroactivity was dealt with in Article 6, which says laws making
actions punishable or increasing penalties are not retroactive, but those
reducing penalties or removing them altogether were. Other noteworthy
points include: (i) the age of criminal responsibility was raised to 16,
14 for more serious crimes; (ii) participation had to be committed
'intentionally and jointly', while previously it could be done negligently;
(iii) deprivation of political and civil rights, banishment from the USSR
and being declared an enemy of the working people were no longer
included in the list of possible punishments; (iv) the death penalty, not
applicable to under-18s or pregnant women, is still considered to be
'exceptional' measure; and (v) deprivation of liberty was reduced from
a maximum of 25 years to 15 (10 for less serious crimes), but the
concept of an 'especially dangerous recidivist' was introduced and this
attracted the heavier limit.[124]

Section 20 set out the aims of punishment as

> not only retribution for a committed crime, but also has the aim of
> correction and re-education of the convicted in a spirit of an honest
> attitude to labour, the precise fulfilment of laws, and also the
> prevention of the commission of new crimes by those convicted
> and by others. Punishment does not have the aim of causing physical
> suffering or humiliation of human dignity.

This is the usual mixture of aims that one has now come to expect, very
different from early formulae with their strong emphasis on
re-education. Also, the list of protected interests has become more
detailed and state-orientated, with the observance of law playing a
prominent part.

Article 33, listing the mitigating circumstances, has dropped any reference to harm causing danger to the state and regime, as does the list of aggravating factors in Section 34. Whether this change has much effect in practice is questionable, as the wide definitions abounding in the law allow an unusual degree of flexibility, but the change may be significant. Consideration of the Principles cannot be completed without reference to the lack of an article on analogy. There is no specific rejection of it, this being implied by Sections 3, 6 and 7. Romashkin[125] rather mysteriously says that the exclusion of analogy and the inclusion of an exhaustive list of crimes would 'fully accord with the socialist nature of Soviet criminal law', in answer to which one can only say that this was not always thought to be the case. One must not overlook the fact that this principle of analogy is not as important as at first may be thought, for the wide definitions in themselves allow for considerable flexibility and reliance on analogy would not be so necessary. However, the formalisation of the law and the exclusion of the analogy provision do perhaps show a change of thought – although this could be more external than internal, one of theoretical rather than practical importance.

The Fundamental Principles introduce some important changes into the law and its practice, and in many ways could be considered as 'liberal'. In some respects, particularly in the protected interests, purposes of punishment, and the more formal approach in the definition and elsewhere, they are a move away from the earlier 'revolutionary approach' to law, with more stability and certainty introduced. One should not overlook the new emphasis on personal rights and freedoms, but the best guarantee of these is not the provisions in themselves, which can always be circumnavigated, but the change of attitude that supposedly lies behind them.

The Law on State Crimes[126]

This law, together with the Fundamental Principles of Criminal Legislation, of Procedure, the Law on Military Crimes, and other laws of lesser importance, was passed at the December 1958 session of the USSR Supreme Soviet.

This new law on state crimes does not use the term 'counter-revolutionary crime', but divides itself into two parts, entitled 'especially dangerous state crimes' and 'other state crimes'. A noticeable feature of the law is the increased precision used in the definitions, but one has to remember that this in itself would not be difficult, as the previous practice was to use the widest of formulations.

Polyansky, the Chairman of the Legislative Proposals Committee of the Council of the Union, reported that the new law was needed because

> some of the provisions in existing legislation have become outdated and therefore lost their practical value; others need clarification because they are not precise and clear enough; still others, because of their nature in present-day conditions, should be excluded from the catalogue of state crimes.[127]

The 'changed situation', not a particularly helpful concept, and increased certainty then, are the main reasons for the change. There are still phrases which are reminiscent of the old approach; for example, Article 5 defines sabotage as various acts committed 'for the purposes of weakening the Soviet state', and 'wrecking' is used in Article 6. The definition of anti-Soviet agitation and propaganda has an imprecise – 'for the purpose of undermining or weakening Soviet rule' – and precise part – 'or of committing especially dangerous state crimes'. Article 1 increases the penalty for treason from death or ten years' deprivation of liberty to death or fifteen years, but according to the 1934 law, treason could be 'any act' while now it had to be 'an act committed deliberately'. Divulging a state secret was not to be considered as treason unless it was passed to a foreign state, and Article 12 indicates that in the absence of treasonable intent, the crime can now only be committed by 'a person who was entrusted with this information or who gained it in his official capacity or work', while previously it could be committed by anyone.

A terrorist act, which had previously come to mean any violent act against an official or close relative, was now defined as the murder or severe bodily injury of 'a state or public figure or government representative committed in connection with his state or public activity for the purpose of undermining or weakening Soviet rule' (Art. 3). Article 4 extended this to similar acts against the representative of a foreign state 'for the purpose of provoking war or international complications'.

Again, as is so often the case with these new important laws, 'revolutionary' definitions were dropped. For example, rendering assistance to that 'portion of the international bourgeoisie which, not recognising the equal rights of the communist system which is replacing capitalism' etc. was replaced by the more prosaic 'helping a foreign state

to carry on hostile activity against the U.S.S.R.' (Art. 1). The concept
of counter-revolutionary sabotage was eliminated in name, but the
relevant penalty was raised from death or not less than one year's
deprivation of liberty to death or from eight to fifteen years.

The most noticeable aspect of this decree, later to become the first
chapter of the Special Part of the RSFSR Code, is the aforementioned
increased certainty of definition, a move away from 'revolutionary'
terminology, and in some cases increased penalties. This was not such a
liberal decree as many others of the period, which should not be
surprising when one considers its subject-matter.

The Anti-Parasite Laws

The discussions that led up to these laws and the laws themselves are
of importance in legal development, as they indicate the attitudes
prevalent to crime and vagrancy − attitudes that usually reflect
intolerance and annoyance, as well as raising questions of increased
social control in a more general sense. The implementation of those
decrees occurred in two stages, one in 1957 involving the smaller
republics, and the other in 1961 for the major republics.

As to the former, the draft law[128] for the Azerbaidzhan Republic
began with a long preamble stressing the importance and virtues of
work, 'the fundamental source of the Soviet state's might and of the
steady growth in the well-being of the masses', and adds:

> there are still people who lead an antisocial, parasitic way of life.
> Such persons either find jobs for appearances' sake, while actually
> living on unearned income and enriching themselves at the expense
> of the working people, or, although able-bodied, do not perform
> any useful work either in society or in the family, but are vagrants
> or beggars and often engage in crime.

Such people are thoroughly condemned, even Lenin is invoked against
them, and the decree allows exile for from two to five years with work,
to be awarded by general meetings of the majority of adult citizens in
the street, apartment block, village, etc. Warnings can be given as an
alternative to exile. The subjects of the crime are not closely defined −
'adult, able-bodied citizens leading an antisocial, parasitic way of life,
deliberately avoiding socially useful labour, and likewise those living on
unearned income'. Article 4 says that 'adult, able-bodied citizens

engaging in vagrancy or begging are subject to sentence by a people's court to exile for a term from two to five years, with obligatory engagement in work at the place of exile'.

The debate surrounding the decrees was an event of some importance, with many readers' letters printed in the various periodicals, usually supporting the introduction of the law and giving examples of person(s) they knew to be parasitic. Often they speak of persons who queue to buy more goods than they require, with a view to resale.[129] In any case, the campaign had an effect. Beermann reports:[130]

> In his speech on the law at the Supreme Soviet of the Uzbek SSR the chairman of the drafting commission stated that in the month between publication of the draft and the session of the Supreme Soviet, in the Sredne-Chirchik raion the number of people active in kolkhoz production had risen from 7066 to 8078; in the Tashkent oblast a thousand applications for employment had been received in twenty days of this period.

However, many attacks were made on the laws. Bolshakov[131] complained that the concepts of 'antisocial' and 'parasitic' acts were too broad; that the basis for liability seems to be suspicion rather than proof; and that there is no right of appeal. Sevlikiants[132] says there is doubt as to who would be liable under the decree, as it would seem to apply to persons who work normally but do other work in their spare time. Also, the meetings which decide the cases could be influenced by minorities, but one should mention that Soviet executive committees at the appropriate levels are to check all the sentences involving exile, so some measures of uniformity and control may be possible. Other suggestions include using comrades' courts rather than meetings to decide the cases,[133] or allowing the local Soviet executive committees to sentence the offenders.[134] These suggestions and criticisms provoked their own ripostes, and debate does seem to have been widespread. Indeed Beermann[135] reports that:

> In Kirgizia, which has a population of 2.1 million, some 200,000 persons are said to have attended meetings on the draft law and 326 suggestions were sent to the newspapers and the legislative commission, while the press published 300 letters and articles on the subject.

One should particularly note a fundamental criticism made by

Arenberg[136] *et al.* that a penalty is being applied when perhaps a
definite crime has not been committed, which is a deviation from the
usual practice that has prevailed from the 1940s.

The Georgian decree 'On Intensifying the Struggle against Antisocial,
Parasitic Elements' was adopted on 5 September 1960[137] and
established that

> able-bodied citizens of full legal age living in cities and urban
> settlements of the Georgian Republic who are deliberately avoiding
> socially useful work and are leading an antisocial, parasitic way of
> life may be banished for a period of six months to two years upon
> decision of the appropriate Soviet executive committees on the basis
> of petitions of general meetings of citizens, public organisations or
> offices of the militia.

Work at the place of exile was required, and the decree was
implemented

> with a view to further strengthening the safeguarding of public order
> and enlisting in work persons who deliberately avoid participation
> in socially useful labour, and taking into account the numerous
> proposals and wishes of citizens and public organisations concerning
> the necessity of intensifying the struggle against antisocial, parasitic
> elements.

Many distinctive elements are exhibited by this decree: working is not
enough in itself, it must be 'socially useful work'; the public are
involved, but now in an instigatory capacity; the problem of parasitism
is basically urban, which is understandable as the opportunities would
be greater for the would-be parasite; and these decrees are part of a
popular movement to uphold or strengthen legality, in the sense of
conformity with the accepted social ways of living. The increased
importance of the role of the executive committee in the proceedings
reflects the great concern centred on the power of the public meetings
in the earlier decrees (this was one of the last of the first group of
republics to issue this legislation). It had been felt that a lack of trained
personnel at that stage would produce an unacceptable number of
unsound conclusions, and this was especially problematic as there was
no right of appeal.

On 4 May 1961[138] the RSFSR introduced its decree, and this
instituted the introduction of the second group of these decrees. The

RSFSR decree, 'On Intensifying the Struggle Against Persons who Avoid Socially Useful Work and Lead an Antisocial, Parasitic Way of Life', had a sizeable preamble that spoke of the 'full-scale building of communism', towards which most citizens were 'working with enthusiasm', but 'there are still individuals who are stubbornly opposed to honest work'. It was a problem in both rural and urban areas, involving those who 'hold jobs for appearances' sake while in actual fact living on unearned income and enriching themselves at the expense of the state and the working people'; and those who

> although able-bodied. . .may hold no job at all but engage in forbidden businesses, private enterprise, speculation and begging, derive unearned income from the exploitation of personal automobiles, employ hired labour and obtain unearned income from dacha and land plots, build houses and dachas with funds obtained by non-labour means and using illegally acquired building materials, and commit other antisocial acts.

In the particular context of collective farms, home-brewing and undermining labour discipline are mentioned, and in most cases drunkenness is said to accompany parasitism. For those who do not have a job of work, the penalty is

> on order of a district (or city) people's court, to deportation to specially designated localities for a period of from two to five years, with confiscation of the property acquired by non-labour means, and to mandatory enlistment in work at the place of deportation.

Those who had taken jobs but were still parasitic are subject to the same measures, prescribed as before, or 'by the working people's collective of an enterprise, shop, institution, organisation, collective farm or collective farm brigade'. The measures were to apply after a warning had been given by a public organisation or a state agency, and were not subject to appeal. The exposure of the persons and the verification of the relevant circumstances were to be carried out by the militia and procuracy.

This decree is more descriptive than the Georgian, but the list of prescribed activities is not definite, being more of an illustrative nature, and there is still a high degree of subjectivity in the application of this decree. It could be noted that the drafts of the law did not contain such a detailed list of possible offences in their preambles, with the change due to criticisms made during the debates. At this time, there was great interest in combating the effects of alcohol and the Ukrainian and Estonian anti-parasite laws, passed at the same time as the Russian, act more specifically in this direction, the 'systematic use of drink' being a sign or constituent of parasitism.

Beermann[139] makes the interesting point, easily overlooked, that the type of behaviour prohibited by these decrees was already prohibited by the Code, but that a 'law is enforcible only if it is acceptable to the prevailing ethical code of a society at large. One way of making the new rules and laws acceptable is to let the population participate in their inception and enforcement', hence their reintroduction.

Morgan[140] gives a useful collection of cases on the subject, including that of a young Moscow mother who had 'transformed her apartment into a place for constant drunken gatherings', and on the demand of the residents of the apartment block and the children's clinic, a court deprived her of the rights of parenthood and exiled her from Moscow for three years (*Moskovskaia Pravda,* 11 June 1961); one Ignatov, who by illegally enlarging his agricultural plot, made a fortune in fruit and vegetables, which led to five years' exile in 'a specially designated place' and confiscation of his property (*Leninskoe Znamia,* 12 July 1961); and finally, Nerodin and wife had had proceedings instituted against them three times for violations of public order, and now received exile for four years (*Leninskoe Znamia,* 19 August 1961).

As the measures taken against offenders are classed as administrative, the safeguards of the Code of Criminal Procedure did not automatically apply. However, in September 1961[141] the USSR Supreme Court issued a decree criticising irregularities in the procedure used, such as the use of closed sessions of the court and the use of anti-parasite legislation when the ordinary law should have been used. Directives against these actions were issued, and the educational aspects of the law were emphasised.

It has been stated that the formulations used in these laws allow them to be used against a wide spectrum of behaviour. An important example of misuse is the case of Joseph Brodsky,[142] a Leningrad poet whose poetry led to a sentence of five years' exile in Arkhangelsk. Sentenced in March 1964, he worked as an agricultural labourer until September 1965, when he was released, perhaps in answer to the revisions to the 1961 decree that took place in that month.

The amended decree[143] differed from the original in many respects. The preamble had dropped references to specific modes of life and simply spoke of 'individuals who stubbornly refuse to work honestly, who lead an antisocial, parasitic way of life'. Generally, the penalty of exile was replaced by 'mandatory enlistment in socially useful work at enterprises (or construction projects) situated in the district where they reside permanently or in other places within the given province, territory or autonomous republic'. The older penalty of two to five years' exile remained for residents of Moscow, Moscow Province and Leningrad.

The warning by the militia or public organisation still applied, as did the role of the militia in verifying the circumstances of the case. The People's Court dealt with cases of exile, the executive committee of the local Soviet with the mandatory enlistments. The public had no role except in the initial declaration to the militia on the existence of a possible parasite. Non-compliance with these penalties could result in application of relevant articles of the Code. These changes stopped any possibility of the anti-parasite legislation being used in preference to the Code in an attempt to avoid the safeguards offered by the Code of Criminal Procedure, which could be less equitable than normal court practice; and took note of the serious problems that had arisen in the localities that had previously had to receive the exiles, for now they were to stay at home (except in Moscow, etc.). The month's warning that now had to be given was not entirely new, but the procedure had been clarified, as irregularities had previously given rise to complaints.

On 25 February 1970, two decrees of interest were issued. The first[144] amended the parasite decree yet again, the major change being an acceleration of the sequence of events by shortening time limits – for example, the previous month's warning was now to be fifteen days. The other[145] introduced Article 209-1 into the RSFSR Code, applying a penalty of up to one year's deprivation of liberty or correctional labour for 'malicious avoidance' by a person of the job placement decree of the executive committee of the local soviet, and so changing parasitism from an administrative to a criminal offence. A repeated offence was to lead to up to two years' deprivation of liberty, and 'systematic participation in vagrancy or begging' was given on a first offence from six months' to one year's corrective labour, and for a repeated offence up to four years' deprivation of liberty – previously, under the decree of 25 July 1962, the penalties had been corrective labour for six months to one year, or deprivation of liberty for not more than two years, after a warning by the administrative organs. The obvious connection between these two offences was emphasised by the decree of 7 August 1975[146] which referred to 'systematic vagrancy or begging or other chronic parasitic styles of life' and awarded penalties of up to one year's deprivation of liberty or corrective labour for a first offence, and up to two years of the former for a repeated one.

In concluding exactly why it was felt necessary to use these decrees in emphasising conformity in society, a useful overview of the history of such legislation in prerevolutionary Russia is offered by Beermann.[147] He points out that decrees as early as 1663, 1760 and 1765 allowed administrative deportation for a variety of persons, for example 'girls and widows of idle and indecent behaviour'. Their somewhat dubious nature was recognised by some, and perhaps only the opposition of the landowners stopped their abolition in Alexander II's reforms. In 1900, a law limiting the grounds for deportation was introduced, and the implementation of the law was tightened up, for example the decision to apply deportation by the village community had to be by a majority in a two-thirds quorum. Comparing the pre- and post-revolutionary practice, Beermann says:

> The relevant point is that a law unpopular among the more liberal sections of society has been able to survive and has reappeared at times when social insecurity was mounting due to the onset of the industrial revolution, to the emancipation of the serfs, to the post-revolutionary upheavals and now after destalinisation.[148]

The measures are always termed 'preventative' and this in itself reflects the anxiety caused by a 'maladjusted' minority for the majority. However, by 'majority' we may really mean that group which says it represents the majority, and the anxiety may be caused by any feelings the group has that its rule may be threatened. A group that attempts to control all or most aspects of social behaviour will be more susceptible to such anxiety. Certainly the use of the laws in contemporary Soviet society is not so surprising, for although a more liberal outlook is now usual, the method and effect of the laws do not conflict with the general practice. Juviler[149] believes that

> Khrushchev was attempting to instill a socialist work ethic and force all available people power into the planned, controlled socialist sector of the economy at the same time. Ideological-moral ends seemed inseparable from more practical ends of social discipline and mobilisation.

Berman[150] says it is part of 'the Soviet conception that it is a primary function of law to help form the character of the people, including their consciousness of their legal and moral obligation to society', and is in accord with the Russian tradition of collective responsibility for individual wrongdoing. Fainsod[151] summarises this type of law's use by saying

> The Khrushchevian desire for political homogeneity seeks to mobilize the forces and pressures of social coercion as a supplement to and substitute for police coercion. The revival of comrades' courts, the antiparasite laws with their dependence on neighborhood assemblies to identify and exile persons not engaged in socially useful labor, and the use of voluntary people's detachments (*druzhiny*) to aid the militia in maintaining public order represent Khrushchev's effort to enlist the energies of the 'activists' in Soviet society in a major campaign to eliminate drunkenness and hooliganism, speculation and idleness, imitation of Western dress, and all deviant varieties of social behavior which Soviet ideologists lump together as the survivals of capitalism in the consciousness of Soviet man.

In conclusion, it would seem that although these laws cause some unease amongst Western observers, and for that matter among some Soviet authors too, the basic fact of their use should cause little surprise. Fundamentally, they are to be used to enforce a certain degree of conformity on members of society. In any society a balance has to be drawn between allowing suitable variations in behaviour — for the needs of different individuals, and their qualities, vary so very much, and yet to stop those actions that if allowed to go unchallenged would in some way harm others. In Soviet society the line is likely to be far nearer the side of conformity than that of a Western society, as the goal of the former is supposedly more definite, more distinct. If the society knows, or feels it knows, what it wants to achieve, then any actions which it decides are detrimental to that aim can be prohibited. The ideology of the Soviet Union offers this, and has been one of the reasons for the altogether more controlled society existing there. The use of these laws, the grounds for action under which are unusual,[152] is an attempt to mould the attitudes of the population, bringing their attitudes into line with those of the regime, as Berman says, 'to lessen the distance between official law and unofficial law-consciousness'.[153] This is particularly noticeable in the introduction of the decrees and the surrounding debates, as these amounted to a reintroduction; and in the use made of social rather than judicial agencies to implement the decrees. The fact that this latter practice was found to be unsuitable is

more probably due to the advantages of a well run court system rather
than to any particular drawbacks in the Soviet situation. It is generally
held that the measures used are administrative rather than penal,
because the offences are not crimes, the measures are not applied by
courts, there are no criminal records, and the conditions for early
release are different from those used in the case of crimes. Berman[154]
feels they are different from administrative penalties in that no specific
act is prohibited, the measure of resettlement is more severe than an
administrative penalty and escape is a crime, and the Code applies if
parasites refuse to work at the place of banishment. It may be as well
to conclude that they differ from both of these, and could be classified
as 'measures of social pressure'.

The image projected by these decrees is that although certain types
of petty criminal would be successfully dealt with, generally the
prohibited behaviour was not so much criminal as unacceptable.
However, this is not to say that the anti-parasite laws are comparable to
the previous methods of illegal pressure, for although they may be in
some way basically similar, the difference of quantity is such that it
amounts to one of quality.

Events before the 1960 RSFSR Code

A decree [155] of 29 January 1960 lowered the penalties for the illicit
manufacture and possession of alcohol to correctional labour for three
months to one year with confiscation of property (previously, it had
been one to two years' correctional labour under a decree of 7 April
1948[156]). The decree did not deal with sales of alcohol, so the heavy
penalties of six to seven years' correctional labour, applied by the 1948
decree, still applied; and measures of public influence are
characteristically emphasised – first offences are to be considered
before meetings of workers, employees or collective farmers. It is
somewhat amusing to read that the primary reason given for the
adoption of this decree is not the delinquency caused, or damage to
health, but the ensuing waste of sugar, grain and other agricultural
products used in the manufacture of the alcohol.

In an interesting decree of 2 March 1959, 'On Participation by the
Working People in Safeguarding Public Order',[157] the USSR Council of
Ministers and the Party Central Committee gave the public a greater role
to play in crime control. The joint authorship of this particular decree is
rather unusual, and is not an arrangement provided for in the

Constitution, but can be used, it seems, for basic policy statements that are to affect future legislation. The decree makes the usual statements on the great achievements made, the decline in crime and the strengthening of legality, but then adds that violations do occur and individuals as well as agencies should be involved in trying to deal with these offences. 'Voluntary people's detachments' are to be formed from workers, collective farmers, students, etc., and will be directed by a district headquarters, drawn up from Party and Soviet agencies, detachments commanders, and trade union representatives. State and local agencies, for example the procuracy, are to conduct public hearings, involve the public in the movement, and assist the detachments.

The newspaper report[158] of the decree states that 'The main functions of the detachments will be to safeguard public order, combat hooliganism and participate in the explanatory work carried on by public organisations among the people for observance of the rules of socialist society.' The detachments are to be guided by the 'requirements of Soviet laws' and their practical duties will include 'defending the honour and dignity of citizens, taking the necessary measures to stop violations of public order and restraining violations, primarily through persuasion and warning.'

The Supreme Court Plenum adopted various decrees related to the implementation of this policy, one of which commences with statistics that show the effect of the legislation:

> in the first nine months of 1959 there was a general decrease in the number of persons sentenced for criminal acts compared with the same period in 1958; convictions for hooliganism dropped 10.9%, for petty theft of state property 19.2% and for theft of private property of citizens 19.7%.[159]

Although courts are using a more diversified approach, heavy sentences are still being occasionally applied to first offences of a petty nature, and many courts have not established close ties with the public and explained their work. Too much emphasis on deprivation of liberty 'even in cases where the individual who has committed a violation of law can be put on the path of reform without isolating him from society' is 'intolerable'. The earlier resolution, 'On the Application of Measures of Criminal Punishment by the Courts',[160] with its references to the individualisation of punishment and de-emphasis on the use of deprivation of liberty, was not being implemented. The courts are recommended to explain their work to the public and more fully involve them in the campaign.

The 1960 RSFSR Criminal Code

Drafts of this Code appeared in 1959, some of which were issued only a short time after the Fundamental Principles, and as one cannot see any real possibility that codes could have been drawn up *ab initio* in so short a time, the belief that these drafts may have been reworked older versions gains credence. It may seem surprising that the Uzbek and Kazakh Republics brought out their Codes before the RSFSR, but Feldbrugge[161] believes the greater degree of central control exercised by the central authorities over the Russian Republic may be of significance; and one should also remember that the public participation campaign would cause delays. Feldbrugge does not think that a prototype code was circulated to the republics, with a view to making each of them accept it with suitable and necessary changes. Uniformity would be guaranteed by the widespread discussion that took place, the inter-republican conferences on codification that were held in 1959, and by the existence of superior federal law affecting the general part, military and state crimes. The General Part of the Code was of course closely derived from the Fundamental Principles, but there are certain differences. Article 24 of the Code defines in detail the concept of an 'especially dangerous recidivist', and the list of possible penalties in Article 21 adds two more to those available, 'dismissal from office' and 'imposition of duty to make amends for harm caused'. Article 38, listing the possible mitigating factors, specifically mentions 'Commission of a crime for the first time, as a result of the fortuitous concurrence of circumstances, if such crime does not represent a great social danger'. Added aggravating factors (Art. 39) are intentional false denunciations, drunkenness, breaking surety regulations, and acting against a dependant. The public discussions prior to the adoption of the Code had an effect on the importance attached to comrades' courts, with Article 51 allowing relief from criminal liability in minor cases, and Article 62 allowing them to deal with certain situations involving alcohol or drug addiction. Public discussion also had an effect on the increased importance attached to conditional sentences. Regarding the General Part, one should finally mention the addition of an entirely new chapter — 'Compulsory Measures of a Medical and Educational Character', applying to the mentally ill, alcoholics and drug addicts, and minors.

The Special Part[162]

Chapter One, 'Crimes Against the State', is derived from the federal legislation, which has already been considered. Compared to the 1926 Code, this is more lenient, with the maximum sentence of deprivation of liberty reduced from 25 to 15 years, social organisations induced to deal with minor offences, minimum sentences tending to disappear, and while 'recidivists' get heavier sentences, penalties are generally lighter. For example, the basic penalty for stealing state property falls from seven to ten years, to three months to three years (Art. 89), with various technical differences between theft, open stealing, assault with intent to rob; and degrees of guilt, all of which had been obscured by the 1932 and 1947 laws, were reintroduced. Article 144 reduced the basic penalty for theft of personal property from five to six years under the law of 1947 to up to two years, but recidivists were to receive up to ten years.

The concept of economic crimes was retained, but penalties were generally reduced, as were those relating to administrative and official crimes. In this last-mentioned chapter, an important change was made limiting the subject of an official crime. Previously, an official was

> any person occupying a permanent or temporary post in any state (Soviet) institution or enterprise, or in any organisation or association entrusted by law with definite duties, rights or powers for the execution of any economic, administrative, trade-union or other public task

– a very wide category. Now, according to Article 170, the places of work are still varied, but the person must be 'exercising functions of representatives of authority' or 'occupying offices. . .which are connected with fulfillment of organisational-executive duties or administrative-economic duties'.

Hooliganism (Art. 206) was basically defined as before, but now had three categories, each with its own penalties – petty hooliganism, with correctional tasks or a fine; hooliganism, with deprivation of freedom up to one year; and malicious hooliganism, with deprivation of liberty for up to five years. Before, since 1940, the penalty had been imprisonment for one year.

In this code, there is a significantly greater emphasis attached to personal rights. Chapter Four, 'Crimes Against Political and Labour

Rights of Citizens', included the offences of obstructing the right to vote, equal rights for women, secrecy of correspondence, and upheld the inviolability of the home. Article 151 protects the property of 'associations not constituting socialist organisations', with the penalties in Chapter Five, resulting in this type of property being treated as personal, not socialist, and so incurring the more lenient penalties for its violation. As has been stated, apart from recidivists, the applicable penalties in this code were generally decreased, but some were increased, such as those in Article 102, in which the circumstances that aggravated intentional homicide were also widened. The basis of the liability for not helping a person in danger of death (Art. 127) was widened from persons obligated to care for the person to include anyone who could help without endangering himself or others, or if he did not inform the appropriate authorities. Failure to report a crime, previously covering certain state crimes and assault with intent to rob, was extended by Article 190 to cover a very wide category of crimes. As a final point, one could note the chapter order in this Code, as that is usually taken to indicate the relative importance attached to the types of crime contained in each chapter. The 1926 Code had ten chapters to the Special Part, the 1960, twelve. 'Personal Property of Citizens', 'Crime Against Justice' and 'Political and Labour Rights of Citizens' had been added, this last chapter incorporating the church-state relationship, which was, in the 1926 Code, covered in a separate chapter.

In the new Code, three chapters were demoted: 'Crimes Against the System of Administration' went from second to ninth; 'Official Crimes' from third to seventh; and 'Economic Crimes' from fifth to sixth. Promoted was 'Crimes Against the Person', which went from sixth to third; and the newly added chapters, mentioned above, came fifth, eighth and fourth, respectively.

This rearrangement suggests the new importance attached to personal, *vis-à-vis* state, rights, but one should not overlook that 'Crimes Against the State' are still in first position.

In conclusion, one can say that this Code had a generally more liberal approach to crime than was the previous practice, with many penalties lowered, definitions restricted and required levels of intent, etc., raised. However, some areas, notably the important general area of hooliganism, were treated more severely. The General Part was, with a few changes, derived from the Fundamental Principles and so contained little of further interest, apart perhaps from the use made of comrades' courts. It is true to say that there is a greater emphasis on individual rights in the Code, with the overall impression that the post-

Stalin reforms have had their effect.

Developments after the 1960 Code

As would seem to be usual after the adoption of an RSFSR Criminal
Code, many changes were introduced in the period following its
introduction. Generally, the changes introduced new crimes or increased
penalties, and indicated a more severe attitude to crime on the part of
the regime, but there were lenient measures, and some directed at
improving the workings of the law. On 20 January 1961, a decree[163]
concerned with the introduction of the new laws dealt with offences
under the old, and as would be expected, said that offenders convicted
of actions not considered as criminal under the Code were to be freed,
and similar cases in progress were to be dismissed. Penalties were to be
reduced to the new levels in all cases except for certain serious offences
such as those especially dangerous to the state, banditry, aggravated
premeditated murder, large-scale theft of socialist property, robbery,
and those involving especially dangerous recidivists.

This familiar attitude is reinforced by the decree[164] of 5 May 1961,
'On Intensifying the Struggle against Especially Dangerous Criminals,'
which considerably widened the possible application of capital
punishment to include

> cases of high treason; espionage; sabotage; terrorist acts; banditry;
> making for the purpose of issuing, or issuing, counterfeit money
> and securities, conducted as a business; premeditated murder under
> aggravating circumstances. . .and the pilfering of state or public
> property in especially large amounts.

Other crimes were to be so treated in time of war. Those convicted of
such serious offences, and habitual offenders, were not to be considered
for parole or remission, and if they terrorised or attacked other
prisoners or the administration at places of detention, they were to be
penalised by eight to fifteen years' deprivation of freedom or death. The
increased use of the death penalty in this decree – a penalty still said to
be used 'pending its complete abolition' – is the precursor of later
decrees introducing the death penalty for violating currency regulations
and for speculation in foreign currency or banknotes conducted as a
business or in large amounts, as well as for violation of the regulations
on foreign currency operations by a person convicted of such crimes;[165]

attempts on the life of a militiaman or people's volunteer if accompanied by aggravating circumstances;[166] rape when committed by a group, an especially dangerous recidivist, committed on a minor, or involving especially grave consequences;[167] and for bribery involving 'an official person occupying a responsible position, or one who has been previously tried for bribery or has taken bribes repeatedly, or if accompanied by extortion of a bribe with especially aggravating circumstances'.[168] The decree starts by saying bribery is 'one of the shameful and abominable survivals of the past', and suggests a particular concern over the problem.

Just as these serious crimes were so treated by the regime, the theoretically minor but practically very serious offences involving hooliganism and alcohol – the two are often linked – received considerable attention. On 19 April 1961, a decree[169] of the Praesidium of the Russian Supreme Soviet made some amendments to the earlier decree of 19 December 1956[170] on petty hooliganism, which dealt with offences that did not come within the scope of the Code. A fine of ten to thirty roubles was to apply as an alternative to the three to fifteen days' detention previously applied to petty hooligans, and 'taking into account the personality of the violator and the nature of the act committed by him', measures of public influence could be applied by public organisations, collectives or comrades' courts. Article 4 punishes with an administratively applied fine of 3 to 5 roubles an 'appearance in the streets or in other public places in an intoxicated state'.

Home manufacture of alcohol was punished in a decree[171] of 8 May 1961, by deprivation of freedom up to one year or a fine of up to 300 roubles if sale was not the aim, and one to three years' deprivation of liberty with or without property confiscation if it was. The effects of alcohol, always the cause of debate and concern in the Soviet Union, led at this point to various decrees and discussions. In October 1964, *Kazakstanskaia Pravda* reported that the Republic had adopted a decree instituting 'labour-therapy centres' for the compulsory treatment of alcoholics:

> Inveterate drunkards who, after the application of measures of public and administrative influence, continue to abuse alcoholic beverages and to violate labour discipline, public order and the rules of socialist society will be subject, by decision of a people's court, to commission to a labour-therapy centre for a term of from six months to one year.[172]

In the following year, Anashkin[173] wrote in *Izvestiia* on the twin
problems of hooliganism and alcohol abuse, saying that the former was
a 'widespread and dangerous crime' but was on the decline, the number
of people sentenced 'was reduced by almost 50% in our country
between 1961 and 1964'. The fight against hooliganism must continue,
as should that against alcohol misuse, as 'more than 80% of hooligan
acts are committed by persons in a state of intoxication'. Anashkin
considers alcoholics and drug addicts together and says it should be
possible to send them for compulsory treatment.

A new decree on hooliganism, introduced on 26 July 1966,[174] was
preceded in *Pravda* and *Izvestiia* by a report[175] on discussions that had
taken place in the Central Committee, etc., on the need to strengthen
public law and order. Severe measures had to be taken, but offences still
occurred due to 'poor work' and 'lack of concern' in the appropriate
agencies. Educational work amongst the population had to be improved,
the struggle intensified, and to that effect a Ministry for Safeguarding
Public Order (All-Union) was to be set up.[176] In the USSR,

> which is pursuing the path of the construction of communism and
> which guarantees to all citizens the right to work, education, rest and
> social security, there can be no place for criminal manifestations and
> other violations of socialist law and order.

The decree itself, 'On increased liability for hooliganism,' began by
saying that 'in conditions of expanded communist construction, any
antisocial manifestations, particularly instances of hooliganism causing
great harm to society and insulting the honour and dignity of soviet
citizens, are becoming even more intolerable', and could lead to the
commission of more serious offences.

The penalties for petty hooliganism were raised to fifteen days'
imprisonment (from three to ten days), and the possibility of using
corrective labour for a period of one to two months with 20 per cent
deduction from wages was introduced. Part Two of the decree dealt
with ordinary hooliganism, saying that petty hooliganism became
ordinary hooliganism after administrative penalties had been applied
once before within a year (previously it was twice). The penalties were
increased to six months' to one year's deprivation of liberty or
correctional labour, or a fine of 30 to 50 roubles (previously three
months to one year, no lower fine limit). Malicious hooliganism —

> i.e. the same actions, but marked by their exceptional cynicism or

special influence, or connected with resisting a representative of
authority or of the public who is fulfilling his duty in safeguarding
public order, or other citizens engaged in curbing hooligan actions

— and repeated offences are to be punished by one to five years'
deprivation of freedom (before, the minimum was three months), but
three to seven years if there is a weapon involved.

The compulsory treatment of alcoholism, mentioned above in
connection with the practice in Kazahkstan, was introduced into the
Russian Republic by a decree of 8 April 1967.[177] Habitual drunken
offenders who will not undergo treatment, or for whom the treatment
has failed, are subject to be sent to 'treatment-labour medical
institutions for compulsory medical treatment and labour re-education
for a period of one to two years'. A people's court decides upon this
course after petition by a public organisation, collective or state agency.
A reduction of up to half the period of treatment is possible if
successful. This decree is a good illustration of the confusion in Soviet
thought on the nature of alcoholism. Whereas in the West it is treated
as a disease, Soviet practice attaches guilt or blame to the alcoholic,
with the recuperative effects of work not overlooked. Later,[178] this
type of treatment applies to drug addicts who are to undergo a
'complete course of specialised treatment at the medical and
preventative-treatment institution of the Russian Republic Ministry of
Public Health' in their local area. If they evade this treatment, or it
fails, and they continue to violate 'labour discipline, public order or the
rules of socialist communal living despite the disciplinary, public or
administrative sanctions', they are subject to committal to a 'medical
and labour preventative clinic for compulsory treatment and labour
re-education for a term of one to two years'. The procedure for the
application is as above.

A very comprehensive law[179] designed to strengthen the law on drug
addiction was adopted on 25 April 1974. It applied heavy penalties for
the illegal manufacture, acquisition, possession, transportation, mailing
for sale, or for the illegal sale of narcotics — up to ten years' deprivation
of freedom, plus possible confiscation of property; such actions, if
repeated or involving a group conspiracy, led to six to fifteen years plus
confiscation; and theft of narcotics, up to five years with possibility of
confiscation, for a first offence. Many other activities in this area were
similarly dealt with.

Berman[180] gives a noteworthy example of repressive legislation,
concerning religious worship. Article 227 of the RSFSR Code was

originally aimed at the 'creation of a group that causes harm to the
health of citizens' and was directed against groups that 'under the guise
of preaching religious doctrines' engaged in practices harmful to health
or sexual morality. In 1962 this was expanded to include 'active
participation' in a religious group which is 'connected with. . .inducing
citizens to refuse social activity or performance of civic duties'.

Article 142 of the Code was concerned with the separation of church
and state, but gave no clear indication of what would be considered as
a breach of the regulations. Such guidance was given by a decree of 24
March 1966,[181] which included disturbing public order, collecting
tithes, the holding of classes to teach religion, fraudulently inciting
religious superstition, and 'the preparation for purposes of mass
dissemination, or the mass dissemination of handbills, letters, leaflets
and other documents making appeals for the nonobservance of the
legislation on religious cults'.

At the same time as the introduction of this law, another[182] awarded
up to three years' deprivation of liberty for a repeated offence involving
the regulations separating church from state. The law in this area has
been used to suppress members of the Initiative Group of the Baptist
Church.

The repressive legislation on the church has an interesting social
background, as the fact that such laws were felt to be necessary arose
from a revival of interests in religion among Soviet youth in the late
1950s. In the campaign that followed, half of the remaining 20,000
Orthodox churches were closed, and only approximately fifteen
monasteries were allowed to function.[183] With the prison sentence
awarded to the Archbishop of Kazan in June 1960, the first show trial
of an orthodox priest had taken place since 1927. Under Brezhnev the
situation eased a little and about 500 churches were allowed to reopen,
and laws on the regulation of religious practices were clarified
somewhat — however, the above-mentioned attacks on the Baptists also
occurred, and the domination of religion, a very important factor
indeed, was maintained. This attack on, or defence from, religious
dissent parallels that on the more general form, a particularly important
example of which was the Siniavsky-Daniel trial in February 1966.
They were charged with violating Article 70 of the RSFSR Criminal
Code, which covers anti-Soviet propaganda and agitation, in their stories
and books. Apart from the fact that these had been published abroad,
and were therefore not obviously under the Article at all, in deciding
whether authors were to be held liable in this way for statements made
by characters in their works[184] the integrity of the Code was being

tested and important questions concerning artistic freedom asked. The Code was found wanting, and artistic freedom limited, by the sentences of seven and five years' hard labour respectively. Their anti-Soviet intent was said to be implied in their writings and confirmed by the sending of works abroad for publication. This trial, attracting a great deal of attention at home and abroad, led to additional methods of suppressing criticism being made available on 16 September 1966,[185] when three additional subsections were added to Article 190 of the Code. They punished the circulating of known falsehoods derogatory to the Soviet state and social system (up to three years' deprivation of liberty or up to one year corrective labour, or up to a 100-rouble fine); abusing the state emblem or flag (up to two years' deprivation of liberty, up to one year corrective labour, or up to a 50-rouble fine); and the organisation or participation in group actions that 'grossly violate public order, involve clear disobedience of the lawful demands of representatives of authority or entail disruption of the operation of transport, state or public enterprises or institutions' (punishment as for circulating falsehoods).

Some of the legislation was directed towards elucidating doubtful points of law. For example, on 11 July 1969 a decree[186] defined the concept of 'especially dangerous recidivist', centring the explanation on the repeated commission of crimes, with most serious crimes needing only a single repetition, while lesser ones needed two or three.

A decree[187] of 18 May 1972 introduced the concept of a 'grave crime' as 'intentional acts representing increased social danger' and then gave a list of such acts, including state crimes, rape, theft, etc. The practical importance of the measure was that higher punishment levels were to apply — fifteen rather than ten years' deprivation of liberty. Some of the aspects of this complex decree are reorganisational rather than innovatory, but personality, motives and circumstances and danger have to be considered and reasons given. A decree of 3 January 1973[188] dealt with the topical problem of hijackings, awarding penalties of three to ten years' deprivation of liberty. If it was accompanied by violence, resulted in the crash of the plane, or in other grave consequences, then the penalty was increased to from five to fifteen years, with or without confiscation of property. Death, or eight to fifteen years, applied if loss of life or grave bodily injury ensued.

The use made of the death penalty in this decree seems to be typical of this time, as many such sentences were handed out for a variety of situations. A poacher who caused a death by murder,[189] Second World War 'criminals' who murdered,[190] murder in course of robbery,[191] murder when drunk,[192] and, more unusually, bombers,[193] all receive this penalty.

Amnesties issued on 28 December 1972[194] – to commemorate the fiftieth anniversary of the formation of the USSR – and 6 May 1975[195] – to commemorate the victory in the war, fitted the usual pattern. Humanitarianism and a desire to draw the offenders back into society were the stated reasons for their promulgation. The earlier applied to those sentenced to five years' and less deprivation of freedom who had been awarded orders and medals in fighting for the homeland, to pregnant women and those with children under 17, those who committed crimes before the age of 17, men over 60 and women over 55, and to certain categories of invalids. It was not to apply to those convicted of state crimes, especially dangerous recidivists and those guilty of serious crimes such as premeditated murder, robbery, theft, drugs, etc. Alcoholics and addicts were to complete their course of treatment, and those who had violated rules while serving their sentences were not to be released. The later amnesty was written in the same terms, but also applied to all war widows and wives of disabled war veterans, regardless of their length of sentence, and it halved all other sentences, apart from those usually prohibited. As usual, those considered to be of no further social danger are being released, and the others are not.

Changes of an administrative nature were forthcoming in 1977, partly based on an increased reliance on non-custodial methods of treatment.[196] Terebilov, the USSR Minister of Justice, contributed an informative article to *Pravda* of 20 May. Discussing changes introduced by decree earlier in the year,[197] he says that 'In view of the increase in overall state discipline and the population's rising social awareness and cultural level, it has been deemed possible to improve and expand the practice of employing social and administrative means of influence.'[198] The earlier changes reflect this with their suggestion that deprivation of freedom should be less used; probationary sentences could apply to all cases under three years (or five if negligence the cause); if less than one year is involved, then proceedings could be terminated and administrative penalties used. Juveniles, it was suggested, could have sentences of less than three years deferred for six months to two years, and if there was no further trouble, they could be released from further liability.[199]

This last-mentioned point suitably introduces the decree later this year[200] that establishes offices for the counselling of juveniles and their supervision. Public and educational agencies were to liaise with them, and local soviet executive committees were to have overall control over them. Juveniles were of concern throughout this period, with many articles written, complaints made, etc. One of the more informative articles was written by Voronstev[201] in 1969, in which he referred to studies of juvenile offenders in rural and urban areas showing similarities: (i) the structure of the crime – 60 per cent of the crimes were theft of state and public property and hooliganism; (ii) the prevalence of group crimes – 78 per cent urban, 70.4 per cent rural; (iii) alcoholic intoxication – 66.6 per cent urban, 64.2 per cent rural; (iv) most offenders were aged 16-17; (v) low educational levels of the offenders; and (vi) the relatively high educational levels of the offenders. Differences discovered included: (i) theft and robbery were more widespread in cities than in rural areas – 14 and 3.6 per cent as opposed to 9.4 and 0.9 per cent; and (ii) a larger number of adults were involved in rural offences – 23 per cent compared with 16 per cent. Any explanation of the figures was said to be forthcoming from the study of the factors shaping the personality of the offenders, a mixture of the social and non-social causes typical of the times, and upheld in the book *Prichiny Pravonarusheniia*, written by Kudriavstev, as late as 1976.[202]

As regards sentencing policy, recent cases show a continued use of heavy sentences. Embezzlers of 30,000 roubles from a state dry-cleaning business received thirteen and sixteen years' deprivation of freedom plus confiscation of property;[203] five years' deprivation of freedom in a strict regime corrective labour camp was applied to one Kharchuk for drunkenness and idleness;[204] Taratukhin[205] got thirteen years' deprivation of freedom as an especially dangerous recidivist for breaking into a hospital safe and taking 12,500 roubles, three months after release from a previous sentence; and the death penalty, already considered, was used with regularity. Both hard and soft approaches to sentencing have been supported, Anashkin[206] praising the present law for being humane and mentioning the measures for minors, mitigating factors, use of early release, maximum limits, etc., as examples of this. Nikiforov[207] wrote in defence of humanism, saying that the belief in extreme penalties was unfounded. The belief that they worked was totally false, as evidenced by their repeal. The present law is severe, and too much emphasis is placed on deprivation of liberty, which can disrupt lives and cause more harm than good. It is necessary to punish offenders, but 'at the same time we must not forget that humanism expresses the very essence of socialism; therefore, along with the development of socialism, the humanism in our life is developing and deepening.' The general trend of convictions in the USSR is difficult to

Table 7.1: Approximate Number of Convictions in USSR, 1955-71

1955		1,015,000
1958		1,421,000
1959	more than	1,130,000
1960	less than	942,000
1961		825,000
1962		1,080,000
1963		905,000
1964	less than	815,000
1965		755,000
1966		998,000
1967	more than	835,000
1968		922,000
1971	more than	870,000

Source: P.H. Juviler, *Revolutionary Law and Order* (New York, 1976), p. 132.

predict accurately because of lack of hard information, but it is perhaps worth noting what Juviler approximates convictions to have been.

Even these and similar statistics have to be viewed carefully, as they are of court convictions only, and any trend, which here would seem to indicate a slight decline in numbers over the operative period, has to take into account that a change in the administration of certain offences can alter the figures. If, for example, for certain offences administrative measures are to apply in future, then they will no longer be included in the table, even though the action in question may still be committed — perhaps even in greater numbers.

The 1977 Constitution

On 4 June 1977 the draft of the Constitution was issued for discussion.[208] It is a complex detailed document running to seven sections with a total of 173 articles.* Many of these are of interest.

The introduction to the Constitution contains many by now familiar points — the achievement of socialism, the alliance of the friendly classes, the dictatorship of the proletariat (now over) and the leading role of that class in any alliance, and the overthrow of capitalism are all included. The present position is said to be a 'state of the whole people' and 'The leading role of the Communist Party, vanguard of the whole

* Alterations made between a draft and its adoption often result in a mis-alignment of one article number.

people, has grown.'

Article 1 speaks of 'the will and interests of the working class, and peasantry and the intelligentsia', and so incorporates the change of view since the earlier references to a 'state of workers and peasants'.[209] The class references, and that is what they are, seem to admit that society has grown more complex, not less, an odd situation for one that is supposed to be withering away! The Communist Party is said to be the vanguard of the 'whole people', while previously it was that of the proletariat only.

Article 6 recognises the importance of the Party's position, 'The Communist Party of the Soviet Union is the leading and guiding force of Soviet society and the nucleus of its political system, of all state and public organisations. The Communist Party exists for the people and serves the people.'

The future development of society is seen in terms of further involving the public in the administration and generally bringing state and people closer together – 'further unfolding of socialist democracy. Increasingly broader participation of the working people in the administration of the affairs of society and the state,. . .intensification of control by the people' (Art. 8). Saying that this is the case does not, of course, mean that it is true.

If the state is meant to be withering away, it is still a central concept in much of the Constitution. Property is defined into various types, the principle form of socialist ownership being 'state property' – 'property belonging to the whole people' (Art. 10) – and 'The state shall facilitate the development of collective-farm - cooperative ownership and its approximation to state ownership' (Art. 11).

The old reason given for the existence of the state is included in Article 31, which says 'Defence of the socialist motherland is a most important function of the state.'

There is a great deal of consideration given to law and legality. Article 4 has the state and state organs functioning 'on the basis of socialist legality,' and assuring 'the protection of law and order', and Article 34 makes the basic statement that citizens are equal before the law in all respects 'irrespective of origin, social and property status', etc. This is in agreement with the view that society consists of friendly classes and that internal class enemies have been overcome. One could deduce that as 'social or property status' is not to be taken into account, then (i) it exists, and (ii) it is recognised as existing.

Mechanical aspects of law are covered in Article 72, which gives the Union the right of the 'Establishment of uniformity of legislative regulation throughout the territory of the USSR and definition of the principles of legislation of the USSR and union republics' (and for state security). As would be expected, USSR laws prevail over conflicting Republican legislation (Art. 73). Safeguards are supposedly included in Article 150: 'In the USSR justice shall be administered exclusively by courts of law'; 154 – 'Judges and people's assessors shall be independent and subject only to the law'; 156 – proceedings are to be public (unless the law provides otherwise); 157 – right of defence guaranteed; and 159 – 'No person shall be considered guilty of commission of a crime and subjected to criminal punishment other than by a verdict of the court and in conformity with law.' The powers of the Procuracy are outlined in Article 163,

> Supreme supervisory power over the precise and uniform execution of laws by all ministries, state committees and departments, enterprises, institutions and organisations, executive and administrative organs of local Soviets of people's deputies, collective farms, cooperative and other public organisations, officials and citizens.

If the Procuracy was a totally independent force it may have fulfilled the role of a free court system and made sure, or tried to, that the Constitution was enforced. The fundamental problem with the rights in the Constitution is that they are unenforceable. Needless to say, an independent Procuracy does not exist for the same reason that an unshackled court system does not.

The final important area within the Constitution that must be considered concerns individual rights. These fill a separate section of the Constitution, headed 'The Basic Rights, Freedoms and Duties of Citizens of the USSR', and as we shall see, the word 'duties' is appropriately included. The attitude to rights is stated by Article 39 – rights are guaranteed, but 'Exercise by citizens of rights and freedoms must not injure the interests of society and the state, and the rights of other citizens.' In the articles that follow, several rights are listed, for example work, leisure, health protection, maintenance in sickness and old age, housing, education and cultural achievements (access to). After each right is stated to exist, there usually follows a section on how it is 'ensured', for example the right to work is 'ensured' by the '41 hour working week' etc. (Art. 41). These statements seem quite pointless in the context of safeguarding the right, as they are merely referring to the present situation. If this is meant to include that in the Constitution and therefore make it permanent, then (i) this has not stopped changes before, (ii) the Constitution could be changed legally, and (iii) some of the statements are not so precise.

Article 50 'guarantees' freedom of the press, speech, assemblies and demonstrations, but says they are so 'in conformity with the interests of the working people and for the purpose of strengthening the socialist system', which does not sound totally unrestricted. The duties side of the equation comes after Article 59, which says, 'Exercise of rights and freedoms shall be inseparable from the performance by citizens of their duties.' These are 'to observe the constitution of the USSR, Soviet laws, to respect the rules of socialist behaviour' (Art. 59); to work conscientiously in a socially useful occupation and strictly observe labour and production discipline (Art. 60); to protect socialist property (Art. 61); 'to safeguard the interests of the Soviet state, to contribute to the strengthening of its might and prestige' (Art. 62); and 'to respect the rights and lawful interests of other persons, to be intolerant of antisocial behaviour, to contribute in every way to the maintenance of public order' (Art. 63). Others, such as correctly rearing children, are also included. The outcome of including these duties and saying that they cannot be divorced from the rights, or rather the rights from them, means that the rights are not guaranteed within the accepted meaning of that term. In any case, with no supervising independent body to see that the Constitution is properly enforced, the old view that law is not to fetter the regime still applies, and the rights are actually illusory.

There does seem an attempt to introduce the concept of the rule of law, but this has been the case before — and under the Stalin Constitution the rights were not limited by the addition of duties, although they were of equally doubtful worth — and perhaps the move has to be considered as an attempt to deceive. There may have been a relative change, but not an absolute one.

However, despite feeling that this is the true picture, one is not surprised that this view is not held by official Russia. The usual comments and articles have been forthcoming. Petrukhin[210] comments that Article 160 — on presumption of innocence — emphasises that the accused is innocent until proved guilty under Soviet law. The presumption is not new, and was there before the Constitution, but its inclusion in the latter upgrades its standing and importance, and reaffirms that it is a workable concept in Soviet criminal trials. As well as this type of more personal critique, major new laws have started to refer to the Constitution and the importance of legality. For example, the Law on the USSR Council of Ministers[211] would have that body guided by 'the USSR Constitution and USSR laws', and ensuring 'the steadfast observance' of both as one of its functions. The continued interest and open recognition of the significance of law continues,[212] but this does not automatically mean that reality will change – witness the trial of Yuri Orlov for what might be termed 'upholding' the Helsinki agreements.[213]

Conclusions

Developments in the beginning of this period were affected by the reaction to the death of Stalin. Change was seen to be necessary or wanted, and in varying degrees was forthcoming.

In the field of theory, not surprisingly, there was a great amount of continuity – incidentally made easy by the fact that such an amount of special pleading was necessary to link theory and practice that any desired explanation could be achieved, regardless of any particular factual situation. The superstructure was still recognised as being an active, partially independent force, so continuing the excuse for a wide variety of developments in the legal and state systems. The dictatorship of the proletariat, which of course had never existed, was now supposedly at an end, and this necessitated the evolution in state theory of such non-Marxist notions as a 'state of the whole people'. In an attempt to dispel any possible contradictions in a situation where two originally class-based entities, the dictatorship of the proletariat and the state – and for that matter, law – have not disappeared together with classes, the Soviet explanation introduces important qualifying factors such as the disappearance of antagonistic classes, not classes *per se*, and the need for a state where the external situation demands one. This last factor has been used to raise the possibility of the existence of a state when communism has been achieved, a possibility totally alien to the teachings of Marx, who may certainly have foreseen some form of regulatory organism in the future society, but not at all one like this – it was to be fully part of society, not ruling over it. This is yet another mutation caused by the impossible task of trying to graft Marx's theory on to the Russian situation.

The withering away is still seen in terms of social self-administration, and some of the particular developments involving the public in this area no doubt believed to be part of this, when in reality this process has to be a genuine part of the growth of communism before it is significant in this way. Communism cannot be artificially constructed by crude social manipulation.

In the 1930s, it was said that 'stability' had become more important in society and law. This could be said also of this period, but now the 'stability' was not a rejection of 'revolutionary' ideas such as a reliance on legal consciousness rather than decrees, but one of turning away from the more blatant abuses of Stalinism and moving towards a system based on the rule of law. This is evidenced by the rejection of many theories postulated by Vyshinsky — for example on evidence and procedure — and the increased emphasis on individual rights. However, it should be immediately noted that this is more of a relative than absolute change, as the much-debated rights of the individual are not really protected, as they can only be exercised in certain approved ways. If this was a state of the dictatorship of the proletariat, then this might be excused, as the state would have the true interests of the majority of the people at heart, but as it is not, it simply gives the state uncontrolled power. State rights are distinguished from personal, and are sometimes even contrasted with them, but it is said that the two cannot basically conflict. State rights are seen as a sort of superior form of personal rights and any 'conflict' is seen in those terms, not as a clash of separate competing interests. As stated, this may well be the case if this was the dictatorship of the proletariat, but it is not, and the point that state and individual interests cannot be in conflict is true for quite different reasons.

Perhaps the involvement of the public in the administration of society can be considered as one aspect of the supposedly coincidental nature of these interests, but in any case it played an important role in the legal developments of the period.

Morgan,[214] when considering the comrades' courts, volunteer militia and anti-parasitism, concludes that although the involvement was always said to be important in the transition to communism, the real reasons were more prosaic, and include the curtailment of the seemingly growing tendency of the people to indulge in 'bourgeois' activities — although their growth was to some extent fostered by the more liberal attitudes of the regime — and the implementation of labour discipline and other more general social controls. Morgan feels the institutions

are directly traceable to problems encountered by the regime in the implementation of its policies, and that any phraseology employed to present them in terms of Marxist ideology and the transition to communism is simply a rationale employed by the regime to conceal the utilitarian functions of these three institutions.[215]

One would certainly agree with this view, and in any case this cannot in itself be the significant part of the withering away.

The Party had to some extent suffered under Stalin, as his very personal method of rule necessarily meant that any other guiding forces were eclipsed. It is interesting to note that his eventual successor, Khrushchev, attained this position from that of Party Secretary, which shows the inherently important position held by the Party, despite its temporary setback. In an attempt to improve the lives of people in general, and particularly those on the collective farms, emphasis was laid on the production of consumer goods and a variety of innovations tried. Too many of the latter were a cause of Khrushchev's fall. Since this event, the general picture of agricultural production has been one of increase, and the differences in status between workers and peasants has eased, but one must conclude that real differences do exist, and the society cannot be said to be homogeneous. Due to the imprecise nature of the term 'friendly classes', it is difficult to see whether this albeit non-Marxist concept has any factual basis in society. The various groups within Soviet society are controlled to an unusual degree compared with Western countries, and in that situation one cannot see any too obvious antagonisms being allowed to develop. However, this does not preclude a certain amount of competition for privileges and material goods, and especially with the formation of Djilas' 'new class' and the enormous disparities of earnings and life-styles that exist, one cannot conclude that this is a society moving towards classlessness. In the period following Stalin, the recruitment of workers and peasants to the Party, always of intermittent interest, was emphasised yet again. The continuing weakness of Party representation in the countryside received more attention, but although the position improved, it is difficult to draw clear comparisons on class, etc., as so many institutional changes were introduced. In any case, the percentage of white-collar members remained very high — over 40 per cent.

The tasks of the Party, as reflected in the resolutions adopted at Congresses and in the Rules, are similar to what they have always been. The hold of the Party on the governmental functions continues, with a very high saturation rate of Party members in influential posts, which often contrasts greatly with membership levels amongst ordinary workers and peasants (although of course there are more of these): for example, 94 per cent of collective farm chairmen, and 5 per cent of peasants (see above). Recruitment continues at a reasonably high level, making the Party very different from that of Lenin in this respect, but its size is indicative of its role, and cutting down on intake would involve perhaps unacceptable changes in the aspirations of a section of society for whom Party membership is an accepted and expected part of upward social mobility.

There was supposedly, especially after 1958, an increased interest in the protection of the rights of the individual. We have seen that this was not really so, as the rights were qualified. As part of this movement, a reaction to what had gone before, other changes occurred which on their face value may be thought to be legality orientated, for example with the procuracy and Code of Criminal Procedure. Various liberal measures were also formally introduced, such as legal abortions, the removal of liability for unauthorised absence from work, restrictions on movement being lifted, the usual series of amnesties issued, many penalties lowered and special procedures ended.

While this was undoubtedly an improvement, the new attitude must be seen for what it really is, for the improvement amounted to one on previous practice, *not* on the underlying principles. Many severe measures were brought in, notably the wide use made of the death penalty — although still an 'exceptional measure' — theft of socialist property, effects of alcohol, hooliganism, state crimes were still heavily punished, and after the 1960 Code a series of penalty increases occurred. As well as these more specific changes to laws, two more general aspects of the treatment of dissent have to be noted. Anti-parasitism should be viewed as a throwback to Stalinist practices, as a definite act did not have to be committed before punishment applied, and although some of the definitions of the Code do not use precise definitions, the anti-parasite laws were special in that they applied to a wider variety of acts and were directed in an altogether more general way.

One also has to consider the treatment of dissenters, of which there are several types: 'neo-Leninists' and 'neo-Marxists', such as Medvedev and Grigorenko, although declining in numbers, receive some protection — perhaps because they may be needed in the future; the liberals and humanitarians, such as Litvinov, Sakharov, and evidenced by the Chronicle of Current Events, and the liberal Russian nationalists such as Solzhenitsyn, exist, which would not have been the case under Stalin, but are persecuted. The regime is willing to allow the exercising of 'rights', but only within certain confines which, to a Western observer, are so limiting as to negate the right itself. The outcome is not a system under the rule of law, but simply an improvement on what has gone before. Reddaway[216] concludes:

Although the regime's greatest weakness is the inflexibility of itself
and its *apparat*. . .opposition can and does. . .exist at the higher
levels. It is different in character from extra-systematic opposition,
being, despite the party's ban on factionalism, less illegitimate and
also more shifting and fluid.

The extent to which this 'opposition' can really be considered as such
is very debatable, but the basic approach does explain why
neo-Leninists receive some protection, while national minority group
dissidents would not. One believes that it would clarify the situation to
say that while *opposition* would not be tolerated, *dissent* in some
circumstances will. This is supported by dealing with the former under
Articles 70 and 72 of the RSFSR Code as anti-Soviet agitprop or
activity — with very heavy sentences including death, while the latter is
treated under Article 190-1 (up to three years' deprivation of freedom).
Historically, this is akin to Lenin's attitude to opposition, for he
tolerated some discussion and debate, but was emphatically against
serious factionalism within the Party, as that might threaten the
continued existence of its rule.

The changes in some areas of substantive law show an increasing
intolerance on the part of the regime towards offenders, and this
attitude prevails to some extent in criminology. This subject had
suffered under Stalin, but study had resumed after his death and
progress was being made. However, one of its problems was that to be
acceptable, any theory of crime causation had to be based on the
'vestiges of the past' approach, so ensuring that no crime-causing factors
were attributed to the present Soviet society. Although overtly
biological theories are rejected with vehemence, psychological factors
are considered by some, but they are still linked to social causes and
are introduced carefully by their supporters.

Too much attention is paid to circumstantial, mechanical aspects of
crime causation, and too little to the question of why one individual
commits a crime and another does not. As crime is supposed to die out
as communism develops, a study on individual cases may lead to
embarrassing difficulties, which is probably why this type of study has
been left alone.

In some respects, 'vestiges of the past' may be a biological
explanation, as they could be in the mind rather than in society, but in
the way used by Marx one has to see them as the latter. The basic
criminological approach is 'Marxist' in the sense that the causes of crime
are said to be in society, but two points have to be mentioned: (i) as

Soviet society is not about to become communist, one cannot say that there are no causes of crime in that society — and that is what the accepted theory says as it blames previous society; and (ii) not all crime necessarily need be explained in this way, as some sort of infringements may well occur in the future society — only they will not be caused by imperfections in society.

Theory in this period is still working on the premiss that society is moving towards communism — in fact communism is supposedly near. This is, as it has always been, patently untrue. The regime has rejected some of Stalin's worst practices and generally one has to say that the situation has improved, but there are still many objectionable features to the system, which are extensions and continuations of previous practices. An appropriate illustration of the underlying attitude is provided by the Resolution, 'On Overcoming the Cult of Personality and its Consequences', published in *Pravda*, 2 July 1956. It said:

> The cult of personality unquestionably inflicted serious damage upon the Communist Party and Soviet society. But to reach conclusions about some sort of change in the social structure of the USSR because of the existence of the cult of personality in the past, or to seek the origins of this cult in the nature of the Soviet social order, would be a crude error. Both one and the other would be absolutely erroneous, would not correspond to reality, would contradict the facts.[217]

Notes

1. G. Hodnett (ed.), *Resolutions and Decisions of the CPSU*, vol. 4 (Toronto, 1974), p. 8.

2. T.H. Rigby, *Communist Party Membership in the U.S.S.R. 1917-1967* (Princeton, 1968), p. 52.

3. A. Brown and M. Kaser (eds.), *The Soviet Union Since the Fall of Khrushchev*, 2nd edn. (London, 1978), p. 97.

4. *Basis and Superstructure* (Moscow, 1955). M. Jaworskyj, *Soviet Political Thought* (Baltimore, 1967), p. 405.

5. 'Nekotorye osobennosti razvitiia sotsializma', *Vop. Fil.* (1966), no. 3, pp. 14-24.

6. Ibid., p. 15.

7. There are some pertinent differences between state and collective farm peasants, such as those to do with wages and the private plot.

8. 'Preobrazovanie sotsial'noi prirody krest'ianstva SSSR', *Vop. Fil.* (1967), no. 12, p. 3.

9. 'O klassovoi sushohnosti sovetskogo obshchenarodnogo gosudarstva', *SGiP* (1976), no. 1, p. 10.

280   *From 1953 to the Present Day*

10. 'K. Marks o gosudarstve kak politicheskoi organizatsii obshchestva',
Vop. Fil. (1968), no. 7, p. 38.
11. 'Problemy analiza mezhklassovye otnoshenii v razvitom sotsializme',
Vop. Fil. (1977), no. 8, p. 8.
12. 'Na puti k besklassovomu obshchestvu', *Vop. Fil.* (1971), no. 5, p. 22.
13. 'Sotzializm i politicheskaia vlast'', *SGiP* (1974), no. 5, pp. 11-13.
14. *Vneocherednoi XXI S"ezd KPSS*, I (Moscow, 1959), p. 20.
15. *State and Law* (London, 1964), p. 63.
16. 'Leninskoe uchenie o sotsialisticheskom gosudarstve i sovremennost'',
Vop. Fil. (1960), no. 4, p. 24.
17. Ibid., p. 26.
18. 'Programma KPSS i nekotorye voprosy teorii sovetskogo
sotsialisticheskogo gosudarstva', *SGiP* (1961), no. 12, p. 4.
19. Ibid., pp. 4-5.
20. Ibid., p. 10.
21. 'Kvoprosy o vraimootnoshenii ob'ektivnogo i sub'ektivnogo prava', *SGiP*
(1958), no. 5, p. 271.
22. 'Sotsialisticheskaia democratiia i lichnost'', *Vop. Fil.* (1958), no. 9, p. 34.
23. 'O primeneii sovetskogo zakona', *SGiP* (1966), no. 11, p. 22.
24. 'XX s"ezd KPSS i zadachi sovetskoi pravovoi nauki', *SGiP* (1956), no. 2,
p. 5.
25. Ibid., p. 6.
26. 'Soviet Justice and its Role in Strengthening Legality', *Kommunist* (1956),
no. 7. *CDSP*, 1956-40-6.
27. 'Ukreplenie sotsialisticheskoi zakonnosti i nekotorye teorii sovetskogo
ugolovnogo prava i protsessa', *SGiP* (1956), no. 4, pp. 26-38.
28. 'Some Questions of Soviet Jurisprudence', *Izvestiia*, 1 Mar. 1957. *CDSP*,
1957-8-30.
29. See R.A. Rudenko, 'Zadachi dal'neishego ukrepleniia sotsialisticheskoi
zakonnosti v svete reshenii XX s"ezda KPSS', *SGiP* (1956), no. 3, pp. 15-25; and
V.S. Tikunov, 'Sotsialisticheskaia zakonnest' – rukovodiashchii printsip v
deiatel'nosti organov gosudarstvennoi bezopasnosti', *SGiP* (1959), no. 8,
pp. 13-26, which makes the extraordinary suggestion that this was so until Beria
subverted them.
30. *State and Law*, p. 56.
31. 'Liberty, Law and the Legal Order' in *North Western University Law
Review*, (1963-4), vol. 58, at p. 643.
32. Translated in L. Schapiro (ed.), *The USSR and the Future* (New York and
London, 1963), as Appendix A.
33. Ibid., p. 299.
34. Ibid., p. 305.
35. 'Voprosy razvitiia gosudarstva i prava v proekte programmy K.P.S.S.',
SGiP (1961), no. 10, p. 26.
36. Ibid., p. 27.
37. Ibid., p. 32.
38. Ibid., p. 33.
39. *State and Law*, p. 73.
40. Ibid., p. 104.
41. 'Soviet Court is an Important Weapon for Strengthening Soviet Law',
Pravda, 12 Nov. *CDSP*, 1954-45-12.
42. 'K voprosy o prichinakh prestupnosti v SSSR i merakh borb'y s nei',
SGiP (1959), no. 3, p. 88.
43. 'Ob izuchenii i preduprezhdenii prestupnosti', *SGiP* (1968), no. 7,
pp. 78-88.

44. 'Izuchenie lichnosti prestuplika po materialam kriminologicheskikh issledovanii', *SGiP* (1965), no. 9, p. 93.

45. See Kriminologiia, pp. 120-4.

46. See W.D. Connor, *Deviance in Soviet Society* (New York, 1976), p. 46.

47. Moscow, 1961, at p. 231.

48. Ibid., p. 232.

49. For details on this see P.H. Juviler, *Revolutionary Law and Order* (New York, 1976), pp. 148-55.

50. Ibid., pp. 180-1.

51. Ibid., p. 94.

52. 'K voprosy izucheniia lichnosti osuzhdennye k lisheniiu svobody', *SGiP* (1965), no. 5, p. 98.

53. Ibid., p. 86.

54. 'Sotsial'no-psikhologicheskie posledstviia urbanizatsii i ikh bliianie na prestupnost'', *SGiP* (1975), No. 8, p. 67.

55. Ibid., pp. 74-83.

56. 'Sotsialno-psikhologicheskie aspecty antiobshchestvennogo povedeniia', *Vop. Fil.* (1974), no. 1, p. 104.

57. 'Problemy prichinnosti v kriminologii', *Vop. Fil.* (1971), no. 10, p. 84.

58. *Problema Prestupnosti* (Moscow, 1969), p. 53.

59. P.H. Solomon in *Soviet Criminologists and Criminal Policy Specialists in Policy-Making* (London, 1976), tends to emphasise the contrary.

60. *Ved. SSSR*, 9-222. Trans. in H.J. Berman and J.B. Quigley, *Basic Laws of the Soviet State* (Cambridge, Mass., 1969).

61. *Izvestiia*, 8 Apr. 1954. *CDSP*, 1954-14-15.

62. *Soviet Criminal Law* (Cambridge, Mass., 1972), p. 100. See Art. 49 of Constitution.

63. *Zaria Vostoka*, 31 Mar. 1956. *CDSP*, 1956-13-3.

64. *Izvestiia*, 9 Feb. 1962. *CDSP*, 1962-6-6.

65. 'Ob izvrashcheniiakh Vyshinskogo v teorii sovetskogo prava i praktika', *SGiP* (1965), no. 3, p. 24.

66. See Berman, *Soviet Criminal Law*, pp. 47 *et seq.*

67. G. Hodnett, *The Khrushchev Years, 1953-1964* (Toronto, 1974), p. 131.

68. *Ved. RSFSR*, 26-371 (Berman and Quigley, pp. 265-74).

69. 'Comradely Justice in Eastern Europe', *Current Legal Problems* (1972), XXV, p. 213.

70. *People's Justice*, Law in Eastern Europe, no. 7 (Leyden, 1963), pp. 67-8.

71. See above.

72. Juviler, *Revolutionary Law and Order*, p. 203.

73. 'Otvet serditym oponnentam', *Lit. Gaz.* 20 Nov. 1968.

74. H.J. Berman, 'Soviet Law Reform', *Yale L.J.*, vol. 66, p. 1192. Obviously this particular abolition would not be highly publicised, as the existence of the Board in the first place was somewhat delicate.

75. Ibid.

76. *Vedomosti SSSR*, 11-221.

77. *Kommunist* (Armenia), 7 Dec. 1954. *CDSP*, 1955-1-27.

78. *Sovetskaia Moldavia*, 12 Dec. 1954. Ibid.

79. *Vedomosti SSSR*, 15-334.

80. *Vedomosti SSSR*, 1955, 22-425.

81. *Vedomosti SSSR*, 1955, 5-114.

82. Ibid., 8-193.

83. See *CDSP*, 1955-35-3. From *Izvestiia*, 18 September.

84. *Vedomosti SSSR*, 10-203.

85. Ibid., 9-193.

86. Not published. See Berman, *Soviet Law Reform*, p. 1203.
87. See *Ugolovnyi Kodeks RSFSR* (Moscow, 1957), pp. 143-5.
88. *Vedomosti RSFSR* (1957) 1-5. *CDSP*, 1957-3-18.
89. F.J. Feldbrugge, *Soviet Criminal Law General Part* (Leyden, 1964), p. 37.
90. Under Law of 10 November 1932, see above.
91. *Pravda*, 2 Nov. 1957. *CDSP*, 1957-44-21.
92. 10 Apr. 1954. *CDSP*, 1954-15-3.
93. *CDSP*, 1954-21-25.
94. *CDSP*, 1955-16-14.
95. *CDSP*, 1954-24-23.
96. See cases of Glazunov, *Kazakhstanskaia Pravda*, 15 Nov. 1955. *CDSP*, 1955-49-21; Vashchenko, *Sovetskaia Moldavia,* 9 Sept. 1955. Ibid., 38-23; Zotov, *Bakinsky rabochy*, 4 Aug. 1955, ibid., 34-19.
97. Parviz, *Kom. Tad.*, 26 May 1955, ibid., 22-20; Bite, *Sov. Lat.,* 18 Aug. 1955, ibid., 36-19; Samorodov, *Mosc. Prav.*, 29 Sept. 1955. Ibid., 41-22.
98. *Sovetskaia Latvia*, 25 Jan. 1955. *CDSP*, 1955-5-30.
99. *Kommunist Tadzhakistana*, 1 Oct. 1955. Ibid., 46-19.
100. *Sovetskaia Rossia*, 20 Dec. 1956. *CDSP*, 1956-49-18.
101. 'Soviet Law Reform', p. 1203.
102. *CDSP*, 1956-49-18.
103. *CDSP*, 1956-52-9.
104. Ibid., 52-10.
105. *Pravda*, 11 July 1954. *CDSP*, 1954-29-5.
206. *Komsomolskaia Pravda*, 4 Aug. 1954. Ibid.
107. Ibid., p. 7.
108. See *CDSP*, 1955-44-5.
109. *Bloknot agitatora* (1955), no. 24. *CDSP*, 1955-34-9.
110. *Leninskaia Pravda*, 13 Dec. 1955. Ibid., 51-23.
111. *Sovetskaia Estonia*, 28 Dec. 1954. Ibid., 2-29.
112. *Turkmenskaia Iskra*, 23 Jan. 1955. Ibid., 5-30.
113. *Kazakhstanskaia Pravda*, 2 Oct. 1955. Ibid., 46-19.
114. *Sovetskaia Latvia*, 22 Sept. 1955. Ibid., 41-22.
115. *Turkmenskaia Iskra*, 27 Nov. 1955. Ibid., 49-21.
116. *Pravda Ukrainy*, 26 Dec. 1954. Ibid., 2-30.
117. *Vedomosti SSSR* (1957), nos. 4-63.
118. 'Some Questions of Criminal Legislation', *Izvestiia*, 27 July 1957. *CDSP* 1957-30-6.
119. *Ved. SSSR* (1959), no. 1-6.
120. 'Provided for' is in Russian the verb 'predusmotret'' and here has the meaning of 'forbidden by'.
121. See Article 32.
122. See Article 43.
123. See *Sotsialisticheskaia Zakonnost'* (1958), no. 6.
124. For more details on juveniles, exile and banishment, etc., see Berman, *Soviet Criminal Law*, pp. 38-9.
125. Ibid.
126. *Pravda* and *Izvestiia*, 26 Dec. 1958. *CDSP* (1959), no. 5, pp. 3 *et seq.*
127. Ibid. in *CDSP* 1959-1-3.
128. *Bakinsky rabochy*, 17 Apr. 1957. *CDSP,* 1957-17-16.
129. See *CDSP* 1957-27-7 for examples.
130. R. Beermann, *Soviet Studies* (1957), vol. 9, p. 221.
131. *Kommunist Tadzhikstana*, 17 May. *CDSP* 1957-27-3.
132. From ibid., 18 May. Trans. ibid.
133. *CDSP* 1957-27-6.

134. Ibid.

135. *Soviet Studies* (1960), vol. XI, p. 454. From *Sovetskaia Kirgizia*, 20 Jan. 1959.

136. *Pravda Vostoka*, 18 May 1957. *CDSP*, 1957-27-7.

137. *Zaria Vostoka*, 6 Sept. 1960. *CDSP*, 1960-44-12.

138. *Sovetskaia Rossia*, 5 May 1961. *CDSP*, 1961-17-8.

139. 'The Parasites Law', *Sov. Studies*, vol. XIII, at pp. 199-200.

140. G. G. Morgan, 'People's Justice: The Anti-Prasite Laws', in *Law in Eastern Europe,* vol. VII (Leiden, 1963), p. 54 *et seq.*

141. *Bulletin' Verk. Suda SSSR* (1961), no. 5, p. 8.

142. Berman, *Soviet Criminal Law*, p. 78.

143. 20 Sept. 1965. *Ved. RSFSR*, no. 38-364. *CDSP*, 1965-44-13.

144. *Ved. RSFSR*, no. 14-255. *CDSP*, 1970-16-32.

145. *Ved. RSFSR*, no. 14-256. *CDSP*, ibid.

146. *Ved. RSFSR*, no. 33-698. *CDSP*, 1975-45-21.

147. 'Soviet and Russian Anti-parasite Laws', *Soviet Studies*, vol. XV, pp. 420-9.

148. Ibid., p. 426.

149. *Revolutionary Law and Order*, p. 76.

150. H.J. Berman, *Justice in the U.S.S.R.* (Cambridge, Mass., 1966), p. 297.

151. *How Russia is Ruled* (Cambridge, Mass., 1970), p. 451.

152. An omission, not working, plus a status, that of leading a parasitic way of life. Berman, *Soviet Criminal Law*, p. 30.

153. *Justice in the U.S.S.R.*, p. 297.

154. See *Soviet Criminal Law*, pp. 80-1.

155. *Ved. RSFSR*, no. 5. *CDSP*, 1960-5-21.

156. *Ved. SSSR*, no. 14.

157. *Izvestiia*, 10 Mar. 1959. *CDSP*, 1959-10-3.

158. Ibid.

159. *Sov. Iust.* (1960), no. 2. *CDSP*, 1960-13-32.

160. 19 June 1959. *CDSP*, 1959-41-14.

161. F.J. Feldbrugge, 'Soviet Criminal Law – the Last Six Years', *Journal of Criminal Law, Criminology and Police Science* (1963), vol. 54, p. 253. However, as the Party would be directing operations, this may be an over-elaboration.

162. Translations of the Code appear in (i) *Soviet Statutes and Decisions* (1964), vol. I, no. 1; and (ii) Berman, *Soviet Criminal Law* (1972); latter used here.

163. *Ved. RSFSR*, no. 2-123. *CDSP*, 1961-7-28/9.

164. *Izvestiia*, 7 May 1961. Ibid., 17-8.

165. *Izvestiia*, 2 July 1961. *CDSP*, 1961-25-21.

166. 15 Feb. 1962. *Ved. SSSR*, no. 8-83.

167. 15 Feb. 1962. *Ved. SSSR*, no. 8-84.

168. 20 Feb. 1962. *Ved. SSSR*, no. 8-85.

169. *Ved. RSFSR*, 16. *CDSP*, 1961-17-9.

170. See *CDSP*, 1956-49-18.

171. *Ved. RSFSR*, no. 18-139. *CDSP*, 1961-19-22.

172. See *CDSP*, 1964-47-16.

173. 3 Mar. 1965. *CDSP*, 1965-9-24, and see Feldbrugge, 'Last Six Years', where 50 per cent theft of private property, 95 (96) per cent hooliganism, 70 per cent murder, 67 per cent rape committed under influence of alcohol.

174. *Ved. SSSR*, no. 30-595.

175. 27 July 1966. Ibid., p. 3.

176. A resolution to this effect was incorporated into a decree of 26 July 1966. *Ved. SSSR*, no. 30-594.

177. *Ved. RSFSR*, no. 15-333. *CDSP*, 1967-15-11.

178. 25 Aug. 1972. *Ved. RSFSR*, no. 35-870. *CDSP*, 1972-37-7.

179. *Ved. SSSR*, no. 18-275.

180. *Soviet Criminal Law*, pp. 73-4.

181. *Ved. RSFSR*, no. 12-221.

182. *Ved. RSFSR*, no. 12. *CDSP*, 1966-14-41.

183. D.W. Treadgold, *Twentieth Century Russia*, 4th edn. (Chicago, 1976), p. 478.

184. A disparaging comment about Lenin was termed 'blasphemy' by the judge! See Berman, *Soviet Criminal Law*, p. 81.

185. *Ved. RSFSR*, no. 38. *CDSP*, 1966-41-43.

186. *Ved. SSSR*, no. 29-249.

187. *Ved. SSSR*, no. 22-176.

188. *Pravda* and *Izvestiia*, 4 Jan. 1973. *CDSP*, 1973-1-7.

189. *CDSP*, 1973-5-27.

190. Ibid., 24-23 and 32-15.

191. *CDSP*, 1974-27-23.

192. Ibid., 28-19.

193. *CDSP*, 1977-7-8.

194. *Pravda* and *Izvestiia*, 29 Dec. 1972. *CDSP*, 1972-52-31.

195. *Izvestiia*, 7 May 1975. *CDSP*, 1975-18-19.

196. A.E. Nataskev, 'Zakonnost' i gumanizm − osnova ispravleniia i perevospitaniia osuzhdennykh', *SGiP* (1977), no. 3, pp. 79-87.

197. *Ved. SSSR*, no. 7, items 116-20.

198. *CDSP*, 1977-20-1.

199. See *Ved. SSSR*, no. 8, items 137 and 138.

200. *Ved. SSSR*, no. 8-138.

201. 'O prestupnosti nesovershennoletnikh v gorode i sel'skoi mestnosti', *SGiP* (1969), no. 3, pp. 103-8.

202. Moscow, 1976.

203. Ibid., pp. 2-21.

204. Ibid., pp. 4-27.

205. Ibid., pp. 6-23.

206. 'Gumanizm sovetskogo ugolovnogo prava', *SGiP* (1963), no. 8, pp. 44-52.

207. *Izvestiia*, 4 Apr. 1975. *CDSP*, 1975-14-11.

208. Published in *CDSP*, 1977-22-1, and *The Times*, 6 June 1977; latter used here. Draft adopted on 7 Oct. 1977.

209. References to the 1936 Constitution are from the Co-op. Pub. Soc. of For. Workers, Moscow, 1937, as before.

210. *SGiP* (1978), no. 12. Trans. *CDSP* 1979-9-14.

211. *Izvestiia*, 6 July 1978. Trans. ibid., 1978-27-20 *et seq.*

212. N.B. After calls for a new USSR Code of Laws at the 25th Party Congress, it was announced in *Izvestiia*, 25 April 1978, that there would be a Code, to be published from 1981-5 (*CDSP*, 1978-17-18).

213. Orlov was sentenced to seven years' deprivation of freedom, to be followed by five years of exile. For details of the trial and some official comment, see *CDSP* 1978-20-1.

214. *People's Justice*, pp. 69 *et seq.*

215. Ibid., p. 71.

216. 'The Development of Dissent and Opposition' in Brown and Kaser, *The Soviet Union Since the Fall of Khrushchev*, at p. 123.

217. Hodnett, *The Khrushchev Years*, p. 65.

8 CONCLUSIONS

Marx believed that the fundamental agency of social development was economic. The economic infrastructure decided the form of the superstructure, part of which was state and law. This basic relationship may seem to be simple, but in reality many subtleties are involved. It is usually accepted that the superstructure is not an entirely passive entity, and that although in the final analysis it is determined by the base, it does have some effect itself. It is not completely clear which areas it does so affect, for although it is generally allowed that it can influence itself, the question arises as to whether it reacts on the base. Of the two originators, Engels is more precise in this — one is thinking of his four letters — but this is only to be expected, as he tended to take a more 'scientific' view, treating the work as a theory, while Marx had a more philosophical view, treating it as an 'approach'. In these 'four letters', Engels admits that it may have appeared that the relationship between base and superstructure was a one-sided determinism, but this was only because of misunderstandings and the fact that Marx and himself had not fully set out the real relationship. Although it is impossible to quantify this affinity, one believes that the superstructure is finally determined by the infrastructure, but that the former can and does have an effect on itself and to some extent on the infrastructure.

What does this mean in terms of later Soviet practice? One important thing one can say is that the deterministic part of the theory tends to emphasise the substance rather than the form of decrees, etc. If the structure and reality of society are decided by the economic base, then any imperfections in the legal and state systems will be relatively unimportant, as they are really minor variations caused by human, or perhaps local, conditions.

This line of reasoning illustrates one of the fundamental balances in Marxism, that between determinism and individual action, that exists in various areas, for example the causes of crime, and on the more general level, the development of history. Put simply, the question is, to what extent can particular human action affect the course of historical development? This question can best be answered after consideration has been given to other aspects of state and law theory.

An extremely important part of Marxist theory relates to the 'withering away' of the state. Basically, the state was to start withering away at the beginning of the transition period, and by the end of the period, when communism had been achieved, was no longer to exist. Since this premiss was made, a tremendous amount of thought has gone into deciding what precisely it means.

Careful examination of what Marx and Engels actually wrote, and the reasons why they wrote particular works and phamphlets, leads one to conclude that some form of organising force was to exist in the future society. The difference between this 'organisation' and the 'state' in nineteenth-century societies investigated by Marx and Engels is partly practical, and partly more philosophical. The future organisation was not to have repressive police forces, and rule over society, but was to be an organic part of society, fully integrated, supply the necessary regulatory functions, and would act in the interests of all society.

To understand the nature and mechanism of the change from one to the other the concepts of 'class' and 'ruling class' have to be introduced. In capitalist society, the state was the instrument of the ruling class, which meant that it furthered the interests of that class and helped continue their rule. It was used as a weapon by that class against exploited classes, as was law, often termed the 'will of the ruling class'. One should not forget that this 'will' is itself finally determined by the mode of production — the infrastructure. Classes were non-existent in the future society; they are to wither away as well. One therefore has a situation in the transition period where state and law, paralleled by class are all dying out. It is suggested that the link between the two is 'political power'. When reference is made to the state 'loosing its political power', that is exactly what is meant, and the result is the aforementioned 'organisation'. When one applies this same reasoning to law, one is left with 'rules', which are to supply the necessary regulation when communism has been achieved. Can one go so far as to say there might be some form of non-political classes? This is probably not the case, as Marx describes classes in terms of their relationship to the means of production. As these means are to be 'owned' by all society, there cannot be any classes. There may be differentiated 'groups' in communist society, but they should not be based on economic differences.

During the transition period, it is recognised that there will be classes. It is to be the period of the dictatorship of the proletariat (as opposed to that of the bourgeoisie, and *not* true democracy, which will only come with communism), and the proletariat will be the ruling class, exercising power over the old bourgeoisie. From this one can easily deduce that there will be a state and law, both of which will be basically similar to the prerevolutionary entities, but be directed against the minority, not the majority. The importance of the transition period must be fully appreciated, as it is such a significant stage of development. It has similarities — and this includes bad points — with earlier society, and is yet a superior stage, as the majority are being benefited and society is moving towards communism. (Of course this latter point can always be said to be true, the difference being one of time — the transition period indicated that it was 'about' to happen, or perhaps 'arrive' would be a better word.) One should note that the transition period is of unknown duration: it is impossible to say it will last a certain number of years, after which communism will exist. This is perfectly reasonable, as although Marx believed such a stage would occur, he would obviously not be able to deduce exactly how long it would last.

In Soviet terms, if the October Revolution was really the socialist revolution, then the period following it is the transition period and the above should be happening: state and law should be withering away, as should be classes and political power. The state should be becoming part of society, not separate, ruling over it. It was a major part of this study to see how and why this was not the case.

Marx and Engels did not say very much about crime and criminals. Their basic proposition was that crime was caused by imperfections in society. These imperfections were inherent in capitalist society, they would not exist in communism, and therefore crime would not exist. This view has been attacked by many as being a crude one-sided determinism, and one has to admit that it does seem remarkably open to this criticism. Moreover, the few comments on what would now be termed 'labelling theory' and 'social reaction' are so truncated that few hard deductions can be made from them. Saying that Marx and Engels did not have a purely deterministic approach may or may not be true, but is not positively constructive.

Deductions of a more interesting nature can be drawn from their attitudes to the lumpenproletariat, a group which includes the criminals. They are considered as totally unreliable, practically worse than the bourgeoisie, a view which must be explained by their political complexion. As they are politically unreliable — Marx gives examples about this in France — they are condemned and rejected. Although it is recognised that this is not an altogether satisfactory explanation, it would seem to be the best available. Criminals are not to be blamed for their actions, as they are the product of the system, but on the other hand, because of their danger, political and otherwise, to society, they are far from being a favoured group.

In the transition period, with the development of communism and change in society, the causes of crime will disappear, and there should be no crime or criminals in communist society — or will there be? Just as one had to make special allowance for the effect of class and politics in state and law theory, does one have to make a parallel differentiation for types of crime? One can make the tautological statement that the type of crime caused by capitalist society will not exist under communism, but to be constructive one has to go further. If one accepts Marx's beliefs about the nature of the future society, one concludes that crime caused by economic imbalance, social friction, etc., will not exist, but does this mean that there will be no crime at all? If it can be said that all crime in capitalist society is caused by the nature of the society, then the answer will be 'yes'. However, on such 'minor' transgressions such as traffic rules one cannot see any link with the nature of society, but more with simple human error. This sort of occurrence would almost certainly exist in communist society as it would in any other, and might be termed 'deviations' or 'transgressions'. Are they the same as crimes without a political content? In so far as they are not caused by inequalities connected with the class aspect of capitalist society, one could say that they were, but it is difficult to decide what exactly Marx intended, as little was said about crime, and although much about law has to be deduced from state theory, this cannot be so readily done with crime as the concepts are not so closely or obviously connected.

To conform to previous practice, one might add that for the Soviet situation, if it is or was the transition period, then crime should be dying out, or changing in nature, and whether or not this is actually happening must be carefully considered.

In the Soviet Union, it is recognised that Lenin added to Marx's original theory, hence the term 'Marxism-Leninism', but this connecting of the two names should also indicate that any additions made by Lenin are believed to be true extensions of the original theory, not revisions of it. A major problem Lenin had to face was how to apply Marx's statements to the Russian situation. It may be remembered that Marx had been consulted on this problem by Vera Zasulich, and had given a positive reply, but attached certain qualifications that were not followed. This, together with general deductions one can make from Marx and Engels' work, should lead one to believe that Russia was not sufficiently developed to begin the final stages of advancement to communism, and this was the generally held belief in Lenin's circle.

However, this was not always to be the case, and after the April Theses the February Revolution was the bourgeois, the October was to be the socialist. Despite initial opposition and surprise, this came to be the accepted view – primarily, one supposes, because it was so much more palatable. Is this view true or not? The answer to this question is not going to lie in the labels attached to various events. The socialist revolution can only happen when society has developed to the correct stage: it depends on the economic forces, not on whether a group of people want it to happen. In the nineteenth century, especially the final part, Russia did undergo considerable capitalist growth, and one might assume that it would have eventually emerged as a significant capitalist power. However, when one compares the various statistics on the economy with those of other countries, it is apparent that this stage had not been reached by 1917. A further period to allow for more growth was required. Seen in context, the idea that the February Revolution could be bourgeois, and the October socialist, appears to be pure nonsense, which is of course exactly what it is.

Having decided that the October Revolution was the socialist revolution, this meant that the period following was supposedly the transition period. What had Lenin said about this? In his writings, the importance of the transition period and the dictatorship of the proletariat was emphasised at length, until it became the 'essence' of the theory. The withering away was seen as a lengthy process (this was probably true), and a great deal had to be done in the meantime to reform and generally prepare society for the future.

This view is not altogether opposed to that of Marx, as he did not underestimate the importance of the transition period, but two important connected points must be noted: (i) Lenin's whole attitude is relying too much on individual action, for although there is a balance between this and determinism in Marx, allowing for choice, a certain degree of acceleration and de-acceleration in development, one cannot cause developments not warranted by the condition of the economic base; and (ii) this was not the transition period and would not end in communism.

The Party, its role and structure, was an extraordinarily important area of innovation for Lenin. It was to be instrumental in the revolutionary process, both as an organisation and as the importer of needed class consciousness. The later development of the Party into a guiding force pervading all aspects of society was an extension of Lenin's concept of it being the vanguard of the proletariat. This confuses the Party with the proletariat whose dictatorship it was supposed to be. These references to the proletariat must be matched with some comment on one of the uppermost problems in applying Marxist theory to Russia: the peasantry.

This class made up the greater part of society, and such a situation seems particularly inappropriate in a socialist stage of evolution, as the proletariat was to be the primary class of that period. The socialist revolution heralding in this stage was to liberate the majority of capitalist society, which was to be the proletarian class. One should note that in Marx's scenario, there do seem to be only two classes, the bourgeoisie and the proletariat, each defined by the relationship to the means of production. This could be criticised as being too simplistic, as every member of capitalist society does not easily fall into one of these two classes, so some allowance may have to be made for other classes. However, it has to be accepted that these two classes have to be the main ones in society, and in Russia, as well as the bourgeoisie being underdeveloped, which has already been implied by the restricted level of capitalist growth, the proletariat was also small-scale for the same reason. The society was rural and agricultural, mainly consisting of peasants. In theory, they did not fit into the picture, and in practice they were a conservative force that wanted certain changes but were not highly revolutionary by any means.

Lenin's answer to this problem was to offer the idea of an alliance of workers and peasants, with the former having the 'leading role'. As the Party had to inject class consciousness into the proletariat, perhaps it did not seem too daunting for it to have to do this for the peasantry too! As Marx's alternative path for future development could not be followed – the village communities having decayed – the existence of such a preponderance of peasants was a definite problem, and one not adequately dealt with by Lenin.

As his emphasis on the importance of the transition period and the dictatorship of the proletariat should have suggested, Lenin believed that state and law would play an important role after the revolution. This was by no means totally unlike what Marx himself had outlined, as the transition period was one which had a state, law and a ruling class. Any difference is one of emphasis, and one has to consider whether the difference is significant or not. As all these factors are impossible to quantify, one would probably have to give this and other variations the benefit of any doubt, but only if the circumstances supported such an action. In this case, they do not, for this is not the transition period, and this is not the state and law of a 'new type' that was to exist. Lenin is, therefore, upholding the use of state and law in a 'normal' situation.

However, his actions do not uphold the rule of law, as enemies were to be treated severely with little regard to formalities. Law was considered to be revolutionary, in a revolutionary situation, but although the latter point was in one way true, it was not the situation set out by Marx. One has to conclude that the situation is in no way comparable to that of law and state in the transition period, and Lenin is attaching Marx's labels to situations to which they do not apply.

From these comments made about Lenin's work and approach, one can see that they are very different from those of Marx. When drawing from theory, Lenin treated Marx and Engels as a monolith, and tended to quote Engels rather than Marx. This resulted in a more rigid, 'scientific' approach, emphasising the inevitability and determinism of the original. He wrongly applied Marx's concepts to the Russian situation, one to which they did not relate, and with his concept of the Party laid the foundations for the party-state bureaucracy that was to develop, which was particularly ironical as Marx rejected the idea of political parties, saying the working class would be their own party. In 'State and Revolution', one can see a Utopian side to Lenin, one which he tended to suppress, but if he believed his predictions, he was mistaken: the time was not right.

The fact that the revolution was not the socialist one colours the events of the first period with special brilliance. The nature of the revolution itself, more palace than social, showed the amount of wishful thinking that had taken place, but this went on to allow for the 'construction of communism'. This consisted of the introduction of a series of what could be loosely described as 'socialist' decrees covering many aspects of social, political and economic life in the country. The fundamental weakness in this was that one cannot 'construct' communism. If society is ready for it, then it will happen, and although a certain degree of freedom of action can occur, a society that is unready cannot be altered to one that is. Therefore these measures may or may not improve the quality of life in society, but cannot be significant steps towards communism. This mistaken attitude still prevails in the Soviet Union, phrases such as 'building communism' abound, and show that too great an emphasis is being placed on the power of individual action. In any event, the system they set out to introduce, that came to be referred to as 'war communism', was a disaster, and after the warning of Kronstadt change had to be forthcoming.

Immediately after the revolution, the position of the Party could be said to be 'contained', that is, it had a defined area of action within which to exercise its role. The government agencies were still separate entities, Party influence being carried out by factions within these agencies. However, this process is expanded successfully to such an extent that the Party and the government to all intents and purposes merge. Other agencies that may have developed competing influential roles, such as trade unions, received similar treatment. The omnipotence of the Party was especially serious, as internal opposition was by no means guaranteed a future. When one compares Stalin's actions with Lenin's, the latter is usually seen as liberal in outlook, but he only supported 'constructive' opposition, and none that might seriously jeopardise the continued rule of the Party. This exception, however understandable or not, had the eventual result of stifling all debate and dissent, although one should say that this did occur under Stalin, not Lenin.

If the Party had genuinely represented the people and had their class consciousness, the situation, while not perfect — for discussion would surely be advantageous in these circumstances — could have perhaps been acceptable, but it was totally unacceptable in the reality of what had happened. The Party was separate from the people, in function, composition, social background, etc., and did not relate to them in any special way. The Party did not rule for the proletariat, it ruled over them, and the cessation of internal criticism, and the suppression of external, was obviously likely to lead to disaster.

As previously mentioned, Lenin believed law would be of great use in this period. Was this the case? To begin with, the prerevolutionary legal system was not entirely abolished, although certain important qualifications were attached to its use. Many new laws were issued, by many, perhaps too many, agencies. Usually they were direct rather than carefully considered, and definitions were imprecise. They were directed against particular problems requiring solution, and had a distinctly *ad hoc* appearance.

Some concepts were given a more extended and careful treatment, for example the use of revolutionary legal consciousness, which was to affect the substance and application of the law. It is suggested that this had only an illusory existence, but the use of similar notions occurs in other legal systems and doubts on its function here concern the extent of its use rather than the use *per se.* In practice, its application is sure to be varied, and the result somewhat unpredictable, although not necessarily unacceptable. However, the tendency was to limit the use of revolutionary legal consciousness by the issuing of decrees and codes or guides. The question was raised that the legal consciousness of the people was not the same as that of the regime, which can be seen as one aspect of the process of imposing a particular system on a society unsuited for it, although one must admit that this could happen in the transition period proper too, but on a lesser scale.

Prerevolutionary law exercised considerable influence over post-revolutionary, not only in the period before it was formally abolished, but in the formation of revolutionary consciousness. To begin with, the persons administering justice were often officials or lawyers of the former system, and their judgement was formed via connected concepts. In later years this law was to affect the codes, and even now some usages can be traced back to the old system. These connections are evidence for the view that although many aspects of the new system were innovatory, it was not one of an entirely new type. It was still akin to a traditional system with changes made, some good some bad: it was on a new direction.

Explanations of crime, at this stage, rested on the 'vestiges of the past' approach, with a basic leniency for ordinary offenders and severity for counter-revolutionaries − who were widely defined. This is similar to Marx's view, but is not in the same context. Counter-revolution was linked to class, for if any non-bourgeois offenders committed such crimes, it was explained by saying they had been misled or forced to do so. The social and political system was 'theirs', working for them and therefore they would not offend against it.

Summarising, one has a Party in control rather than the proletariat; a tendency towards dictatorship, and not one of the proletariat; considerable upheaval caused by the revolution; an embryonic legal system that differentiated offences on class lines; and little sign of any rule of law. The continued existence of law and state is explained in pseudo-Marxist terms, this being historically supported by the fact of the revolution (although not the correct one), and crime is similarly excused and treated with a distinct class aspect. The fallacy of the time can be summarised in one sentence: Lenin said this was the transition period and it was not.

The 1920s, the period of the NEP, were in many ways one of the most interesting in Soviet history. The policy itself reversed the trends of war communism which had been disastrous for the country and threatened the position of the regime. It was criticised for being a retrogressive step, reintroducing capitalism, and despite valiant arguments to the contrary by Lenin, one believes it was a return to capitalism, a definite change of direction for the regime. However, it should not be termed 'retrogressive', as it was in compliance with Marx. The country was not ready to begin the latter stages of development to communism, so the introduction of measures to lead to this (on such a scale, of doubtful orthodoxy in any case) predictably resulted in adversity, so the NEP should be seen as a return to normal development. If such matters can be judged on results, then this interpretation would appear correct, as economic conditions improved greatly.

It was in this period that the gap between Party and government closed, and the infiltration of the latter by the former totally succeeded. The differentiation between the Party and the people continued, for although the Lenin Enrolment curtailed the elitist aspect to a significant extent, the social composition, as would be expected with a governing party, was different from society, having a much higher percentage of white-collar employees. The intake was not experienced, but older members were in the higher posts, a situation that favoured leadership from the top.

If this had been the transition period, various entities and concepts should have been withering away, one of which would be class. Was this happening? As regards theory, of course it could not be, but what was the situation in practice? At the beginning of the period class references continued to be included in the decrees and Codes, and were important in assessing the punishments to be used. After 1927 they tend to be less frequent, but the wide definitions would allow for discrimination if this was wanted. On an economic level, the situation was changing in a Marxist sense as the relationship to the means of production was changing for the various groups in society. Although the means of production were supposed to be owned by the proletariat in this period — they being the ruling class — in reality the formation of a 'new class' may have been beginning, as the upper levels of the administration had a certain control, a certain special relationship, to these means of production.

Djilas, in *The New Class*, says the class is initiated by the professional revolutionaries rather than the Party as a whole, and can be difficult to define, but may be described as being made up of 'those who have special privileges and economic preference because of the administrative monopoly they hold'.[1] If one accepts this thesis, then this period is when the new class begins to consolidate itself, but the more spectacular developments come a little later with the wage and privilege differentials fostered by Stalin in the industrialisation campaign, in an attempt to give them a personal interest in its success.

There was a great deal of legislative activity in the 1920s, and it was an important period of codification. The Codes had wide definitions and were usually liberal in their original form, which was made more severe by subsequent changes – a case of the good intentions of debates and discussions being tempered by cold reality. While the terminology used is not so 'Marxist' as the 1919 Fundamental Principles, their overall pattern works from similar assumptions, with a materialist rather than formal approach, a belief that crime was in one way excusable as it was due to 'vestiges', but severe penalties for 'counter-revolutionaries' who turned out to be anyone threatening the continued rule of the regime; and the use of the concept of social defence. Law did not appear to be about to wither away, and was seen to be important in the short- and medium-term future. Stuchka, and especially Pashukanis, linked law too closely to bourgeois values, useful to begin with, but then of considerable embarrassment, for as time progressed new explanations had to be found to say why events were not following the Marxist pattern, the real reason being, of course, totally unacceptable.

A particularly typical development in this period was the Krylenko-Pashukanis codes, which carried many of the contemporary theories to a logical conclusion by rejecting the definitions of a special part and relying on the broad guidelines of the general. When the stability of law comes to be emphasised, this sort of approach is obviously unsuitable and the codes, and their authors, fell from favour.

Summarising, one has an innovative, stimulating period, that was supposed to be the transition period. Although some important qualifications had started to appear in state theory – notably the theory of socialism in one country – to try to explain the actual situation in what would appear Marxist terms, the withering away of state, law and crime was not happening in practice, with the state being strengthened, reorganised and protected; law becoming more accepted, institutionalised and codified (which meant less faith was being placed in revolutionary legal consciousness); and crime increasing, despite the use of novel ideas such as constructive punishments rather than imprisonment. Criminology was an accepted area of study, and although working from false premises, may have reached instructive conclusions eventually if allowed to develop.

Although the labels of Marx are still attached, they do not apply, and the Party was consolidating its position. The introduction of the NEP can be seen as Lenin's realisation that further development on capitalist lines, with suitable controls to stop excesses, was necessary before Russia could begin to seriously move towards communism. His late work, 'On Co-operation', emphasises the use of co-operatives and seems to indicate a new or renewed belief in the use and need for change within society – as opposed to that imposed from above. It is difficult to pass judgement on Lenin's actions in this period, the last in which he was alive, as he was not in power long enough for him, and us, to see how things would have developed under him.

The 1930s were shaped by two events, the purges and collectivisation. The former affected the Party, and resulted in Stalin gaining complete control. In the process, indeed as a necessary part of the process, he destroyed the Party as an institution. It ceased having the separateness, power of decision-making and importance it had earlier, and became more of a 'conveyor belt' for Stalin's wishes. He had admired Hitler's subjugation of the National Socialist Party in June 1934, and acted similarly. Schapiro,[2] in saying that the Party was not a true bureaucracy, describes it as 'essentially a body of retainers', an apt depiction. A thought-provoking aspect of the purges was the reactions of the purged, Bukharin's unnecessary return to Russia being a spectacular example. Reading the various accounts, one receives the impression that although surprise and bewilderment were widespread, there was no general feeling that something was wrong with the leadership. The horror was not so much due to being purged, but at the thought one may have been disloyal to the Party, showing an almost religious feeling that the rule of the Party and the path followed was right (and inevitable) for society.

During this period, there were further attempts to increase the proportion of workers and peasants in the Party, a worthy but perhaps less important aim now that the Party was less important. The most significant factor concerning the Party in this period was its lessened significance.

If the purges directed themselves primarily at the Party, collectivisation certainly did not act so selectively, with the majority of society affected. It supposedly set out to reorganise agriculture on to more acceptable, socialist and efficient lines, but the effect was different. Production dropped drastically as peasants slaughtered cattle and neglected their work. Much legislation was specifically designed to meet these problems, but was not overtly successful. Of course the peasantry had always been a problem to the regime, as they were a conservative force, hardly suitable in a situation of 'revolutionary advances'. Collectivisation was a useful way of destroying any opposition by breaking up peasant society and organising it on more controllable lines. The kulaks were the alleged enemy, and they would have been a genuine centre of discontent against the regime, and moreover, allowed the instigators of the campaign to say it was not directed at the peasantry as a whole, but only a certain privileged section of it, for an open breach with the peasantry was completely out of the question. Of course in practice this breach did occur, as the collectivisation squads often acted indiscriminately, and legislation affected all — poor, middle or kulak.

Disregarding the inhuman deprivations caused by the campaign, the idea of trying to change the basis of society in this artificial way is totally un-Marxist: change must be organic, not enforced. It did result in an important fundamental change in agriculture, but not the advent of communism, and reflects the reasons for its introduction, some economic, some political, and some personal to Stalin, for he now had the state, a superstructural entity, directing and controlling economic change.

Repressive legislation affected workers too, as labour discipline decrees became stricter and more frequent. This had the most profound effect on the quality of life throughout all society, and even the upper echelons had to deal with strange working hours and whims from above. The various attempts to strengthen the procuracy and temper the worst excesses were better than nothing, but could not alter the basic injustice of the period.

Just as law was fully utilised in this period of its 'withering away', the state was furthered, glorified and protected, with the introduction of treason decrees and the heavy penalties for infringements of socialist property, which was the subject of an almost continuous stream of decrees. As this property was said to belong to society as a whole, the legislation protecting it could be said to be acting for all society, and against the common enemy. However, Djilas[3] says, 'The emergence of the new class has been concealed under socialist phraseology and, more important, under the new collective forms of property ownership. The so-called ownership is a disguise for the real ownership by the political bureaucracy.' Seen in this light, the decrees protecting this 'asset of all society' are really defending the rights of ownership of the new ruling group, which would be entirely in accord with Marx. In this period, the connections with 'Marx' become noticably more tenuous. State and law are stabilised rather than withering, and special pleading has entered fully into the life of theory, with friendly classes, the need to defend the country from outside attack, all used to 'explain' the situation in pseudo-Marxist terms. Many of the worst features of the period are often blamed on Stalin personally, and it seems certain that this is in some way relevant, as he had a suspicious, strange personality. However, one must not consider this a Utopian situation gone wrong, or made to go wrong by one man. The foundation of this Utopia were non-existent.

After the interest of the previous years, the period to Stalin's death does lack in excitement. The most important historical event, the war, had an enormous effect on society, but cannot be judged in our terms, apart from on the general level of saying that if communism was nearing, it should not have happened, and for the leader of the 'progressive' forces in the world, Stalin seemed to find it remarkably easy to come to an accord with Hitler. Many trends appearing earlier were continued, such as the further emphasis on the stability of the law and state, Vyshinsky supplying a theory that would appear to explain this in Marxist terms. The Party remained in the background, with Stalin becoming more reliant on governing via a small group. Labour discipline was tightened even more, with a further worsening in the quality of life of ordinary citizens, but analogy, although not a necessary tool, was utilised in a more restricted way, part of the move to appear more under the rule of law that had developed since the Stalin Constitution. Oddities of a most serious nature occurred with the deporting of certain national groups, and towards the very end of his life Stalin seemed to become more suspicious of others, a most portentous state of affairs. His death, whether mourned or greeted with a sigh of relief, was most opportune, and if not a full stop in history, certainly a semi-colon.

Change was both needed and expected, and to a certain extent materialised – but not in all areas. For example, theory suffered no traumatic reversal. State and law were to continue and there was some suggestion that they may exist under 'communism', a development completely at variance with Marx but not at all surprising when one considers previous products of similar evolution. From this, one can deduce that the withering away was supposedly still to take place. It was seen as further public participation in the administration of state and law, with the comrades' courts and anti-parasite laws as examples of the latter. However, as has already been stated, the true withering away is an organic integral change in society, and cannot be crudely engineered in this way, so while a similar development may well be a significant product of the true withering away, it cannot be a significant part of the withering away in itself.

Part of the mechanism by which the existence of law was continued was the emphasis placed on 'stability', which now implied a rejection of some Stalinist practices (and of Vyshinsky's theories). There was a great deal of talk about the protection, and the need to protect, the rights of the individual, but this did not result in any real safeguard, as state rights and individual rights were seen as complementary, unable to be in conflict. If the situation had been that envisaged by Marx, and this had been the transition period, then at the end of the period there would be no conflict between such interests, the state being part of society. In the actual situation prevailing, it is nonsense; and state and individual rights would tend to be in greater conflict than in many more liberal societies where fewer regulations pervade. This really amounts to a method of theoretically upholding personal rights, a development necessary as part of the rejection of the heritage of Stalin (and useful in itself), while in practice allowing the state the same freedoms as before. As by 'state' one really means the Party leadership, the continuity becomes apparent. They have this power and status *ex officio* — consider Khrushchev's position after his fall — and should be considered as a significant part of the concept of the state. Despite the continuity, the partial change in climate would probably mean that the worst excesses of the Stalin regime would not easily occur again if a comprehensive repressive policy was stepped up. The Party underwent a revival, and took a more significant part in the decision-making process than it did under Stalin. Its Programme of 1961 had many features that were in line with previous developments. One notable point was that the dictatorship of the proletariat was said to be not needed internally, as the exploiting classes were no more. This is yet another extraordinary use of Marx's labels to non-Marxist situations. The dictatorship of the proletariat in truth did not exist, but not because it was no longer needed. It had never existed. If there had been a dictatorship it was of the Party or its leaders, the dictatorship of the proletariat being a transition period phenomenon. The general role of the Party as the guiding force in society remained very much the same as before, and mechanics such as recruitment were basically similar, although in the beginning of the period the intake of workers and peasants had one of its occasional increases. There is still a high percentage of white-collar workers in the Party.

The stated class composition of society also raises awkward questions about orthodoxy with Marx. The position at the moment is that there are supposed to be two friendly classes, of workers and peasants. The intelligentsia form a 'stratum', not a class. This is in many ways a rather ingenious compromise, as it reflects the initial problem of the Russian situation: too many peasants, too few workers; and admits the obvious differences that still exist between the two. The further differentiation between the intelligentsia and the rest of society is also taken into account, which is at least an improvement on any pretence that the society is homogeneous. What is the real picture and what are the conclusions to be drawn?

It is sensible to recognise that differences do exist between the workers and the peasants, and in many other societies the intelligentsia are rather difficult to classify. However, although Marx did not fully expand his ideas on class, the basic point about his view is that one's class is decided by the relationship one has to the means of production. In the simple pattern, if one was a member of that group which owned them, then one was bourgeois, and if one did not, then one was proletarian. This easily applies only to the idealised advanced capitalist society, but usually the picture was more complicated. Would peasants and workers be considered as separate classes by Marx? The former were from an earlier 'stage' of development, and would have evolved into workers (or bourgeoisie) if allowed. In the meantime it would be more correct to consider them as separate classes, but they can in many ways be identified with the proletariat – but not in all. They do have a different, if not exactly opposite, relationship to the means of production. The intelligentsia should be a product of their background and ideally fall into one or other of the classes. It was Lenin who emphasised the concept of *déclassés* – linked to his ideas on the Party and class consciousness.

What has not been admitted by the Soviets is the existence of a new bourgeoisie, for although the means of production are supposed to be owned by all members of society collectively, and used for the common good, this is not the case. Djilas maintains they are owned by the 'new class', a view supported by their access to, and power over, the means of production– and the grotesque variations in salaries and privileges that exist in present-day Soviet society.

Many liberal developments occurred in substantive law, which would be expected when the very severe measures that prevailed under Stalin are remembered. However, they were some harsh measures introduced, some more specific in their action, such as the wide use made of the death penalty, crimes against the state and state property, hooliganism and alcohol misuse, and the changes to the 1960 Code; but some were more general – the anti-parasite legislation. This latter is a rather Stalinist method of dealing with a problem, and showed the continuity that existed between the 'old' and the 'new'. Stalin had been rejected, but not Stalinism, and while there have been rehabilitations of those previously purged and condemned, there have also been periodic threatened rehabilitations of Stalin.

It does not seem that crime is about to disappear, and although criminological research is continuing, difficult if not insurmountable problems are being caused by the inability to admit the existence of any

crime causing factors in present Soviet society other than those
directly or indirectly connectable with 'vestiges of the past'. This is
becoming more embarrassing as the 'past' becomes more distant.

Summarising this period, one has definite links with the past, yet
improvements have been made. Changes have occurred in both theory
and practice, but often these are of degree, not kind. The Party has
been resuscitated and once again has the guiding role in practice which
it has always had in theory — although the leadership is becoming more
obviously separate in deciding policy. State and law are continuing,
with artificial attempts made at 'withering away' and 'communism' is
said to be nearer. Crime does not appear to be decreasing significantly,
and some areas are giving cause for considerable concern.

The fundamental problem that has prevailed throughout Soviet history
is that of relating theory to practice. It seems extraordinary that there
can be any further pretence that the Soviet Union is in the final stages
of the development to communism — in Marx's transition period. Its
problems and drawbacks are simply unconnected with Marx, who
cannot be blamed for what has happened. His concepts do not apply to
the Soviet Union — except in so far as there exists a state, a ruling class,
political power, law and crime. What does not exist, and never has, is a
dictatorship of the proletariat, transition period, socialist revolution
and socialism. Wishful thinking, or a deliberate attempt to mislead, has
resulted in the attachment of certain labels to different concepts, and
the question must be, how long can it continue? This will not depend
on the ingenuity of the regime to think of new explanations for
whatever develops, or what does not develop, as this seems infinite.

Engels sums up the situation very well when, in 'The Peasant War in
Germany', he says:

The worst thing that can befall the leader of an extreme party is to
be compelled to take over a government in an epoch when the
movement is not yet ripe for the domination[4] of the class which he
represents, and for the realisation of the measures which that
domination implies. What he *can* do depends not upon his will but
upon the degree of contradiction between the various classes, and
upon the level of development of the material means of existence...
What he *ought* to do, what his party demands of him, again depends
not upon him or the stage of development of the class struggle and
its conditions. He is bound to the doctrines and demands hitherto
propounded...Thus, he necessarily finds himself in an unsolvable

dilemma. What he *can* do contradicts all his previous actions, principles and immediate interests of his party, and what he *ought* to do cannot be done. In a word, he is compelled to represent not his party or his class, but the class for whose domination the movement is then ripe. In the interests of the movement he is compelled to advance the interests of an alien class, and to feed his own class with phrases and promises, and with the (assertion) that the interests of that alien class are their own interests. Whoever is put into this awkward position is irrevocably lost.[5]

This class was the 'new class'. While Marx's approach is not totally deterministic, the scope for individual action has its limits.

Notes

1. Milovan Dijlas, *The New Class* (London, 1966), p. 49.
2. L. Schapiro, *The Communist Party of the Soviet Union*, 2nd edn. (London, 1970), p. 623.
3. *The New Class*, p. 55.
4. *Herrschaft* – 'rule' (or 'domination').
5. Moscow, 1956, pp. 138-9.

SELECT BIBLIOGRAPHY

Abbreviations Used in this Study

CDSP   − *Current Digest of the Soviet Press*
SGiP   − *Sovetskoe Gosudarstvo i Pravo*
Sov. Iust.   − *Sovetskaia Iustitsiia*
Sots. Zak.   − *Sotsialisticheskaia Zakonnost'*
Vop. Fil.   − *Voprosy Filosofii*
SU see *Sobranie Uzakonenii*, below
SZ see *Sobranie Zakonov*, below
Vedomosti RSFSR, see below
Vedomosti SSSR, see below

Collections of Laws

Sobranie Zakonov i Rasporiazhenii Raboche-Krest'ianskogo
    Pravitel'stva S.S.S.R. (1924-38)
Sobranie Postanovlenii i Rasporiazhenii Pravitel'stva S.S.S.R. (1938-46)
    (a continuation of the above)
Sobranie Postanovlenii i Rasporiazhenii Soveta Ministrov S.S.S.R.
    (1946 to date) (a continuation of the above)
Vedomosti Verkhovnogo Soveta S.S.S.R.
Sobranie Uzakonenii i Rasporiazhenii Raboche-Krest'ianskogo
    Pravitel'stva R.S.F.S.R. (1917-38)
Sobranie Postanovlenii i Rasporiazhenii Pravitel'stva R.S.F.S.R.
    (1938-48) (a continuation of the above)
Sobranie Postanovlenii i Rasporiazhenii Soveta Ministrov R.S.F.S.R.
    (1948 to date) (a continuation of the above)
Vedomosti Verkhovnogo Soveta R.S.F.S.R.

Abramovitch, R.R. *The Soviet Revolution 1917-1939* (George Allen and Unwin, London, 1962).

Acton, H.B. *The Illusion of the Epoch* (Routledge and Kegan Paul, London, 1973)

Adamiak, Richard 'The "Withering Away" of the State: A Reconsideration', *Journal of Politics*, vol. 32 (1970), pp. 3-18

Adams, Will 'Capital Punishment in Imperial and Soviet Criminal Law', *American Journal of Comparative Law*, vol. 18 (1970), pp. 575-94

Akhapkin, Yuri (ed.) *First Decrees of Soviet Power* (Lawrence and Wishart, London, 1970)

Amnesty International *Prisoners of Conscience in the USSR: Their Treatment and Conditions* (Amnesty International Publications, London, 1975)

Anashkin, G.Z. 'Gumanizm sovetskogo ugolovnogo prava', *Sovetskoe Gosudarstvo i Pravo*, no. 8 (1963), pp. 44-52

Antonian, IU.M. 'Sotsialno-psikhologicheskie posledstviia urbonizatsii i ikh vliianie na prestupnost'', *Sovetskoe Gosudarstvo i Pravo*, no. 8 (1975), pp. 67-73

Avineri, Shlomo *The Social and Political Thought of Karl Marx* (Cambridge University Press, Cambridge, 1968)

Babb, Hugh W. (trans.) *Soviet Legal Philosophy* (Harvard University Press, Cambridge, Mass., 1951)

Baitin, M.I. 'O klassovoi sushchnosti sovetskogo obshchenarodnogo gosudarstva', *Sovetskoe Gosudarstvo i Pravo*, no. 1 (1976), pp. 5-13

Barry, Donald D., Ginsburgs, George, and Maggs, Peter P. *Soviet Law After Stalin*, Part I, Law in Eastern Europe, no. 20/1 (A.W. Sijthoff, Leyden, 1977)

Beermann, R. 'A Discussion on the Draft Law against Parasites, Tramps and Beggars', *Soviet Studies*, vol. IX (1957/8), pp. 214-22

——, 'Law Against Parasites, Tramps and Beggars', *Soviet Studies*, vol. XI (1959/60), pp. 453-5.

——, 'The Parasites Law', *Soviet Studies*, vol. XIII (1961/2), pp. 191-205

——, 'Soviet and Russian Anti-parasite Laws', *Soviet Studies*, vol. XV (1963/4), pp. 420-9

Belov, G.A. *et al.* (eds.) *Iz Istorii Vecheka 1917-1921rr.* (Gosudarstvennoe Izdatel'stvo Politicheskoi Literatury, Moscow, 1958)

Berlin, Isaiah *Karl Marx*, 3rd edn. (Oxford University Press, London, 1963)

Berman, Harold J. 'Soviet Law Reform – Dateline Moscow 1957',

Yale Law Journal, vol. 66 (1956-7), pp. 1191-215

——, *Justice in the U.S.S.R.*, 2nd edn. (Harvard University Press, Cambridge, Mass., 1966)

——, and Quigley, John, B. Jr. *Basic Laws of the Soviet State* (Harvard University Press, Cambridge, Mass., 1969)

——, and Spindler, James W. *Soviet Criminal Law and Procedure: The RSFSR Codes*, 2nd edn. (Harvard University Press, Cambridge, Mass., 1972)

Blackstock, P.W. and Hoselitz, B.F. (eds.) *The Russian Menace to Europe* (The Free Press, Glencoe, Illinois, 1952)

Bloom, Solomon F. 'The "Withering Away" of the State', *Journal of the History of Ideas*, vol. 7 (January 1946), pp. 114-21

Bober, M.M. *Karl Marx's Interpretation of History*, 2nd edn. (Harvard University Press, Cambridge, Mass., 1948)

Bodenheimer, Edgar 'The Impasse of Soviet Legal Philosophy', *Cornell Law Review*, vol. 38 (1952-3), pp. 51-72

Bottomore, T.B. (ed.) *Karl Marx: Early Writings* (Penguin Books, London, 1975)

——, and Rubel, Maximilien (eds.) *Karl Marx: Selected Writings in Sociology and Social Philosophy*, 2nd edn. (Pelican Books, London, 1973)

Bowden, W., Karpovich, M. and Usher, A.P. *An Economic History of Europe Since 1975* (American Book Company, New York, 1937)

Brown, Archie, and Kaser, Michael (eds.) *The Soviet Union Since the Fall of Khrushchev*, 2nd edn. (Macmillan, London, 1978)

Brzezinski, Zbigniew, and Huntington, Samuel P. *Political Power: USA/USSR* (Penguin Books, London, 1977)

Bukharin, N., and Preobrazhensky, E. *The ABC of Communism* (Pelican Books, London, 1969)

Bulatov, S. 'Khuliganstvo i mery bor'by s nim v rekonstruktivnom periode', *Sovetskoe Gosudarstvo i Pravo*, no. 4 (1933), pp. 63-74

Bunyan, James *Intervention, Civil War and Communism in Russia: April – December 1918* (The Johns Hopkins Press, Baltimore, 1936)

Cambridge Economic History of Europe, The (H.J. Habbakkuk and M. Postan (eds.)), vol. VI, Part II (Cambridge University Press, Cambridge, 1966)

Carew Hunt, R.N. *The Theory and Practice of Communism*, 5th edn. (Penguin Books, London, 1963)

Carr, Edward Hallett *A History of Soviet Russia: The Bolshevik Revolution 1917-1923* (3 vols., Pelican Books, London, 1966)

——, *The Interregnum 1923-1924* (Pelican Books, London, 1969)

——, *Socialism in One Country 1924-1926* (3 vols., Pelican Books, London, 1970)

——, and Davies, R.W. *Foundations of a Planned Economy 1926-1929*, vols. 1 and 2 (Pelican Books, London, 1974)

Chertkov 'Novye formy klassovoi bor'by kulachestva', *Sovetskaia Iustitsiia*, no. 30 (1931), pp. 14-16

Chkhikvadze, V.M. *Sovetskoe Ugolovnoe Pravo: Chast' Obshchaia* (Gosudarstvennoe Izdatel'stvo Politicheskoi Literatury, Moscow, 1952)

Christman, Henry M. (ed.) *Communism in Action: A Documentary History* (Bantam Books, New York, 1969)

Cohen, Stephen F. *Bukharin and the Bolshevik Revolution* (Vintage Books, New York, 1975)

Collection of Yugoslav Laws, vol. XI (The Criminal Code) (Institute of Comparative Law, Beograd, 1964)

Communist Party of the Soviet Union:

K.P.S.S. v Rezoliutsiiakh i Resheniiakh s"ezdov Konferentsii i Plenumov TsK (Izdatel'stvo Politicheskoi Literatury, Moscow, 1970)

'KPSS v tsifrakh', *Partiinaia Zhizn*, no. 10 (1976), pp. 13-23

Resolutions and Decisions of the Communist Party of the Soviet Union. General editor, R.H. McNeal (University of Toronto Press, Toronto, 1974)

    Vol. 2: *The Early Soviet Period, 1917-1929* (ed. Gregor)

    Vol. 3: *The Stalin Years, 1929-1953* (ed. McNeal)

    Vol. 4: *The Khrushchev Years, 1953-1964* (ed. Hodnett)

Vnoecherednoi XXI S"ezd Kommunisticheskoi Partii Sovetskogo Soiuza, I (Gosudarstvennoe Izdatel'stvo Politicheskoi Literatury, Moscow, 1959)

'XX S"ezd KPSS i zadogi sovetskoi pravovoi nauki', *Sovetskoe Gosudarstvo i Pravo*, no. 2 (1956), pp. 3-14

Companion to Russian Studies I: An Introduction to Russian History, R. Autry and D. Obolensky (eds.) (Cambridge University Press, Cambridge, 1976)

Connor, Walter D. *Deviance in Soviet Society* (Columbia University Press, New York, 1976)

Conquest, Robert (ed.) *Justice and the Legal System in the USSR* (Bodley Head, London, 1968)

——, *The Great Terror*, rev. edn. (Pelican Books, London, 1971)

——, *Lenin* (Fontana, London, 1972)

Constitution, USSR (Co-operative Publishing Society of Foreign Workers in the USSR, Moscow, 1937)

Criminal Code of the R.S.F.S.R., translated by O.T. Rayner (UK Foreign Office, London, 1925)

Criminal (Penal) Code of the R.S.F.S.R. (UK Foreign Office, London, 1934)

Daniels, Robert V. *A Documentary History of Communism* (2 vols., Vintage Books, New York, 1960)

De George, Richard T. *Patterns of Soviet Thought* (University of Michigan Press, Ann Arbor, 1970)

Denisov, A.I. *Istoriia Gosudarstva i Prava SSSR* (Chast' II, Iuridicheskoe Izdatel'stvo Ministerstva Iustitsii SSSR, Moscow, 1948)

Deutscher, Isaac *The Prophet Armed* (Oxford University Press, London, 1954)

——, *Stalin*, rev. edn. (Pelican Books, London, 1966)

Djilas, Milovan *The New Class* (Unwin Books, London, 1966)

Dobrin, S. 'Soviet Jurisprudence and Socialism', *Law Quarterly Review*, vol. LII (1936), pp. 402-24

Draper, Hal 'Marx and the Dictatorship of the Proletariat', *New Politics*, vol. 1, no. 4 (1961), pp. 91-104

Durmanov, N.D. *Poniatie Prestupleniia* (Izdatel'stvo Akademii Nauk SSSR, Moscow-Leningrad, 1948)

Engels, Frederick *The Peasant War in Germany* (Foreign Languages Publishing House, Moscow, 1956)

——, *Anti-Duhring* (Lawrence and Wishart, London, 1969)

——, *The Condition of the Working Class in England* (Progress Publishers, Moscow, 1973)

Erickson, John *The Soviet High Command* (Macmillan, London, 1962)

Estrin, A. YA. *Ugolovnoe Pravo R.S.F.S.R.* (Iuridicheskoe Izdatel'stvo Narkomiusta, Moscow, 1923)

——, *Sovetskoe Ugolovnoe Pravo: Chast' Obshchaia* (Gosudarstvennoe Izdatel'stvo Sovetskoe Zakonodatel'stvo, Moscow, 1935)

Evans, Michael *Karl Marx* (George Allen and Unwin, London, 1975)

Fainsod, Merle *Smolensk Under Soviet Rule* (Vintage Books, New York, 1963)

——, *How Russia is Ruled*, rev. edn. (Harvard University Press, Cambridge, Mass., 1970)

Federal Criminal Law of the Soviet Union, The, Law in Eastern Europe, no. 3 (A.W. Sijthoff, Leyden, 1959)

Feldbrugge, F.J. 'Soviet Criminal Law – the Last Six Years', *Journal of Criminal Law, Criminology and Police Science*, vol. 54 (1963), pp. 249-66

——, *Soviet Criminal Law: General Part*, Law in Eastern Europe, no. 9

(A.W. Sijthoff, Leyden, 1964)

——, *Codification in the Communist World*, Law in Eastern Europe, no. 19 (A.W. Sijthoff, Leyden, 1975)

Ferimov, D.A. 'Liberty, Law and the Legal Order', *North Western University Law Review*, vol. 58 (1963-4), pp. 643-56

Footman, David *Civil War in Russia* (Faber and Faber, London, 1961)

Franklin, Bruce (ed.) *The Essential Stalin* (Croom Helm, London, 1973)

Freeborn, Richard *A Short History of Modern Russia* (Hodder and Stoughton, London, 1966)

Fuller, Lon. L. 'Pashukanis and Vyshinksy: A Study in the Development of Marxist Legal Theory', *Michigan Law Review*, vol. 47 (1948-9), pp. 1157-66

Gernet, M.N., and Trainin, A.N. (eds.) *Ugolovnyi Kodeks: Prakticheskii Kommentarii* (Izdatel'stvo 'Pravo i Zhizn'', Moscow, 1925)

Gertsenzon, A.A. *Sovetskaia Ugolovnaia Statistika*, 2nd edn. (Iuridicheskoe Izdatel'stvo NKIU SSSR, Moscow, 1937)

——, 'Ob izuchenii i preduprezhdenii prestupnosti', *Sovetskoe Gosudarstvo i Pravo*, no. 7 (1968), pp. 78-88

——, *et al.* (eds.) *Kriminologiia*, 2nd edn. (Gosudarstvennoe Izdatel'stvo Iuridicheskoi Literatury, Moscow, 1968)

——, and Vyshinskii, Z.A. *Sovetskoe Ugolovnoe Pravo: Chast' Osobennaia* (Gosudarstvennoe Izdatel'stvo Iuridicheskoi Literatury, Moscow, 1951)

Ginsburgs, George, and Mason, George 'Soviet Criminal Law Reform: Central Uniformity versus Local Diversification' in G.O.W. Mueller (ed.), *Essays in Criminal Science* (Sweet and Maxwell, London, 1961), pp. 409-46

——, and Rusis, Armins *Soviet Criminal Law and the Protection of State Secrets*, Law in Eastern Europe, no. 7 (A.W. Sijthoff, Leyden, 1963)

Gladkov, I.A. *Sovetskoe Narodnoe Khoziastvo v 1921-1925rr.* (Izdatel'stvo Akademii Nauk SSSR, Moscow, 1960)

Goliakov, I.T. *Sbornik Dokumentov Po Istorii Ugolovnogo Zakonodatel'stvo SSSR i RSFSR, 1917-1952* (Gosudarstvennoe Izdatel'stvo Iuridicheskoi Literatury, Moscow, 1953)

Gregor, see Communist Party of the Soviet Union

Grey, Ian *The First Fifty Years: Soviet Russia, 1917-67* (Hodder and Stoughton, London, 1967)

Gringauz, I.K. 'K voprosu ob ogolovnom prave i pravovorchestve mass v 1917 i 1918rr.', *Sovetskoe Gosudarstvo i Pravo*, no. 3 (194), pp. 80-91

Hazard, John N. 'Reforming Soviet Criminal Law', *Journal of Criminal Law and Criminology*, vol. 29 (1938), pp. 157-69

———, 'Trends in the Soviet Treatment of Crime', *American Sociological Review* (1940), pp. 566-76

———, 'Soviet Wartime Legislation', *Russian Review* (1942), pp. 22-30

———, *Law and Social Change in the USSR* (Stevens and Sons, London, 1953)

———, *Settling Disputes in Soviet Society* (Columbia University Press, New York, 1960)

———, *Communists and their Law: A Search for the Common Core of the Legal Systems of the Marxian Socialist States* (University of Chicago Press, Chicago, 1969)

———, Schapiro, Isaac, and Maggs, Peter B. (eds.) *The Soviet Legal System: Contemporary Documentation and Historical Commentary* (Oceana, Dobbs Ferry, New York, 1969)

———, and Weisberg, Morris L. *Cases and Readings in Soviet Law* (Parker School of Foreign and Comparative Law, Columbia University, New York, 1950)

Henderson, W.O. (ed.) *Engels: Selected Writings* (Pelican Books, London, 1967)

Hirst, Paul Q. 'Marx and Engels on Law, Crime and Morality', *Economy and Society*, vol. 1, no. 1 (1972), pp. 28-56

Hodges, Donald Clark 'Engels' Contribution to Marxism', *Socialist Register* (Merlin Press, London, 1965), pp. 297-310

Hodnett, see Communist Party of the Soviet Union

Hook, Sidney *Towards the Understanding of Karl Marx* (London, 1936)

Istoriia Gosudarstva i Prava SSSR (2 vols., Izdatel'stvo 'Iuridicheskaia Literatura', Moscow, 1967)

Istoriia Sovetskoi Konstitutsii 1917-1956 (Gosudarstvennoe Izdatel'stvo Iuridicheskoi Literatury, Moscow, 1957)

Jaworskyj, Michael (ed.) *Soviet Political Thought* (The Johns Hopkins Press, Baltimore, 1967)

Johnson, E.L. *An Introduction to the Soviet Legal System* (Methuen, London, 1972)

Juviler, Peter H. *Revolutionary Law and Order* (The Free Press, New York, 1976)

Kamenka, Eugene *Marxism and Ethics* (Macmillan, London, 1969)

Karev, D.S. *Ugolovnoe Zakonodatel'stvo SSSR i Soiuznykh Respublik* (Gosudarstvennoe Izdatel'stvo Iuridicheskoi Literatury, Moscow, 1957)

Karnitskii, D. *et al.* (eds.) *Ugolovnyi Kodeks R.S.F.S.R.*, 4th edn.

(Sovetskoe Zakonodatel'stvo, Moscow, 1931)

Karpets, I.I. *Problema Prestupnosti* (Gosudarstvennoe Izdatel'stvo Iuridicheskoi Literatury, Moscow, 1969)

Kelle, V. ZH. 'Nekotorye osobennosti razvitiia sotsializma', *Voprosy Filosofii*, no. 3 (1966), pp. 14-24

Kelsen, Hans *The Communist Theory of Law* (Stevens and Sons, London, 1955)

Kolakowski, Leslak *Marxism and Beyond* (Paladin, London, 1971)

Korsch, Karl *Marxism and Philosophy* (New Left Books, London, 1970)

Kosolapov, P.I. 'Na puti k besklassovomu obshchestvu', *Voprosy Filosofii*, no. 5 (1971), pp. 17-30

Kozhevnikov, M.V. *Istoriia Sovetskogo Suda* (Gosudarstvennoe Izdatel'stvo Iuridicheskoi Literatury, Moscow, 1957)

KPSS, See Communist Party of the Soviet Union

Krylenko, N.V. *Sudoustroistvo RSFSR* (Iuridicheskoe Izdatel'stvo N.K.IU., Moscow, 1923)

——, *Safeguarding Public (Socialist) Property* (Co-operative Publishing Society of Foreign Workers in the USSR, Moscow, 1933)

——, 'Proekt ugolovnoe kodeksa Souiza SSR', *Sovetskoe Gosudarstvo i Pravo*, no. 1/2 (1935), pp. 85-107

——, 'O sude i prave v epoky sotsialisma', *Sovetskaia Iustitsia*, no. 19 (1936), pp. 8-10

Kucherov, Samuel *Courts, Lawyers and Trials under the Last Three Tsars* (Frederick A. Praeger, New York, 1953)

——, *The Organs of Soviet Administration of Justice: Their History and Operation* (Brill, Leiden, 1970)

Kudriavstev, V.N. 'Problemy prichinnosti v kriminologii', *Voprosy Filosofii*, no. 10 (1971), pp. 76-87

——, 'Sotialno-psikhologicheskie aspekty antiobshchestvennogo povedeniia', *Voprosy Filosofii*, no. 1 (1974), pp. 98-109

Kurskii, D.I. *Izbrannye Stat'i i Rechi*, 2nd edn. (Gosudarstvennoe Izdatel'stvo Iuridicheskoi Literatury, Moscow, 1958)

Kurylev, S.V. 'O primenii sovetskogo zakona', *Sovetskoe Gosudarstvo i Pravo*, no. 11 (1966), pp. 21-9

Labour Correctional Code of the RSFSR, trans. Hsinwoo Chao (Sweet and Maxwell, London, 1936)

Laird, Roy D., and Betty A. *Soviet Communism and Agrarian Revolution* (Pelican Books, London, 1970)

Lapenna, Ivo 'Socialist Legality: Soviet and Yugoslav', *Soviet Survey*, no. 25 (1958), pp. 53-60

——, 'The New Russian Criminal Code and Code of Criminal Procedure',

International and Comparative Law Quarterly, vol. 10, no. 3 (1961, pp. 421-53

——, *State and Law: Soviet and Yugoslav Theory* (University of London, The Athlone Press, London, 1964)

——, *Soviet Penal Policy* (The Bodley Head, London, 1968)

Lashko, V.T. 'K voprosu izucheniia lichnosti osuzhdenykh k lisheniiu svobody', *Sovetskoe Gosudarstvo i Pravo*, no. 5 (1965), pp. 98-101

Lefebvre, Henri *Dialectical Materialism* (Jonathan Cape, London, 1968)

Lenin, Vladimir Ilych *Sochineniia*, 5th edn. (Gosudarstvennoe Izdatel'stvo Politicheskoi Literatury, Moscow, 1958)

——, *Collected Works* (Lawrence and Wishart, London, 1960-70)

——, *O Sotsialisticheskoi Zakonnosti* (Gosudarstvennoe Izdatel'stvo Politicheskoi Literatury, Moscow, 1961)

——, *Selected Works* (3 vols., Progress Publishers, Moscow, 1975)

Leninskie Dekrety 1917-1922. Bibliografiia (Izdatel'stvo 'Izvestiia Sovetov Deputatov Trudiashchikhsia SSSR', Moscow, 1974)

Lepeshkin, A.I. 'Programma KPSS i nekotorye voprosy teorii sovetskogo sotsialisticheskogo gosudarstva', *Sovetskoe Gosudarstvo i Pravo*, no. 12 (1961), pp. 3-14

Lichtheim, George 'Marx and the "Asiatic Mode of Production"', *St Anthony's Papers*, vol. XIV (1963), pp. 86-112

——, *Marxism*, 2nd edn. (Routledge and Kegan Paul, London, 1964)

Liebman, Marcel *Leninism under Lenin* (Jonathan Cape, London, 1975)

Lukacs, Georg *History and Class Consciousness* (Merlin Press, London, 1971)

——, *Lenin* (New Left Books, London, 1972)

Malafeev, A.N. *Istoriia Tsenoobrazovaniia v SSSR (1917-1963)* (Izdatel'stvo Sotsial'no-Ekonomicheskoi Literatury 'MYSL'', Moscow, 1964)

Mal'kovich, T.K. 'K istorii pervykh dekretov o sovetskom sude', *Sovetskoe Gosudarstvo i Pravo*, no. 7, pp. 94-107, and no. 8/9, pp. 164-79 (1940)

Mamut, L.S. 'K. Marks o gosudarstve kak politicheskoi organizatsii obshchestva', *Voprosy Filosofii*, no. 7 (1968), pp. 29-39

Mandel, Ernst *The Formation of the Economic Thought of Karl Marx* (New Left Books, London, 1971)

Man'kovskii, V. 'Voprosy ugolovnogo prava v period perekhoda ot sotsializma k kommunizmu', *Sovetskoe Gosudarstvo i Pravo*, no. 3 (1939), pp. 88-101

——, *Sovetskoe Ugolovnoe Pravo v Period Otechestvennoi Voiny*

(Ucheniye Zapiski, Leningrad University, Leningrad, 1948), no. 106

Mannheim, Karl *Ideology and Utopia* (Routledge and Kegan Paul, London, 1960)

Marcuse, Herbert *Reason and Revolution*, 2nd edn. (Routledge and Kegan Paul, London, 1955)

——, *Soviet Marxism* (Pelican Books, London, 1971)

Marx, Karl and Engels, F. *Werke* (Dietz Verlag, Berlin, 1956 onwards)

Marx, K. *Pre-Capitalist Economic Formations* (Lawrence and Wishart, London, 1964)

——,   and Engels, F. *The German Ideology* (Lawrence and Wishart, London, 1965)

——,   and Engels, F. *Selected Works* (3 vols., Progress Publishers, Moscow, 1969)

——, *Theories of Surplus Value* (3 vols., Lawrence and Wishart, London, 1969)

——, *Contribution to the Critique of Political Economy* (Lawrence and Wishart, London, 1971)

—— and Engels, F. *On Ireland* (Progress Publishers, Moscow, 1971)

——, *Articles from the Neue Rheinische Zeitung 1848-49* (Progress Publishers, Moscow, 1972)

——, Capital (3 vols., Lawrence and Wishart, London, 1974)

—— and Engels, F. *Selected Correspondence*, 3rd edn. (Progress Publishers, Moscow, 1975).

——, and Engels, Frederick *Collected Works* (Lawrence and Wishart, London, 1975 (in progress))

——, and Lenin, Vladimir Ilych *On Scientific Communism* (Progress Publishers, Moscow, 1967)

Matthews, Mervyn *Class and Society in Soviet Russia* (Allen Lane, The Penguin Press, London, 1972)

—— (ed.) *Soviet Government* (Jonathan Cape, London, 1974)

McLellan, David (ed.) *Karl Marx: Early Texts* (Blackwell, Oxford, 1971)

——, *The Thought of Karl Marx* (Macmillan, London, 1971)

——, *The Young Hegelians and Karl Marx* (Macmillan, London, 1971)

——, *Marx Before Marxism*, rev. edn. (Pelican Books, London, 1972)

——, *Karl Marx: His Life and Thought* (Macmillan, London, 1973)

——, *Engels* (Fontana, London, 1977)

McNeal, see Communist Party of the Soviet Union

Medvedev, Roy A. *Let History Judge: The Origins and Consequences of Stalinism* (Macmillan, London, 1971)

Men'shagin, V.D. *et al.* (eds.) *Ugolovnoe Pravo: Obshchaia Chast'* (Iuridicheskoe Izdatel'stvo Ministerstva Iustitsii SSSR, Moscow, 1948)

Meyer, Alfred G. *Leninism* (Harvard University Press, Cambridge, Mass.,

1957)

Miliband, Ralph 'Marx and the State', *Socialist Register* (Merlin Press, London, 1965), pp. 278-96

Morgan, Glenn G. 'Lenin's Letter on the Soviet Procuracy', *American Slavic and East European Review*, vol. 19 (1960), pp. 10-27

—— ,'Peoples' Justice: The Anti-Parasite Laws, Peoples' Volunteer Militia and Comrades' Courts', *Law in Eastern Europe,* no. 7 (A.W. Sijthoff, Leiden, 1963)

Morton, Henry W. and Tokes, Rudolf L. (eds.) *Soviet Politics and Society in the 1970s* (The Free Press, New York, 1974)

Natashev, A.E. 'Zakonnost' i gumanizm — osnova ispravleniia i perevospitaniia osuzhdennykh', *Sovetskoe Gosudarstvo i Pravo,* no. 3 (1977), pp. 79-87

Nikiforov, B. 'Fundamental Principles of Soviet Criminal Law', *Modern Law Review*, vol. 23 (1960), pp. 31-42

Nove, Alec *An Economic History of the U.S.S.R.*, rev. edn. (Pelican Books, London, 1976)

Ollman, Bertell *Alienation* (Cambridge University Press, Cambridge, 1975)

Orlovskii, P.E., Pavlov, I.V. and Chkhikvadze, V.M. *Voprosy Sovetskogo Gosudarstva i Prava 1917-1957* (Izdatel'stvo Akademii Nauk SSSR, Moscow, 1957)

Ostroumov, S.S., and Chugunov, V.E. 'Izuchenie lichnosti prestupnika no materialam kriminologicheskikh issledovanii', *Sovetskoe Gosudarstvo i Pravo*, no. 9 (1965), pp. 93-102

Pethybridge, Roger *The Social Prelude to Stalinism* (Macmillan, London, 1974)

Piontkovskii, A.A. 'K voprosu o vzaimootnoshenii ob'ektivnogo i sub'ectivnogo prava', *Sovetskoe Gosudarstvo i Pravo*, no. 5 (1958), pp. 25-36

—— , 'K voprosu o prichinakh prestupnosti v SSSR i merakh bor'by s nei', *Sovetskoe Gosudarstvo i Pravo*, no. 3 (1959), pp. 85-98

—— , and Chkhikvadze, V.M. 'Ukreplenie sotsialisticheskoi zakonnosti i nekotorye voprosy teorii sovetskogo ugolovnogo prava i protesessa', *Sovetskoe Gosudarstvo i Pravo*, no. 4 (1956), pp. 26-38

Plamenatz, John *German Marxism and Russian Communism* (Longmans, Green and Co., London, 1954)

—— , *Man and Society* (2 vols., 5th impression, Longmans, Green and Co., London, 1969)

—— , *Ideology* (Macmillan, London, 1971)

Platkovskii, V.V. 'Leninskoe uchenie o sotsialisticheskom gosudarstve i sovremennost'', *Voprosy Filosofii*, no. 4 (1960), pp. 14-29

Polianskii, N. 'Revoluitsionnye tribunaly', *Pravo i Zhizn'*, no. 8 (1927) pp. 67-79

Popper, Karl *The Poverty of Historicism*, 2nd edn. (Routledge and Kegan Paul, London, 1961)

——, *The Open Society and its Enemies*, 5th edn., revised (2 vols., Routledge and Kegan Paul, London, 1966)

Prokopovich, S.N. *Narodnoe Khozaistvo SSSR* (2 vols., Checkov Publishing House, New York, 1952)

Rappard, William E. *et al.* (eds.) *Source Book on European Governments* (D. Van Nostrand Co., New York, 1937)

Rayner, see Criminal Code of the RSFSR

Rigby, T.H. *Communist Party Membership in the U.S.S.R. 1917-1967* (Princeton University Press, Princeton, 1968)

Romashkin, P.S. *Amnistiia i Pomilovanie i S.S.S.R.* (Gosudarstvennoe Izdatel'stvo Iuridicheskoi Literatury, Moscow, 1959)

——, 'Voprosy razvitiia gosudarstva i prava v proekte programmy KPSS', *Sovetskoe Gosudarstvo i Pravo*, no. 10 (1961), pp. 26-39

Rudenko, R.A. 'Zadachi dal'neishego ukrepleniia sotsialisticheskoi zakonnosti v svete peshenii XX S"ezda KPSS', *Sovetskoe Gosudarstvo i Pravo*, no. 3 (1956), pp. 15-25

Sakharov, A.B. *O Lichnosti Prestupnika i Prichinakh Prestupnosti v SSSR* (Gosudarstvennoe Izdatel'stvo Iuridicheskoi Literatury, Moscow, 1961)

Sanderson, John 'Marx and Engels on the State', *Western Political Quarterly*, vol. XIV (1963), pp. 946-55

Schapiro, Leonard *The U.S.S.R. and the Future* (Frederick A. Praeger, London, 1963)

——, *The Communist Party of the Soviet Union*, 2nd edn. (Eyre and Spottiswoode, London, 1970)

——, *Totalitarianism* (Macmillan/Pall Mall Press, London, 1972)

—— and Reddaway, Peter B. (eds.), Lenin: the Man, the Theorist, the Leader. A Reappraisal (Pall Mall Press, London, 1967).

Schlesinger, Rudolf 'Soviet Legal Theory', *Modern Law Review*, nos. 1/2 (1942), pp. 21-38

——, *Soviet Legal Theory* (Sweet and Maxwell, Stevens, London, 1946)

Schwarz, Solomon M. *Labour in the Soviet Union* (The Cresset Press, London, 1953)

Scott, E.J. 'The Cheka', *St Anthony's Papers*, no. 1 (1956), pp. 1-24

Selektov, M.Z. 'Sotsialisticheskaia demokratiia i lichnost'', *Voprosy Filosofii*, no. 9 (1958), pp. 23-38

Serge, Victor *Year One of the Russian Revolution* (Allen Lane, The Penguin Press, London, 1972)

Select Bibliography 315

Shlyapochnikov, A. 'Zakon 7 Avgusta ob okhrane obshchestvennoi sobstvennosti i praktika ego primeniia v RSFSR', *Sovetskoe Gosudarstvo i Pravo*, no. 5 (1933), pp. 21-31

Shub, David *Lenin: A Biography*, rev. edn. (Pelican Books, London, 1966)

Simush, P.I. 'Preobrazovanie sotsial'noi prirody krest'ianstva SSSR', *Voprosy Filosofii*, no. 12 (1967), pp. 3-14

——, 'Problemy analiza mezhklassovykh otnoshenii v razvitom sotsializme', *Voprosy Filosofii*, no. 8 (1977), pp. 3-15

Sofinov, P.G. *Ocherki Istorii Vecheka* (Gosudarstvennoe Izdatel'stvo Politicheskoi Literatury, Moscow, 1960)

Solomon, Peter H. (Jr.) *Soviet Criminologists and Criminal Policy Specialists in Policy Making* (Macmillan, London, 1978)

Solzhenitsyn, Alexander *The Gulag Archipelago*, vols. 1 and 2 (Fontana, London, 1974 (vol. 1), 1976 (vol. 2))

Sontag, J.P. 'The Soviet War Scare of 1926-27', *Russian Review*, vol. 34 (1975), pp. 66-77

Sorok Let Sovetskogo Prava (2 vols., Izdatel'stvo Leningradskogo Universiteta, Leningrad, 1957)

Stalin, J. *Sochineniia* (Gosudarstvennoe Izdatel'stvo Politicheskoi Literatury, Moscow, 1946 onwards)

——, *Collected Works* (Foreign Languages Publishing House, Moscow, 1952-5)

Starosolskyj, Jurij *The Principle of Analogy in Criminal Law: An Aspect of Soviet Legal Thinking* (Research Program on the U.S.S.R., New York, 1954)

Steinberg, I.M. *In the Workshop of the Revolution* (Victor Gollancz, London, 1955)

Stuchka, P.I. 'Otchet Narodnogo Kommissariata Iustitsii', *Proletarskaia revoliutsiia i pravo*, no. 1 (August 1918)

Sudebnoe Nastol'noe Rukovodstvo, 2nd edn. (Tipografiia Kommissariata po voennym delam goroda Petrograda i Petrogradskoi gub., Petrograd, 1919)

Taylor, Ian, Walton, Paul, and Young, Jock *The New Criminology* (Routledge and Kegan Paul, London, 1973)

Taylor, Laurie *Deviance and Society* (Michael Joseph, London, 1971)

Tikhomirov, IU.A. 'Sotsializm i politicheskaiia vlast'', *Sovetskoe Gosudarstvo i Pravo*, no. 5 (1974), pp. 11-19

Tikunov, V.S. 'Sotsialisticheskaia zakonnost' — rukovodiashchii printsip v deiatel'nosti organov gosudarstvennoi bezopasnosti', *Sovetskoe Gosudarstvo i Pravo*, no. 8 (1959), pp. 13-26

Timasheff, N.S. 'The Impact of the Penal Law of Imperial Russia on Soviet Panel Law', *American Slavic and East European Review*, vol. XII (1953), pp. 441-62

Treadgold, Donald W. *Twentieth Century Russia*, 4th edn. (Rand McNally College Publishing Company, Chicago, 1976)

Trotsky, Leon *On Lenin* (Harrap, London, 1971)

——, *Revolution Betrayed* (New Park Publications, London, 1973)

Tucker, Robert C., and Cohen, Stephen F. *The Great Purge Trial* (Grosset and Dunlap, New York, 1965)

Ugolovnoe Ulozhenie (St Petersburg, 1912)

Ulam, Adam B. *Lenin and the Bolsheviks* (Fontana, London, 1973)

Ushakov, IA. 'Sozdanie pervogo narodnogo suda v Petrograde', *Sovetskoe Gosudarstvo i Pravo*, no. 1 (1957), pp. 3-12

USSR Constitution, see Constitution, USSR

Vasil'ev, V.I. *et al.* (eds.), see *Leninskie Dekrety*

Von Laue, T.H. *Sergei Witte and the Industrialisation of Russia* (Columbia University Press, New York and London, 1963)

Voronstov, V.S., Gukovskiia, N.I., and Mel'nikova, E.B. 'O prestupnosti nesovershennoletnikh v gorode i sel'skoi mestnosti', *Sovetskoe Gosudarstvo i Pravo*, no. 3 (1969), pp. 103-8

Vyshinskii, A. YA. (gen. ed.) *The Law of the Soviet State* (Macmillan, New York, 1948)

Westwood, J.N. *Endurance and Endeavour* (Oxford University Press, London, 1973)

Wetter, Gustav *Dialectical Materialism* (Routledge and Kegan Paul, London, 1958)

——, *Soviet Ideology Today* (Heinemann, London, 1966)

Wilson, Edmund *To The Finland Station*, rev. edn. (Fontana, London, 1974)

Wittfogel, Karl A. *Oriental Despotism: A Comparative Study of Total Power* (Yale University Press, New Haven, 1957)

Wolfe, Bertram D. *Three Who Made a Revolution* (Pelican Books, London, 1966)

——, *An Ideology in Power* (George Allen and Unwin, London, 1969)

Wright Mills, C. *The Marxists* (Pelican Books, London, 1963)

Zelitch, Judah *Soviet Administration of Criminal Law* (University of Pennsylvania Press, Philadelphia, 1931)

Zhogin, I.V. 'Ob izvrashcheniiakh Vyshinskogo v teorii sovetskogo prava i praktike', *Sovetskoe Gosudarstvo i Pravo*, no. 3 (1965), pp. 22-31

Zile, Ziguds L. *Ideas and Forces in Soviet Legal History*, 2nd edn. (College Printing and Publishing, Inc., Madison, Wisconsin, 1970)

INDEX